D1266208

LOST LOVE

The Untold Story of
Henrietta Szold

LOST LOVE

The Untold Story of
Henrietta Szold

Unpublished Diary and Letters

BAILA ROUND SHARGEL

Copyright © 1997 by Baila Shargel

All rights reserved. No part of this publication may be reproduced or transmitted in any form or by any means, electronic or mechanical, including photocopy, recording, or any information storage or retrieval system, except for brief passages in connection with a critical review, without the permission in writing from the publisher: The Jewish Publication Society, 1930 Chestnut Street, Philadelphia, PA 19103.

Manufactured in the United States of America

Library of Congress Cataloguing-in-Publication Data

Szold, Henrietta, 1860–1945.
   [Selections. English. 1997]
   Lost love : the untold story of Henrietta Szold : unpublished
diary and letters / [edited and translated by] Baila Shargel.
     p. cm.
   Includes selections from the author's diary (1903–1908) and an
exchange of letters with Louis Ginzberg.
   ISBN 0–8276–0629–X
   1. Szold, Henrietta, 1860–1945—Correspondence. 2. Jewish women-
-United States—Correspondence. 3. Ginzberg, Louis, 1873–1953-
-Correspondence. 4. Jewish scholars—United States—Correspondence.
5. Szold, Henrietta, 1860–1945—Diaries. 6. Unrequited love.
I. Shargel, Baila Round. II. Ginzberg, Louis, 1873–1953.
Correspondence. Selections. III. Title.
E184.J5S9613   1997
973'.004924'00922—dc21   97–2517
                                                 CIP
                                                 r97

Contents

For Nahum

Preface and Acknowledgments

Henrietta Szold has played a role in my life ever since I was young. My mother, a native Baltimorean like myself and a Hadassah enthusiast, took personal pride in her. Szold, who founded Hadassah, attended our alma mater when it bore the fusty nineteenth-century title: "Western Female High School." Her father, Rabbi Benjamin Szold, officiated at the wedding of my mother's parents.

When I was conducting research for my first book, a biography of Israel Friedlaender, Szold again claimed my attention. Szold and Friedlaender were close Zionist associates who signed their personal correspondence "with Zionist greetings." They shared the belief that education was the key to Jewish renaissance and labored together with uneven success on behalf of organizations dedicated to those convictions. Szold solicited Friedlaender's advice for Hadassah's motto and gratefully accepted his suggestion: "The healing of the daughter of my people."

I did not become interested in writing about Szold, however, before I gathered data about Friedlaender's colleagues. Browsing through the extensive archives of the Jewish Theological Seminary, I found her letters to Ginzberg. They fascinated me. Jerry Schwartzbard of the library staff kindly retrieved a microfilm copy of the other side of the correspondence. When I first started to think about how to structure this project, I intended to publish the letters only. But something bothered me. Biographies of Szold mentioned that she traced the course of the Ginzberg friendship in a journal. Even though it was written after the correspondence ended, I felt that for the ideas and feelings expressed in the letters to be understood, the journal had to accompany them. But for a long time the journal was unavailable to me. I am deeply indebted to M. Jastrow Levin and his wife Alexandra for granting permission to publish it, as well as Ismar Schorsch and Eli Ginzberg for arguing my case before them so effectively.

It is my pleasure to thank the people who aided my research and writing. Dr. Schorsch deserves credit for suggesting that I publish the letters in the first place. Jack Wertheimer and Jonathan Sarna supported my early efforts, as did Mel Scult, who read and commented on the entire manuscript. Chava Weissler advised me to consult the writings of Carolyn Heilbrun. At Alan Dawley's suggestion, I named Szold's 1908–1909 journal "A Meditation on Lost Love."

This book relies upon archival treasures from various collections. First and foremost are materials from the Central Zionist Archives in Jerusalem, where Yoram Majorek and his fine staff were a great help to me. They comprise the bulk of this publication. I spent many fruitful hours in the Rare Book Room of the Jewish Theological Seminary, aided by Jerry Schwartzbard and Seth Gershauer. Other documents come from the Jewish Publication Society Archives at the Philadelphia Jewish Archives Center housed in the Balch Institute. Lily G. Schwartz, in charge of the collection, was more than helpful in granting access to letters as well as photographs. Virginia North of the Maryland Jewish Historical Society showed me the Szold records housed there and permitted use of the Szold family pictures. Julie Miller of the Ratner Center for Conservative Judiasm, Sharon Liberman Mintz and Elka Dietsch of the JTS graphics department supplied additional photographs. Ira Daly was my guide to resources at the (now sequestered) Hadassah Archives in New York. The staff of the Schlesinger Library at Radcliffe College in Cambridge, Massachusetts, showed me the Szold papers housed there, including a complete if mistake-ridden transcription of Szold's journal. I am grateful for the warm reception I received at all these places.

I acknowledge with gratitude the aid of Carmel Friedlaender Agranat of Jerusalem and the late Maxwell Whiteman of Philadelphia, who allowed me to select pertinent materials from their autograph collections.

Thanks are also due Herman Dicker, Anne-Marie Gordon, and Norton Shargel for helping decipher the old German script and translating tricky German phrases; as well as Emanuel Goldsmith, who made sense of some Yiddish expressions. Vikki Battaglia typed the "Meditation." At the onset of the project, Michael Monson of JPS extended needed encouragement. Without the editorial support of Ellen Frankel of JPS, who supervised the project from start to finish, the book could not have been written. I appreciate the efforts of Christine Sweeney of JPS and Becky Barnhart of Shepherd, Inc., who prepared the manuscript for publication.

I would especially like to thank the Memorial Foundation for Jewish Culture for supporting this project.

An early draft of the Epilogue appeared in the June 1990 issue of *Hadassah Magazine*.

Family members warrant special recognition. I am indebted to the linguistic sensitivity and editorial proficiency of my daughter Dina Projansky, the successful effort of my son Raphael to ferret out the elusive Madison Cawein, and their sister Rebecca's participation in an academic session where I spoke about the material in this book. My husband Rabbi Norton Shargel patiently endured my immersion in the early years of the twentieth century at a time when he came to grips with personal and communal problems of its final decade. To him I dedicate this volume with great love.

Tragedy in our own family heightened my respect for journal writing. In 1986 our son Jonathan died suddenly during a routine surgical procedure. In the months that followed, I went through the motions of mourning in accordance with Jewish law and tradition, but remained tight-throated and numb. In the summer of 1987 I attended a teachers' seminar sponsored by the Melton Foundation. Several sessions were exercises in journal writing, directed by the very talented Eduardo Rauch. Putting my thoughts about the tragedy on paper for the first time, I found I could let my emotions rise to the surface. At last I was able to articulate the twenty-four-year ordeal of caring for a handicapped child along with his healthy brother and sisters and my suppressed feelings about his death. I returned from the seminar refreshed and ready to take on the world.

Throughout my work on this project, I have struggled with the realization that I was setting before the world a piece never intended for publication. Yet I know that it had to be done, if only to dispel the general impression that Szold was born at age sixty. Here I should add that the wonderful exhibition, "Daughter of Zion: Henrietta Szold and American Jewish Womanhood," curated by Barry Kessler of the Jewish Historical Society of Maryland while I was still laboring over the manuscript, shared my purpose. That display, however, covered the public events of Szold's life, while the very intimate "Meditation on Lost Love" affords a glimpse into her soul. The words of Nigel Nicolson, who published the admittedly more embarrassing journal of his mother, Vita Sackville-West, express my sentiment exactly: "Far from tarnishing the memory . . . it burnished it."[1] Szold's journal is a contribution to the literature of love, set in a thoroughly Jewish context during a critical period of recent history. As such, it demands publication.

[1]*Portrait of a Marriage* (New York: Atheneum, 1973), p. viii.

INTRODUCTION

The Exceptional Friendship
of Henrietta Szold
and Louis Ginzberg

L ove is one of life's profoundest mysteries, and an accomplished
woman's obsession with a man who rejects her is an especially baf-
fling conundrum. Such a drama was enacted in New York City just
after the turn of the twentieth century between a young Talmudic
genius and a multi-talented middle-aged woman. Their intimate,
complex, and ultimately aborted friendship has been a matter of
record for nine decades, yet the relationship has more often been sub-
jected to whispers than disinterested examination.

Since the 1920s Henrietta Szold (1860–1945) and Louis
Ginzberg (1873–1953) have functioned as icons in the Jewish world.
Szold, founder of Hadassah, has inspired women by her selfless devotion to Zionism, modern medicine, and the rescue of children from
the Nazi inferno. Ginzberg's peerless Talmudic erudition still stimu-
lates scholars. This study aims to consider with dispassion six years
near the midpoint of their lives, 1903 to 1909. It was a pivotal period
for each of them, but for different reasons. During this interval
Ginzberg won his reputation in the pantheon of Jewish scholars. For
Szold it was a season of self-redefinition through suffering, of belated
yet peremptory expulsion from an Eden of sexual ignorance and personal innocence.

I. *The Seminary Milieu, 1903–1909*

Louis Ginzberg and Henrietta Szold dwelled in the heart of several concentric circles. The largest was Ashkenazic Jewry, then in the process of relocation in both a material and a cultural sense. Its nucleus was the great Jewish mass of East Europe Jewry, of which nearly one-third was midway through its hegira to the New World. In 1903 the Kishinev pogrom produced brutal attacks upon Jews and their homes and businesses. About fifty Jews were killed, five hundred were injured, and much of local Jewry's economic base was destroyed. Kishinev soon became, in a contemporary historian's words, "the most potent metaphor for East European Jewish misery."[2] Jewish immigration was only nine percent of the total immigration to the United States in 1903; between 1904 and 1908 it rose to an average of nearly thirteen percent. More than one hundred thousand Jews settled here in each of these years. This number was achieved again only on the eve of the Great War and in the final window of opportunity before immigration restrictions were imposed in its aftermath.[3]

To borrow an expression that echoed far beyond Hebraist and Zionist society, the issue was not only "the problem of the Jews," in other words, legal disabilities, poverty, sporadic pogroms in eastern Europe, and the unanticipated resurgence of antisemitism in the west European lands of Emancipation. It was also "the problem of Judaism," a religion and a culture threatened from within by intellectual impotence and undemocratic communal arrangements and threatened from without by modernist ideas of every stripe—academic and religious, political, social, and economic.

The second circle was the Jewish population of New York City, then experiencing the fastest growth in the history of the diaspora. Contemporary scholars marvel at the flowering of Jewish self-expression: mutual aid societies; trade unions struggling to be born; hundreds of new synagogues and prayer groups; and high and low cultural and political expression in newspapers and journals, discussion groups, and the theater. But New York Jewry also suffered the consequences of dislocation, especially in the bustling Lower East Side. Oppressive crowding and job uncertainty were most pressing concerns. People feared losing their children to boorishness, assimilation, and even crime.

Szold and Ginzberg were more specifically stationed in a third, much smaller Jewish circle of turn-of-the-century New York—a religious and national-minded intelligensia, mostly newcomers from Europe, a few from other parts of the United States. More precisely, they belonged to the elite of the newly recast Jewish Theological Seminary of America, where classes began in the very year of the Kishinev pogrom. Solomon Schechter, the world-famous discoverer of the Cairo Geniza, had been lured from Cambridge, England, to New York, in 1902. He assumed academic leadership of the seminary, which had been reorganized with funding by Jacob Schiff and lesser lights of the New York German-Jewish patriciate. Schechter immediately recruited a stellar faculty. First was Ginzberg, already living in New York. He helped Schechter secure two European colleagues, Alexander Marx and Israel Friedlaender. The three men represented different segments of Ashkenazic Jewry. Friedlaender grew up in Warsaw, Marx was a product of Königsberg, East Prussia, and Ginzberg of Lithuania. More importantly, they shared exemplary qualities: youth—all were in their twenties; a well-developed critical intelligence; early promise as masters of biblical and rabbinic texts; systematic education on the doctoral level at top German universities; a dedication to Jewish religious practice coupled with an understanding of *halakhah* as the product of evolutionary modification and change; and a commitment to the renewal of Jewish life and learning in the modern idiom. Israel Davidson, another brilliant young scholar born in Europe but educated in America, cherished the same values. He was recruited in 1905, thereby completing the major faculty.[4]

All five professors distinguished themselves through pathbreaking scholarship during their lifetimes on the seminary faculty, abetted by long summer vacations in European libraries and archives. Nevertheless, Louis (or Levi) Ginzberg possessed the strongest "yihus" as well as earned credentials. His mother, Zippe Jaffee, was the great-grandniece of Elijah, the "Gaon of Vilna," the quintessential Lithuanian savant. At age twenty-nine, slightly older than the other young men when he assumed his position, Ginzberg was already on the road to an enduring reputation as a scholar unmatched in the field of Talmud. He had mastered both the Babylonian Talmud and the Jerusalem Talmud in Europe and in America would ultimately produce monumental Talmudic analyses. But during his first years in this country, 1900 to 1902, he composed short pieces; no fewer than 406 articles in German, which were translated for the new English-language *Jewish Encyclopedia*. At the same time he was recruited for a second, even more ambitious project. The *Legends of the Jews* merged all the rabbinic fables and parables about the central biblical figures into a seamless, continuous narrative.[5]

5

II. The Szold-Ginzberg Friendship

The *Legends* could not have been completed without the services of Henrietta Szold. Three years before her first face-to-face encounter with Ginzberg she received a letter from Mayer Sulzberger suggesting the young professor as author of the projected work, with two important caveats:

> *Whether Dr. Ginzberg who is connected with the Encyclopedia could find time or inclination for the work is of course a question, though I doubt whether he writes English.*[6]

At that time and through the rest of her working career, Szold bore the title "Secretary to the Publication Committee of the Jewish Publication Society," located in Philadelphia. For this position she had been enlisted in 1893, after having served on the committee in an unpaid capacity for the five years since its inception. At the time of her recruitment, she was thirty-two years old and unmarried, the eldest of the five daughters of Benjamin and Sophie Szold. The couple had emigrated from Hungary in 1859 to Baltimore, where Rabbi Szold, a moderate Reformer, had assumed rabbinic leadership of the Oheb Shalom Synagogue. Henrietta, born at the end of the following year, was her father's favorite "son,"—actually he claimed that all five of his accomplished daughters were "sons"—but she remained first among equals.[7] From her earliest days she had expedited his Hebrew scholarship, even conducted serious academic discussions with him at table in German while the younger girls chatted about lesser matters in English. She was deeply devoted to both her parents, and so comfortable in the family home that her emotional development lagged even as her intellect matured precociously.

The young woman's first career was that of teaching, and throughout her long life she would devote effort to education on many levels. She graduated first in her class from Western Female High School, then became an instructor of Greek, history, and less daunting subjects at the Misses Adams School, a fashionable nonsectarian local female academy. At seventeen she became a published author, initially with the contribution of articles to the *Jewish Messenger*, a New York publication; her pen name was "Sulamith." A respectable number of articles for other journals and the *Jewish Encyclopedia* and numerous public lectures followed.

During her late twenties, she was drawn to two new movements and in one became a pioneer. Unlike many American-born Jews steeped in German culture, Szold was captivated by the immigrants from eastern Europe and charmed by their fierce Jewish passion. In East Baltimore, the Russian Jewish neighborhood, she created one of the nation's first night schools to aid in their Americanization. At the same time, she joined the Issac Bar Levinson Hebrew Literary Society, a local branch of the proto-Zionist *Ḥibbat Zion* movement. She was an active member, lecturing on such topics as religious tolerance in Maryland and the poet Emma Lazarus.[8]

At the Jewish Publication Society her immediate superior was Judge Mayer Sulzberger, titular head of the publication committee, but the preponderance of the work fell upon "Miss Szold's" compliant shoulders. Years later one of her critics admitted the enormous scope of her labors: "the editing [and] or translating of its manuscripts, the proof-reading of the galleys and the pages, the compiling of indexes and appendices, the preparation of advance notices, the motherly [sic] care of rejected and accepted manuscripts."[9] In the period under consideration here, she assumed two additional responsibilities. First with Cyrus Adler, then alone, she edited four volumes of the *American Jewish Year Book*, a formidable task that required tact and fortitude in soliciting articles, then following them up, and tiresome, tedious drudgery compiling statistics from every American Jewish community.[10] To honor her father's memory she took on an additional editorial job unconnected with her work for the Publication Society, the revision of a prayer book composed many years before by Benjamin Szold and Marcus Jastrow.[11]

For unremitting toil over a period of twenty-three years, the reward was little more than a decennial tribute.[12] On the job Szold suffered many indignities. The salary was low—the Society had been prepared to pay her as much as $200 per annum above her starting pay of $1000[13]—and intermittent pleas for increased remuneration produced delaying tactics or curt denial.[14] In everything but name Szold was editor, but, because of the structure of the publication committee, the Society was free to refuse her suggestions. A case in point was Gustav Karpeles's book on Jewish history which to Szold was sloppy and unoriginal, in part a repetition of the author's previous book, "the rest plagiarized from Graetz, Zunz, and Kayserling." Not mincing words, she called the author "a 'smart' journalist, who dares unload his literary refuse upon the Jews in Yankeeland." When she enumerated his mistakes, however, the response was that he was too busy to change the manuscript. To her great chagrin, Sulzberger backed Karpeles rather than his indignant "secretary."[15]

For ten years Szold endured this treatment in silence, just as she had deferred to the benevolent partriarchy of her parental home. Soon after the death of her father, however, she made a move that would change her life. With her mother Sophie she left Baltimore and established a household in Morningside Heights in Upper Manhattan, across the street from the new building of the Jewish Theological Seminary. The time was chosen to coincide with the opening of the reorganized seminary. Szold had attracted the admiring attention of Schechter during a visit to Baltimore in 1895; after that, the two corresponded. In December 1900, Schechter wrote to her announcing his decision to accept the seminary presidency and proposed a personal visit the following April to Baltimore even before the arrival of his wife and family.[16] It is not surprising, therefore, that he willingly acceded to her request to enroll in the seminary as a special student, and obtained the acquiescence of the board of trustees. At the same time she notified Sulzberger of her move and received permission to attend classes even as she carried on her duties for the Publication Society.[17]

For their part, the regular students were content to sit by her side. Herman Rubenovitz, a distinguished Boston rabbi, later reminisced:

> We students looked upon (Szold) with awe—twenty years lay between us—but all formality was soon forgone and we thought of her as one of the boys, so unassuming and endearing did we find her.[18]

Nor did the fact that she was female create difficulties, except in one instance, to be discussed. She was not even unique. Another woman, Myra Mildred Frienderich of San Francisco, registered for classes in 1906.[19]

To Rubenovitz and perhaps other students as well, Szold was "a savant."[20] Despite her double duty as full-time student[21] and editor, the work did not tax her unduly. Henrietta Szold was a woman of iron discipline and in good health, with years of experience in deciphering ancient Jewish texts with her father and editing and translating modern ones for the Publication Society. Jewish history had always interested her; indeed, she had reworked the British edition of Graetz's famous *History of the Jews* for the JPS even before assuming a professional position there.[22] Soon after classes began, a letter to her friend Elvira N. Solis indicated: "One almost feels as though one could have delivered the lectures oneself."[23]

In no way, however, did this generalization apply to the classes of Professor Louis Ginzberg; through them she discovered "an entirely new world."[24] Vaster than the sea of the Talmud that his lessons enabled her to navigate, it was a universe that enlisted her entire being. For the first time in her life, Henrietta Szold, forty-three years old and a guileless virgin, experienced erotic passion.

It was love at first sight, unanticipated, imprudent, and entirely out of character. Only once, in her early twenties, had she seriously countenanced the courtship gestures of one man, a cousin. It was during a trip to Europe, but her father quickly whisked her away, for fear of losing his eldest "son."[25] After that, as she witnessed her sisters' marriages, one by one, her spinsterly dress and schoolmarm mannerisms—including an index finger outstretched to make a point—and reticence about personal matters effectively eliminated nuptual prospects.

The main obstacle to matrimony for this woman, however, was neither appearance nor deportment but age. Born in 1860, Szold reached maturity before the migration to America of a substantial Jewish intelligensia whose participants shared her academic interests, critical acumen, and refined sensibility. The seminary professors, born in the 1870s, though bachelors, seemed too young for consideration as possible mates. At any rate, they soon married, Marx and Friedlaender in 1905 and Davidson in 1906. The equally youthful Judah Magnes and Samson Benderly, important nonacademic colleagues and close friends, soon followed them down the bridal path.

Ginzberg, however, remained a bachelor. At the time when he stormed into her life, Szold maintained an idiosyncratic position; a woman in a man's world, an editor deprived of the title and of final decision making, a middle-aged female in a circle of young males, a spinster in a married world, a student of rabbinics who promised not to seek ordination.

Aware of the additionally anomalous situation of her infatuation with the youthful Talmud professor, Szold initially discouraged what she innocently labeled his "advances." These, of course, were not the approaches of a man seeking intimacy with a woman but those of a foreigner in need of a translator.

English was indeed a problem for all the foreign professors. For this reason, they were permitted to lecture in German during the 1903–1904 school year, with the understanding that they would soon switch to English. Classes posed no problem for Szold, raised in a household where German was frequently spoken and consistently read, or to her classmates, for whom Yiddish, rooted in medieval German, was "mamma loshon." But everyone in the seminary circle—the president, the board, and the instructors themselves—realized the need to replace German with English as quickly as possible. For their avowed mission was to transmit Jewish piety and wisdom in the modern idiom to the children of the East European immigration, who were already immersed in the American language and street culture.

As a service to the seminary's major faculty, Szold offered informal lessons in English every Saturday evening. The motive may have been gratitude for permission to audit their classes. More likely, it reflected an altruism honed at her family table and in the Baltimore Night School. Shortly before Lillian Bentwich's London marriage to Israel Friedlaender, Szold welcomed her into the seminary circle and explained her course of action:

> *When you come to live in America, and see how many fine minds fail to gain recognition, fail, indeed, to reveal their force and ability, because they happen to lack the common medium of expression, you will understand why it has become second nature for me to give of the store of English which I owe to the mere accident of birth in a country of English-speaking folk.*[26]

Ginzberg at first was not included, ostensibly because he had been living in America for some time. In reality it was because Szold was desperately trying to maintain a distance from him. But he soon joined Friedlaender and Marx at Saturday evening study sessions in her home. Still, she absented herself from his Talmud class, first out of belief in his discomfort with female students. After that misunderstanding was cleared up, she hesitated to attend when the subject matter was the tractate *Kiddushin*, which deals with male-female relations. Ginzberg, however, assured her that she was more than welcome, because she was his best student.[27]

Flattery was in order, as Ginzberg was already enlisting Szold for English translations of his German letters and journal articles, and lectures delivered in class and before the wider public. At the same time, she facilitated the translation and organization of raw data into four volumes to be published between 1909 and 1913, to wide acclaim. Of all these tasks, only the *Legends of the Jews* was a project of the Jewish Publication Society. Szold was more coauthor than mere translator of parts of this magnum opus; she passed judgment upon which biblical references warranted inclusion, how entries were to be annotated, and the general organization of the volumes. In private conversation, moreover, Ginzberg referred to the *Legends* as "our book."

Far beyond any obligation, Szold helped Ginzberg create articles for the *Jewish Quarterly Review* based upon his research on fragments from the Cairo Geniza that Schechter had transported from Cambridge, England, to New York. An excerpt from her journal portrays her as much more than a proofreader:

> He actually dictated all the English matter, and for four years, I
> put as much time and thought upon it as he himself did.

These articles would form the core of the second volume of *Geonica: the Geonim and Their Halakic Writings*. The first volume, "The Gaonate,"[28] was equally a product of Szold's expert editing. They became showcases of seminary scholarship, the first two books published under the rubric "Texts and Studies of the Jewish Theological Seminary of America."

Frequent contact with Ginzberg plunged the normally even-tempered Miss Szold into a flurry of mixed emotions, experiencing ecstacy when he praised the translation of a word or a phrase and agony when she observed maidens of blossoming youth—including her own little sister Adele. As she peered into an unforgiving mirror, she compared their willowy forms to her own plump buxom body barely five feet tall and their fresh faces to her own serious, bespectacled face.

What she called her "bittersweet happiness" was reinforced by frequent strolls with Ginzberg along leafy Riverside Drive, brisker walks in Morningside Park, and occasional forays into the immigrant section of New York for a Purim service or a light repast. Most of the meals taken together, however, were enjoyed in the comfort of the Szold dining room, where Ginzberg was a frequent and always welcome guest. Summers found Ginzberg either in Tannersville, a Catskill resort which catered to Zionistically inclined intellectuals and academicians, or in European libraries, where he carefully copied out medieval manuscripts. In 1905 and 1906 the two exchanged weekly letters; his displayed comradely affection but nothing more.

During three years of study at the seminary, 1903–1906, Szold remained sober minded about a future with Ginzberg. The best she could hope for was his remaining unmarried and in continuing need of her services. Still, as early as 1906 everyone regarded Szold and Ginzberg as a permanent twosome, if not an engaged couple. Furthermore, even after she left the classroom that September, Szold remained within the seminary orbit, regularly attending Sabbath morning services followed by a long constitutional with Ginzberg, listening to public lectures delivered there, and attending life cycle events of the faculty and others in the seminary circle.

The spring of 1907 brought new promise. Ginzberg was summoned to the bedside of his father, then painfully dying of cancer in Amsterdam. Letters to Szold reveal a man in crisis, tormented not only by his father's physical distress and but also by guilt over not fulfilling parental expectations. Szold's comforting responses nearly crossed the boundary between empathetic friendship and pulsating affection. Ginzberg, for his part, seemed genuinely concerned with her health and well-being, paradoxically advising her to demand a lighter load from the Publication Society even as he bombarded her with new requests for his own benefit.

With Ginzberg's return from Europe three months after his father's death, the relationship advanced a notch. He became an almost daily guest at the Szold table and in her study. Walks taken together were of longer duration. The two friends often sat on a bench overlooking the Hudson and the Jersey shore. They observed passing boats and birds, and enjoyed long periods of silence, for Szold more eloquent and promising than any conversation.

When Ginzberg sailed for Europe in July 1908, Szold was confident of his deep affection for her. For this reason, her letters of that summer made no effort to veil her feelings. Boldly, she employed the poet's device of the pathetic fallacy to express her great sorrow at his departure:

> New York has today consoled itself. From Thursday noon until Sunday morning the heavens dripped, and showered, and poured. The purpose of all the water that came down must have been to bemoan your going away.[29]

Following the progress of his ship as it approached the continent, she declared, was the most exciting activity of the week.[30] Another letter announced:

> I cannot promise to lend you any of my time. I can only give it to you outright when it can be transmitted into such work as I am able to do for you. In that form you know by this time, I hope, you can

have it almost for the asking or without asking. No matter how you may feel about the amount of it, your friends cannot but be gratified that your ability is being recognized everywhere. As I wrote you recently, such a life as yours is the only sort worth living.[31]

By the time this excerpt was penned, however, Ginzberg already belonged to another woman. It appears that his family was unhappy with his bachelorhood and his association with the elderly American bluestocking. What better way to change the situation than to expose Ginzberg to an attractive girl from a good family and then let nature take its course? After traveling to a scholarly conference, Ginzberg spent a Sabbath in Berlin. Friends seated him strategically in the synagogue with the winsome and vivacious Adele Katzenstein in full view. Inquiries led to a meeting, then another, and, after a third, a marriage proposal.[32]

In New York, Szold became apprehensive, waiting for mail that was too slow in coming. Those letters that did arrive intimated a change of heart that she discerned but refused to recognize. The final three, she noted with misgiving, referred to her as "victim." Anxiety kept her away from the port on the day of Ginzberg's return. When he came to see her, her worst suspicions were confirmed: he was engaged to be married!

Cruelly, he asked her if she was happy for him. Convention demanded that she say yes. He then went so far as to request a letter of congratulation to his fiancée. Incredibly, he proceeded to conduct himself afterward in his accustomed manner, dining with Szold's family, working with her on his publications, and strolling with her in the park. For three weeks she went along with the charade but, finding these activities impossible to sustain, confronted him for the first time with her true feelings. Ginzberg claimed shock and surprise, and cavalierly assured her that the infatuation would soon pass.

He was wrong. Her peace of mind was not quickly restored; instead she plunged into a prolonged depression. Even in her tortured state, however, Szold continued translating the *Legends of the Jews* for the Jewish Publication Society. Now Ginzberg communicated with her only in writing and snubbed her when they met by chance, signifying the termination of a fruitful friendship. To make matters worse, as their story circulated in the Jewish world well beyond the seminary orbit, Szold became an object of pity and Ginzberg a subject of scorn. Within the group, the common reaction was best expressed by Israel Friedlaender: "The cad!"

It is an irony of American Jewish history that the story of Henrietta Szold's unrequited passion has become an enduring legend, more familiar to some than the *midrashim* that she and her beloved carefully stitched together. This volume intends to unsnarl the tangled web of misinformation about an American Jewish fable and questionable interpretations of its significance. I will speculate about Ginzberg's motivations only insofar as Szold pondered them, as she is my primary focus.

III. 1900–1910: A Transitional Decade

Szold's eighty-four years were about evenly split between the nineteenth century, when she was identified as a Baltimore rabbi's daughter, and the twentieth, when she lived independently in New York and Jerusalem. As a woman, she was a transitional figure, poised between the expectations of the earlier era and the anticipations of the new. During her first forty-two years she acquired conventional feminine skills of the needle and the keyboard but also learned Hebrew and delved into sacred texts, a male preserve in normative Judaism.

Although she could not have known it at the time, the move to New York in 1903 inaugurated the second half of her life and set the stage for the infatuation that is the subject of this volume. Surviving evidence of her friendship with Professor Ginzberg consists of their correspondence and Szold's private journal recounting the course of their association during a period of societal transformation. For the historian these sources serve a dual purpose. Even as they trace the tribulations of a despairing yet indomitable woman, they also offer evidence of the mind-set and mores of the early twentieth century.

In the journal, certain articles of outer apparel that were indispensable in an age of sartorial standards take on metaphoric significance. Ginzberg's fedora, innocently perched on a rack in her apartment hall, received surreptitious strokes whenever Szold passed it. Her hats—their seasonal variety, susceptibility to moisture, and disposition to fly in the Manhattan wind—compelled his consideration and excited her expectations. At one point Szold found it necessary to explain her gloveless condition during the "fierce" heat of a New York summer when Ginzberg inadvertently touched her hand.

Summertime, when the two were mostly apart, prompted the written communication that is integral to this study. The Szold-Ginzberg correspondence signified societal transformation; for the first time convention permitted exchange of familiar letters between single women and bachelors, particularly if there were also business matters under consideration.

In a certain respect, the letters were beholden to new technology in the form of rapid and inexpensive ocean travel. Though Ginzberg did not relish living in the United States, he had accepted the seminary position partly because long academic vacations allowed for frequent visits to family and research facilities in Europe.

With the development of newer forms of transportation, the pace of life accelerated. In 1908, the final year of the Szold-Ginzberg collaboration, the Wright brothers' invention, previously regarded as an exotic toy, flew seventy-five miles in 113 minutes. It was evident that the "aeroplane" would one day revolutionize travel, perhaps warfare as well. The same year saw the first Model T car raise the possibility of a new mode of transportation for the average family.[33] For Henrietta Szold all this progress was a mixed blessing. Though she marveled at the speed of auto travel, she maintained her reservations. "The fast automobiling," she complained after a spin in a Pierce-Arrow, "kept me in an uncomfortable humor. Emphatically, I am not fast."[34] Letters from an ocean liner prompted more musings in the same vein: "I have been trying to decide all day long whether I like the *Lusitania*. It shortens one interval, but it may have the effect of lengthening the other."[35]

There were additional indications that a fleet new world was replacing the more leisurely universe of Szold's youth. The telephone figures prominently in the Ginzberg friendship; after her move to Jerusalem in 1920, she would find its absence discomfiting. Radios were not yet household items, but steamships plying the Atlantic now featured wireless equipment. One of the few incidents stirring enough to distract Szold from her personal troubles was a maritime near-disaster of 1909: two steamers collided in Nantucket Bay with minimal loss of life because several vessels responded to an SOS transmitted by wireless.

Much as Szold welcomed technology's benefaction to human welfare, she was equally cognizant of the price exacted by modernity, most particularly its toll on Jewish life. In a Jewish version of Henry Adams's contemporary paean to the unitary and pristine medieval Christian world (the "Virgin") replaced by the "Dynamo," symbol of the multiplicity and the chaos wrought by modern technology,[36] she mourned the loss of "the type of the simple, single-hearted and single-minded Jew," and inquired rhetorically: "What has robbed us of such simplicity—the telephone or the Darwinian theory?"[37]

Unlike Adams, however, sophisticated Judaic scholars welcomed new inventions—Schechter noted the benefits of electricity to night study. On the other hand, "Darwin"—i.e., scientific theories that challenged traditional religion and sometimes fueled antisemitism—prompted ambivalence. Still, as principled and self-respecting moderns, members of the seminary circle could not ignore prevailing assumptions about nature and society. They retained close relations with other rabinically trained scholars who developed expertise in fledgling academic disciplines; some were rabbis' sons. The fact that Szold's sister Rachel was married to Joseph Jastrow, a pioneering psychologist, helps account for psychological terminology in her self-analysis, e.g., "suppressing instincts," and "realizing subconsciously." With admiration, she reported how Paul Radin, a budding anthropologist, regaled other Jewish intellectuals with reports of personal encounters with Winnebago Indians. Schechter himself was a good friend of Sir James George Frazer, world-famous author of *The Golden Bough*. Szold compared Ginzberg's self-reproach after his father's death with "our savage ancestors" whose response was "cutting and gashing our bodies."[38] For his part, Ginzberg indicated familiarity with Eastern religions when the death of Szold's old dog prompted musings about metempsychosis.[39]

At a time when new and sophisticated disciplines enriched the academy, an old-fashioned sentimentalism permeated popular literature and penetrated even the finer journals. In her despair, Szold was not immune to its blandishments. In 1905 she read "The Solitary," a treacly poem by popular author Madison Cawein in *Harper's Monthly* and copied it out. She saved this portrait of a fictional virgin crushed by the dynamo of disappointed love. Four years later she appended it to her account of the Ginzberg calamity. Little did she realize that her spontaneous reflections evoked the pain of unrequited love more honestly than Cawein's artificial construction. Her prose account, unlike his verses, would still ring true at the close of a fluctuating and turbulent century.

IV. The Correspondence and the "Meditation"

As previously noted, two sources testify to Henrietta Szold's transformation from aspiring lover to humiliated victim: a journal and a series of letters. Letters, written with the opinion of the recipient in mind, inevitably censor some of the truth. Journals, intended for the writer's eyes alone, are generally less self-conscious, revealing an inner world of thought and feelings; yet they too are limited insofar as they construct an artificial and narcissistic universe, carrying on dialogue only between the writer's "I" and her "myself." Epistolary historian Mary S. Favret finds greater truth in familiar correspondence, arguing that its intricate *entre nous* breathes the less rarified air of true dialogue, revealing actual interplay between writers.[40]

Thanks to conscientious families and meticulous archivists, both kinds of data have survived as witnesses to the Szold-Ginzberg friendship. The letters especially paint a rich and variegated portrait of American Jewish life during the first decade of this century: domestic details; books read and appraised; immigrant adjustment; the trials of Jewish publication; relations between the reorganized Jewish Theological Seminary, its uptown supporters, and its downtown detractors; struggles within the Reform movement; the birth of Dropsie College; and the plight of Zionism between the death of Herzl and the First World War.

Far more subjective is the narrative account of the relationship. In 1908–1909 Henrietta Szold constructed a unique and poignant chronicle, quite unlike the more conventional diaries of her 1909–1910 visit to Europe and Palestine and the aftermath. This piece defies categorization; it is part journal, part memoir, but conforms to the norms of neither. The typical journal documents diurnal thoughts and events. This one does not; entries seldom enumerate Szold's actions on a particular day but ponder her state of mind at irregular intervals. Furthermore, the relationship with Ginzberg is the sole concern. Other people and events are included only insofar as they touch upon it. Yet this very limitation facilitates more penetrating observation than the conventional chronicle of a person's comings and goings, for Ginzberg was the central fact of Szold's life during five tumultuous years. Current conditions which are mentioned serve a Proustian purpose. Just as the smell of a madeleine evokes memories from Marcel Proust's youth, so does a rainy Tuesday, a central trope in Szold's narrative, call to mind Tuesday mornings and evenings at her desk with Ginzberg at her side.

Although a remembrance of things past, this document also fails to qualify as memoir. Memoirs are commonly written long after the fact, recalling even the most disquieting episodes in tranquility. This narrative, by contrast, begins just four weeks after Ginzberg revealed his engagement to another woman and continues for eight more months, during which time Szold absorbed additional aftershocks of his rejection. To avoid the pitfalls of categorization, I have entitled the piece "Meditation on Lost Love."

V. Meditation on Lost Love

Henrietta Szold was a gifted writer; it was therefore appropriate for her to seek solace from disappointment in writing. What is surprising is the timing of her journal: between November 1908, soon after she learned of Ginzberg's engagement, and July 1909, shortly before her six month's leave of absence from the Jewish Publication Society. "Meditation on Lost Love" is a highly personal account designed to exorcise the demon of her passion.

> *If I put all my memories down, not necessarily in order of time, but only so as to have them before me as an object, so to say, outside of myself, instead of keeping them inside of me as a subjective pain—perhaps it will help me to adjust myself to the new cold loveless life I must henceforth live.*

By making herself a spectator on her own life, Szold followed a practice recommended by some psychotherapists in current practice. "Diaries involve a communion with deepest aspects of the conscious self away from the object world," observes Leonard Pearson. By unself-consciously writing down what they hesitate to utter aloud, he maintains, patients objectify their problems, an enormous first step toward self-understanding. For Michael White and David Epson, journal composition is a "narrative means to therapeutic ends." Through "storied therapy" their patients accomplish the externalization and objectivization of their predicaments. The act of writing itself functions as a rite of passage that proceeds systematically, from "separation" to "disorganization" to "reincorporation."[41]

Szold's written exercise in self-examination helped her through a painful passage. Her deliberate effort to create a distance between her ego and her injured feelings corresponds to White and Epson's "separation" phase. Szold's "Meditation" represents what they call the "betwixt-and-between" stage of "disorganization." In excruciating detail, the narrative reveals both paralyzing torment and quite reasonable efforts to make sense of her own actions and those of the object of her affection. It would be gratifying to report that when

Szold laid down her pen on July 21, 1909, she had expunged bitterness and self-reproach and recovered her self-esteem, i.e., achieved "reincorporation" or reintegration of her personality. Her personal correspondence and the journal of 1910, written after her return from abroad, indicate that this, unfortunately, was not the case; healing would be prolonged and painful. But the process had begun.

In the written recapitulation of her association with Ginzberg, four themes predominate: the elemental human concerns of death and love, and the impact of social convention and moral principle upon the relationship.

Death, like an undulating stream, rises at the beginning of the piece, then courses beneath the surface, to bubble forth fitfully and sporadically. Her life has been a tragedy, Szold exclaims, suspended between two losses, one of her father and the other of Ginzberg. This statement is probably the source of a central thesis in Irving Fineman's biography of Henrietta Szold, namely that her love for Ginzberg is best understood as the displacement of affection for a beloved father. It is impossible to discount Fineman's thesis; Szold's return to the family home even after work took her to another city suggests the immature if not pathological need of a grown woman for parental proximity. Nevertheless, in the narrative, the two deaths are not at all equivalent. Ginzberg's rejection looms as a far greater catastrophe than Benjamin Szold's death, which she claims to have borne with equanimity. When Szold initiates the written self-analysis, her father has been dead for little more than a year, yet she never restates any connection between her two "loves." October 20, 1908, the infamous day when Ginzberg "killed" her with news of his engagement, on the other hand, is the "Meditation's" primary trope; the date is repeatedly noted without further explication. It symbolized the termination of hope for the happiness experienced by most people as well as unbearable personal humiliation.

The shattering of her only chance for marital felicity triggered a process of mourning. Szold experienced distress common to people who have lost loved ones: sleeplessness, poor appetite, bouts of tears, and self-pity. Like a newly bereaved widow or orphan, she was inconsolable, despite kind efforts on the part of family and friends. "Has (Ginzberg) enough imagination to realize," she wondered, "what it means for a person like myself to have to say every morning on rising, 'I must live, I must live.'"

If death lurks in the background, it is overshadowed by love, the journal's most prominent motif. Szold's infatuation for Ginzberg exhibited three features never associated with this prim, scholarly woman: obsessive passion, masochism, and sensuality. Dorothy Tennov, a contemporary psychologist, has coined a word for the first quality: "limerence," defined as

> . . . an involuntary passionate yearning for another person in which the subject experiences intrusive cognitive activity, acute longing for reciprocation and interpretation of the loved one's every action with respect to the probability of reciprocation. The mood of the limerent is tied up with the loved object; it is buoyant when reciprocation seems more likely and morose when it seems less likely. The limerent possesses a remarkable ability to emphasize what is truly admirable in the other and to respond with compassion for the negative, even to the point of rendering the negative into a positive attribute.[42]

Henrietta Szold was a textbook illustration of limerence. Thoughts of Ginzberg informed her daily existence and governed her every action. Even as she performed her duties for the Jewish Publication Society, she arranged her schedule to conform to his needs, to the point of uncharacteristically breaking prior appointments whenever he summoned her. She stopped attending seminary classes in 1906 not, as a letter to Israel and Lillian Friedlaender intimated, to gain time for leisure activities,[43] but, as she confided to her journal, because of her hopeless infatuation for Ginzberg. Faithfully, the narrative recalls her shifting moods: melancholy in 1904, 1905, and 1906, when she harbored few hopes for reciprocation of her passion; sanguine during the summer of 1907 when confidences exchanged with Ginzberg crossed the ocean with great frequency; and exuberant in 1908, when she became convinced that he returned her affection.

Most astounding was this limerent's capacity for construing her beloved's abuse of her abundant talents and limited means as a virtue. Ginzberg was a permanent guest at the Szold table, dining there once or twice a week in the early years and, in the last season, 1907–1908, almost daily. During time away from the classroom, the library, and her study, the two friends took walks, seldom dining out or enjoying the cultural attractions of New York. Shamelessly, Ginzberg borrowed money, paper, and stamps, almost never repaying, and virtually every moment of her leisure. Dutifully, she purchased scrapbooks and filled them with his articles. Yet he never thanked her for her services. All this she interpreted in a positive light; for her they were signs betokening "no mine and thine between us," unspoken emblems of their troth.

What she deemed "the reckless generosity" of her passion was hardly the love of a mature woman seasoned in the ways of the world; indeed, her reported love at first sight is reminiscent of a teenage "crush." Like a schoolgirl, Szold sensed a new consciousness, unlike anything in her previous experience. How did this come about? It was not so much a displacement of affection for a dead father, I think, as the search for an anchor in a new world. Years before, when she had assumed professional duties for the Publication Society, she had moved to Philadelphia, where the Society was located, and commuted to Baltimore on weekends. Unhappy in her new surroundings, she had soon returned to the parental home, claiming the imperative to comfort the ailing and ultimately dying Benjamin Szold. After the Szolds set up housekeeping in New York, she found herself in a much more cosmopolitan environment, for the first time heading the rump family, perhaps frightened by the boldness of the undertaking, and a little lonely. For the rest of her life, she would look back upon the patriarchal family in which she was raised as a kind of utopia. In Morningside Heights, far from the Baltimore Eden, Szold assumed the position of student, a lesser status than the wonted ones of teacher, lecturer, and editor. This only confirmed feelings of inferiority already entertained because of her lack of formal higher education and her limited literary output. From any objective standpoint this was a false judgment. If Szold did not attend college, she read as widely and as intelligently as anyone who did, subscribing to periodicals written in German, French, and English. She excelled in her studies at the Jewish Theological Seminary, intended for college graduates. Proof of her broad education were frequent allusions to classical and modern literature and a generous sprinkle of Hebrew, Latin, German, and French in both the "Meditation" and the letters. For the Jewish Publication Society she translated books written in German and French and for which the knowledge of Hebrew and Aramaic was essential. Against the originals she checked other books written in those languages as well as Yiddish. The correspondence with Ginzberg, moreover, demonstrates a broad and easy familiarity with the Jewish classics. It was Szold who first noticed glaring errors in a book by William Rosenau, a Baltimore rabbi and Hopkins Semitist, thus initiating one of Ginzberg's most scathing reviews. The "Meditation" also reveals acquaintance with Christian terminology; several entries identify her "crucifixious" suffering with that of Jesus of Nazareth.[44]

Furthermore, if work at the Jewish Publication Society deterred prodigious expansion of her literary oeuvre, her duties involved far more than selecting books, casting translations, and proofreading. Her own translations were felicitous and the directories of Jewish communities serviceable. Many articles published under Louis Ginzberg's name were given final English form by Henrietta Szold. "Meditation on Lost Love" itself is a serious literary effort worthy of publication nearly ninety years after its composition.

Withal, a sense of inferiority prepared the ground for initiation into the maelstrom of all-encompassing romantic passion. Psychologist Theodor Reik has shown that even highly worthy people are unconsciously drawn to those next to whom they feel mediocre.[45] In Szold's mind, her subordination to Ginzberg, the savant, was evident; even her revered father's scholarship was no match for his.

In Ginzberg, Szold found her own perfection—a man equal to her self-imposed demands and demonstrating erudition far beyond her capacity. To identify with him was to realize her own ego ideal. To succor the man whom she secretly considered "my darling who let me imbibe somewhat at the source of his learning," was therefore to realize her own unfulfilled personality. Willingly, she became a partner in what she acknowledged as "the annihilation of my whole personality." In her subordination, her "worship," she exemplified the masochistic personality. To Ginzberg she ministered as a mother to a spoiled son, peeling his oranges, cracking open his boiled eggs, doing without her entrée so that he might enjoy a second portion, supporting his valetudinarianism (which disappeared after his engagement). She went without sleep in order to function as a "hod carrier" who abetted the construction of his "monument." When he telephoned a request to see her after she had prepared for bed, she quickly dressed and met him at the door.

Masochistic gestures such as these reflected the density and intensity of Szold's passion. To her personal amazement, Ginzberg awakened a long-suppressed sensuality, belatedly arousing what she called "that peculiar young happy feeling." Their very first encounter initiated her into what she termed "the cosmical mystery of sex." The controlled and prudish spinster became obsessed with this man's every lineament. In her mind's eye she continuously reviewed Ginzberg's sparkling blue eyes, his guttural giggle, his face framed by "a little silk cap" or a mortar board—and his body. "Next to him," she confided to her journal, "all other men seem to me like sawdust stuffed into coat, vest, and trousers."

Awareness of his body brought a new sense of her own. "I am a dependent woman with a keen emotional nature," she exclaimed, "a distinctly feminine woman, not an intellectual abstraction"; "a woman with red blood running in my veins." Attention from Ginzberg became the font of her happiness. Every encounter with him produced a somatic reaction. When they barely knew each other, she "thrilled" when her sister Rachel addressed him. Szold described herself as "quivering and palpitating" at the very sight of him and trembling at each physical contact, however inadvertent, however innocent. A veil he once knotted to prevent her hat from flying into the wind became a precious keepsake. She became a bundle of nervous energy. Whenever he called she "flew" to the telephone or the door. She kissed his books and clasped his letters to her heart. And when she thought he loved her she "jubilate(d)" and "sang." A graphic example of her very physical ardor is the following memory from 1905:

> There were times when my passion absorbed and mastered me. One evening, it had been snowing and raining and sleeting, but it stopped, and a high whistling wind arose. I could not stay in, the pain at my heart drew me out at eight o'clock in the evening, and I raced around Morningside Park screaming at the top of my voice whenever the wind was noisy enough to drown my agony.

A sensual image marked Szold's reconsideration of the relationship, when she compared her distress to that of

> . . . a man (who) lives on with a wound from which the missile that has produced it has never been removed, and everybody that passes and everything that happens, knocks against the protruding handle of the dagger, and gives it a painful wrench.

Here was a clear if unconsciously phallic metaphor. The "missile," of masculinity had not brought about personal fulfillment. To the contrary, initiation into the "cosmical mystery" of sexual desire exacted a price redolent of death rather than new life. It appeared that pain and suffering would continue to plague her for the remainder of her days.

Fortunately, there are two other themes in "Meditation on Lost Love" that partially alleviated the soreness, summarized in the following declaration from the "Meditation's" opening section:

> Unless I can see myself innocent and see him innocent, both of us victims of conventions . . . I do not know how to go on living worthily.

Throughout her life but especially at this critical juncture Henrietta Szold was alert to social convention, which she defined as "historical, organized common sense, handed down for the safeguarding of those laboring under strong emotion." That it became the third motif of her "Meditation on Lost Love" was in part an outgrowth of her own ambiguous social role. Within her own milieu, she was at once the most and the least conventional of women. Modest in dress and deportment, never one to stoop to feminine wiles, she was a religious woman devoted to traditional values. At the same time, this rabbi's daughter also surmounted boundaries, both professional and personal. Women were beginning to enter the work force, but seldom did they achieve the prestige of Szold's position at the JPS. Few women knocked at doors of theological seminaries, Christian or Jewish.

Outside the family circle, moreover, she functioned in a world of men. Before the turn of the century, when young people were discouraged from corresponding with members of the opposite sex, she freely exchanged chatty, easy-flowing letters with Joseph Hertz, Harry Friedenwald, and Morris Jastrow, bachelors of her own age.[46] Her work life during the years under consideration centered around the Jewish Publication Society, the Jewish Theological Seminary, the Federation of American Zionists, and a little later, the New York Kehillah, where virtually all her peers were men. During the years spent in the seminary milieu, Szold would enjoy the camaraderie of old friends such as Elvira Solis and Rose Sommerfeld and her cousin Miram Schaar, and companionship with the wives of seminary professors Schechter, Marx, Friedlaender, and Davidson. But throughout her long life she continued to cultivate male friends as well, e.g., Magnes, Benderly, Marx, and Friedlaender in America, and Palestinians Aaron Aaronson and Hans Beyth.[47]

Many lines, however, remained to be crossed. Before the Great War shattered societal mores, a rigid formality governed personal relations, even overrunning gender lines. Neither in written correspondence nor in cordial discourse did friends address each other by given names. For fifty years, Marx and Ginzberg, inseparable after the Szold imbroglio faded from view, called each other "Marx" and "Ginzberg," never "Alexander" or "Levi." Even when Szold and Ginzberg worked together and dined at her house almost daily, they remained "Miss Szold" and "Professor Ginzberg." Societal correctness was no trivial matter. It informed their entire relationship and helps explain why Szold never expressed her feelings in so many words, though she was often tempted to do so, and why Ginzberg could blatantly ignore the many obvious tokens of her affection.

Relations with members of the opposite sex remained fundamentally asymmetrical; men were expected to seize the initiative and women to respond, but not too eagerly. When Szold looked back upon her second meeting with Ginzberg, she marveled at her brazen act of extending her hand to him rather than waiting for him to approach her. She regretted her accession to one of his early requests for aid in translation "with such unwomanly avidity." After inviting him spontaneously to dinner, she fretted over her "unwomanly boldness." In 1907 once opportunity for life-altering boldness beckoned, when announcement of Ginzberg's departure for Europe created such despondence on her part that he inquired about its cause. Even then, she could not reveal her true feelings in the absence of a script dictating the proper procedure.

Nevertheless, in her fevered imagination, she already *was* "in the eyes of God," Ginzberg's "affianced wife." Like a loyal spouse, she absorbed his ideas, acceded to his tastes—i.e., lightening her lecture schedule because he considered this activity unseemly for a woman— and coddled him when he was ill. The October 20 announcement could not immediately transform this apperception. Now enjoying walks with him made her feel like an adulteress. Ruefully, she identified the wedding trip with the new Mrs. Ginzberg as "my honeymoon." Truth to tell, she regarded herself not as a rejected would-be wife but as an *agunah* (deserted wife unable to remarry). In self-laceration, she revised her former status to that of "intellectual mistress" and her service to Ginzberg as "four prostituted years."

Belatedly, Szold berated herself for not having risen above convention and informed Ginzberg of her feelings. Only then did she recognize his self-absorption to the point of disregard for common courtesy. Only then did she condemn his inconsideration in submitting numerous pages for proofreading just days before a deadline (a practice continued long after October 20). His demanding the return of the scrapbooks without a word of thanks for the many hours put into them brought the issue to the forefront. His obliviousness to her obvious distress led her to question his profession of continued friendly feelings.

The convention which she had most fervently hoped to defy, of course, was the most fundamental discrepancy in their relationship, the thirteen-year gap in their age. When she contemplated the happy marriage of Ginzberg's old friend to a woman fifteen years his senior, she cried out in pain, "Is it possible that he alone, he, my ideal, could not rise above convention?"

It was Ginzberg's ultimate convention flouting that hit the hardest: his leaving the impression that he was obligated to one woman and then conducting a whirlwind courtship with another. As the Szold-Ginzberg friendship soured in the wake of her degradation and his sullied reputation, a most curious transaction took place. Ginzberg passed his professed "best friend" on the street and did not tip his hat. Instead of censuring his rudeness, Szold justified his performance. His refusal to hew to customary forms, she realized, was proof of the sexual dimension of their relationship.

Fortunately there was a fourth motif that assuaged her painful plight to some degree: the question of culpability. Crushed as she was under the burden of unrequited love, Henrietta Szold was not prepared to discard everything that she held dear. Like other refined and advanced women of her station she cherished the qualities of "restraint, sympathy, and unselfishness."[48] Her entire existence had been animated by dedication to education, humanity, and the Jewish people. Had she found these values wanting in Ginzberg, it is unlikely that she would have succumbed to his charms in the first place.

From their first meeting, Szold had considered Ginzberg her "ideal," a man of unimpeachable character as well as superior intelligence. It followed that if she could efface this image of the ideal man, then she could successfully maneuver through her perilous rite of passage. Not once but many times she posed the question: "Is he guilty?" A positive answer to this question, though insufficient to dispel her love, would inaugurate the process of recovery.

The moral issue is key to "Meditation on Lost Love." The first two sections are a narrative describing contacts with Ginzberg, in person or by mail, in chronological order. After the narration of the October 20 climax and its immediate aftermath, the form changes. The concluding section is a jumble of rambling thoughts wherein Szold reviews the events of the previous five years, sometimes adding narrative tidbits but no longer hewing to chronology. The themes of societal convention, her own obsessive, masochistic, and ultimately disappointed passion, and the underlying murmurs of death surface and resurface, but in no special order. Not so the motif of Ginzberg's guilt. Like the others, it pervades the narrative. But the other themes appear, willy-nilly, whenever a phrase, a season, a date, or a current event conjures up their memory, whereas ruminations about guilt and innocence proceed along a linear trajectory. Gradually Szold amasses evidence of Ginzberg's guilt, beginning with the trifling and ending with the most damaging. It is this that gives structure to the narrative.

Just what constituted guilt in her eyes? At first Szold found Ginzberg blameworthy only of requesting small translation favors beyond those performed for the other professors. After some reluctance, she admitted, she became a full and equal collaborator in her own exploitation.

Advancing and intensifying their relationship were all those walks and talks in Morningside Park and along Riverside Drive. But as Ginzberg became as willing a student of Szold's store of knowledge as she of his, as the amateur botanist "opened his (Ginzberg's) eyes to read the book of nature"[49] as the two sat in wordless silence gazing upon river and sky, they displayed an intimacy more common among lovers than friends. The strongest evidence of reciprocal love, to Szold's mind, emerged during the 1907–1908 academic year, when the two met almost daily and she perceived a "lovelight" in his eyes. Were not these tokens of romance rather than light-hearted friendship? On that question hinged Ginzberg's guilt or innocence.

In Szold's disordered imagination, had Ginzberg admitted his affection for her before his departure for Europe, he would not have been guilty of betrayal. Nor would she have faulted him for succumbing to amorous infatuation for the young and pretty Adele Katzenstein. Then, at least, she could take credit for "unlocking his heart," even if someone else took possession of it. What she could not abide was his insistence that he had never considered their friendship anything but platonic and his professed blindness to abundant evidence of her infatuation.

As she continued to ruminate on the failed relationship, she unearthed specific examples of mendacity unsuitable for an ideal man. One was the opacity of Ginzberg's final letters at a time when love gushed out of hers. Another was his insistence that he had taken Marx rather than her into his confidence during the time when he spent every day with her and hardly saw the other faculty outside of the seminary. A third was his declaration that the source of his 1908 personal crisis was familial when it really sprung from the decision to marry the girl from Berlin. The deciding blow was his insistence that he had been totally ignorant of her passion until she told him of it, though her bizarre behavior after the announcement of his engagement betrayed her depression to all around them.

After Szold uncovered Ginzberg's mendacity, her "ideal man" began to slip from his pedestal. Though she could not yet escape her limerent emotions, she finally acknowledged resentment at his self-serving capitalization of them. Friends contributed additional information that raised questions about Ginzberg's character and his sexual integrity: he had always boasted indifference to public acclaim, yet he informed the *American Hebrew* of his 1909 publications; for no apparent reason, he had destroyed Israel Davidson's relationship with a woman; advances to the adolescent Ruth Schechter had resulted in his banishment from the Schechter home. A personal affront was his joking about a breach of contract suit with two colleagues.

Those findings, however, were insignificant next to the disclosure that functions as the "Meditation's" denouement. Mutual friends revealed that in Europe and perhaps even in America Ginzberg had consorted with loose women. (Upon hearing this, Szold's fevered [and virginal] imagination even conjured up an illegitimate child.) Though she questioned the veracity of the information, it nevertheless permitted her to indulge in *schadenfreude*, satisfied that her distress was sullying Ginzberg's reputation, gloating over his difficulty in locating a new translator.

Then, at last, she admitted that he had acted dishonorably toward her and entertained the prospect that her impending trip to Europe and Palestine would cure her passion and restore her mental health. She had already decided not to continue translating what became the third volume of the *Legends of the Jews*—a wise move—and to remove her name from the fourth volume, which she did translate, and keep it out of *Geonica* altogether—self-defeating gestures discouraged by close associates.[50]

The termination of the Szold-Ginzberg literary collaboration again invokes Szold's masochism, a personality trait that transcended her surrender to Ginzberg's exploitation. To toil to the point of exhaustion was to conform to a lifelong pattern. In Baltimore, Philadelphia, New York, and later in Jerusalem, Szold was a workaholic. Furthermore, the fact that 1903 to 1908 were the years when she felt herself most alive supplied another masochistic motive for journal writing that actually contradicted the stated intention. While her rational side wanted to eliminate pain through objectivization and externalization, her emotional side clung to the pain and the joy of her "bittersweet happiness." But this seemingly masochistic motive was, paradoxically, to pave the way for her redemption. Rationality and the exercise of the will were not what Szold needed at this time. Friends' advice to drive the Ginzberg episode into the background and lose herself in literature or scholarship proved ineffective. It was almost as useless to record the events in chronological order; for this reason the first two sections of the "Meditation" were of limited value. The third section would prove more beneficial. By abandoning system and chronology, Szold forced herself to confront her inner reality.

Willy-nilly, she stumbled upon a procedure taught in contemporary journal workshops. For the past thirty years Ira Progoff and his followers have helped people move through personal crises by composing "intensive journals." The technique of journal writing empowers them to draw upon inner resources and find new meaning in their lives. Because Szold concentrated on only one episode in her life and did not probe relations other than those with Ginzberg or speculate about a future without him, her eight-month stint of journal writing did not complete her passage to the safe shore of mental health. The "Meditation" was not the beginning of the end, but the end of the beginning of her healing.[51]

"Meditation on Lost Love," then, is an effort to negotiate between numerous complexities and contradictions. It pulsates with conflicting sensations of eros, disappointment, and anguished yearning for a man who would never be hers, alongside candid introspection and good common sense. With the European voyage just weeks away, Szold needed to anchor her thoughts in a simpler and more consistent literary effort of her own. She found it in words written four years before. That summer (and every summer since 1904, with the exception of 1908), as Ginzberg departed New York for vacation, she had imagined his returning with a bride. To prepare herself for this eventuality, she had copied a poem about a rejected woman, then composed a letter of renunciation that acknowledged her infatuation but relinquished Ginzberg to a more appropriate mate. When the anticipated event had happily failed to materialize, she had stored the two pieces away. To recover them in 1909, after the dreaded deed had actually taken place, was a wise move. The renunciation especially helped disentangle a real rather than an imagined predicament, thereby initiating a long-delayed passage into emotional maturity.

MEDITATION ON
LOST LOVE

EDITOR'S NOTE: SOURCES AND STRUCTURE

The next three chapters contain an account of the frienship between Henrietta Szold and Louis Ginzberg in the words of the protagonists. As printed, it is an amalgam of Szold's reflections after the frienship's abrupt termination ("Meditation on Lost Love") and the Szold-Ginzberg correspondence. The "Meditation" supplies the framework; letters are inserted whenever the narrative reaches the point at which they are written. To differentiate them from Szold's narrative, they are indented on both sides of the page.

I have included the complete text of all letters available to me, excluding only some detailed and technical discussions about publishing and the very few sentences that are fragmentary and unclear. Deletions are indicated by three dots (. . .). In preparing the correspondence for publication, I regularized the position of addresses and dates at the top center. All salutations and final greetings are included. Wherever parentheses appear, they are found in the original text. Words in square brackets are mine; they include explanatory transitions, transliterations of Hebrew and Aramaic in the Ashkenazic pronunciation familiar to Szold and Ginzberg, and translations from these languages as well as German, French, Latin, and Yiddish. Phrases demanding full sentence explications are translated in footnotes. I have retained original punctuation, underlining, Szold's archaic spelling and word divisions (e.g., to-day, staid, learnt, programme), and Ginzberg's original variations on English spelling and word usage (klippings, sightshowings and wifes). All this is intended to recreate the social and cultural atmosphere of Jewish New York during the first years of our now waning century.

I am responsible for the title, "Meditation on Lost Love," the tripartite division, and all section and subsection headings.

Awakening Love,
1903–1906

Tuesday, November 17, 1908

Today it is four weeks since my only real happiness in life was killed by a single word. Since then I have hardly been conscious of living. There has been only suffering, nights and days, and days and nights of suffering. Today for the first time I have been calm, at least outwardly. For the first time I have been aware of what I was doing at a given moment. Almost I slept all night. All these weeks composed of minutes of misery I have done nothing but remember—and it has been a thorny crown of sorrows, this remembering bittersweet days.

Today the thought comes to my mind that if I put all my memories down, not necessarily in order of time, but only so as to have them before me as an object, so to say, outside of myself, instead of keeping them inside of me as a subjective pain—perhaps it will help me to adjust myself to the new cold loveless life I must henceforth live. Something I must do to wipe out what I now recognize as folly in the past and prevent it from becoming wickedness in the future.

It would be easy enough to sum up the tragedy of my life in a sentence: For eight years, from 1894 to 1902, I said to myself every night when I went to bed: You may be awakened this night and summoned to your father's bedside because his last moment has arrived. Be prepared and be strong. Then catastrophe came, and I was not there to see him pass away, I was neither prepared nor strong. Life was no longer ideal and full of content. Then, after an interval, for four years, from 1904–1908, I said to myself daily, not once but a thousand times, at any moment you may be told that he is affianced to another woman. Be prepared and be strong. That blow came, too, as inevitably as the other, and again I was neither prepared nor strong.

Why am I not satisfied with this brief statement of my tragedy? Because I must, if I can, work out a justification for myself and for him, I needed no justification of the ways of God, when my father was taken from me. Whatever they may say, I have a truly religious nature to that extent. But unless I can see myself innocent and see him innocent, both of us victims of conventions, let me say for the sake of completing the thought in a formal way, since I do not know how my facts are going to complete it—unless I can see ourselves, each one of us innocent, I do not know how to go on living worthily.

I met him[1] February 11–12, 1903, at the Clara de Hirsch Home.[2] Dr. Jastrow[3] had prepared me for the scholar, Adele[4] for a conceited coxcomb, and I at once saw only the man—the idealist, the single-minded searcher for truth, the free-thinker so radical that he was conservative—this side he showed to me then and always.

The next day, or was it the same afternoon? I saw him at a meeting of the American Jewish Historical Society. For some reason I left before the meeting was over and as I passed out of the room, I caught a sight of him sitting on the end seat of one of the benches. As I brushed by, I extended my hand to the man I had seen only once before, instead of merely nodding to him. I was frightened and abashed. For weeks the memory of it would return to haunt me, and shame me.

In the fall of 1903, the end of September, we moved to New York. I do not think he had returned from Europe at the time, but he must have landed within a week, for Rachel[5] and myself spoke to him after the Synagogue services on Saturday, the third of October it must have been, at all counts the second Saturday we were living here, and we asked him the way to Cooper Union, where the delegates to the Basle Congress were to give their report that evening. He offered to call for us and to take us there, but mindful of the strange attraction he had exerted upon me I repulsed him. Rachel, afterwards reproached me for having been so brusque, and I could offer no defense, except that I wanted to be brusque. That incident at the Historical Society meeting still frightened me. It frightened me, too, that I thrilled when Rachel addressed him, and he spoke. Up to that time I had never loved a man, was I to begin then? So late in life?

[That there was written contact on a professional level before 1903 is indicated by the following letter:]

November 6, 1901

Dr. Louis Ginzberg
New York City

My dear Sir:—

Your letter of September 18 submitting your plan for the proposed work on "Jewish Legends relating to Biblical Matters," was put before the Publication Committee by the Chairman early in October, and by it approved and recommended for adoption to the Board of Trustees. The latter has now had its meeting, and I am instructed to write you that your proposition has been accepted, together with the terms you suggest. The understanding is that you will write, in German, a book on the lines laid down in your proposition, to contain approximately one hundred thousand words, and to be available for the use of the Society in the year 1903, all rights in the book to be ceded to the Jewish Publication Society of America for a honorarium of $1000.

The Committee suggests that, as the manuscript must be handled by a translator, it be written in ink and only on one side of the paper.

Awaiting your reply, I am, my dear Sir,

Yours very truly,

Henrietta Szold,
Secretary to the
Publication Committee[6]

[That Szold, in her professional capacity, had to deal with Ginzberg harshly is indicated by the following:]

528 West 123d Street
New York, October 20, 1903

Dr. Louis Ginzberg
60 West 115th Street
New York City

My dear Dr. Ginzberg,

Your letter of October 9 was duly submitted to the Publication Committee of our Society at a recent meeting, and the

Chairman of the Committee instructs me to write you that the Committee could not see its way to granting your request for a readjustment of terms. The Committee realizes the position in which you are placed, and appreciates the fact that your labor will be greater than you had anticipated, and perhaps, under the circumstances, could have anticipated. On the other hand, the Society will be put to much greater expense in providing for the translation and publication of your book than it had planned. In view of this additional expense, the Committee had to decide that no revision of the arrangements entered into with you could be made in justice to the Society.

Furthermore, the Committee wishes me to say that it hopes the completion of the book will not be too long delayed.

Yours very truly,

Henrietta Szold
Secretary to the
Publication Committee

I cannot remember, perhaps I never know, why I did not enter his Talmud class, was it arranged between him and Dr. Schechter?,[7] and I never asked. I don't know. At all events, I went to him only for a few history lessons, until Dr. Marx[8] arrived from Europe, and throughout the session for a lesson once a week in Aramaic grammar. For a large part of the time he was sick. But even the comparatively few times I saw him, I forced myself into antagonism to him. I held it up against him that he occasionally was late for his classes. When I learned that he actually did object to my being in his class, that naturally counted against him, not because he opposed the higher education for women, but because I felt he must have known that I was seeking something to bring me into accord with my dear father even after his death.

Meantime all the advances were made by him—made in the same way as advances have been made to me all my life. On the last day of the holidays, Dr. Jastrow died, and Louis[9] asked him for a short eulogy. He wrote it in German, and one day he stopped me in the hall and asked me to translate it for him. I demurred—not over graciously, either. And that was surely against my nature and my habit. He made a little plea, and I gave in. I did the work, and handed him the paper, again in the hall of the Seminary, simply in passing, pointing out, however, a change I had made because I thought it necessary.

So far as I can remember I had little other intercourse with him all winter—once I met him at Mr. Hoffman's,[10] and all but quarreled with him, and Seder evening at the Schechter's, at the end of which the first gracious word was exchanged between us. It was a wild night, and Dr. Marx and Dr. Friedlaender[11] proposed to take us home. He excused himself for not going with us too, on the plea of not yet being strong enough to expose himself unduly. How emphatically I repudiated the idea of his having even thought of doing it!

Meantime, his two colleagues had been coming every Saturday night for English instructions. One evening, Dr. Friedlaender accused me of having written the article in the Comment[12] on the personal characteristics of the Seminary faculty. His chief reason for attributing it to me was that scant justice had been done to him. He was wrong—I had not written the article—and yet how right he was that I could not have done justice to him. When I defended myself, the question was asked, why I had not invited him to join in the English evenings. How could I offer instruction, I said, to a gentlemen who had been in this country several years? That was honest, not a subterfuge, but I was glad at the time that I could honestly not invite him.

In the spring I had a severe attack of earache, and I could not go to the synagogue one Saturday morning. In the afternoon, Dr. Marx and Dr. Friedlaender came to inquire about me and to find out whether they were to come in the evening. With them he came too. And that was the beginning of my real struggle with myself on account of him, of my bitter-sweet happiness and of my present humiliation.

What could I do, when they left for the afternoon service, only to return for supper and an evening of English, but turn to him, too, and ask him—the words stuck in a dry throat—whether he would not come with the others for supper and for a lesson? From time on he came regularly, and my torture has never ceased from that hour until this. Will it ever cease?

The next occasion that I remember as a distinct impression was the Commencement at the Seminary. On the platform I saw only him—his face that meant and means so much to me, everything that is ideal in life. After the exercises he came over here, with the Nathans[13] and Elvira Solis[14] and others. It was a hot day and we served lemonade, and over the lemonade a discussion arose as to the higher education of women. It was evident he didn't even want me to go into his class.

His South-African brother[15] visited him that summer (1904) and he took a trip with him. On his return—I was in the thick of the Year Book[16]—he came to my house and asked me to write a letter for him to the Commissioner of Immigration on account of a relative of his detained at Ellis Island.

I put down such slight services as these that were asked for to justify myself in anticipation for the advances I may be charged with having made later, along the same lines.

Late in September or early in October—it was a golden day—I was invited on a Monday, the day the Seminary opened for regular work, to the Schechter's for a luncheon in honor of Professor Goldziher.[17] He was there, and with him and Dr. Friedlaender I walked back to the Seminary. On the way Dr. Friedlaender asked me whether I was not going to be present at the Seminary dinner for Professor Goldziher, and I reiterated my principle, not to go to the Seminary dinners, though I *was* a student then. He said he could not understand the distinction I drew. Then—I still thrill at the recollection as I thrilled at the time—he shot forth "Ridiculous!" with that dear little guttural gurgle that is so eloquent in my ears. How happy I was—he recognized my womanhood.

On the same walk from 115th Street up, he said that he had expected to see me in his *Kiddushin* class, and I reminded him of the opinion he had uttered at our house on Commencement afternoon, and asked whether they did not suffice to keep me away.— Next morning at the breakfast I had his letter. I trembled so I could not at first open it, and the letters danced before my eyes. He said he wanted me to come to his class—he would he had more disciples of my kind.

JTS, October 10, 1904

Dear Miss Szold,

I just finished going through the part of the treatise *Kiddushin*[18] which I intend to take up in the class and I am quite satisfied that there is nothing in it that should prevent you of being present at my Talmud lecture. I am writing you these lines and informing you of the fact mentioned because I don't want to be misunderstood as if I had any objection to your being present at my lectures. It is against my character to make any compliments, not even to a lady, but I answer you that I wished I had a class of *Talmidim* [students] like you, that I could realize "*U-mitalmidai yotair mi-kullam.*"[19]

Yours very truly,

Louis Ginzberg

Not by what he said was I made crazy—his words were conventional, and in all my transport I knew them to be so. But the fact that he had written at all, and that he would have me in his class, would tolerate me!

[That Szold still felt uncomfortable with the subject three months later is indicated by the following:]

528 West 123rd Street
New York
January 16, 1905

Dear Dr. Ginzberg:—

An innocent word dropped inadvertently in my presence warned me of the approach of an awkward passage in Kiddushin, to be omitted, it seems, on account of me. I am not writing because I do not trust your tact and judgment implicitly. I want merely to assure you that if you exercise your right to exclude me from the class when my presence is trying, I shall only take it as an indication that ordinarily I am persona grata. You need not refer to this, unless it be to tell me to absent myself from your class.

Yours very truly,

Henrietta Szold[20]

At the end of the first lesson, he called me aside, and asked me whether I would correct his errors in English at the end of every hour. Was that my fault? No, but it was my undoing. And it *was* my fault that I did it so conscientiously. Need I to have done it absolutely every day? Need I to have done it so thoroughly? And all that time I was commending myself inwardly for never remaining with him a single minute after I had finished explaining to him! That was a sop to my Cerberus of a conscience. But it did not neutralize the danger I was exposing myself to.

Exposing? How long was it before I was in the clutches of the danger, a victim? I don't know—I cannot remember. My brain was in a constant whirl then hardly less tumultuous than its condition now. Oh, how long it is since I have known a calm moment! For even when happiness came, it was far from tranquil. And now, shall I ever be at peace? All I know is the result—unprepared as I was for the study of the Talmud, I was often the only one in the class to understand him. The intricacies of the subject, involved still more by his awkward English, lay open before me, without an effort on my part. Whatever he said, he seemed to say for me. And then, how quickly I learnt to distinguish his footfall in the corridor. As I sat with my back to the door, and heard the scuffling of feet outside made by the students, I could pick out his step, as he came in with the big folios under his arm and the little silk cap on his head. Never did I make a mistake. Soon I began to notice—or was I mistaken?—that he both averted his eyes from me and sought me again. When a knotty point came up, he always looked in my direction—when he felt my intense gaze resting upon him, he half turned away.

That torture went on until about January or February (I think February, because we had to hurry), when he again made an advance. One evening he came with the half and inadequately translated lecture "The Talmud Student"[21] done by Mr. Hoffman and to be delivered soon. He asked me to help him with it. I helped him as I was henceforth to help him always, I did the translation, I had the typewriting done, I fixed it up, and I did it by sacrificing sleep, and fool that I was, I was happy over it. Again was it my fault that he came with this piece of work, showing me how I might make myself useful to him? No, it was again not my fault, but why did I grasp the opportunity with such unwomanly avidity? Why was I willing to make substantial sacrifice? Why was I so willing to meet him half way? Why did I then offer to teach him how to read the lecture? Why did I besides, go to hear him deliver it, when I knew every word by heart? Was that the lecture delivered at Dr. Asher's synagogue,[22] at which his sister-in-law met me, and thanked me for what I had done for him, for coming besides, and for inviting him to the house for lunch, instead of letting him take a cup of wretched cocoa at an eating-house? Or was that the following year? Whenever it was, I was honest enough to say to myself, "You little know how little disinterested I am in all this, you little know how happy I am to make every sacrifice in the world to secure his presence by me!"

It must have been then, or soon after, that he asked me to read the proof of one of his Genizah Studies articles in the *Jewish Quarterly*.[23] I was innocent again, so far as the suggestion was concerned. But was I so innocent as to the way it was carried out? The second or third time it was not proof reading merely, he actually dictated all the English matter, and for four years I put as much time and thought upon it as he himself did, again sacrificing sleep to do the work as thoroughly as I knew how.

The Jewish Theological Seminary of America
531–535 West 123rd St.
New York City

6 May (1905)

Dear Miss Szold,

Your "remnant" as my ["]remainder" did not remain long with me as I mailed my article for the J.Q.R. as soon as I left you. There "remains" nothing for us to do than to have my "remainder" "remain" in its present state as the article will "remain" in England and I do not even expect to get the proofsheet of it.

I remain as ever

Your

Louis Ginzberg
a remnant of the
remainder[24]

Of course, I was doing the same sort of services for Dr. Marx and Dr. Friedlaender, and Dr. Schechter, and Dr. Schloessinger,[25] and half a dozen students—the more fool I. But did he not notice the difference? Did I really succeed in hiding my preference? I was afraid at the time that I was not circumspect.

I can attach a distinct state of mind to Purim, 1905. Once again it was not my fault that he should ask to be permitted to go with me when I said I was going downtown to a synagogue on the East Side to hear the Megillah [Scroll of Esther] read. But that evening I learnt the whole extent of my misfortune. When I reached the women's gallery, I found I was on the same side with him and could not see him. Am I suffering so keenly now because I wickedly crossed over to the other side and sat where I could see his face? On the way down there had been a delay and I feared we should come too late for the reading, and I told him it would be on his conscience if for the first time in my life I did not read the Megillah. We came in time, none the less I did not read the Megillah, I read his dear face only.

But was it my fault that he asked me one Saturday morning after the services to stop a moment—he had a favor to ask of me? Would I take down the lecture he was going to deliver on the holidays? No, it was not my fault. I could not have invented the welcome opportunity to be working for him. But did I have to sit up night after night working out my notes? Did I have to feel jubilant when I wore myself out for him? And wasn't that the time when I began to consult him at every point on his Legends? Was that absolutely necessary? Or am I too hard on myself? And how did I come to write up the Halakah lectures[26] for him—at my own or his instigation? This very summer just ended, with what joy I corrected the typewritten copy of those holiday lectures! And how true I thought it, when his niece told me I had been a fool for working for her uncle as I had, adding that I would probably do it again. And now I may never do it again if I want to maintain a vestige of self respect—so at least they tell me. As though I cared for self respect in the face of annihilation of my whole personality.

"Saturday after the services?" I said. When did those happy Saturday walks begin? I cannot remember. Were they my fault, my suggestion, I mean? I cannot remember. But they must have begun some time that spring, because I remember when he came home the following fall from his European trip, I escaped to the other side on the first Saturday after his arrival, and he came after me and asked for a walk, and I said: "Ah! this is good to resume the old ways!" And he returned: "Why shouldn't we resume?"

Even then I began to notice something that made me exquisitely happy. He never thanked me for anything I did for him. What could he mean by dropping a convention that was deeper than the ordinary convention?

Passover came, and I gave the Seder at the Clara de Hirsch Home. How enthusiastic they all were about my manner, my language! Was I flattered by their admiration? Have I ever been flattered by such admiration? But in this case, I said to myself, you do not know that you are admiring my darling, who let me imbibe somewhat at the source of his learning! You admire him and not me. And I was happy. More than that, I realized that slowly some of the idealism that I had lost with my dear father was coming back to irradiate my life.

That was not all. I had to spend the night at the Home, but the next morning I walked up to the synagogue. I have promised myself to confess everything here, therefore I must admit that three-fourths of the impulse to walk uptown so early in the morning was my burning desire to see him on the holiday—for then as now and always in the interval I had to wrench my eyes forcibly away from his face to my prayer book. At the synagogue it always seemed doubly fine, kind, and noble to me. But—I thought at the time—was ever woman more royally rewarded for an effort than I that beautiful Passover morning? As I entered with Miss Sommerfeld, he raised his eyes, they lighted up, he stirred in his seat and called Dr. Schechter's attention to my presence.

Numerous recollections crowd in upon me of that spring. For Purim he had sent me the Hebrew book of legends, with a poem on the fly-leaf. I sat in the dark for two hours holding my hand upon his writing, my whole body vibrating painfully. In the evening I met him at Schechter's, and for my shame I could not look him in the face, nor could I swallow a bite, until a word from Dr. Schechter about my lack of appetite brought me to my senses, and I heard him say that he (unlike Dr. Marx) could flirt with any women he chose—he was heart-whole.

How often I sat over my work in the same way as over this book of legends—incapable of thought or work. The whole of me a sensation, a painful one at that. How often I had to give up sleep in order to make up time lost in this way. And my friends now recommend all sorts of intellectual effort to drown the sorrow in my heart! That is my misfortune. No one knows, I apparently could never convey to anyone by word or manner that I am a dependent woman with a keen emotional nature, a distinctly feminine woman, not an intellectual abstraction.

It was either that spring or a year later that something happened that made even me laugh at my folly. Mrs. Eli Strouse was at the Seminary synagogue, and she said "What a fine, noble face!" and I returned with ardent enthusiasm, "Isn't it, and it expresses the man!"

But she meant, it soon appeared, Mr. Jacobson, the reader[27] and I meant *him!*

Long before this I had begun to preach to myself that my feelings were absurd in a woman of my age, and in relation to him, so many years my junior. I examined my face in the mirror, and went away saying, never again shall this foolish, hopeless feeling master me—only to succumb the next time I saw him. And then things got worse, I even got jealous—of all sorts of young girls, of my own sister Adele. He came one day and asked her to take a walk with him. She refused. He turned to me and said, "I do not ask you, because you are too busy!" Thus it has always been, never too busy to do work, but too busy for a walk. I began to study every young girl's face I met, to envy her—the round contours, the fresh color, the light laugh, the lineaments unmarked by experiences, the buoyant step, the insouciance of manner. How I prayed—fool, fool!—for youth or its semblance. Sometimes I saw his eyes rest upon a young girl, a beautiful girl, at the synagogue, and I despaired. Such has been my torture for three years.

But chiefly I was jealous at that time of Adele. One day they had a discussion about nationalities, and Adele asserted her scorn of Germans. I noticed a catch in his throat at that. Did he consider himself a German? I asked. To the very last, even after her marriage, I thought he treated Adele with more piquancy—she was the young woman, and I the old.

Again I remember the Commencement—his face under the cap and above the gown. And how I almost scratched his face, because he said something derogatory to his own appearance. I had to laugh, when I realized that it was he saying it of himself.

I think it was soon after this second Commencement, before he went to Europe, or it may have been the following year, that Miriam Flexner came to supper one Sunday with her brother. It was a hot day, and I saw him at the Seminary library window working. I went over and made him come to supper. He seemed grateful and even happy about it. And I worried myself nervous and sick over my unwomanly boldness.

If I did wrong, I expiated it all over and over again that summer. He went to Europe and when he bade us farewell, he said he would write occasionally if we permitted it. I thought I was included only that he might write all the more naturally to Adele. Before a letter could come, to confirm my fears or disabuse me, indeed, before the card came from the steamer for both of us, I was to learn the strength of my passion. The night following the day he left, I gave way entirely to my feelings. For days and nights I wept and wept and renounced him, because I saw the folly of it all. And then I wept and wept again, until I was grayer than I had been, and older looking, and thin. Adele had several weeks before by accident discovered my plight, I think she caught me weeping. But from that time until November 10th of this year no one, as I thought, knew anything about it except her. It now turns out that everybody in my world knew it.

My love swept over me like a torrent for several weeks. All the time I was doing Yearbook work, dry-as-dust work, I was in a turmoil. Day after day I hoped for a letter and none came. Finally, I tried to end the whole commotion within in the same way I am trying to end it now—I sat down and wrote out a renunciation. It helped me, I grew calmer. I saw that he could not feel any love for an old woman— he was too normal for such aberrations. It did me good to pretend, as I did, that chivalry had led him to offer himself to me when he noticed my plight. Love, I made myself realize, he could not give me, and chivalry I would not have. But I could not help hoping for a letter—and it came, and joy of joy, I had one and Adele had none. And I had a second before Adele's came, and I had a third that summer, the last in German.[28]

Paris, July 3, 1905

My Dear Miss Szold,

You will undoubtedly be very much surprised to receive my first letter from Paris. But you know the saying: "bad company spoils good manners" and having had for ten days exclusively the company of women—the men did nothing but gambling all the time—I acquired some weaknesses of the fair sex, among others the custom of changing the mind. When we came near Cherbourg it suddenly occurred to me that it would not be a bad idea to visit Paris, and so I am again in *"la ville lumière."*

The weather and the sea were splendid all the time of my voyage. I spent all my time in sleeping, walking and dreaming. I believe that I might have entered in a sleeping match with Miss Adele without great risque of losing it. As to my dreams in the state of waking, they were not of a very pleasant mind. The grandeur and monotony of the sea has always a melancholy-producing effect on me, and it is very good for me to be in the gay city of Paris again. I have met here Mrs. Friedenwald[29] and her children who asked to be remembered to you.

With kind regards, to you, Mrs. Szold, and Miss Adele, I am

Your

Louis Ginzberg[30]

Amsterdam, August 17, '05

My dear Miss Szold,

I still think in cycles of thousands of years and measured by this standard there elapsed a moment hardly between the time I received your kind letter and my answer. This is only *tov al derekh ha-pilpul,* as for *tov al derekh ha-pshat*[31] I will confess that I do not dare to write to you but English and you know it belongs to my characteristic immodesty rather not to do a thing at all than to do it badly. Now as no other choice is left to me than either to do injustice to my pride or to my friends, I can't help preferring the first evil. What a shining example of modesty I am! I can ascribe this feeling only to the effect of my seasickness which I termed "melancholy." By this I understand the feeling which comes over me when I confront nature in its grandeur and vastness. Such a sight is the best demonstration of how little and insignificant this little creature is which in its stupidity calls itself "homo sapiens." Of course I do not deny that moral indignation at the men gambling below and resentment of being left in the company of chattering geese drove me to Paris. This is again an illustration for the philosophical theory according to which there is neither evil not good in itself. The bad company had the good result for me to enjoy the art treasures of Paris. I arrived now to the point which enables me to examine the account given of myself in my last letter.

I stayed in Paris for about a week and then I tell you that I visited the Bibl[ioteque] Nat[ionale] only once for do not doubt that I found this city delightful. The Louvre is still the greatest art collection in the world and after spending several years in the American desert one needs "a strong dose" of it. From Paris I went to Hamburg V.D.H. where my parents drank the waters and I stayed with them a fortnight. Unexpectedly I met there Dr. and Mrs. Marx on their wedding tour. Mrs. Marx is a very nice little woman—the adverb modifying both adjectives—and she will be a great addition to the Seminary.[32] I did not go further East as Marx had arranged the printing business with Itzkowski[33] in Berlin and I am spending a great part of my time in reading proofs . . . I intend to spend about a month in Oxford and Cambridge and return to NY about the end of October.

I am very thankful to you for the news you were kind enough to inform me of. If a [I] were rude I would have said what a pity that Dropsie[34] did not die a few years earlier, but as I am too gentle to make such remarks I will deplore only the fact that his will was not known four years ago. We would have had a Jewish academy instead of a theol. Sem. But *das Geschehene lässt sich nicht mehr ungeschehen machen* [What has been done cannot be undone]. Let us hope that the Sem[inary] will benefit by it not only pecuniarily but also spiritually.

I do not understand such indignation at Krauskopf's remark that the thread uniting the Jews is purely social.[35] This fool "*sprach ein grosses wortgelassen aus*" [let something slip out of his mouth]. One of the greatest German historians defines history as following: "*Die Geschichtsewissenschaft is die Wissenschaft, welche die Thatsachen der Entwickelung der Menschen in ihren Bethatigungen als sociale Wesen in kulturem Zusammenhange erforscht und darstellt*" [The science of history is the discipline which depicts the evolution of human beings as social creatures in their cultural context {paraphrase}].

If I were in America I might have written on the subject: What is social? The Zionistic movement is mainly due to social reasons and if Krauskopf were not a fool or a charlatan he might have become a Zionist. Speaking about Zionism, you know probably by this time I did not go to Basel.[36] I could give you a number of reasons why I stayed at home but the real reason was this: I was elected delegate to the Congress and the credentials were sent to me. Now I do not think that I who is not connected with any Zionistic organization ought to be elected a delegate and as I did not care to go as a *Zuschauer* [observer], I remained home. Of course I do not need to tell you that I am delighted at Zangwill's *mappoloh* [defeat][37] and I hope only "*ken yovdu.*"[38].

I was very glad to hear of the mutual spoiling of grandmother and child. But you do injustice to Benjamin by calling him an adulator. Children are free of this fault they really believe their exaggerations and in the case of Benjamin's grandmother he is still more to be excused for a little exaggeration.

My mother sends her regards to you, *unbekannterweise* [though she has never met you] and my father also said that if it were not against the Talmudic law *ein shoalim bi'shlom ishah* [A man shouldn't inquire about a woman's well-being], he would like to send his regards to you. As for myself I only hope you will punish me for my long letter by writing a much more longer one to your

Louis Ginzberg

P.S. Please remember me to Mrs. Szold and Adele. I hope to write next week to Miss Adele and she may prepare herself for a treat.

Amsterdam, September 1, 1905

Dear Miss Szold,

When on the steamer I thought more than once of your Drama,[39] especially when the men in their extreme egotism used to leave their seasick wifes [sic] on the deck and plunge themselves into the depth of a "poker" and did not emerge from it before the dinner bell sounded. But my wrath against the gambling men abated the more I was left over to the company of the crown of creation, seeing that also the weaker sex—but strong when knowing their weakness—was playing its game all the time.

And don't you think that your Margaret—is this her name? was playing? From the moment she declared her love to Gilbert she became unfit for real work, her socialism and all other "isms" were only her playthings, while poor Gilbert was going on planning, scheming, and working. In other words, I believe that a woman can't master more than one strong feeling at once. When in love nothing but the object of her love exists for her, while the man is strong enough to love a woman and have other passions at the same time. The love affair between Margaret and Gilbert was bound to take an unfortunate turn and neither of the two lovers was to blame for it.

Of course, my judgment is adequate to that of the Rabbi who, on hearing the pleadings of one party, exclaimed "You are right," and the same time he did on hearing the pleadings of the other party, and asqed [asked] [sic] by his wife, the Rebbetzin, how it is possible that both parties are right, he answered, "You are right too!" But how can you expect literary judgment of a person who spends half of his time in preparing Geniza Fragments for the printer and the other half reading the proofs of them?

I have nevertheless a surprise for you. In the last four weeks I have read Labriola: *Essais sur la conception materialiste de l'histoire*[40]; Kautsky, *Was will und kann die matarialistische Geschichtsauffasung Leisten?*[41] and Bernstein, *Das Realistische und das ideologische Moment in Socialissmus.*[42] Now what do you think of me reading the works of three "*Genossen*" [comrades]? I consider it needless to say that I am still opposed to the socialistic conception of history. I am still the old aristocrat who can't and will not believe that Caesar, Alexander the Great, Napolean, etc. did *not* make history but that it was the headless, heartless, mindless vulgus who produced civilisation. I was glad to see, however, that even in socialistic circles the dogma set up by Marx, according to which "*Die Ideen war the Reflexe der okonomeishchen Verhaltnisse sind*" [Ideas are reflections of economic forces] is now given up. Kautsky writes—it is not a literal quotation, "*Wenn einmal ein mehr nicht ökonomisches Monument durch andere schliesslich ökonomische Ursachen in die Welt gesetzt ist es nun sind selbstandig auf seine Umgebung und sogar auf seine eignene Ursachen—die ökonomischen Elemente—zuruckwirkt.*" [If in one period of time noneconomic facts were the products of economic causes, they later became independent and themselves influenced economic

aspects of society]. Bernstein goes still so far [as] to acknowledge independent character to the ideal forces. But then the
basis of Socialism is given up!

Knowing how busy you are, I do not consider it proper to
make you read long letters, *und daher schluss* [with this, I close]!

With best regards to you, Mrs. and Miss Szold

I am yours very truly,

Louis Ginzberg

Then he returned. I had to go downtown the morning of his
arrival, a Monday morning, and I saw in my neighbor's paper that his
vessel had had an accident. Ah! my renunciation was wearing off.
When I came home he was at the house, and he brought me the ink
well, some Dutch china. I wished he hadn't. I didn't want gifts to
come between us, or any conventionalities. That year I wrote out
the notes of his Halakah lectures for him. I believe that was my own
suggestion. It brought us together a great deal, because he had to go
over each lecture to see whether it was correct. But on the whole I
behaved well. I kept my age, my gray hair, my lined face before me
all the time, even when that peculiar young happy feeling took possession of me in his presence. On the other hand that was the year
in which he began to come to the house regularly for Tuesday meals,
and other meals, and our walks increased. My Sunday morning tor-
tures began then. I was always waiting for a message to come that he
wanted to take a long walk in the afternoon. Yet I kept myself well
in hand. Of course, there were times when my passion absorbed and
mastered me. One evening, it had been snowing and raining and
sleeting, but it stopped, and a high whistling wind arose. I could not
stay in, the pain at my heart drew me out at eight o'clock in the
evening, and I raced around Morningside Park screaming at the top
of my voice whenever the wind was noisy enough to drown my
agony. That calmed me, and I came back to my desk, feeling as
though I could never again give way. What a mistake! How many
nights since then I have prayed and wrestled with myself, and
writhed on my bed, and been in utter blank despair for days at a
time.

Either late in December 1905 or early in January 1906, something happened. He made an engagement with me to take a walk
on a Sunday afternoon, and I went, though a visitor was here from
Baltimore, Mr. Hartogensis.[43] Anyone who knows me will realize

what power he had over me if for his sake I excused myself to an out-of-town visitor. It was a bitter cold day, and we walked on Riverside. The wind cut my face cruelly. He had brought with him the first three or four pages of his lecture "The Rabbinical Student"[44] and he read them to me as we walked along, and we discussed the development of the ideas they broached the whole afternoon. As a matter of course, he handed the manuscript to me for me to translate it. There was no question as to whether I was to do it—it was my privilege, my duty, my joy. Moreover, he had begun so late to prepare it that I had to work night and day to get it done. Did that mean anything? No, a thousand times no, I said to myself, and no, it will ever be and must be. But the afternoon was to yield me another pleasure. The wind became fiercer and fiercer, and I had to pin my veil on, but every time I caught it up, the wind tore it out of my hands. Then he bade me sit down on a bench, while he tied it on. When I came home, the veil was removed without opening the knot, and since then it lay in my drawer where I could caress it from time to time. Now I have taken it away, and put it with his letters, not to be touched again.

In the fall before Adele had translated an article for him on Isaac Hirsch Weiss, how I envied her, and how I envied her the inscription in the copy he gave her, that he was "giving her of hers." That winter Adele read her paper on Emma Lazarus. Another occasion for heart burning! He came to hear it, he praised it so enthusiastically, he sat by her in the car on the return from the hall, and I sat opposite smarting with pain, and hating myself for it. A seat beside him became vacant, and with a little light in his eyes that I was to know only too well later, he invited me to take it. But I still smarted.

No matter what memory I summon, as, for instance, my visit to the Magneses[45] at Brooklyn, I always feel myself quivering, palpitating. When he was not near me, I was restless, when he came I grew calm and satisfied.

It was on Purim of that year, I think, that he gave me the Jalkut[46] and the inscription spoke in the last line, of his hope that our friendship would never be ruptured. Alas! the binder lost the inscription, and I have always had a superstitious feeling connected with that incident. It boded ill. This terrible passion actually made me superstitious, and too much love ruptured friendship. How satisfied I would be with friendship now. But they tell me that is impossible, and they tell me, too, that I am a patient and cannot judge what I need.

I cannot now recollect anything definite connected with the spring of 1906, except that I trod the earth with a sore feeling, in my chest. At Pesach I collapsed, and went to Baltimore, but that was due to Publication Society worries. In spite of the sore feeling, I cherished no hopes, I kept my age steadily before my eyes, and I insisted to myself that only a miracle could keep him at my side for life.

The summer went on placidly. The Year Book was a nightmare as usual, but for me it yielded me heart-satisfaction, because he interested himself in my getting away from my desk, and took me on walks. But I kept myself well in hand, that does not mean that I ever succeeded in banishing his dear face from before me—there it was night and day for four years and more. All I mean is, I did not indulge myself—I remembered my years.

In July I went down to Long Branch to visit Miss Solis. All summer he had been talking of going there, but he did not. As soon as he heard I was going, he said he would go on the same train—on a Friday afternoon. My blood leapt so violently that my temples felt as though they were bursting. But I calmed myself. If I hadn't, a little incident would have done it. I asked him three times where he was going to stop in Long Branch, and always, it seemed to me, he evaded the question. He denied the charge when I made it on his return to the city—he said moreover, that he might have sought me at the Solisis, but he did not think it right to "bother" me there, too. And what did I do those days in Long Branch? Think of him and of him and of him. When I was being whirled up and down in the automobile, my eyes almost popped out of my head, as I sought him in the crowd on the beach, up the quiet streets. What did I care for the Seligman and Guggenheim palaces? The whole of Elberon I would have given for a word from him. And how happy I was, when in the middle of the week, a picture postal came from him with a word.

On the following Saturday I was reading alone, the bell rang, I opened the door. It was he, and I screamed "You?!" If he had had ears to hear the joy in that one syllable, he would not have done what he has done. I went with him to Riverside, and so far as I can remember that was the first of our many silent sittings there—those silent sittings that made me feel that we understood each other perfectly, though I did not then indulge in such extravagant feelings, and not for more than a year to come. Then I had made up my mind that if I could keep his friendly companionship, forever, I would be happier than I ever thought it possible to be.

Next came that wonderful Saturday morning in Central Park, when we watched the birds and the squirrels. And next that wonderful Friday evening at his house when coming to fetch me, as he said, he met me, and when he took me home, he asked me to sit with him in Morningside. We spoke of parents and children, and one's first born, I remember.

Then came Tisha be-Ab [Jewish fast day in mid-summer]. We went to a down town synagogue together, and both of us came away unsatisfied. The next day late in the afternoon he unexpectedly came in, and he staid and broke his fast. How sick my poor friend was, and how frightened I! How I took him home, hungry as I still was, and too weary myself to carry the heavy books I wrested from him.

The next thing was that we worked together on the letter to the Nation about cruelty to animals and the Jewish law.[47] I remember that we took supper together at a restaurant on 124th Street and I was so happy that I influenced him to do something of the sort. And how happy I was later when he wrote me from Tannersville that for my sake he was glad people had spoken of the article approvingly—it was due to the form I had given it. It was not true, but I was happy at any rate. It required so little to raise me to the seventh heaven.[48]

There must have been many walks that summer, for when he bade me good-bye the evening before he left for the Catskills, I had the temerity to say, or I was sad enough to say, that I would miss him, and he begged me to take walks by myself.

I recall a little incident connected with his going to the Catskills. He mentioned that he would have to go to his down town bank. It was hot and rainy, and I begged him to take the money I had in the house. He came the next morning and took it. I mention the incident, because it illustrates my tendency, which became more and more pronounced, to save him every step I could.

His four weeks at Tannersville, were again one long-drawn-out period of waiting for me—a letter, a letter, a letter, was my cry morning, noon and night. He wrote weekly and I was satisfied. He came back for Mrs. Davidson's wedding.[49]

August 3, 1906

Rosh ha-Shanah
V'Yom Ha-Din
The New Year's Day
and
Day of Judgment
of the Jewish Calendar
by
S.N. Deissard A.M., Ph.D.
Rabbi Cong. Shaare Tov of
Mineapolis [sic], Minn. and Ass't
Professor of Semitics at the
University of Minnesota
The title of the book takes up the
entire postal card so that very
little space is left for writing
Wishing you a *Shabbos M'nuhoh* [restful Sabbath]

Your Louis Ginzberg[50]

"The Fairmont," Tannersville, NY,
August 10, 1906

Dear Miss Szold,

I do not believe that the reading of my letter is an *Oneg Shabbat* [Sabbath pleasure] but as I have not written to you since I left NY, I think I ought to do it before the end of this week. As a *"caputitis benevolentia"* [obliging person] I will remark at the start that Dr. Benderly[51] is sitting to my right while Dr. Marx spreads his wings to my left and in such surroundings you cannot expect from me a well [w]ritten letter. Poor Dr. Benderly did not tell an anecdote for the last twelf [sic] hours and it would be cruel and against the general conception of hospitality if I would not listen to him.

About myself I have very little to tell you. For the last week I tried to become a pupil of the Hindus i.e. to worship "the great nothing," and *borukh HaShem* [praise God] I succeeded. My modesty however forbids me to claim all the credit for me and *"suum cuique"* [to each his own].

Dr. Malter from Cincinaty [sic] deserves great praise. Dr. Malter is next to me the only idler in our society.[52] Dr. Schechter, Marx and Magnes do some work while we two try to pass our time in talking and walking. But when I happen to look at the well fed and well dressed Jewesses sitting in the park I can not help asking with the prophet Eziekiel *Ha-tyhyenoh ha'azamos ha-eyleh?* [Can these bones live?][53] Is there any hope for Israel if its representative elements are so degenerated?

And now how are you? Do you take your daily walks at the Riverside Drive? Many a time I thought of our walks which I would prefer to those in the mountains. Did Miss Adele return from Maine? I found among my papers a letter written by me to her which I never sent off and as it contains a eulogy of *Wahlverwandtschaft* [congenial relatives] I think I'll rather keep [it] for myself.

With kindest regards to you, Mrs. Szold, and Miss Adele.

Your *Louis Ginzberg*

P.S. The Schechters, Marxes, Magnes, and Benderly send their kindest regards.

The Fairmont, Tannersville
August 16 [1906]

My Dear Miss Szold,

At the risk to appear banal I must begin my letter with the statement that your letter was not a *ta'anug Shabbos* [Sabbath pleasure] for me. In the first place it did not reach me on *Shabbos* and in the second because it contained things which gave me just the opposite feelings from *ta'anug*. I was very sorry to hear that you suffered of the hot weather and that you did deny yourself even a walk at the Riverside Drive. I am not so much surprised at you as at Anna[54] who certainly did not forget my words spoken at departing from your house. Or is even the authority of Anna of no avail with you?

I think I may well congratulate you and Miss Adele at her very clever decision to resign her position. But please do not tell to her as it may add a new reason for her classification of me as "antiquitatis species."

Your remarks concerning the Radins[55] gave me much pleasure as I am fully convinced that it is not what *I* said that pleases the people but the form in which *you* expressed it.

Have you fixed the day for the commencement of your vacation? I have told our mutual friends that you are going to take a vacation this year and I hope you'll not have me appear again telling lies (Is this a correct translation for *lügenstrafen?*) And how about the place where you intend spending your vacation?

About myself I have very little to tell you. I am still trying to live the life of the Hindu but I am sure it would be easier for me to adopt the mode of life of the Dervish than of the Hindu. A great part of my time I spend in discussing scientific as well Jewish matters with Benderly, Magnes, Malter, Marx and Dr. Schloessinger. This morning I made an onslaught on Ahad Ha-am[56] for his anti-legalistic views. Of course you know "A *Litwak spart sich immer*" [A Lithuanian Jew always argues] . . .

With kind regards to you, Mrs. Szold and Miss Adele.

Your

Louis Ginzberg

"The Fairmont," Tannersville, NY
August 22, 1906

Dear Miss Szold,

It is not Christian love but Jewish justice which dictates me this letter to you. I waited with my answer till today that I may be able to give you a Sabbath delight in return for the one you gave me last week. Of course human justice is never complete, at least it never can consider the individual value of things which can neither be measured nor weighed; "*Si duo facient idem non facient idem*" [If two people do the same thing, they will not conduct themselves in the same fashion]. And indeed it was the individualistic tendency of the rabbis of old which forced them to deny the verbal meaning of the Biblical laws regarding "*jus talionis.*" Now I am not better than my fathers and I hope you'll accept my poor letter as if it were equal to yours.

This introduction is a specimen of *pilpul* [circumlocution] while if I were to give you some *pshat* [simple explanation], I would have to confess that I had a very hard week and therefore did not like to write to you. It was not so much physical illness which befell me as my *Seelenzustand* [state of mind] which caused me many a painful hour and more than one sleepless night. The reasons therefore are manifold.

First the "notoreity" of my letter to the "Nation" annoyed me extremely. Why, I asked myself, in the name of all the saints of American Judaism, so much noise about a trifle? What reasons are there for the *Jewish* press to reprint such articles? Either the Jews know the meaning of *tzar baale hayim* [concern for all living things] and then my letter was superfluous for them or they do no longer know it and then my letter has no justification. I hope you understand me [my] feelings well enough and you'll not accuse me of ingratitude. I fully appreciate your kindness in this matter, even more than this, I am glad to have written it, but the Jewish papers disgusted me.

My main trouble however came from another source. Dr. Pereferkovich[57], a Jewish scholar and author, arrived here from St. Petersburg a few days ago. This concrete illustration of the misery of the Jews in Russia made me so miserable that for days I could not think about any other thing than the Jewish situation in Russia. To complete my misery I was induced to read—*Ha-batolloh m'veeoh beyedai Shamayim* [Idleness can lead one to Godly acts]—the speeches made at the last meeting of the ITO[58] and you can imagine how edified I felt after Zangwill's Lubhoelder of Rothschild and our diplomats' eulogy of America.

I think I'd rather stop right here as my letter contains enough to make it to the approach of a *Erev Shabbos* [the onset of the Sabbath].

With wishes of *Gut Shabbos* to you, Mrs. Szold, and Miss Adele,

I remain,

Your

Louis Ginzberg

P.S. I have decided to leave next Friday for N.Y.

Critical Years, 1906–1908

November 27 1908

How happy I was a year ago! I who hate, abominate going downtown, went on a special expedition to the Flat Iron Building to get him a cigar for his birthday. I did not dare get him a real gift. And only a few days before I had been downtown to seek book rests for his new desk. That idea his sister-in-law[1] took from me, and superstitiously I interpreted that to be a sign that it would be too bold to give him a gift. Tomorrow he will be thirty-five years old, and I may as well be one hundred and thirty-five for all the value life has in my eyes without him. And this year I may not even congratulate him, even though I do wish him happiness without me.

At Mrs. Davidson's wedding,[2] I was unhappy, for I was to leave next day for a two week's stay in Maine.[3] That evening, after the wedding, he came, tired as he was, to bid me good-bye. He could hardly stand upon his feet, and still he came. Dr. Benderly came too, to persuade me to do some educational propaganda work. The three of us walked together, and when Dr. Benderly absented himself to telephone, he told me how he felt about the Nation article. He was careful to say that my part in it was all right, and that he was glad we had done it together, but he abominated the fuss that had been made of it in the Jewish press. The palaver about it seemed a refutation of his thesis. He was right, and yet I gloried in the notice everybody had

61

taken of it, and God knows, I cared little enough about my part in it, except inasmuch as he was, or said he was, pleased with it.

And how, on the other hand, I hated the idea of that trip to Maine! There were to be no letters, upon that I had resolved. In my ascetic way I reasoned that the opportunity for discipline was too good to be disregarded, and as it was I who was going away, it would depend upon me to start the correspondence. A brave resolution, but how I suffered under it. How I went to the post office at night and in the most inclement storms, in the hope there would be a scrap. There never was! The country was beautiful, but I saw him, and him only everywhere. How often on our walks, I failed to follow the conversation for unending thoughts of him. Then I allowed myself to be persuaded to stay alone at the hotel for a week, and my walks were solitary. Even now the memory comes back to me of clear skies, deep blue sea and intensely green country, and the memory cuts into me like a knife, because with it comes back my longing for his companionship, my intense desire to enjoy with him the beauties of the country life I was leading, to speak out all the thoughts that rushed upon me during my unwonted leisure. And still no letter, and still I remained stoical toward myself. At last, his little nephew acknowledged my box of green things, and he added a single line for the New Year, enough to call forth a long letter from me—I have the impression somehow that he never read that letter of mine. He asked me questions about my stay there that were anticipated in the letter.[4] How I remember the ride down from Boston with Corinne Jackson, and how desolate I was! But when I reached home, my pulses leaped high, because my mother told me at once he had telephoned twice that day to know whether I had come back.

For a few weeks I gave myself up to the magic of his companionship without putting the usual restraint upon myself. I had been deprived of it so long. I remember I had the audacity to walk with him from the synagogue on *Shemini Azeret* evening, and he had to send me home before I went too far, because his brother was indisposed, and he could not take me back. How different, I said to myself, that was from the evening not so long before when I was invited to his sister-in-law's house, and he did not even take me to the car,[5] but let his brother do it. And on Yom Kippur he had come down during the intermission to talk to us!

It was on that *Shemini Azeret* evening that he outlined to me what his criticism of Dr. Rosenau's book was to be.[6] I had spoken to him about the book early in the summer indeed, I believe I had been the one to point out that Baraita nonsense to him. Now he was determined to castigate. The "Tannersville group" of friends had wrought him to a proper pitch of excitement about it, and nothing I could say would dissuade him. And yet, though I hated his doing it, I could not but translate it for him, and alas! I translated it in his spirit. I felt crestfallen about it, and when Adele asked me whether it had occurred to me that he was in a measure taking up Papa's cause, I could only smile assentingly, but there was no joy, and I began again to discipline myself, for I felt that if he had cared for me, he would have desisted.[7]

I am speaking now of the winter of 1906–1907. In January 1907 he lectured on the Jewish Primary School[8]—it seems to me we labored together over that lecture more than over anything else I did for him. Again it was translating in a hurry, and practicing how to read the lecture at the Seminary. That was the lecture he read in the dark, the lights had gone out. All that winter too the Genizah Studies brought us together.

Jewish Theological Seminary
531–535 West 123rd St.
New York City

February 5 1907

Dear Miss Szold,

The editors of *Haro'eh U'mvaker*—not *V'hamevaker*—are Jacob Badek and Nachman Isaac Fischmann; the author of *Herev Nokemeth*[9] is Meir Isaac Bresselau, not Bresele.

Your

Louis Ginzberg . . .

I forgot to put down that I left the Seminary in the spring of 1906, and I was glad to do it. I felt I had no business there on account of my passion. But leaving the Seminary seemed to bring us closer. There were many, many walks, and not a Saturday after the Synagogue did we miss. One of the Saturday walks stands out in my memory, because it is closely akin to my present turmoil. It was toward the end of March. There had been snow and ice, but that morning a wonderful thaw had set in, converting the streets into riverlets under a magic sky. It was so wet we could not go through Morningside Park, and we turned northward, on St. Nicholas Avenue. For weeks he had been telling me, with the difficulty he always had when he had to speak of something that affected him deeply, of his father's precarious health, and there can be no mistake about his having realized my intense sympathy. On this March Saturday walk, when we had about reached its northern most limit, he suddenly told me he was going to embark for Europe in the last of April, and that he would be away for at least five months.[10] There was no sunshine anymore for me. All the ice was back. My mouth was locked with an iron grip, my head hammered, my eyes swam—was it possible to exist without him for five months? All I could press out was, "Do you mean that you are going to leave in five weeks or so?" He assented. It was all I spoke on the way home, and I felt his eyes rest upon me from the side several times inquiringly.

The next day was Philadelphia Sunday,[11] and something unpleasant happened, I don't know what. Or perhaps it wasn't unpleasant per se, perhaps my depressed mood made it seem so. I returned on Monday, still unable to shake off my dejection. On Tuesday he came for dinner—still I could not speak, every word had to be forced out with difficulty. He was very gentle with me. Wednesday my gloom lifted somewhat, and late in the afternoon I went for a solitary walk, only to find that he was before the house talking to my mother. He had come to fetch me for a walk, and his first word after my mother left us was a question as to my depression, and I told him of my business troubles, and I continued, there is something else which I dare not tell you—of course, I meant his long absence in Europe.

In my present state it is easy for me to recall what I endured in the weeks before his sailing. But there was a compensation! He was to sail on Saturday, and he would have to walk down to the dock. After many days, amid quaking and trembling, I asked him whether I might walk down with him. It seemed to me he was pleased. Then I heard that Dr. Marx wanted to go with him, and I offered to give up the project if he would rather walk with someone else who might offer. His reply was: "No one else would be such a f——" I stopped him before he could finish the objectionable word, fool, but I was pleased, nevertheless.

When the time came for him to go, the big Census Year Book[12] was in full blast, and during the few days preceding his departure, he found time to help me identify some of the Russian and Hebrew names of congregations in New York. On Friday he came for the last time to bid my mother good-bye. The typewriters were making such a racket that the three of us retired to the middle room. There he told us that his father was most desirous of seeing him married. I remember that I had myself so well under control that I did not shiver, inwardly or outwardly. I even said to myself, he will come back engaged to please his father, and I will be sad, but not in despair. It is to be expected. On the way out, he bade Anna take care of me, and force me to take walks!

THE WALK TO THE DOCK![13]

No, I must go back first and finish my account of the winter, because there were more joint activities, and these that are left to mention are the ones in which I was the recipient. I had to write an article for the Hebrew Standard, and at his suggestion I tackled the Judeo-German Weiber literature.[14] He got all the books together for me, and I talked over bits of information I derived from them with him. When I was putting my material into shape, he asked me whether I would let him see the article before it went to the printer. He praised it, not very warmly, I must confess, and he hoped it would encourage me to do some independent work. Did I care for the praise? Even if it had been enthusiastic, it would not have been a circumstance to compare with the fact that he had been interested in a concern of mine. That same winter he helped me with the revision of Helena Frank's Perez translation.[15] Will I ever again have such happy hours! I certainly never had any such before as were those Tuesdays, when he used the time between dinner and his afternoon lectures to go over the manuscript with me. And sometimes there was a bit of time left, and he would read me a Yiddish tale, in Yiddish, in his dear little gurgling way.

I speak of what he did for me, as though I wanted to balance my desires over against his, God knows that is not in my mind! *He* made me happy—and unhappy—but happy above all, and it seems I gave him nothing in return for that, at all to be compared with it. And yet he took so graciously, so without thanking me, that I thought it meant something to him that I was devoting all my strength and ability to him. When he left for Europe that summer, he even left in debt to me for half a dozen typewriter jobs, for cigars, and the debt sat lightly upon him, and I thought what a small expenditure of money was bringing me a rich harvest of happiness.

And now the walk to the dock! It was a Corot-like spring morning. At first it felt like rain, and his sister-in-law told me how solicitous he was about my hat—and I was happy. We walked down Fifth Avenue, and the trees in their misty green were so beautiful that it hurt me to look at them, but if I averted my face from them, my eyes devoured him, and that hurt me still more. How fortunate it was that Dr. Marx was with us! What might I not have said or done, had there been no restraining third presence.

We stopped at the Astor Library for a rest, and then a number of his friends joined us. From there we were to go for lunch at twelve, but we waited for Adele and Thomas,[16] and as they delayed to come, I urged him to go off with his friends, and leave me there to wait for my sister. He refused with an assumption of masterfulness, and I pleaded, and he returned: "You know you cannot make me do anything, you never have." All I could press out, hindered as I was by quick-coming tears, "Then do something I want, at least this last day." Adele appeared upon the scene at that moment, fortunately, else I might have lost my self-control. He need not have been so incisive. I did not then yet claim him as my own.

At lunch I sat next to him, and, of course, could not eat.

On the way to the dock I disgraced myself in my own sight. I had not wanted to go at all, because I was not sure of my ability to behave decently. But Dr. Marx would otherwise have walked home. If I went along, he could spare himself and stay downtown with me until the end of the Sabbath. As we turned into the street leading to the ship, he came to walk with me alone, and I said under my breath, "Don't be persuaded to stay in Europe," and he returned, "Oh, if only I could stay, how happy I would be!" And I pleaded, "But I would be so unhappy."

When we reached the boat, his sister-in-law said with a significant look, "I knew you wouldn't be able to stay away." My heart almost jumped out of my breast, when he defended me, with just a twinge of indignation in his voice. And later, when after seeing his room, we all stood on the deck awaiting the signal for departure, I happened to stand alone, while he was joking with Adele and her party, Thomas, Dr. Magnes, and others. He accidently glanced in my direction, and seeing, I suppose, my utter dejection, he cruised over to me at once and remained at my side the rest of the time.

When we descended the bridge, it was all up with me. The tears would come, in spite of Adele's rebuke. And when he came down again and walked to the other bridge with Dr. Marx, I could not move a step towards him.

And what did I not tell Dr. Marx that afternoon about him! Did I speak of anything or anyone else! If I did, it was only because my companion insisted upon it. That afternoon, as that whole summer, was only one long thinking of him.

A couple of weeks before he left, the Halakah lectures were copied, and I corrected one copy and filled in the Hebrew sentences. I wonder whether he had any idea of the many many hours I spent over it. The work was done, however, and he had the set bound and sent to Judge Sulzberger. I did permit myself to wonder whether he told him that I had written out the notes. Before sailing, he asked me to fill out two more copies, one for Dr. Marx and one for his uncle-brother-in-law in South Africa. Though I was working nineteen hours a day on the Year Book, I did it promptly. Dr. Marx had his before *he* went to Europe, and still earlier his uncle's was finished. He wrote me a word of thanks and, I believe, a little demurrer about my working on this when I had so much else to do.

"A WHOLE SUMMER THINKING OF HIM": THE 1907 CORRESPONDENCE

That summer the letters came regularly and frequently. He seemed to need mine. He was in distress, and people in distress have always found me. But I was satisfied that I could be something to him.

Amsterdam, May 8, 1907[17]

Dear Miss Szold,

I arrived yesterday after spending a day with my sister at Antwerp, and I am sorry to say that I found my father in a very serious state. The nature of his illness is not quite clear to me and I intend to go over with him to Leiden that I may hear the opinion of the professor who treats him.

My voyage was a very pleasant one, especially as the rough sea kept most of the people in their staterooms, and the deck was left to me and a few others. Due to this fact is my escape of meeting Miss American, who looked at me daggers but left me alone. In Antwerp the president of "the Ezra," a society for the protection of the Emigrants, came to see me, and in the course of his conversation, asked me whether I would not come to the office of the society to meet Miss S. American, who announced her visit to them. He

described the lady as a very rich woman and a great philanthropist. My answer was, I despise the rich and hate philan-
thropists and I stayed.[18]

I am enclosing the letter of Mr. Hart concerning the
printing of the Geniza Studies . . .[19]

Have you brought before the Publication Committee the
matter of your vacation? What are the new developments in
Cincinnati? If you find something in the Jewish press of
America that you think may interest me, please send me it.
My interest in American affairs increases in inverse ratio to
the distance in which I find myself from this country. The
farther away from it, the more American am I.

With kind regards to your mother and the Seltzers.

Louis Ginzberg

---

528 W. 123rd St.
New York, May 16, 1907.

Dear Dr. Ginzberg,

We in America have always been accustomed to hear of
"*Europa-Müde*" [weary of Europe]—I had a postal[20] this
evening from one who is blatantly "*Europa-froh*" [takes
pleasure in Europe]. Every line of it, from your "silly" pun
down to, or up to, your enjoyment of the rough sea speaks
of your satisfaction at having put a few thousand miles
between yourself and the hated land of sensationalism and
humbuggery. Well, I don't care. Surely, your happiness shall
not make me unhappy. Besides, I console myself with your
promised letter from Amsterdam, and I wish with all my
heart it will sound equally buoyant, and will contain the
best of news.

On the day you wrote your postal, I was in Philadelphia
discussing your title-page with Judge Sulzberger. At least he
had no criticism to make. Dr. Jacobs was there, and he continues to object to "The Legends of the Jews" as the title.[21] . . .

According to programme, my mother went over to
Philadelphia with me, stopping off for a two days' visit with
the Jastrows. Consequently, my trip bore an altogether different character from its usual stern business aspect. With

her wonted enthusiasm, my mother watched, and made me watch, the gradations in spring developments as we flew southward. And it *was* remarkable. Every added mile had its added garlands. Even a backward season has its peculiar charm, for only such a one could have made the climate of each mile visible to the eye. In Baltimore, from the vantage ground of my sister's suburban porch, my mother continues to enjoy the birds and the plants—not to mention the two dear little human plants. I must not forget to make my report to you. Mrs. Ginzberg[22] sent me the two sets of lecture notes, and I am transcribing the Hebrew into them little by little, a lecture or two every evening. A few days ago, Dr. Marx was good enough to bring me (together with a bound copy of "The Primary School," for which many thanks) the bound copy of the notes returned by Judge Sulzberger. That facilitates the transcription considerably. I have arranged with Dr. Marx to have him "hold copy" for the English. So I must hurry up and get through with the Hebrew before he goes off to Europe. The Marxes have taken pity on my lone estate, Jewishly speaking, and have invited me to their house for the holiday meals. I fancy Dr. Marx and myself got to know each other better during the long spring Sabbath afternoon in Seward Park after you sailed. That Saturday I became fully convinced of what I had always suspected—that the East Side is not half as interesting and inspiring as its devotees and condescending, slumming patrons would have it. There is squalor, to be sure, and to spare, but it is not picturesque squalor—and the misery of it!

If I had not registered a vow inside of myself not to bother you with long letters, I'd tell you about a gentlemanly though public altercation between Dr. Magnes and Dr. Silverman, after a sermon by the former, in which he touched upon the Cincinnati muddle[23]—I didn't write much. But no! This letter *shall* not extend to the bottom of the fourth page. Only this once more —I hope you will have reassuring news to write. The Seltzers—who were here when your postal came—send their regards and good wishes to you.

Sincerely yours,

Henrietta Szold

Amsterdam, May 16, 1907

Dear Miss Szold,

Assuming that you expect a supplementary note to my last letter I will inform you today that I was in Leiden and had a long talk with the professor. To my great sorrow however I am now more discouraged than before seeing the professor, as he prepared me for the worst. My intention to go with my father to Berlin and Vienna cannot be carried out, as his weakness would not allow to undertake such a journey. There is absolutely nothing to do but to wait patiently. *V'la-shem Ha-yeshuoh* [(and hope) for salvation from the Lord].

I have very little to tell you about myself. You can imagine how much I suffer mentally and physically to see others suffer. I gave up my diet that my parents should not notice there is aught wrong with me, which would make them feel very unhappy. The consequences of it are not pleasant.

Did you get the *T'khines?*[24] I have written to Dr. Marx reminding him of it and I hope he was able to find them for you.

I was reading lately my Legends and it strikes me as if we had to[o] many references to the Bible in the text. I am of the opinion that the knowledge of the Bible, i.e. of the narrative part of it, must be taken for granted. Don't you think I am right?

I have received a letter from Judge Sulzberger complementing [sic] me on my lecture at the Primary School, but adding that he wished I would have gone to Hillel's *ḥeder* [school] and learned a little patience. He objects strongly to page ten concerning the mission of Israel. He does not know that if not for this, I would not write a line in [the] popular manner. I think that it is not too egoistic if the writer tries to enjoy a few lines in his writings.

I have written to Dr. Marx to hand over to you the bound copy of my halakha lectures [lectures on Jewish law] which the judge has returned. And when you have filled in the Hebrew in the blue set you have to send it to Mr. A. Ginzberg, P.O. Box 3158, Johannesburg, S. Africa.

And how are you and the other members of your family? Did your mother go to Baltimore? I would like to write to her but in the present state of affairs, I think I'd rather not write.

Did the Publication Committee take official cognisance of your intention to take a long vacation next year?

With kind regards to you and the S.S.[25]

Your

Louis Ginzberg

---

528 W. 123rd St.
New York, May 20, 1907

Dear Dr. Ginzberg,

My pleasure in your letter on this second day of the holiday was considerably tempered by the few words you say about your father. Knowing your habits, I realize that the brief sentence holds much pain and anxiety. I had been hoping all the time that you would find the reports of his condition had been magnified by the distance they had travelled. It would be carrying coals to Newcastle for me to preach patience and fortitude to you. But I do venture to continue to preach hope.

The University Press estimate is very reasonable as compared with American prices . . .

So you really want to know about my affairs? Or do you ask about them, because I was selfish enough to force them on your attention when, being face to face with me, you could not avoid listening to me? Well, here goes—it's your own fault. I had a long and satisfactory talk with Judge Sulzberger. I told him many a thing I had kept bottled up within me for years. The upshot was that he said he saw no reason why I should not have a fourteen weeks' holiday next year. As for the Year Book, I was to write him a letter about it, such as could be put upon the agenda of the American Jewish Committee's convention, to take place here at the end of the month. I have written the letter, and it was a document! It set forth why it was impossible for the Publication Society as now constituted to carry on statistical work, and on the other hand, how important the statistical work was. Judge Sulzberger had agreed that the American Jewish Committee was the proper agency, but he seemed to have some doubt as to its survival. This he did not say, but I take it he had in mind that recently a conference had taken place between the I.O.B.B., the U.A.H.C. Board of Delegates, and his committee, and the only outcome seems to have been that Mr. Adolph Kraus and Mr. Simon Wolf will resign from the last.[26] However, if the American Jewish Committee do[es] not take the Year Book over for the next year, I am to have the privilege of closing down the work very early, say in June, so that I can get off by August 1. Meantime, the Year Book work is as stupendous as ever, and I see my way as little clear as ever to get through with it, in as thorough a manner as I should like, in the alloted time. Last week I collapsed entirely over it, but I revived at once after moving the type-writer out of my room. It was the incessant clicking right next to me that completely demoralized my usually well-behaved nerves. And these three days of holiday, sunshine, and un-strenuous living have quite restored me. You must remember that after a long day at work at the Directory, I gave the evening to the Prayer-Book,[27] the first proof of which came today. If I don't go to pieces this summer—well, I won't do it again, and if I do go to pieces, I surely won't do it again.

But let me pass on the more interesting Cincinnati imbroglio.[28] It has been all of six weeks since I have read the Jewish papers in my accustomed way. They are piled high on my radiator. When I go through them, which I hope to do in a few days, I shall clip them for you. The developments have been interesting. Take only this week's budget: 1. An open somewhat prolix letter addressed by Dr. Magnes to Mr. Gold-man, the President of the Union of American Hebrew Congregations, complaining of the Board of the Governors of the College, who refused to issue an explanatory statement.[29] 2. A letter, published, like the first in all the better papers, and signed by Dr. Harry Friedenwald as president, and Dr. Magnes, as secretary of the Federation, denying Dr. Kohler's oft repeated statement, in his series of articles on Zionism that Zionists are unpatriotic Americans.[30] 3. A letter written by a Mr. Gorfinkle, a senior student at the College, explaining why he, as a non-Zionist, feels himself forced, one year before his graduation, to leave the college which makes it impossible for Zionists to belong to its teaching staff.[31] 4. A letter in the American Israelite, from Dr. Max Heller,[32] charging Kohler with bad faith, and 5. An editorial article, probably by Leo Wise,[33] in the Israelite, quoting paragraph after paragraph from Emil Hirsch,[34] in response, to prove that he cannot be made a member of the Board of Governors of the College.

In Letter No. 1 Magnes again quotes the sentence with which you furnished him. And in the Israelite editorial they also refer to you, of course, to prove I.M. Wise's conservatism.[35]

When I wrote you the other day, I referred to an altercation between Dr. Magnes and Dr. Silverman. The former has in his sermon mentioned the "deposed" professors of the College. When he sat down, his colleague crossed over to him, and asked him exactly what he had said. Dr. Magnes: *Dibarti* [I have spoken]. Then Silverman called upon him to retract, which he refused to do. Silverman then threatened to make a counter-statement from the pulpit, which Magnes told him would be a very foolish thing to do. But Silverman would not be diverted from his purpose. At the end of the service, he announced to the congregation that what they had heard "his honored colleague" say was merely his "personal interpretation." In reality, the professors had "voluntarily resigned." Tableau, commotion among the worshippers, a hastily summoned board meeting, at which Dr. Magnes' warmest friends had great ado in restraining those who had hitherto not been ardent supporters of his, from suspending Dr. Silverman. More moderate counsels finally prevailed, and by a vote of five to four, it was decided to write a letter of rebuke to the offender, who at once, it is said, became meek and submissive, and acknowledged himself to have been unduly influenced by Dr. Kohler. Dr. Magnes seems to have gained many friends by his self restraint, when he and Silverman were summoned before the board. I seem to hear you say: How characteristically American! I should add that I have the early facts from Dr. Magnes himself, and the later facts from Dr. Marx, who derived them from Mr. Marshall,[36] via Dr. Schechter—an overwhelming array of authorities acknowledged in good Talmudic style. Dr. Magnes was at Dr. Marx's to bid us all goodbye. This very evening he leaves for California and his sister's wedding.

You have heard, have you not?—that the Zionist Congress meets at The Hague.[37] A half dozen of your friends have already made up their minds to take the opportunity of looking you up in your own home.

I do not deign to commend upon the "American" episode, because I might be tempted to tell you that you were rude. To make up I'll tell you this: Yesterday an acquaintance of mine from Baltimore was at the synagogue and she asked me to point out the notabilities. I called her attention to the professor of history[38] and then to the professor of exegesis,[39] and she wanted to know which one was the savage man who had belabored Dr. Rosenau so atrociously.[40]

I paid a visit to your sister-in-law yesterday and found her looking very well, and this morning she and her trio of sons were at the synagogue. I told her I found Mr. Nast's letter had betrayed to your home people, long before you had wanted them to know, that you were coming.

And thus do I keep my resolution not to bother you with the long letters you abominate! They vanish into the air or rather into thick paper. It's a little bit your own fault; you asked tempting questions. As for myself, I hope to hear, from you or through Mrs. Ginzberg, better news than today's letter contained, as the result of the Leyden professor's examination.

---

528 W. 123rd St.
NY, May 24, 1907

Dear Dr. Ginzberg,

It is good of you to have taken the trouble to let me know how distressed you are. Need I tell you that I understand the full depths of what you are undergoing? To see those suffer whom one holds dearer than oneself is to realize the terrible isolation of the human soul. One stands by and can do nothing. Each bears his burden unaided—the sufferer his physical pain, the onlooker his mental anguish. There-fore I do not dare mention sympathy. Even if I were near you, instead of thousands of miles away, my "feeling with you" would not puncture the armor of resignation in which you are clothing yourself. I hope you will at least find com-fort in the thought that you are permitted to be with your father.

What I should like to have courage for, is to admonish you to take care of yourself. Exactly for your parents' sake, you must. If hard days are ahead of you, they will need you and all you can give them from the abundance of your spir-itual reserves, and though God has given you a strong spirit, it cannot altogether rise above the frailties of the flesh. Write me that I am right, and that, for once, you are taking my advice.

Dr. Marx is keeping the *Tehinnot* in mind, and the lec-tures will soon be on their way to South Africa . . .

I cannot agree with you about the Biblical references in the "Legends." It is true, a knowledge of the Bible narrative must be assumed, and I have a note to that effect for your preface. But your references are usually to the more recondite points of the narratives. They were very helpful to me in doing the translation, and I should think I'd be a good "*Probekannichen*" [investigator]. In any event, Biblical refer-ences are never disturbing, at least not to the Anglo-Saxon reader, and the "Anglo-Saxon Benny Brittes," as the irre-pressible Dooley[41] dubs the American Jews, needs them badly, besides.

Judge Sulzberger spoke to me also about your little ironies and I disagreed and disagree with him wholly. Not only has an author the right to enjoy a few lines of his own productions, as you put it, but those are the very lines that make the material most eagerly studied by posterity. It is not true that even the dry-as-dust scholar, delving in the past, is pleased beyond the ordinary when, amid his antiquarian finds, there is one specially well preserved by reason of its attic salt—is *Lebensanschauung* [outlook on life] and *Lebensweisheit* [worldly wisdom] I looked at the "mission" passage again—it is all right. Judge Sulzberger promises sig-nificantly that "you will get older," but if his wisdom in this particular is the wisdom of age, stay young. In fact, stay young anyhow.

Here comes only my little office force—good girls they are, they work with a will for me—and I must stop. I hope you have received the Hart letter. I forgot to put my address on it.

Take care of yourself, and do not entirely lose heart in spite of the Leyden professor.

Sincerely yours,

Henrietta Szold

---

528 W. 123rd St.
New York, May 28, 1907

Dear Dr. Ginzberg,

I have just finished the lectures, and they are lying next to me tied up and addressed to South Africa. As soon as one of my assistants comes, the package will be sent to the post office, and registered as "commercial papers." The lectures are not bound, as I wrote they would be, because Dr. Marx goes away too soon to see the job through to the end, and I am not sufficiently experienced to superintend it.

Frankly, the above is only a pretext for writing to you. I want to preach to you. You and your anxieties have naturally been much on my mind, but also your folly in abandoning your diet, after you had observed it so faithfully for so many months. Please resume it and be careful of yourself. Will you? Make that my pay for having fixed up the lectures.

From Baltimore we had good news a few days ago. A still nameless niece[42] arrived safe and sound at Mr. Levin's house. My mother, of course, describes the little worm as a perfect beauty.

With kind regards, and in the hope that your father is passing these days with you in freedom from pain and suffering.

Sincerely yours,

Henrietta Szold

Amsterdam, June 6, 1907

Dear Miss Szold,

Your kind letters are a further corroboration of the truth that there is nothing absolute, neither good [n]or bad. My present very unhappy state brought me your deep sympathy which in its true form is not of a negative but of a positive character. It does not only assist us in carrying our burden but also affords us a positive pleasure. Of course, the orthodox evolutionists will maintain that sympathy is nothing but dependence upon others and one ought to try his best to make himself independent. It is however the cardinal mistake of the evolutionists to overlook the simple fact that a combination of elements do not reproduce themselves but produce something new. The primitive nature of our feelings may have been of a very materialistic nature, but they gradually changed to something entirely different. I am therefore not ashamed to tell you how great a pleasure your letters gave me and hope that you will continue to let me enjoy that pleasure.

The condition of my father did not change, at least no change is visible to us. The physician however maintains that there is a gradual change for the worse. One consolation is that my father is mentally very fresh. He studies his *Gemorah* as soon as his pain allows him and is extremely interested in the Yerushalmi tr[actate] *Bekhoroth*,[43] which he began to investigate very carefully. He also discusses with me some problems in the Yerushalmi fragments, and I must confess that he called my attention to some facts which have escaped me. . . .

I do not dare to leave Amsterdam and, being here, I work to kill time. My parents wish me to go to some summer resort and if I understand your letter correctly, you advise me the same. But I really do not see how I can leave Amsterdam at the present conditions, it be perhaps to some small place in the neighborhood of Amsterdam. The weather is for the present very hot and it would not be advisable for me to go to the country but as the physician is against father's travelling, I am unable to leave Holland.

The controversy Magnes-Silverman was not entirely new to me as my brother had sent me a clipping from the *Times*.[44] Of course what you told me about the trustees was not in the paper.

My comment was: "How characteristically American!" One may be a *b'haymoh t'mayoh* (unclean beast) and lecture from the pulpit of a synagogue about Trilby, but beware of the decorum!

Is Magnes going to the Congress? I would like to know before hand who are coming. I might be able to arrange quarters for them. Is Dr. Friedenwald coming here? Zionism is dead here! Holland Jewry produces now only Kosher Kase [cheese] and Yomtovdig Shokoladt [chocolate for the holidays].

I do not feel hurt at your criticism of my remarks about Miss American, but I do not understand how you could be in doubt whether I really want to know all about your affairs. I can assure you that the news you informed me about your arrangements with the Publication Society gave me great pleasure and delight. I only hope that you remain firm in your refusal to issue the Yearbook Directory. If the Committee of 50 is to disappear, I will not shed tears for them; there is no reason why you should do the work. Let them form a permanent society for the study of Jewish statistics and issue [a] statistical [directory] later.

Aren't you to take any rest at all this year? I should think that from the middle of August till the middle of September the work in the office is not so urgent that you could not rest for a few weeks. How about the next year's publications? Will Philo be ready?[45]

I am sending you under separate cover a set of the Geniza Studies, which you'll be kind enough to return to the printer with the request to have the printed pages sent to Amsterdam. I went through very carefully these pages but under no circumstances would I take the responsibility for all the diacritic points and other "Kraenk" [headaches].

I assume that Dr. Malter is now in New York and I would ask you to let me know his address as I would like to write to him. I am writing today to your dear mother which I did not do till now, not wishing her to grieve about me.

With kind regards to the Seltzers and yourself

Your

Louis Ginzberg

P.S. How is Fraulein Anna? Do not forget to give her my very respectful regards . . .

Amsterdam, June 7, 1907

Just a few lines postscription to my letter which I sent you yesterday afternoon. Accept my sincerest wishes to your new niece; you are a threefold aunt *V'haḥut Ha-meshulash lo bim'haroh yinosek* [May the threefold cord never be severed].[46]

It was very kind of you to finish up the lectures but it was unkind of me to burden you with the new work as if the Yearbook were not enough. In my own favor I must add that I left the lectures with you, thinking you may take them up when the rush in the office of the J.P.S. will be over. Now of course I cannot refuse you your labors reward and I will try to observe my special *Shulḥon Arukh*, but I'll do it in the same way as the Orthodox Jew does in observing certain prescriptions of the *Shulḥon Arukh* among gentiles.

With kindest regards,

Louis Ginzberg

528 W. 123rd St.

June 10, 1907

Dear Dr. Ginzberg,

At Ruth Schechter's wedding, Mrs. Ginzberg told me you were not well—that you were sick, in fact. Your anxiety, to be sure, is sufficient to account for a breakdown. But do you not see that you must be particularly careful of yourself? Won't you be good to yourself, and not add to the apprehensiveness your friends already feel in your behalf?

The wedding was beautiful, a notable success—the bride lovely to look upon, the ceremony long and solemn, the feast well-arranged, the guests brilliantly gowned and gay, the mother proudly sad, the father in one of his most benignant, leonine moods—everything happy and complete.[47] Did *I* enjoy *myself*? I had had to interrupt my Year Book work for half a day to go, and in the crowd I remembered keenly that I was all alone in New York, for the Seltzers have left, too. To-day I worked harder than ever to make up for the time lost. All feelings vanished—I am again a machine. It is better so.

I hope your father is fairly comfortable. And will you take care of yourself?

Sincerely yours,

Henrietta Szold

---

528 W. 123rd St.
New York, June 16, 1907

Dear Dr. Ginzberg,

I have just returned from Philadelphia. A special Publication Committee meeting was ordered for the first hot day of the season. Even now that it is over and done with, I do not understand why there was need for it. It is rather late to write a letter, but to-morrow will be crowded with all sorts of tasks, such as proof reading of Dr. Schechter's book,[48] proof reading of Dr. Margolis's book,[49] writing out minutes, correspondence galore, and above all directory tinkering, not to mention prayer book revision as a diversion in the evening. With such a fine catalogue before me, I feel that I must tell you before I forget how it went—you know what a sieve-like memory I have—what was said about you in my hearing, *to* me in fact. Of course, I know you don't care, but———! I saw Judge Sulzberger in the morning before the meeting, and he was at his best—talking kindly, and wisely, and brilliantly, and suggestively critically. Among other subjects came up the writing of popular books, by scholars, for the Jewish public. Judge Sulzberger expressed his disappointment at a certain piece of recent work, and I agreed, and remarked that Dr. Schechter was a shining exception among Jewish scholars. He knew what aspect of a learned subject to present to the uninstructed layman, and he was aided by flashes of insight that amounted to prophecy or genius. Judge Sulzberger did not dissent by any means, but he hastened to add that in respect to ability for popular presentation you were quite as unique, if different. I was quite taken aback to hear him say what you will remember I have told you a dozen times. Please do not charge me with having been unfaithful to you and to my estimate of you. Judge Sulzberger simply did not give me a chance to mention you. He snatched the word out of my mouth. If I thought of Dr. Schechter first, it was because he has an advantage over you—his masterly handling of the English language! And you always wait for a halting translation.

At the meeting itself Dr. Schechter (by letter) reported, had secured your consent to write the Volosin article and add it to your book of essays and lectures.

And after the meeting, one of the gentlemen to whom your proposed book had been assigned—was it a year ago?—stopped to ask me how it had been that it had never reached him. He had been absent from the meeting at which the explanation had been forced from me, that you refused to submit manuscripts to examination. When he was told the reason, he exclaimed with some vigor of manner and expression, that your stand was entirely correct—you were not the man to subject yourself to such tests as are devised for the general.

I know, I know, you don't care. But can you blame me for being pleased at hearing my own views corroborated? It is to please myself, not to please you, that I write all this to you. I hope that long before this you have regained the lost tone of your nerves, and that you are able to be a comfort to your father, instead of an anxiety. Now I must stop, if I am to be up early.

Sincerely yours,

Henrietta Szold

528 W. 123rd St.
New York, June 17, 1907

Dear Dr. Ginzberg,

I closed my letter to you early this morning and in the first mail came your two of June 6 and 7, together with the proof of the Geniza Studies. The latter I shall dispatch soon, tomorrow probably . . .

Don't worry about giving me things to do. You know, in the first place, that I like to do them for you, especially if they set your mind free for better work; and in the second place you give me the opportunity to show the Year Book that it cannot absorb my whole personality. That is my great objection to the drudgery I suffer—that there is no margin left for such little courtesies as friends should show one another. You cannot faintly imagine how at this point I am repressing myself to keep from pouring myself out to you and telling you how thoroughly unhappy I have been about the Year Book, and everything connected with the Publication Society. The Year Book will in all probability be taken over by the American Jewish Committee. The matter is now under consideration by its Executive Committee. But my mind is not yet at rest. Some of the impotent rage possesses me that inspires the opposition of labor to capital—unreasoning and probably baseless rage in my case, but I fear it is going to lead to a breach. A little more initiative, a little confidence that I can make a modest place for myself in some other position, and I'll cease to be their secretary. If I could put down the conversation I had yesterday with Judge Sulzberger—O I guess you'd shrug your shoulders and smile a superior smile at my sensitiveness and dependence upon the approval of others. If he hadn't said the nice things about you, I would have come away from his house with murder in my heart. But enough of this!

You did not read my letter aright, if you thought I advised your leaving your father. On the contrary, I say, keep yourself well and strong, by sensible living, so that you can be with him every moment of your time while you are in Europe. From what you write of his occupations, his vigor of mind and serenity of soul, his interest in your interests, it is evident that your nearness to him is a joy. No, I believe you must make even the sacrifice of your own health to stay with him. What I deprecate is a momentary sparing of other people's feelings only to hurt them deeply and for long. Enough of this, too! I certainly do not want to preach in return for your fine letters, which by the way, contained some remarkably good English, as though to rebuke me for my criticism of you less than an hour before their arrival.

You ask about various things. Dr. Magnes, in company of Mr. Lewin-Epstein[50] and Dr. Lubarsky, sailed last Wednesday en route for the Holy Land. All three and Dr. Schloessinger and Dr. Margolis (no wry faces allowed!) expect to be at The Hague.[51] Dr. Friedenwald says he is not going. But I fancy his resolution will weaken when the time comes. The Hague seems so close—one could do the whole trip in less than four weeks—the length of the vacation you kindly assign to me. And yet you need not provide quarters for me! Mr. Lubarsky left with a heavy heart, on account of the bad news from Ahad Ha'am.[52] At the last moment America sickened him, because no message of sympathy had been sent from here to the victim of Odessa brutality. And the Duma is dissolved! A foregone conclusion since Russia raised a loan.[53]

Your second inquiry is about next year's publications and Philo . . . But please let's go on with the Legends as though they had to come out at once . . . You should have seen Anna when I gave her your message. She trod on air all day. And I don't wonder. I am sure she is even cogitating whether there are any other dishes besides beans that can be made acceptable to you and your doctor by the substitution of lemon for vinegar. For the rest, her temper is as vinegary as ever, and she is as efficient as ever. She needs and deserves a husband—that's all there is to it.

I am glad you wrote to my mother. In the letter I last received from her two days ago, she said that I hadn't mentioned you for some time, and she wanted to know if there had been no news. All I could write her was the disquieting report your sister-in-law had given me of you.

I do not hesitate to send my regards to your mother. But I have been wondering whether your father would resent a message to him. Give him my best wishes, and tell him I feel as though I know him, and therefore I can rejoice that he has the pleasure of having his son with him for so long a time.

You write of his suffering pain. I pray you and he are not having much of that to undergo—he the reality and you the sight. That is the bitterest of all things.

Now a little more proof reading, and then to bed.

Sincerely yours,

Henrietta Szold

Amsterdam, June 5(?),[54] *1907*

Dear Miss Szold,

My letter to you of June the 27th had the same fate as yours from the 17th. Two hours after sending it off, I received your letter with a full description of the meeting of the J.P.C.[55] I did not reply immediately because I wanted to have some time to think the matter over and when I made up my mind to write to you, my father's state of health took such a turn to the worse that we feared the worst has now come. Even today, the last 24 hours haven't been very alarming, (yet) I am hardly in a position to collect my thoughts.

Now so much for the day. Your grievances against the J.P.S. are partly real, partly imaginary. I have no doubt that Judge Sulzberger and his associates know your great value to the J.P.S., but as "good Jews" they try to make a bargain and make you do work which its not at all in the domain of a secretary. Whether the directory is to be published by the American Jewish Committee or by the J.P.S. is of very little interest to me, but I am sure it is not the duty of the secretary to furnish his society with books. Whether my *Legends* is a fit book for the J.P.S. I do not know—I doubt it very much—but since when is it the duty of a secretary to act as translator of books! Of course the J.P.S. is not entirely to blame. You yourself is [sic] responsible for a great deal of your troubles. You ought to have your work and duties exactly defined. If the J.P.S. expects you to be *"ein maedchen für alles"* [a woman for all (tasks)]: translator, author and collector of statistics, then let them look for somebody else. You see, I do not shrug my shoulders but look at the matter from an entirely practical point of view, and you ought to do the same. You are un-American and un-Jewish in your business transactions, and never so for your own interest is concerned. Being at blaming and scolding you, I will add that your second letter, in which you excused yourself to have "bothered" me with your affairs, has hurt me very much. I might add with Job: *et ha-tov l'kabel v'et ha-ra lo l'kabel?"* [Should we accept the good and not the bad?] Is our mutual friendship of the kind that I am to pour out to you my heart while you are to keep anything unpleasant from me? I do not like to attack your sex, else I would say that only a woman is able to act this way.

Yesterday I received from Rome a specimen of the Vatican Manus[cript] of the Yerushalmi[56] . . . For your corrections of the Geniza Studies, many thanks . . .

I am surprised that you do not mention anything about your mother's health. I hope she is enjoying herself with the grandchildren, though I should think a little rest would do her good. Where did the Seltzers go to?

It was very kind of Fraulein Anna to take interest in my diet but I am afraid that next winter she will have more trouble than ever. In all events my very respectful compliments with the hope that she also may loos[e] some acid, the lack of which is my main trouble. By the way, what do you mean— it is a question of English by saying she needs and *deserves* a husband; does it mean she deserves it as a punishment or a reward?

Dr. Radin who had announced his intention of visiting Amsterdam did not show up but I hope that Dr. Schloessinger will keep his word.

Your allusion to Achad Ha-Am being a victim of Russian antisemitism was not intelligible to me until today when I happened to look at a Jewish-Dutch paper, where I find that he was approached by some of the hooligans.[57] If you would know the Jewish press in this country, you would not be surprised at my ignorance of Jewish affairs.

With kind regards to your dear mother, the Seltzers and yourself.

Your

Louis Ginzberg

Amsterdam
June 19 (1907)

Dear Miss Szold,

Just a few lines, as it is near *Shabbes* to inform you that I have absolutely nothing new to write to you. My father's condition is the same and we begin to be satisfied if it only does not grow worse.

I am feeling much better since I took up again my diet but which was forced upon me by you and by the fact that I had a very severe attack of stomach trouble.

With kind regards,

Your

Louis Ginzberg

---

528 W. 123rd St.
New York, June 20, 1907

Dear Dr. Ginzberg,

As I suspected, the Genizah proof has to go back to you . . .

So much for business. I feel as though I owed you a few lines in addition, because my mother sent me, this morning, the little note you wrote to her, and it was almost like having a letter direct from you. But though I am much serener than I was when I wrote to you last, I am still not tranquil enough to talk impersonally. As it is, I feel ashamed for having bothered you, who have real troubles and anxieties, with even a mention of my stupid grievances. But of this you may be assured—no matter how foolishly excited I may be about my petty affairs, I think of you and your father every day, and many times a day and I keep hoping and praying for the good.

Sincerely yours,

Henrietta Szold

Amsterdam, June 21, 1907

Dear Miss Szold,

It was very kind of you to think of me but it was also very unreasonable of you to worry about me. I do not know who has spread the rumor that I am ill. I can assure you that there is no truth in this rumor. Of course my nervous state did not improve since I am here but I am thankful to G. that it did not get worse, considering what I had to go through lately. As if the measure were not full yet, my mother was taken ill three weeks ago and her state was so serious that the physician feared the worst. Her precarious state affected the health of my father considerably and you can imagine what I suffered. Now thank G. mother is gradually improving and she is out of danger but no change for the better in father's health; we hope very little but fear much.

The weather is cold and unpleasant and I would not go to a summer resort even if everything here were in its ordinary state. As it is, I have no thought at present to leave Amsterdam. Itzkowski has actually printed three sheets and I hope to have the rest of the fragments finished by the end of July . . .

Besides this I have not my library with me and although there are books enough in Amsterdam I find it very uncomfortable to work here as I am accustomed to.

You see, without a Yearbook one may have his troubles if one is foolish enough to publish books of which the one half will not be read and the other not understood. I hope you'll be kind enough to let me know your opinion in this matter.

You may be right with regard to the Biblical references in "The Legends," but I'll be merciless against all references, brackets and parentheses, of which I found quite a number. I also found that the book lacks in many respects uniformity. Take for example the expression Tetragrammation, the Name, and the Ineffable Name for one and the same idea.[58] I am trying now to read the book through with an eye upon these and cognate matters.

I know I have no right to take away so much of your time in making you read my letters but I can not close this letter before admonishing you to be a little more careful about your health. You must try to have your walk every evening and think that if I were in NY you would have to leave by far more time, by walking and talking.

With kind regards to your dear mother, the Seltzers, and yourself.

Yours very cordially,

Louis Ginzberg

Amsterdam, June 27, 1907

Dear Miss Szold,

The hot afternoon, the heavy aroma of the H[illegible] and the brilliancy of Judge Sulzberger are *die mildende Umstände* [mitigating circumstances] in your case. To be sure, there is a strong case against you to be brought not by me but by Dr. Schechter. You know my notion of modesty, but you wrong Dr. Schechter in comparing "my popular gift" to his. Let me tell you that neither you nor Judge Sulzberger knows properly what popular is, indeed no "intellectual" can know what popular is. If you or Judge Sulzberger read something about a matter the details of which are not known to you and the representation helps you to understand it the matter without studying the details, then you call it popular. I understand by popular to make the populus *feel*, a gift which Dr. Schechter possesses but which I entirely lack. I reason lucidly and therefore can explain some difficult matter to those who know how to reason but entirely fail to make people feel. As a member of the J.P.S. I strongly oppose to the issue of my essay, which will certainly be a failure, but as the Publication Committee might make still a worse choice I will not make known my protest to the public.[59]

How far is your Jewish university progressed? I have read Dr. Adler's address in the American Hebrew and I do not think there is something behind it; it is simply talk and nothing more.[60]

Poor Mrs. Frank! To be the sister of a U.S. senator and to be expelled from a hotel is too much for a poor invalid.[61] Do you think that the restriction against the Jewish guest will result in making them more self-respecting? I am afraid not. Perhaps that it will open the eyes of those who maintain that it is the Jewish exclusiveness which causes anti-Jewish feeling. To eat Jewish pork is really a double *gehinom* [hell]! What remain[s] there from the new theology according to which it is the duty of the Jew to sacrifice his individualism that the brotherhood of men be established? We are certainly "the chosen people" but it is a pity that "the others" do not believe it.[62]

I expect Dr. Radin to be tomorrow here, Dr. Schloessinger also informed me that he will spend a few days here on his way home. But I must confess that though I am glad to see friends here, I feel very little in the humor for sightseeing or sightshowings. Father had again a very bad week and I feel the effects of it mentally and physically. I am glad however to inform you that my mother's health is improving. The physician allowed her to leave her bed for some time. With the psalmist I may say *Lulai Toras'khoh sha'ashuai, oz avad'ti be'onyi* [Had Thy law not been my delight, I would have perished in my affliction],[63] as it is only in studying and working that I can forget myself a little and I am convinced that to rest would be very poor cure for me. I have been very happy and successful in my work so that at one day I spent so much as a fl. for a cigar, the limit. If my Yerushalmi is not published shortly, I am afraid I'll be ruined by my extravagant smoking . . .

And now after having written to you all about me I hope to hear from you about yourself. Did your dear mother return to NY? How are the Seltzers and the Levins? It is a pity that Benjamin and his [. . .] are now in the minority and I hope that no injustice will be done to him by the two females.

If you happen to see my sister-in-law, please try to persuade her to go to a hospital and have the operation she needs performed on her. I know if I were in NY I would have accomplished it but I am afraid that my sister will delay it longer than it is good for her.

And now one question more. I was looking around whether I could get here a *Besamim Büchse* [spicebox] like yours but so far I was not successful. Do you insist on the grater inside of the box or not? I have seen a number of boxes used here for *besamim* without the grater.[64]

With kind regards to your dear mother, the Seltzers, yourself, and your staff, including Fraulein Anna.

I am very cordially yours,

Louis Ginzberg

528 W. 123rd St.
New York, June 29, 1907

Dear Dr. Ginzberg,

This is meant only to reassure you on the subject of my sanity. You must have thought me stark crazy when you received an envelope with practically nothing in it. Miss Sweetman gathered it up from my desk with other letters and mailed it without my knowledge. I had been going through the papers of the last three months, and when I came across an article which I thought might interest you, I clipped it, and in anticipation of others, I addressed an envelope to you, in order to keep your clippings separate from the others, in the hopeless confusion that now reigns my desk ordinarily. When clipping no. 2 presented itself, the envelope was not to be found, and an investigation revealed the mistake. From the fact that I miss several notes I had jotted down, I imagine they must have wandered into your envelope. Tear them up.

One of them had reference to a rather interesting phenomenon—the Central Conference of American Rabbis[65] has issued an Order of Service for Sabbaths suitable for summer resort use![66] I haven't seen it, so I cannot speak of its peculiar tonic and cooling qualities. What would a man and Jew like your father think of such an aberration?

As I am at it, I might as well acknowledge your postal of a few days ago. I am doubtful whether to be glad or sorry I had so potent an ally as an attack of stomach trouble forcing your diet upon you. "Ally," of course, is a mere *façon de parler*. The stomach trouble did the whole business of compelling you back to sense. A distance of several thousand miles does not produce an influence that has no existence when you are in New York. Nothing multiplied by infinity itself still produces nothing. However, I am satisfied to know that you are taking better care of yourself, and I am not sure but that I'd rather have you exactly as independent as you are, and unamenable to influence.

You cannot expect stimulating news and sprightliness from a correspondent who, to quote my sister Adele, is either a demi-god or a horse, the alternative suggested to her by the report that I was working seventeen hours a day, on the average. Isn't it a disgusting record? I'm not a bit proud of it. But just wait and see what will happen another year! I must admit, however, that in spite of heat, work, and many disappointments, I am well—I am not one of the celestials, so I must be the equine.

You could never guess how I spent part of this holy Sabbath day—in reading some of your Legends! And now guess which chapter—the one on Solomon! It goes very well, I think, and I am quite convinced you are wrong about the undue frequency of Bible references.

Sincerely,

Henrietta Szold

New York, July 1, 1907

Dear Dr. Ginzberg,

I can imagine what a distressing time you must have had with your mother ill, too. When one is unstrung by fears and tremors night and day on account of one beloved person, to have another equally beloved person menaced by danger, robs one of all power of self-control. I only hope your mother continues to improve, and that delight in her recovery has wiped out the detrimental effect anxiety had upon your father's condition. In spite of all, I am not astonished to hear that you are bearing up well. However bad nerves may ordinarily be, they respond to responsibilities, if only the responsibilities are great and grave enough to startle them into good behavior.

In the Itzkowski business my advice would be not to work at your notes now . . .

You are not in the least wanting in modesty—if you maintain that the value of the fragments publication will reside in your commentary. I go further and hold that the text may not even appear without the notes, and that you must not make the final plan for them when your condition is not normal. You ought not to subject yourself to unnecessary strain, while the necessary strain is so severe. Of course, I cannot conceal it from you that even when you return to America, it will be very, very hard for you to do anything of an exacting nature. I have often this summer been projecting my sympathy with you forward to the time when stern necessity will bid you leave your father. So long as you are with him, and can observe his every act, and can offer him little courtesies and plan little pleasures for him, even the sight of his suffering is endurable. It is when you come away—Oh I know the feeling so well! But it is wrong of me to borrow your feelings. Fortunately you still have months to be with him, and perhaps a way will be found of lengthening the time . . .

You will receive an envelope filled with clippings. My sending them imposes no duty upon you to read them. Tear them up if they do not suit your mood.

Involuntarily I smiled when I read your complaint about lack of uniformity in your "Legends." What, have I infected you with my little passions?

Continue to take good care of yourself, and continue to be brave and strong. I hope you will not think me patronizing. I counsel, not from my head, but from my heart. I have lived through such solemn days as yours unfortunately are. Above all things, do not go away from Amsterdam—that's what you are in Europe for—to be a companion to your father and a solace to your mother.

Sincerely yours,

Henrietta Szold

---

528 W. 123rd St.
New York, July 9, 1907

Dear Dr. Ginzberg,

On my return from Baltimore a couple of hours ago, I found a letter of yours—the one explaining popular literature— lying on my desk. Even without this invitation justifying my writing to you, a letter would have been inflicted upon you to-night, because I must tell you something that will flatter you—or ought to, or, at least, it would flatter me if a child had done it to me. Saturday evening Dr. Benderly came out to Walbrook[67] to see me. The children had, of course, been put to bed by that time. Next morning I told Benjamin, "A friend of yours was here last night—Dr. Benderly." At once a musing expression came into his big brown eyes, I misinterpreted it and went on: "Don't you remember Dr. Benderly, who gave you your Hebrew blocks?" He said: "Oh, yes! But was Dr. Ginzberg with him?" Wasn't that remarkable? And aren't you flattered? Or do you, in your conceit, take it as a matter of course that everybody should be impressed by your personality, even a little child?

I went to Baltimore last Friday to be with my mother on the anniversary of my father's death, and to visit his grave. Incidentally, I made the baby's acquaintance, and gave Harriet an opportunity to make mine. The baby is a healthy, good animal—sleeps twenty-two out of the twenty-four hours—enviable creature! And Harriet is a graceful little coquette, a really charming companion, at once a baby and a grown-up. Unfortunately my visit was spoilt by the intense heat, which laid me low. I was on my back most of the time. Or it may have been, not the heat, but only the reaction from the hard "galley" work I have been doing. I was particularly happy to be with my mother, whom I had not seen for two whole months. I found her as I expected—tired out by her excessive activity in the house and with the children. Yet she did not come back with me, because my sister Mrs. Jastrow expects to be in Baltimore in a week's time, and she wants to spend a few days with her. Since I have told you so much about our family, I may as well finish up—The Levins are well, my sister looks particularly young and radiant, and the Seltzers are enjoying the cool breezes of Somerville, where they are comfortably installed with the farmers who took us in last year.

As for your sister-in-law, I shall not wait until I happen to see her, but I shall make it my business to call on her for the purposes of persuading her. I can do so with the more grace as I have already spoken to her on the subject several times. And I have returned from Baltimore fortified with an argument in the vigor of my sister, who is a changed person since she underwent an operation.

I was happy to hear of the improvements in your mother's condition. I only wish your account of your father might have been equally satisfactory.

Jewish University! I was not at the Seminary commencement, and I have only the newspaper reports to base my opinion on, which, not very elegantly expressed, is "Tommy-rot." Dr. Adler, of course, was speaking as one who is on the inside track in Dropsie College matters. It appears from what has leaked out that the Dropsie people are formulating a comprehensive scheme of Jewish education, from the primary stages to the highest. And probably when the public will be told the whole now contemplated, Dr. Adler will be in a position to smile a superior, ironical smile at his critics. Nevertheless, I mention that what he said, said in the way in which he put it, was silly verbiage.

Please don't bother about the *Besamim* box. Seeking one for us must be as distasteful to you as the mere thought of sightseeing and sightshowing, as you express it. The only quality we insist on is a negative one—that it shall not be in the shape of a tower, but should be a box. If you have seen one you yourself like, send it, but please make no further searches.

The "popular" business we'll fight out another time. Meantime I hope you will continue to smoke good cigars for legitimate reasons, even if it does beggar you.

Sincerely yours,

Henrietta Szold

Amsterdam, July 12, 1907

Dear Miss Szold,

To be well trained in dialectics has also its drawback. This I found out when I received your clipping containing Heller's letter to the editor of the *Israelite*,[68] accompanied by two mysterious notes. Any ordinary human being would immediately have said that there is no connection between the clippings and your notes, but not I. Being brought up an "*harber Rambams*" [one able to untangle very difficult halakhic problems in Maimonides], I tried to find a *pairush* [exegetical explanation] and of course I could explain your notes in different ways except in the correct ones.

Pairush 1: "Summerresort Prayerbook" will say that it was impossible for you to go to a summer resort as I have suggested to you because your free time is taken up by the revision of the Prayerbook.

Pairush 2: "Sweet country of liberty"[69] etc. was a comment on the condition in the H.U.C. of which the enclosed clipping dealt. You wanted to convey your opinion that the H.U.C. acted against the American spirit as well as against the Jewish. You see I was not at all embarrassed about the explanation and I never doubted your soundness of mind. Even more than this, I did not suspect you of pietistic inclination, else I would have explained "Summerresort Prayerbook" meaning that the prayerbook is your source of recreation instead of the summer resort. It is therefore not kind of you to destroy my *pilpul* [circumlocutory explanation] and declare the whole matter a misunderstanding caused by Miss Sweetman.[70] But I am sure that your good opinion of my *scharfe Sinn* [keen mind] did not suffer on account of it. No same man could have connected the summer resort with the prayerbook in the way the Conference of American Rabbis did. According to the methodological rule of the Talmud *Atu B'shuftani askenan* [Do we have to deal with fools?], one might have accused me of illogicality if I would have guessed the right meaning of your sentence.

Concerning the Yerushalmi, I have a new idea, but which you'll kindly keep a secret . . .

Why not have an Introduction to the Jerusalem Talmud? Of course, an introduction not with some of Mielziner's[71] or Strack's[72] booklets, but a scientific resume of the problems connected with the Yerushalmi. I therefore think it would be the most advisable thing to have two volumes:

I. The Geniza Fragments and the Hebrew notes, with a very short English preface.

II. An introduction to the Jerusalem Talmud.[73]

In all events, you are right that I ought not to set up the Hebrew notes before returning to New York . . .

I have read your letter to my father and he remarked smilingly that you are certainly the daughter of a *Talmid Hakham* [learned Jew], knowing what *ha'aramoh,* "legal fiction,"[74] is and that making use of the same subterfuge, he sends regards to you.

My mother is out of danger but, due to the critical state of my father, she is unable to regain her strength. We had a very sorrowful week, as father is now confined to bed and is very weak so that he can hardly speak. He nevertheless insists that I should leave Amsterdam and go to some summer resort. Fortunately the weather is extremely hot and I can give it as reason for my remaining in Amsterdam.

Dr. Schloessinger was last Sunday here and his information about you was of the kind to cause me great sorrow. Could you not manage at least to take a rest from Rosh Hashonoh till after Succoth? I wished I were now with you and could influence you perhaps that cold writing hardly will do.

With kind regards to your dear mother and yourself.

Very sincerely

Your

Louis Ginzberg

Amsterdam, July 12, 1907

Dear Miss Szold,

I forgot to mention in my last letter to you that I received the klippings out of which I managed to get out some fun, notwithstanding the fact that the whole controversy "*sehr merkwurdiglich*" is [very remarkable]. It tickelt my humorous vein to see myself described in the same issue of the *Israelite* as an Orthodox Jew—Dr. Magnes' characterization—and as a denier of the authority of the Pentateuch on account of which Dr. Wise did not want me at Cincinnati—the statement quoted from Emil Hirsch![75] The difference between Dr. Magnes and Hirsch is that the one told a truth in an inexact way and the other a lie in an exact way. I am not "schadenfroh" [a gloater at other people's distress] by nature but I could not help enjoying the spectacle, "the dirty Pollack"—Dr. Kohler's name for Schulman—defending the German-American Reform. And Dr. Schulman the Ehrendoktor [one who received an honorary doctorate] of the Orthodox Seminary![76] "*Na dir a groschen un sog mir den Pshat*" [Take the coin and give me the answer].[77]

This Yiddish sentence reminds me that my mother gave me for you a nice collection of *T'khines* which I am sure you'll enjoy. Of course, you'll say that I have not no right to rob mother of her literature, but the truth of the matter is that her eyesight is very weak and tears very harmful so that (I) tried some ruse to get the *T'khines* from her.

I am very flattered by the compliment paid to me by Benjamin but for the sake of inquiry I'll show you that I have no reason to be proud of it. Dr. Benderly's personality must have impressed itself with such power upon his young soul that he even remembers such a 'small' detail as "*meine Wenigkeit*" [my humble self] in connection with the strong impression. I am also thankful to you for the report concerning your family.

I hope that by the time this letter reaches you, your dear mother will have returned to New York. I hope this on her account and on account of yourself; perhaps that she will be able to make your next summer more reasonable. Pardon this strong expression, but it is unreasonable and foolish to sacrifice our health for nothing. It is much better the Congregation Anshey Schmilveritz in Poughkeepsie is left out of the Directory than you ruin your health by such conscientiousness . . .

Since a fortnight the state of my father is very alarming and I am mentally and physically near a breakdown due to the fact that I suffer terribly of insomnia. Father is now bedridden and has a day and night nurse; his sufferings are so that he gets twice a day morphine injected. The pleasure to talk to him is denied to me as he is too weak to speak or to be spoken to. It is very egotistic of me to write this to you, but even my strength will have its limitations.

With kind regards to you and your dear mother

Your[s] sincerely

Louis Ginzberg

528 W. 123rd St.
NY, July 17, 1907

Dear Dr. Ginzberg,

I am prepared to meet you more than half-way in your view of my strained relations with the Publication Society. It is not only partly my fault, I am almost entirely to blame. When my nerves are steady, as they now are and I look back upon the years of my secretaryship, I realize that I actually *usurped* duties, if that is possible. And now I expect others to protect me against myself! I was too eager to serve an apprenticeship, and not having had proper and self-respecting confidence in myself, I now enjoy the logical return: the Committee has no confidence in me, only the confidence one places in an upper, well-tried loyal servant with a *"Bedientenseele"* [soul of a servant]. But all this does not help me to throw off the unreasonable irritation that overcomes me every time the subject enters my mind. I wonder how much of it is due to the goading of others, how much to overwrought nerves—thoroughly feminine reasons, I hear you generalize, feminine lack of independence and feminine unsteadiness—which brings me to your second indictment, on which I am not quite as tractable. You charge me with having hurt your feelings. And having hurt them for no less a reason than because I am woman. In the first place, I don't believe you were really hurt, since you knew that there was not intention of being unkind, only a belated realization that I had obtruded petty thoughts upon one who, never given to pettiness, could at present not possibly harbor it. And it actually did turn out that when my letter reached you, you were actively unhappy! I wonder whether you can realize how perfectly I can follow your alternations of feeling as you sit by and watch your father? I know how all your senses are sharpened to detect changes, how you yourself suffer every change in your own body—how your heart sometimes gives a bound that sets every nerve quivering and quailing. And then the quiet happy hours come when the old gentle converse is resumed and you drink it in with the feeling that you are coming into the possession of a something of which the cruelest fate cannot rob you.

I have gotten away from your charge—my "in the first place" was to be followed by secondly and thirdly, though no sermon was intended. But I will not go back to them, only to say that I shall try to mend my ways, and report all the disagreeable things that happen to me—or try to do it, try to be unwomanly.

Instead, I have to confess that my mission to your sister-in-law was a failure. Some time ago, I remember, it was too cold, and then Ruth Schechter's wedding came, or perhaps it was your going away, and now it is too hot (to-night it is too hot for anything), and later the holidays came, and then you are coming back and then the house must be put into order—and then—perhaps—if it isn't too cold—perhaps! That's as far as we got. Mrs. Ginzberg does not know that in the Reform synagogues they have a three years' cycle for the Pentateuch, else she might have gone on telling me reasons for two years more why that operation which is not a serious one, cannot be performed. I suspect it will take your quiet insistence to bring it about. However, I had a pleasant little Sabbath afternoon chat with two-thirds of the family, the two older boys not having been in evidence. It ought to flatter you to know that they all miss you sorely, from the youngest to the oldest, your sister-in-law perhaps most of all. She told me she weeps three days after each letter that comes from you. Queer, what different effects the same causes produce! Now I, for instance, was pleased for at least three days, with no inclination in the direction of tears.

My mother? By this time you have my letter telling about my visit in Baltimore. I may not have told you, however, that her arm is no better, which does not prevent her from doing five times as much as a grandmother with a strong arm. But you are right—she ought to have a little rest. I hope to have her back with me by the end of the week. And then she will be hankering after the trio, and wondering how Harriet gets along without her "*Mütter*," as she calls my mother. You should see my mother's eyes and cheeks when she is playing with that little charmer.

Another sheet! But it is my first offense since you have been away, and I'll try not to do it again. I must this time, if only to congratulate you upon Itzkowski's having made good . . .

In one of your letters you refer to the *American Hebrew* and having read something or other in it, from which I jump to the probably unwarranted conclusion that the paper is sent to you. If so, you will know that Mr. Schiff and Mr. Marshall called a meeting on the East Side to enlist popular support for the Seminary.[78] Everybody has been extolling Mr. Schiff's speech on the occasion. I thought it in abominable taste. He made two points: one was a scolding, that there was more true Judaism to be found in New York forty years ago than now[79]; the other an admonition, that they must support the Seminary even if they don't like the rabbis it turns out, they are the rabbis for their children. If the East Siders refuse for their children rabbis that do not suit them, may that not be an indication that they possess as much of Judaism as the New York of forty years ago? I, too, think that rigid orthodoxy is doing harm, but what right have I to tell a particular man or set of men to abjure rigid orthodoxy? And the other statement, about forty years ago, is not proved. There was much talk of Judaism, but little understanding of it, and little feeling for it, except a sort of Protestant pietism and Anglo-Saxon preoccupation with the subject of religion. The two periods are not comparable. The one practically knew no poverty and struggle, the opposition between the needs and demands of life on the one hand and the behests of religion on the other, was a vanishing factor. And now! I wonder whether Mr. Schiff, whom his intimates describe as a truly large-and-warm-hearted man, has an inkling of the bitterness of life for some people . . .

You will think this is *Megillah* instead of *Echah* time.[80] In a minute I'll be through.

I hope Dr. Schloessinger kept his intentions of visiting you, because I think his personality is of the soothing sort. He will not rub you the wrong way, even if he does not stimulate you.

To-day Anna is with us three years. Now, say whether she does not *deserve* a lord and master? This is a lesson in English for you and in other things, too! Anna, overwhelmed by your courtesy to her, wishes me to give you her respectful regards.

The only sort of regards I can send you is warm regards—
I don't know where the thermometer is, but the humidity
must be 120. It is real *Tisha be-Ab* weather.

Sincerely yours,

Henrietta Szold

---

528 W. 123rd St.
NY, July 22, 1907

Dear Dr. Ginzberg,

Do you remember all the nonsense you wrote on July 12th?
All about prayerbooks and summer resorts? It served the purpose of nonsense—it amused me and my mother, and to have
amused me in these strenuous days is not a little thing. Since
Dr. Schloessinger told you of my fiendish existence this summer, I may as well own up to it. It has been the worst Year
Book craze yet. But now it is all over—this very day I shut
down, that is to say, I am making no more effort to secure
data. I have been a veritable martinet, writing to certain
organizations that would not answer, and writing again, and
still again, all but sending, as you once said, the sheriff
against them. But the stars with which I conscientiously
mark unofficial information remain numerous, in spite of the
eighteen hundred personal letters I have dictated since January 15, not to mention circulars galore. But now the child is
dead, and I weep no more. To-day the first of the galley-
proofs went back to the printer, and the rest follows day by
day until he has all, which I hope will be at the end of the
week. Then the page proof—the book will have 700 pages of
very fine print—and then the three weeks of Government[81]
work, and then I am a free woman, unless I am a mummy. But
do not imagine me suffering. I marvel at my own endurance.
The Year Book and the Prayer Book together kept me at my
desk from sixteen to eighteen hours daily for weeks, and yet
my appetite and my sleep are normal, except that I can
abnormally wake myself up at the end of four or five hours of
deep, refreshing sleep. I must be a fine animal. But no one
will ever guess what a drain this summer's work has been

upon my mind and my *Gemüt* [cast of mind, disposition]. Now that my mother is back, I am not quite so mummified as I was. But practically your letters were all that came my way to stimulate and divert me. Do you feel rewarded, for what I know is an effort for you?

I wonder whether I am going to be permitted to help ever so little with that projected Yerushalmi Introduction? You do not say whether it is to be in English. I think it is a fine plan, because it will be worthy of your critical powers and your scholarship . . . Beside your own pleasure, there will be the real contributions you will be making to Jewish science. I hope you will continue to nurse and cherish the project and carry it out at an early opportune time.

My mother came back last Thursday tired but happy about her stay with the children. For three days she slept away most of the time, resting up after her busy time in Walbrook. To-day, however, she is at her accustomed place, by the window, alternating with the seat and the sewing machine, stitching away industriously. She looks very well, very blue-eyed and very rosy-cheeked.

I wish you could reciprocate my good news with reports of a like kind about your parents. What a patient, gentle man your father must be! The few words you write about his weakness, and his strong insistence at the same time that you care for yourself give me a vivid picture of his personality. Almost I can see him, and you with him. I am emboldened by his forebearance to send my regards to him, this time without any subterfuge, and to your mother, too, and my mother wishes to be remembered to you and your people.

I hope yesterday passed off better with you than *Tisha beAv* did last year. I still get the creeps when I think of it. We had a fine and easy day of it here.

The next time I write I shall probably tell you that I take a daily walk on Riverside. Once the galley proof is off, the crisis is past.

With the wish that this may find your father suffering less than when you wrote, I am

Sincerely yours,

Henrietta Szold

Then the news came of his father's death. For a week, the week of mourning, I wrote him daily. I let myself go, I comforted him with all the comforts I had. In his little note following up the cable, he said in a postscript that as the funeral took place the next day, he would not be able to write to me for a week!

Amsterdam
23 July (1907)

Dear Miss Szold,

The sad news of my father's death will have reached you before this letter leaves Europe, and I only want to assure you that I bear up well. Father lived the life of a saint and died the death of a martyr. His sufferings were so that death came to him as a deliverance from evil. And have I any right to think of what I have lost?

Sincerely yours,

Louis Ginzberg

P.S. Tomorrow 11 a.m. will take place the funeral and I'll not be able to write to you for a week.

LETTERS OF CONSOLATION AT
GINZBERG'S BEREAVEMENT AND RESPONSE

528 West 123rd Street
New York, July 23, 1907

My dear friend,

I have just heard that the bitter and inevitable has happened. May God give you strength to bear the anguish of your bereavement, and in the time to come, when your grief will have lost its first cruel sting, may He turn the affliction into an added source of spiritual power.

I write no word of sympathy, no word of consolation—you are assured of the one without a word, the other must spring from the depths of your own being—and it will.

Sincerely yours,

Henrietta Szold

528 W. 123rd St.
New York, July 24, 1907

Dear Dr. Ginzberg,

If the cruel blow had fallen upon you here, I would have sought to see you every day, and by forcing you to the effort of listening to me, make you at once dwell upon and forget your sorrow. Isn't that one purpose of the *Shiv'ah?*[82] Need I apologize then, to you or to myself, for speaking to you today again, only because you happen to be thousands of miles away? To me at least distance makes no difference in feeling, in sympathy.

When I wrote to you yesterday, I felt that for once—a sad once—we stand upon the same level, eye to eye. I, too, have passed through the experience of having to give up a father beloved beyond words, the inspiration of all my days, so far as my life and actions are raised above the commonplace. To-day, after a little while, I have to admit to myself that even now you stand above me. Our fortunes may be the same objectively, my loss is as great as yours, even our capacities for sorrowing equal, but in one respect you must outreach me. The well-springs of your consolation flow deeper, fuller, more spontaneously. How many "verses" must be coming to your mind now which put your experience into thoughts— compelling, emotion-deepening words? Your memory is stored with situation after situation in history and literature, mirroring your own state of mind, yet different enough to rob your grief of none of its sanctifying power by setting it down as the common lot of man, the consolation offered first and all the time by the vulgar, who deal in phrases instead of get-ting the full value even out of such thoughts and feelings as they are capable of. We all, it is true, are subject to the same fortunes and fate; the elect alone emerge from them, equipped for an ampler life.

Only take care of your health, so that the powers within may not forsake you even temporarily. It is a tribute to the departed to grieve, and noble grief, showing love and forti-tude at the same time—doing honor to the dead and raising you to the heights the dear one would have had you occupy— is impossible if the body asserts itself in pain. So do not let mere physical pain and weakness usurp the place of solemn and justified sorrow.

Sincerely yours,

Henrietta Szold

---

528 W. 123rd St.
New York, July 25, 1907

Dear Dr. Ginzberg,

When I went to see your brother, he told me of a letter he had received from your father only a few days before the cablegram came—a letter instructing him minutely what to do when the tidings foretold by himself should reach him. From what you have told me of your father, I know that he was actuated by the simple desire to have his children act in accordance with the age-sanctified requirements of the faith he loved and lived. But I could not help feeling that this desire of his was inspired by the self-same motives that lie back of the requirements themselves. Unless grief submits itself to laws and customs, it is wild, uncouth, unhuman, and yet the very customs that restrain, permit and suggest a full expression of the otherwise impotent feeling that takes possession of one—to do something, something more than weep and lament, that will give evidence of the sorrow and sadness pent up within. If we were first to cast round for the form in which to display our intense and intensified affection for one who, alas, is removed forever beyond the need of our demonstrations of affection, the intellectual exercise would actually inhibit feeling instead of satisfying and stimulating it. We would shudderingly say to ourselves that the mystical connection that subsists between those who hold each other in affection ceases with life. There is nothing to be done but submit coldly. But if we use immemorial, transmitted forms of mourning, and abstain from our ordinary pursuits, giving ourselves up entirely to thoughts of the departed, then we realize fully the extent of our loss, and while outwardly doing what generations have done, whether learned or boorish, what the coldest and stupidest of those about us do—while doing like them, we are left free to put new content into new form. Thus, as I said, we learn to realize fully the extent of our loss—we learn that, paradoxically enough, the greater the loss, the greater is the inheritance, greater in memories and greater in responsibilities.

July 26

Ever since—I was going to say since you left, but that is not true—ever since your first letter from Amsterdam, I have been rejoicing daily that you were privileged to spend these last months with your father. There was much pain connected with them—how much I felt keenly through your postal from Zandvoort—and for a long time your picture of your father will be connected in your mind with his suffering. But after a while, it will recede into the background, and his last words and acts will be a résumé to you of all the years you knew him.

It was easy for me to rejoice in your privilege, but the beautiful thing is to see your people here rejoice amid their grief. I do not know how to take it—as a tribute to your character, as a recognition of the close intimacy between you in particular and your father, or as a manifestation of their unselfishness. Your brother spoke of his longing to go with you when you left for Europe in the spring—he had not seen his father in more than a quarter of a century, but—he broke off—it was entirely fitting that *you* should have been the one to be in Amsterdam at the end. I hope it is as much of a solace to you as it is a chastened joy to them.

Henrietta Szold

July 27

Before going back to the workday work, I write you a line to assure you that much of the Sabbath leisure was devoted to thought of you and speech of you between my mother and myself. I hope the Sabbath of Consolation fulfilled a mission with you *nosson la-oyef ko-an v'l'eyn onim ozmah yirbeh* [He gives strength to the weary, fresh vigor to the spirit][83]—bringing you consolation with the rest of the mourners of Zion.

July 28

Your sister cried out in her grief the other day: Who is there to say to me now—It made my heart contract, this outcry of hers. It recalled to me all the poignancy of my own grief when my father was taken from me. A world is locked up with every human being that passes beyond our physical ken. Slight our contact with him may have been, but if it was in any way cordial, it means that certain ideas and sentiments of ours needed no explanation to him. A hint sufficed and he knew what we wanted to express, because it grew out of common experiences, the exact counterpart of which we have in common with no other. So one chamber after the other is locked up in our hearts as we go through life, and sometimes the very key is lost. And what a world goes with a beloved father, what a big chamber is locked after he leaves us! To this day when certain ideas come to me or are suggested to me, my mental note is, remember to tell to—and suddenly I realize that he who would have understood and sympathized without a word of explanation is no more.

July 29

What has been passing through my mind to-day, I find it hard to write down—to write even to you at this time. Is it the reserve of the Jew in matters of faith? And yet I write of it—perhaps my experience will grant you a momentary consolation.

When the end came and my father was no more, I for the first time in all my life believed fervently in the immortality of the soul. And exaltation of spirit seized me. I felt closer to him than ever in life. I was almost indifferent at seeing his lifeless body lowered into the grave. I have since then cherished the memory of what passed within me. When I lose faith in myself, in my capacity for ideal living, such as I thought I had when my father inspired me to it, recall those days, and encourage myself to believe that once having reached the heights of faith, the possibility is present within me, and I may reach them again and again, and become truly religious, as your father was, living by a simple faith that permits no going astray from the right path.—

To-day I received your letter telling me of the last days—
how you could not even speak to your father, how you fear a
breakdown for yourself. When the news came, I saw all this
in my mind's eye—these last terrible days—and I have been
anxious about you, lest, as you say, even your strong will
should give way. I wish I could send you some of the superfluous strength I am wasting in the Directory. As it is, I can
only hope and hope that you are at least taking care of yourself to the best of your ability.

Henrietta Szold[84]

After the week of mourning I continued to write frequently, when,
O wonder of wonders! a letter came from him asking me to write as
often as I possibly could. And how broken hearted his letters were that
summer. My poor friend had passed through the severest ordeal, and I
know the ordeal. And when I wrote to him how well I could understand his feelings by reason of my own experience, how tenderly he
regretted that he was recalling my own grief so vividly.

Amsterdam
August 2, 1907

Dear Miss Szold,

My last letter has shown you that I am calm though I must
confess of a calmness that would not please you. I cannot yet
realize the fact that my father is dead. I still suffer with him
as I did for the last three months. I read once that people who
have parts of their limbs amputated still feel pain in the part
amputated. Now I feel about the same. I do not mourn but
suffer indescribably. My father was the embodiment of all the
noble and great Rabbinical Judaism has produced and his
death takes away from me the concrete[ness] of my "*Weltan-
schauung.*" You see how selfish my mourning is.

There is told in the Midrash that a great rabbi lost a son
and four scholars came to console him. The first three
referred him to Aaron's fate who lost two hopefull sons, to
David, who lost his favorite son and others. The mourning
father replied, "Not enough that I weep over my own son
now I'll have to weep over the sad fate of Aaron and David
also." This story came to my mind when I read your second
letter. I feel that my sad fate has awakened in you the old,

never-forgotten grief over the loss of your father. As you said, our cases are so [a]like that at this moment, I feel your loss and I do not doubt that this is the same with you. Now I am asking myself, is it right for me to cause you such pain and open old wounds? But what am I to do?

I was yesterday to see a nerve specialist as I did not like the state of my mind. He made a very grave face and induced me to leave Amsterdam at once. In compliance with his order, I'll leave for Berlin this coming Sunday and will then proceed to the German-Russian boundary—Memel—to meet my grandmother. The poor old woman—she is about ninety—was very much attached to her son-in-law and it was the wish of my father that I shall go to see her.

It is extremely hard for me to write and you'll excuse the way my letter is written. But if you want to confer a favor upon me—and I know you do, please write to me so often your time will allow it.

May I also ask you to inform Dr. Friedenwald in Baltimore of my father's death. I had promised, or to be correct, I had offered Dr. Fr. my services during the stay of his mother in The Hague, thinking that I'll attend the Congress. The physician, however, strictly forbad me to attend the Congress and you'll greatly oblige me if you'll explain to Dr. F. the matter.

With kind regards to your dear mother and yourself

from

Louis Ginzberg

---

528 W. 123rd St.
NY, August 5, 1907

Dear Dr. Ginzberg,

It was very good of you to give me the assurance, in the very freshness of your sorrow, that you were bearing bravely the affliction that has come upon you. If only your physical strength holds out, of your spiritual endurance I have no fear. As I wrote you, I know you are blessed with resources beyond the great majority of men. If you feel more keenly than most, you also have the cunning to force from the very cruelty of fate the solace that removes its sting. You wrestle until the angel of darkness must give you his blessing.

This week I have been thinking much of your mother. I hope she had rallied sufficiently from her recent illness not to be completely broken by this blow, without ability to rouse herself. Measure her sense of loss by your own. Life is practically at an end with her—I mean, there is no future. She will henceforth live only in the past. I know it from my own mother. Cheerful and helpful as she is, all things are in reality indifferent to her. It is good that you can stay with your mother for some time yet. Your presence will comfort her in a way, more, I believe, than the presence of any one else, for I cannot help fancying that you bring back to her vision her lost husband in feature and especially in disposition. You write something about tears not being good for weak eyes. Do not keep hers from flowing—they *are* good, if not for eyes that are weak, for sore hearts and bruised spirits.

Of ourselves here I have little to tell you that would interest you now—unless you are interested to hear that my list of indictments of Mr. Schiff, "the dean of American Jewry," grew by another item this week. He delivered the closing address at the Jewish Chautauqua Summer Assembly, and to my mind it was the arrant nonsense that befits the movement. He described the type of the American Jew of the future. He described his views of "a people of our faith who have thrown off the shackles, the peculiarities, and the prejudices which handicapped their fathers." And how they would be Jews in faith but one in sentiment with their surroundings—do you understand that? Jews in faith, yet one in sentiment with their surroundings! As though that were not the tragedy of the Jew, that because he was a Jew, he could not be one in sentiments with his surroundings—and not only his tragedy, but also his duty and his distinction. And needless to say that Mr. Schiff got in a whack at Zionism.[85] Needless to tell you, too, that the Jewish Chautauqua Society applauded boisterously and voted to have the address printed and fifty thousand copies to be distributed broadcast—for general circulation, that means, I suppose, "among the Gentiles," that they may know what a great, good, and

American people we are. It is the American edition of the Emil Cohn episode in Berlin.[86] To-day, Mr. Schiff said, the Jews in America are pilgrims, to-morrow they will be patri- ots—and that is his view of the future. Let my portion be with those whose epitaph is that they "lived the life of a saint," as you say of your father.

There is no use getting furious at Mr. Schiff. One ought to get furious at the Jewish public which is so ready to pay adulation and honor to the rich man.

I knew without your telling me that it would be a long while before I should hear from you, and your little note came as an unexpected gift, for which I am doubly grateful. But I shall look forward to hearing from you when you feel like writing. Whenever it comes, I hope your letter will com- bine the impression of your note—that you are as quiet and gentle in your sorrow—and as so good a Jew as your father would have had you be.

Sincerely yours,

Henrietta Szold

But not once did my hopes rise. I said to myself, he is in a soft- ened mood, he has the need to talk himself out. When he braces up, physically and spiritually, he will see the lines in your face again. The very fact that you are so experienced that you can give sympathy will stamp you as old—will militate against you.

In one of his letters he complained that he had not been a joy to his father during those months of his decline. His father had wanted him to be a *Lamdan* [traditionally learned Jew] and not a modern scholar, and his father had wanted to see him married, and besides he feared his father had discovered his small piety during the hard months before his passing away. He wrote further that he could not regret having become a Western scholar, and as for marriage (he appealed to me) I know "how happy he was in his bachelorship." So it be! If he is happy as a bachelor, I am satisfied, more, far more than satisfied to go on forever, doing what I had been doing for him and getting his friendly companionship in return.

Several times in our correspondence that summer our thoughts crossed. I would admonish him to merge his grief in good Jewish fash- ion in the general grief of the people expressed in the prayers of the season, and he wrote me of his feelings while he, the Nietszchean, read the *Selichoth!* And he let himself go otherwise in his letters—he told me about himself in various aspects—both incidents and feelings. And some of our correspondence turned on that.

Continental Hotel, Berlin
August 6 (1907)

Dear Miss Szold,

By the paper heading you see that I really left Amsterdam in accordance with the wishes of my physician which, as it happens in this case, was also my wish. I am trying to get my mother away from Amsterdam and this is only possible if I am to be away from there myself.

Do you remember our frequent conversations about my relation to my father as a typical case for the relation between old and young Israel? Now I never realized the depth of the chasm as I did in the last three months. You said in your last letter—July 26—that you and my people in New York rejoyced that it was I who was privileged to be with my father in his last days. So far as I am concerned you may be right in maintaining that time will extinguish the picture of his sufferings from my view and instead it will keep alive the picture of his gentleness and saintliness. But I cannot help thinking that my presence partly increased the mental suffering of my father. My father was a great admirer of mine, not in that usual foolish way of parents but in that of a "connoisseur," so that he never allowed me to perform the smallest service for him because it is against the *din* [Jewish law] to be serviced upon by a great scholar. And yet how many a time did he suppress a sigh that then his son did *not* become a *gaon* [traditional scholarly paragon] as he could, but a scholar! In this summer, he also realized more and more that I am not "*fromm*" [pious]. I do not need to assure you that I did my best to avoid anything which might have offended his religious consciousness but you do not know how difficult it was. Here an instance! We walked once on a Saturday and suddenly we were over the limit of the *eruv* [territory earmarked as within limits for carrying objects on the *Sabbath*]. My father never carried anything with him on a *Shabbes*, not even when there was a *eruv* and he told me that I'll have to throw away everything that I had with me, and I did. But unfortunately I had some money with me—about 20 guilden—by mistake as I ordinarily take out money from my pockets before *Shabbes*. I told father this but it pained him greatly that such a thing of carrying money on *Shabbes* could happen to me. As I spent most of my time in observing him I had time and opportunity to observe the effect of my presence upon him and I doubt whether my presence was beneficial to him. I cannot more. It is the tragic of Israel of our . . .

With kind regards to your mother and yourself

Louis Ginzberg

---

528 W. 123rd St.
New York, August 10, 1907

Dear Dr. Ginzberg,

I understand your paradox perfectly—you do not mourn, you say, but you suffer. Only I know—again from my own experience—that what you ought to say is, that you do not mourn *yet*. Your soul and mind are now filled, to the exclusion of everything else, with the picture of the abnormal circumstances of these last days and weeks—with all the suffering your dear one endured. It takes a long time for the scar made by a white-hot iron to disappear. For weeks and weeks after my father's death, I could not even recall his features. I looked at picture after picture, and they were nothing but paper to my eyes. I remembered nothing but his pain. Gradually only his image came back to me, what he had been in reality, his mental and his physical portrait stood out clear before my inner eye—and then I realized the whole extent of my loss, and realizing it, I was assured of my sanity, of the fact that my affection for him had not been a mockery and an illusion. Perhaps it will be so with you, too. The strain put upon you from the first, here at a distance and there at his bedside, has been too much for your nerves, as your physician discerned. I am glad he sent you away, and I hope that you will meet the Marx's (or that you have met them) in Berlin. They are whole-souled and they have so recently been through the furnace of sorrow and long-drawn-out anxiety, that their companionship will soothe you, and prepare you for what I fear will be another emotional trial—the meeting with your mother's mother. However, I can imagine that this meeting may soothe you, too. The aged are calm with a resignation born, not of callous indifference, but of larger experience, prophetic insight, and a true valuation of life, its gifts, and its problems.

Do not force yourself to write to me. It is enough for me to know that you want my letters—that they are not an intrusion upon the sacredness of your grief. By this time you will have the proofs in your hands that I instinctively anticipated your wishes. But I will confess to you that after I had observed the seven days with you, I shrank a little from resuming my correspondence with you. However well I might know your disposition in ordinary circumstances and relations, and however well my own experiences fitted me to put myself in your place, after all I could not judge whether what I felt impelled to put down on paper would fall in with your mood—whether it would not grate upon your sensibilities. You had undergone a fearful trial, and how was I to know whether it had not changed the man I had known into another? Either I had to look into your face again and hear your voice, hear you say something, even some indifferent words—or I had to have the assurance you have now given me of your own accord, that you want me to continue to write to you.

If your trip and the change of scene do you good, you will write me a line in a picture postal, telling me that the physician's prescription has had the hoped-for effect, and I shall be satisfied.

With this mail, I shall write to Dr. Friedenwald, as you wish. I am quite sure your physician was wise in counseling against your going to the Congress.

My mother sends her regards and good wishes to you. Take good care of yourself.

Sincerely yours,

Henrietta Szold

Köenigsberg
August 10, 1907

Dear Miss Szold,

For a week I tried to drug myself by means of work and company. The result was pretty tolerable days and frightful nights. I consulted a specialist in nervous diseases and he advised me travelling, and as I had the intention to go fast, I followed his advise. I arrived here last night and will remain here or in the neighboring Cranz[87] for a few days and will then proceed to Memel where I hope to find some letters from you. I have booked on the Ryndam which sails Sept. 22 and I hope to arrive in NY *Shemini Azereth* [Jewish festival which follows *Succot*] . . .

The text of the Yerushalmi is now printed . . .

You will have the kindness to excuse me to your dear mother for not answering now her letter. It is entirely difficult for me to answer condolence letters, and I think your dear mother will not insist on formality.

With kind regards,

Louis Ginzberg

528 W. 123rd St.
New York, August 13, 1907

Dear Dr. Ginzberg,

Writing to a European traveller is like trying to put oneself into communication with a disembodied spirit—and I am no Spiritualistic medium. I don't know where to imagine you. At Berlin? At Memel? On your way back? Both these places, like Amsterdam, are but geographical concepts to me. And yet if you could be identified in my mind with a name of a habitation, I could fix you better and feel that you were listening to me. But there you are flitting hither and thither, and the letter will have to follow you and likewise flit hither and thither, and by the time you read it, it will be antiquated, which on the whole is a serious drawback to European correspondence. One would always like to write about eternal verities in a letter destined to travel across seas. One can be reasonably sure of holding the same opinion on them two weeks after writing. But a flippant, or a trivial, or even a humorous mood cannot be expected to last until a letter takes a long ocean trip, and then the reader has a wrong conception of the writer as he actually is.

Talking of geographical concepts reminds me that one of them connected with a tentative itinerary of yours was Hungary. Weren't you to do something about that Kodashim-Yerushalmi manuscript of Friedland-Algazi?[88] I wonder whether you happen to have read that it has been rather emphatically pronounced a forgery by Ratner?[89] I remember that you yourself were somewhat reticent about it; you refused to commit yourself. I did not see Ratner's criticism. I don't even know where or in what language it appeared. But the quotation from it that has been making the rounds of the American Jewish papers left one in no doubt as to his opinion.

And do you know that you gave the death blow to the Jewish Quarterly Review? At all events it is not to appear after the July number, at least not as a Quarterly. I believe the Editors promise that it will continue as an occasional publication. They simply couldn't get along without those Genizah Fragments of yours, and when they were not forthcoming, due to your stubborn—I mean firmness, the Quarterly had to die of inaction. Isn't this the psychologic moment for the American "coterie of scholars" to start a Jewish scientific publication?[90]

To-morrow the Zionist Congress opens, and I feel my biennial regret that fate does not favor me to the extent of permitting me to participate in one. It looks to me as though there could be some sharp passages between the factions this time. By the way, with regard to Mr. Schiff's address I am in a hopeless minority, so far as I know, in fact, I form a party all by myself. No one has yet sympathized with my view of it. On the contrary, the papers are jubilating over its pronouncements, and especially over its outspoken anti-Zionism and its equally outspoken Americanism. Several of them wonder how any one can dare remain a Zionist since the great and only Mr. Schiff has spoken his "ipse dixit." I am keeping the clipping for you until you come back—I count that it will be in seven weeks—and I hope you at least will join my party.

I have written of all sorts of indifferent things in this letter. But you must not think me unmindful of your present state of mind and soul. You must believe that from day to day I can and do follow your emotions. Do not misunderstand me. As I wrote you before, I know I cannot measure the depth or express the force of your emotions. I am a firm believer in the Jewish view, that a boor cannot be truly pious,[91] with the inference from it, that the more intellectual the man, the keener, the deeper, the more effectual his feelings, if he has feelings at all. What I mean is, if I cannot follow you to the highest heights and the deepest depths, I know at least that there are heights and depths, and when their times come and go—in short I can be sympathetic. I can feel with you.

I do not permit myself to worry about your refractory nerves. I insist upon believing that the trip you have undertaken is doing you good physically. But when you write me the picture postal I asked for, you must tell me the exact truth.

Sincerely,

Henrietta Szold

---

528 W. 123rd St.
New York, August 14, 1907

Dear Dr. Ginzberg,

Early this morning—very, very early, for Creole is most exacting in his decrepitude about the hour of his matitudinal stroll—I mailed a letter to you, and the first delivery a couple of hours afterward brought me yours from Berlin. I quite made up my mind not to reply to it for a couple of days at least, even if you *did* give me the privilege of writing often—and here I am late in the evening disregarding my resolution. That is because the letter has been haunting me all day at my work. You must not indulge in such morbid thoughts about your father. Take my word for it—your father knew long ago that you were not of his own stripe of piety, and though he regretted the fact, the knowledge of it did not in the least diminish his admiration of you. The little incident about the money may have given him a momentary shock, but only because it was, from his point of view, a rather drastic confirmation of what he already knew. I am convinced as though I had heard the words from his mouth, that your presence was a solace to him—that to the end you remained his *Gaon* [brilliant expositor of the Talmud]. If now and again you discerned a wistful expression in his eyes as they rested on you, it had another reason. Even those who are absolutely resigned to the will of God cannot ward off the desire to enter the Promised Land, and he knew that his end was too near for him to see the realization of all the hopes and wishes he had centered upon you.

For once the clarity of your judgment has forsaken you. And I do not wonder at it! But you must admit it—you must say to yourself a couple of times daily that the superhuman strain you endured for months had the effect upon you which a lesser strain has upon others—it has rendered you incapable of seeing true, especially where your relation to the father you mourn is concerned. It is a warped way of recognizing the irrevocableness of a bereavement. We torture ourselves with reproaches instead of cutting and gashing our bodies like our savage ancestors. By and by such morbid fancies will lose their mastery over you. Indeed, I hope by the time this letter reaches you, you will not stand in need of my sermon as a tonic for your nerves. Only it is not meant for sermonizing! It is meant to say—I understand your suffering and I assure you it will pass away, and you will again be self-reliant and self-poised.

For the rest, I want to repeat what I wrote the other day—do not write to me if the effort is too severe. If it relieves you to set down what you are thinking of, do it by all means. I need not tell you I shall be glad to have every scrap you feel impelled to send me—and sermonize afterwards. But do it from an inner impulse, not to satisfy an external convention.

Sincerely yours,

Henrietta Szold

528 W. 123rd St.
New York, August 18, 1907

Dear Dr. Ginzberg,

Mr. Blechman is responsible for the fact that you are getting an early Sunday morning letter, instead of the usual Saturday night letter. He came to see me yesterday afternoon, staid for supper, and lingered on until half past nine, and then I had to throw myself—as much of myself as is left at that hour—into the dispatching of some proof that I had not been able to finish up on Friday.

I have had several Seminary visitors lately—Hershman, who has gone from Syracuse to Detroit; Dobrin who thinks he is firmly established in what is a most "beloved" Hungarian congregation in Cleveland; and Blechman, who has just accepted a position in Boston. He goes there confident he will carry the town. Jacob Kohn has secured Hershman's position in Syracuse, and Lubin's socialism and aggressive personality have lost him his in Austin![92] Poor Lubin's wife! Besides these, one of the Raisins[93] has visited me. Not one of the conversations, so far as they related to the Rabbinical office, was inspiring. Mr. Raisin, indeed, is here for the purpose of seeing whether he can't worm his way into some business, so that he can crawl out of the Rabbinate, and if he succeeds half-way, his brother will follow suit. The only one who feels the "call" is Mr. Blechman. He is a veritable Methodist. There you have it! In the same breath, I deplore the lack of inner compelling conviction, and discerning it in a particular person, I call him derogatory names. That characterizes the present situation, and that explains why, in all the small communities of the West and the South, and no less in the colossal, amorphous community of New York, shoals of Jews are streaming into the Christian Science Church. Where faith ends, superstition begins.

It is a principle of mine to be chary of advice to others in important concerns, but after I had heard these various "rabbinical" conversations, I was not sorry for what I had impulsively said to Isidore Blum, the son of our physician in Baltimore, who paid us a ten day visit this summer, and in the course of it poured out his plans and projects for a career to me. He discoursed eloquently—with the eloquence of nineteen—of his doubts and hopes, and then pressed me to help him decide whether he should become a rabbi or a lawyer. It was then I burst out with: "I don't know about your becoming a lawyer, but I can tell you that if you hesitate for an instant between the rabbinical and any other profession, you cannot be a rabbi."

The "call" in these days must be unmistakable, urgent, insistent. Success and satisfaction—real, inner satisfaction—will at any rate reward only one in a thousand. At least the other nine hundred and ninety-nine should feel that whatever fate betide, they could not have done otherwise, so help them God!

You remember how I used to plague you about your attitude toward the Seminary, the students there, and the work it is supposed to stand for? I think you will admit that I let up on the subject somewhat during the last year, and more. I promise you now that I will not bother you any more. I understand better now. It is hopeless—the whole business has no vitality, no viability—no spring, no compelling force. Add to this insinuation(?) from external causes, the dead pressure of economic circumstances, which make Sabbath observance an utter and absolute impossibility, and what have you?

Do you remember the Galician canvasser who offered his services to me for the Directory? Some time ago he presented himself to bid me good-bye. After four years of struggle with American conditions in the effort to live as a Jew, he was returning home. He could not make up his mind to bring his children to this country. He told me the following incident: He was walking, on a Saturday morning, through one of the East Side streets, Ridge, I think, when he saw a man at the open window of an upper story laying Tefillin. Thinking that the man had forgotten it was Shabbes, he called to him, and received the answer in Yiddish: "It's all right to go to the factory today to work, why shouldn't I lay Tefillin?" I am sure that neither Rashi nor Rabbenu Tam could have conceived such a twist of mind and affairs.

I wonder whether this letter reminds you of our walks on Riverside Drive?—when I talk, talk, talk unmercifully, and you listen patiently, you always wearing the tolerant air of "*Nur zu! Ich halt still, wenn Gott durchaus will!*" [Go on! I'll desist, if God insists!] Never mind! There are only three more weeks of letter-writing from me to you, and after that it will lie with you whether we shall walk and talk on Riverside.

With regards from my mother, I am,

Sincerely yours,

Henrietta Szold

---

528 W. 123rd St.
NY, August 21, 1907

Dear Dr. Ginzberg,

May I continue my talk with you about the Rabbinical mix-up? It was brought back to my mind vividly by a letter from Dr. Schechter yesterday. He actually returned the galley proof of the Safed article[94]—and in what condition! The office of the printer will be a sulphurous blue when the compositor tackles the corrections. It was pasted up on big sheets and the extended margins were embroidered with Dr. Schechter's handwriting and Mr. Abraham's,[95] and half a dozen casual visitors'! Then there were Hebrew memoranda, heavily and lightly crossed off, either way they will make the printer desperate. And the successive changes of mind and opinion had left visible traces. In effect, the article is again re-written—I mean the double reduplication—on the proof. However, I wanted to tell you, not about the proof, but about the letter. It seems Dr. Schechter has been engaged all summer, more or less, in composing a scathing review of Dr. Philipson's book on "Reform Judaism."[96] Didn't I send you Dr. Deutsch's review of it, damning it with faint praise, and using the opportunity to fall upon Dr. Schechter?[97] Dr. Schechter's article, it appears, is to be published anonymously, and his friends have been trying to make him desist. In his letter to me, all his fighting spirit is on. He scents antagonism in the air, and he is girding himself and polishing his armor for the fray. Now, what amused,—no, amused is not the word—well, I don't know what word I want, so amused will have to do—what amused me was that in his two pages of fulminations, Dr. Schechter mentioned no names, but to me, who have had the same feeling about it, it was apparent—that he was excited by Mr. Schiff's utterances of which I wrote you some time ago. But heigh-ho! Mr. Schiff is the patron saint of *your* Seminary!

That does not complete the irony of the situation. A few weeks ago Mr. Schiff and Mr. Marshall with Dr. Schechter— it was in June—went down to the East Side and told the Ghettoites they must support the Seminary. Mr. Schiff barbing his arrow with the insulting statement that there had been more Judaism in the small New York community of forty years ago than in all the hundreds of thousands it now consists of.[98] Six weeks later, on that same East Side, there took place a meeting of the Union of Orthodox Rabbis of the United States, and one of the resolutions adopted at the Convention was, that if the congregations whose rabbis were there assembled took a graduate of the Theological Seminary as, well, as something or other, they were requested not to denominate him rabbi, but reverend or doctor, for rabbis meant something quite other than the thing represented by the graduates of the Jewish Theological Seminary.[99] The juxtaposition of these two East Side meetings, and Dr. Schechter's excitement (my own, too) is delicious.—Dr. Schechter is on his way to Detroit, to install Mr. Hershman—Mr. Hershman[100] who, being a Russian and not a little of the *Maskil* [Hebraist and Jewish rationalist] feels these ironic contrasts much more keenly bitterly than I, with the semi-Reform, semi-Protestant influences of my formative period.

Am I mistaken, or does a marshalling of such present-day facts and conditions make your mind revert to your father, as the type of the simple, single-hearted and single-minded Jew, treading the narrow path so clearly marked out by law and tradition, and doing the duty that lies at hand, without *Grübelei* [brooding] but with intense love and devotion! What has robbed us of such simplicity—the telephone or the Darwinian theory?

The clans are gathering at our house. Mr. Seltzer came back some days ago, my sister Adele will be here in a week's time, and to-morrow we expect my sister Mrs. Jastrow for a brief visit. From the children and their parents in Baltimore we have good news, and my mother is regaining her strength after a vicious summer cold. I wish we might be sure of good news from you, too.

Sincerely yours,

Henrietta Szold

528 W. 123rd St.
NY, August 23, 1907

Dear Dr. Ginzberg,

This letter is a Siyum-Siyum Year Book and Siyum Prayer Book.[101] Yesterday I sent off the last page of the Prayer Book and of the Year Book. I have only a few scraps left that will not bother me much—such is the simultaneous ending of a seven months' fiendish parallelism. I use the strong expression not as a matter of habit. It *has* been frightful, and if I had indulged myself, I would have written of it in every letter to you. It was not fear of being unwomanly or non-womanly that kept me from it—you had given me leave to trouble you with my affairs, almost insisted upon it as an earnest of friendship. But I realized sub-consciously that it would be a pity to spoil my chief pleasure of this summer by even thinking of my annoyances while writing to you. Some of my old asceticism asserted itself, too. I have taken both these tasks as disciplines, punishment, I don't know exactly for what, but on general principles. However, if I think hard enough, I can manage to find one or two transgressions so iniquitous that they are not even indexed in the Confession of Sins.[102] Therefore, I shall not confess them to you, either. At all events, the experience has been so chastening—can you conceive what an average of sixteen hours' work daily for a period of seven months means? Work? No, mean unmitigated drudgery!—it has been so chastening that I cannot even be glad it is over with. Not even the end is a satisfaction, for neither piece of work is well done, so well-done as I *could* do it—the prayerbook because I had to carry out other people's ideas against my better judgment, the Directory, because the time was too short, also undertaken, therefore, against my better judgment.

But do not speak to me of the progressiveness of Judaism! Why isn't there one *Techinnah* in all the books to fit my modern case—not one to raise up the spirit of a so-called emancipated woman, Heaven save the mark! To be sure, I don't know myself what I am to look for in the prayer-book—what I am to thank for? Have I escaped a danger, or a responsibility—or my own folly? Danger to my physical person there seems to have been none. On the contrary, lack of exercise has placed about fifteen pounds extra to my credit, which I shall now proceed to walk off vigorously. My sister is right, I *am* a horse! But I do not dare reckon up the cost to my intellectual and spiritual person. I am wrung dry; sometimes I wonder whether I shall ever be able to read a book again.

There! Now I am done with that chapter. You must not even let me talk to you about it when you come back. Instead, you will refresh me by telling me all the details of your plans for the Yerushalmi Introduction, which, I hope, are beginning to take shape in your mind. I won't understand? O yes, I will, if you will have the patience and the desire to explain to me. I *will* to understand!

By this time your second period of mourning has come to an end. There are people who say scornfully that grief has no periods. My opinion is that they do not know real grief. To divide up time does not mean that sorrow diminishes. I take the *Shloshim*[103] as a warning that the time has arrived when we must begin to give the world around us its due. So long as the cause of our grief is new, the world and all our relations to it are submerged. The others have no rights, only duties toward us who are plunged in mourning. But gradually we must acknowledge it has rights as well, and we are called upon to take up the old relations to it, and a sane man's sorrow sanctifies them, besides.

This afternoon my sister Mrs. Jastrow comes, and she brings Benjamin with her. So we shall have gay and lively times here.

With Sabbath greetings, I am

Sincerely yours,

Henrietta Szold

Berlin, August 25, 1907

Dear Miss Szold,

I am on my way back to Amsterdam after spending a few days with my grandmother in Memel. It was a great joy and consolation to me to find my grandmother physically and mentally very well. She is a real grand old lady, her mind serene, her wit ready and her memory remarkably strong. Of course, it was not an easy thing for me to answer her questions relating to my father without betraying any emotion, as I had decided to keep his death a secret from her. The strain on my nerves is so enormous that I fear I may break down every moment, but it seems that I am physically stronger than my physician ever thought. The sleepless nights with the suffering face of my father all the time before me are becoming unbearable! A specialist for nervous diseases whom I have consulted advised me to go to a sanatorium for some time, but imagine, what will become of my poor mother! She is very weak, though she bears her affliction bravely and it is my duty to be with her. I never realized the great strength there is in the fulfillment of a duty as it is the sense of duty which keeps me up and I hope that I'll come out victorious from the struggle.

The news about Mr. Schiff is no surprise. He is a great financeer and in his capacity as such he knows that in giving money for an object you acquire it, and as he spends large sums of money for Jewish institutions, he believes himself the rightful owner of American Jewry. One would laugh at the stupidity he shows were it not for the grave consequences of his stupidity. It is the tragedy of a small class or religious congregation that the influential individual may cause so much harm. Mr. Rockefeller, the richest man in the world, is of very little importance in the Baptist Church, indeed some of the members of this church even refuse his money, but Mr. Schiff is the greatest power in American Jewry. The reason is the smallness and poverty of the Jews. The Baptist can do very well without Mr. Rockefeller, but not the Jews without Mr. Schiff. Of course if the great masses of American Jewry were organized, the moneybag would lose his influence, but who is (to) bring order in this chaos!

I must tell you a little incident which happened to me last week. I met in Cranz near Köenigsberg the Rabbi and Rosh Yeshiva of Tels, where I studied when I was thirteen years old. The old man was overjoyed when I reminded him of the last *kushia* [scholarly question] I put before him the day I said goodbye to him, dealing with a *"harber Tosfos"* [difficult passage in the Tosafist literature] in Sanhedrin. But his joy was only of a very short duration. In the next moment he said with tears in his eyes: "A great gain was lost by Israel in the day you left Russia." Do you remember what I wrote to you in one of my last letters? This was exactly the feeling my poor father had when he saw me for the last time.

Aren't you going to take a fortnight off? I am sure the business of the Jewish Publication Society are [is] not so pressing that you could not take a short holiday. By the way, I met Dr. Perles,[104] who sends his best regards to you and he also declared himself willing to do some work for the J.P.S.

I do not know whether I wrote you that I am to sail on September 21 and it is my intention to stay in Amsterdam till the day of sailing.

With kind regards and *k'sivoh v'hasimoh tovoh*,[105]

Your

Louis Ginzberg

NY, *August 26, 1907*

Dear Dr. Ginzberg,

Yesterday at noon the very very last page went to the printer, and to-day I have done nothing but straighten my desk, and tear up endless memoranda. Miss Sweetman went on her vacation four or five days ago, consequently the clatter of the typewriter is not heard in the land. Altogether my office has quieted down to its wonted peace. The Directory work, in so far as the Census Bureau is concerned, goes on, and will go on for several weeks yet, and simultaneously with it proceeds the installation of next year's Year Book, which I shall put into shape for my blessed successor. For these reasons I cannot take your advice repeated in several of your letters, and take a vacation away from home. The Government work must be done at once, and that will carry on into the holidays, and I have no desire to repeat the goyish experience of last year. Besides, to work normally, as I am now doing, is in itself a vacation, and to keep up to my work, so that it will not pile up and again necessitate a period of rush is all that I want. Immediately on dispatching my proof yesterday, I took a jaunt. I went to see Nellie Wallerstein, Mrs. Jastow's daughter,[106] who has taken a home at Mount Vernon, whither my mother, my sister and Benjamin had preceded me in the morning. The suburb is beautiful, every street shaded with avenues of magnificent trees, and Mrs. Wallerstein has a lovely little daughter, who admires me as much as I do her, and that is very soothing. Benjamin has been doing his best to give me a vacation, too, by his varying swings—an angel now, an imp in a moment, a surprising little thinker now, a mere baby in a moment. He is to be with us over Rosh ha-Shonoh, unless he gets homesick, of which a few symptoms have manifested themselves. The most interesting thing about him is his passion for every Jewish form, and his love for Hebrew. In obedience to the physician's strict orders, he is never permitted to have a book, not even a picture book.[107] He is to lead and does lead the life of a little animal. The only time he has anything printed in his hands is when he says his prayers, and then he seems transfigured.

War has been declared—war between the two factions in American Jewry, the nationalists and the anti-nationalists, and there can no longer be any doubt that Mr. Schiff is, and means to be, the spokesman of the latter. Hard upon his Chautauqua speech, of which I have been writing to you, follows an open letter addressed to Dr. Schechter, who, it seems, had written to him as early as the middle of June. Mr. Schiff's reply appeared in the current issue of the American Hebrew, but simultaneously copious extracts from it appeared in the daily press. The gist and substance of it is that a Zionist cannot be an American citizen of the true stripe, and vice versa, a true American cannot be a Zionist.[108] The old story—the

Jew must out-Herod Herod, must be more royal than the king, more Catholic than the pope. On second thoughts I am sending you the Chautauqua speech and a clipping containing the essence of his letter, the latter being but the logical consequence of the former. To me it now looks like war to the knife.

To-day I received the first two copies of the Congress "*Welt*"[109] but I have not yet had a chance to glance at them. No matter what happened at the Hague, I shall continue to cast my lot with the live Jews, instead of becoming a follower of Schiffian Judaism. Fortunately, I am not a professor at the Seminary!

With kind regards from my mother, I am,

Sincerely yours,

Henrietta Szold

NY, *August 28, 1907*

Dear Dr. Ginzberg,

I had your little note from Köenigsberg last evening, and I determined to wait until the end of the week before replying to it. But somehow or other I feel impelled to write you a few lines on my return home after an afternoon spent rather gaily at the Bronx Zoo with Benjamin, my mother, my sister, Miss Sommerfeld, and several common out-of-town friends here on vacation. In spite of the chatter and small talk and happy teasing of little Benjamin—he is angelic—your note kept me thinking of you, and wondering whether you find any comfort in the beauties of nature. My own feelings are diverse. Sometimes I am soothed and strengthened and uplifted by the reflection that all goes steadily and unceasingly, no matter how topsy-turvy things were inside of me. And again there are times when I rebel against it, that the trees stand in their majesty, rustling their leaves and undergoing the silent changes of the seasons, and the river speeds on, each wavelet glistening, while I am troubled and disturbed and full of seething, unexpressed feelings.

I fancy that you with your equable disposition are always soothed. You wrote me from Zandvoort that the sight of the sea makes one forget his "little self with his troubles and joys." And I know you always look forward with eagerness to the ocean trip, probably because of this very fact, that the infinite grandeur of the marine phenomena banishes petty troubles. If that is so, I wish you could have been with us this afternoon. We went through beautiful country, and the fresh smell of the earth, drenched a night ago by a long-awaited and much-needed rainfall, rose into our nostrils, and sent us back to town made over as good as new. In any event, Benjamin would have brought you out of yourself. I shall have to tell you about him when you come back, in less than five weeks—his wonderful sayings and doings.

I rejoiced to hear about the fine progress of the Yerushalmi. And as for my mother, of course she does not expect a formal reply to her letter. I always give her a share in my letters from you, and like myself she has only the wish that the few remaining weeks in Europe may give you abundant strength.

I hope your nights are improving. If only I could send you some of my capacity for sleep, healthful sleep. The habits which I had to cultivate for Year Book exigencies have robbed me, only temporarily, I suppose, of the power to sleep many consecutive hours—five a night suffice—but while I sleep, I do it thoroughly. By this time you will know from one of my letters that I am as little exacting as my mother—that I do not expect you to force yourself to write to me—a word occasionally is all I ask. But I hope the cards, each one in turn, will tell me that you are regaining the tone of your system.

Sincerely yours,

Henrietta Szold

528 West 123d Street
New York, August 30, 1907

Dear Dr. Ginzberg,

This note shall serve only the one purpose of carrying my greetings for the New Year to you. May it bring you consolation and healing for the sorrows and wounds inflicted by the old, and more than this—may it hold actual happiness in store for you, and strength to execute all the plans your fertile mind has conceived and will conceive.

My mother joins me in the above, and to your mother please wish "a good writing and sealing" in my name.

Sincerely yours,

Henrietta Szold

p.s. Will you address the enclosed to Dr. and Mrs. Marx for me, and mail it to them?

---

528 W. 123rd St.
NY, September 2, 1907

Dear Dr. Ginzberg,

I wonder whether you will detect a peculiar flavor about this letter? It is being written in time stolen from the Jewish Publication Society! The aftermath of the Year Book is so dull, so deadly dull, that I must stop a bit, and I take the time until lunch to chat with you. Imagine the stupidity of my morning's task,—I have been going through the correspondence, not a little bulky, of the last seven months, to pick out the names of persons in all the states and towns who gave me helpful information. These I am cataloguing for the use of that blessed successor of mine (O that I could name him or her by name!), so that he or she may produce a much better Directory than my first attempt has turned out to be, and may then crow over me. Such has been the nature of my work these last two weeks, and it looks as though it and the Government would keep me (gently) busy a couple of weeks more. But I am not really grumbling. I take life very easily with Benjamin around. I wish you knew that child as well as I do now. He is what my father used to call a "Gemorah-Kopf," [analytical mind capable of Talmudic reasoning] and, besides, so affectionate and childlike that one cannot be a drudge while he is around.

Yesterday afternoon I missed a visit from your brother and your sister-in-law, because I was walking Riverside

Drive from end to end. The sunshine was golden, the atmosphere deliciously warmed though yet cool, and all the walks thronged with festively-clad Sunday pleasure-seekers. In the evening my mother and myself paid a visit to the Friedlaenders, the first time I have seen them since Ruth Schechter's wedding. The "domestic" problem is still acute with them, and Mrs. Friedlaender seems dragged out, but the baby is fine, to judge from the account of him given by his parents, and from the more unbiased testimony of photographs taken at Tannersville.[110] The Tannersville rusticators are returning family by family—the Malters came back a few days ago, and dined with us Saturday; and Mrs. Schechter wrote me she expects to leave tomorrow. Also the European travellers are putting in appearances—I hear both Dr. Radin and Dr. Magnes are here. And today four weeks *you* will land!

At Dr. Friedlaender's we discussed Mr. Schiff vigorously. Dr. F., of course, does not sympathize with his anti-nationalistic attitude, but he excuses his course of action—sees in it his obedience to the promptings of a sense of duty. But what a mistaken sense of duty, which insists that you must put the sharpest of weapons into the hands of the Anti-Semites! These are the days when I wish I were a ready writer—I would enter the fray with such gusto! Harry Friedenwald has replied to Mr. Schiff in this week's Jewish papers, and his letter is dignified and not without vigor.[111] It is the letter which the President of the Federation should have written. But now I should like some one else to come along with a caustic pen and a real grasp of the situation—one who would not defend and apologize, but make bold attack.

Did you happen to see an article by Emil Cohn of the *Berliner Gemeinde* fame? It appeared in the *Prussissche Jahrbücher*. It is admirable. *He* could answer Mr. Schiff according to his folly. Indeed, his article *is* an answer to him and to all assimilationists. But Mr. Schiff will not feel himself on the defensive by arguments from across seas. The most interesting feature of Cohn's article is perhaps the editorial notes by Delbrück. He protests that Cohn's article came to him and was accepted for publication before its author had obtained notoriety. Then he goes on to ask what the Berlin *Gemeinde* wants—Fromer's solution of the Jewish problem was met by Fromer's dismissal: Cohn's opposite,—nationalistic solution is again met by dismissal.

Does it bore you to hear about these things so far away from your thoughts? Perhaps I am writing of them of malice aforethought. When this letter reaches you, the holidays will be with us, and each day, whether joyous or solemn, will bring back your grief, and the leisure of the season will tempt you to think again the bitter thoughts with which, according to your own confession, you have been torturing yourself. Is it not customary at this season to combine with personal wishes also wishes for the community of Israel? May I interpret this for you? It means that you must not be too morbid—that you must shake off undue depression, and turn your attention to the work you have in hand, not as a duty, as you say, to divert yourself from your grief, but because it is the work you can do for the glory and the better understanding of our people, and also for the honor of your dear father's name. There is still much excitement in store for you before you settle down to your wonted placid, academic life—your parting from your mother and from Europe, the journey across, the meeting with your people on this side. The holidays are really your last chance to soothe your nerves before returning to work. Please take the chance—don't allow yourself to get more excited than you must. You know that I am a firm believer in grief and in manifestations of grief, but you I would hold back from going too far. It is curious, isn't it? that I who am not at all calm should preach moderation to you who are a model of tranquility—and controlledness. Perhaps what I ought to preach is that you should exercise less self-control—that you should let yourself go a little more.

Whatever may be the right thing for you, I hope this last month will teach you to do it for yourself, and send you back to America invigorated.

Sincerely yours,

Henrietta Szold

528 W. 123rd St.
NY, September 5, 1907

Dear Dr. Ginzberg,

I am sending you a few clippings to show you how the Schiff letter is spreading its virus. I think more and more, it is the greatest piece of Rishus (evil) ever perpetrated. And the worst of the matter is that those who are convinced of the reverse of the axiom laid down by Mr. Schiff keep a cowardly silence. Take our friend "the Judge."[112] In the spring I was invited to a dinner given by Mrs. Marshall to a number of the members of the American Jewish Committee. Among the guests was Judge Mack[113] of Chicago and also Dr. Harry Friedenwald, and the conversation turned upon this very point of the incompatibility of Zionism and Americanism. Before Dr. Friedenwald, in his cautious hesitating way, could begin to formulate a reply, Judge Sulzberger caught up the question raised by Judge Mack and annihilated the arguments he had used. But do you suppose Judge Sulzberger will come out in print against Mr. Schiff, "the dean of American Jewry?" I have heard it rumored that Mr. Marshall will reply—*nous verrons!*[114]

Dr. Schechter displays all the great traits in his character under this trial—for trial it is, it cannot be denied. See how the American Israelite rejoices! It makes the work of the Seminary doubly hard, to speak only of the very undertaking in which Mr. Schiff is supposed to have been interested. As I think I wrote you, I am not surprised by Mr. Schiff's attitude and utterances. The only thing in the letter that truly shocks me, as coming from a man of the world, is the expression he uses in speaking of Dr. Schechter's conversion to Zionism, "since his removal to the United States." These words look like a raising of Mr. Schiff's forefinger in Dr. Schechter's face: as though to say, you deceived me. Had I known of your intention to become a Zionist, you may bet your sweet life I wouldn't have consented to your being brought away from Cambridge. As I said, the two conversations I have had with Dr. Schechter on this subject since his return show him in his character as a sage and man of deep and refined feeling. But we cannot hide it from ourselves—we are on the losing side, for it is money that talks.

So much for today. I have not heard from you or even indirectly about you for ten days. It is true, I have myself repeatedly urged you not to write unless you feel in the humor for it. But now I realize that if your-not-writing indicates that you are not in the humor for it, or not in the condition, mental or physical, your-not-writing, after the way you have spoilt me all summer, makes me anxious and uneasy. I hope, however, it only means that you have been seeing many interesting people, who have kept you so pleasantly engaged that you had no leisure for letter writing, which, I know, is at best not a favorite occupation of yours.

Sincerely yours,

Henrietta Szold

Amsterdam, September 5, 1907

Dear Miss Szold,

This is my first letter from Amsterdam since my return from Germany and of course you expect to hear from me the results of my travelling. Now after all I believe that my physician was wrong in sending me travelling. You know how I hate any display of emotion, especially in presence of people with whom my relation is not very intimate. The consequence was that all the time I was in Germany I had to exercise my power of will forcing myself to be quiet and jolly. Of course I succeeded admirably and I am sure that many who met me thought me rather lightminded. And the consequence was, as I told you in my last letter, frightful nights with physical and mental agony. I feel now much better and I am even able to do some work, while in Berlin even the proofreading was a great strain upon me.

What is your definition of morbid? The law of nature according to which a thing set in motion would continue forever to move if not hindered by some other power holds good for our m[illegible]. If real joy gets hold of us it will, if not hindered, increase to the point of "*Ausgelassenheit*" [wildness, lack of restraint] and grief and sorrow increase to the point to morbidity. Our primitive ancestors tore their flesh and garments in their sorrow; it was, as you correctly remarked, their way of morbidity, and we try to deepen our grief.

As to the facts I mentioned in my letter, they are not creations of an overstrained brain but realities. I know my poor father did not dy [die] peacefully on account of my becoming a scholar instead of a *Gaon* and—on account of my bachelorship! Now you know how happy I feel in my state of bachelorship and I can assure you that I do not regret I did not become a Polish *Gaon* and I only mention these facts to you to show you how much our individual happiness has to do with our relation to Judaism.

Imagine Mr. Schiff, who certainly believes himself a very good Jew—my father died with these words on his lips *Tsadik hu ha-shem ki pihu merekhi* [The Lord is in the right, for I have disobeyed Him][115] —worrying about his son's *Lamdanus* [extent of Jewish learning]. I read his address which you sent me[116] and I stated even before I was not astonished at Mr. Schiff, who is a great financeer and a small man, nor at his adulators. *Kulhu makhn'fai l'malka* [Everyone flatters the King] is an old Talmudic saying—but at the stupidity of our people who do not consider that it requires more intelligence and knowledge to decide the Jewish question than to be a successful *Börsenjobber!* [speculator on the stock exchange]. Now I do not want to become bitter and will drop the subject.

I do not need to tell you how glad I am that the prayerbook and the directory are off your hands. I only hope that the lesson you received this year will not be without effect in the future. Benjamin's presence in NY will give you a very agreeable occupation which you may consider as part of your vacation. Of course you'll see to it that he does not study or try to read. These "Wunderkinder" are delicate plants and require special care. I met lately a number of people who told me what a "Wunder" I was in my youth, that at my seventh year I was already a *Lamdan* [learned Jew]—by the way, they forget themselves; I was older than that—and I told them I wished I would have learned then real gymnastics instead of Talmudic gymnastics.

In my next letter I'll write you my plan for an introduction to an introduction into the Yerushalmi, for I ought to have some consideration for my physician who put his interdict on writing, and I have written today no less than ten letters.

With wishes of a *k'thivoh v'hathimoh tovoh* to you, your dear mother, and the Seltzers.

I am your

Louis Ginzberg

P.S. Your letter to the Marxes I forwarded immediately.

Amsterdam, September 14, 1907

Dear Miss Szold,

If not for your modesty I would say "great minds run in the same direction." I was going to write to you exactly on the same point on which you dwelt in your letter. I was going to relate you the effect the reciting of the *Selichoth* [penitential prayers recited before the holy days] had upon me.

You must know that since the death of my father I am acting as *hazzan* [cantor] sometimes in the "russische Schul" and sometimes in the "hollandisch synagogue" and it is remarkable what a soothing effect the saying of the prayers had upon me. I had not shed a tear during all the time of my suffering. While reciting the *Kaddish* [memorial prayer] at the grave of my father I was nearly unconscious and regained my self-possession only by being shocked by a grammatical fault in the vocalisation of the Aramaic in the *Kaddish!* The mind of man works sometimes very strangely! The grammatical error caused me a real unpleasant feeling while my great misfortune had made me for a utter emptyness of any feeling. The recital of the *Selichoth* with their graphic description of Israel's sufferings and misfortunes makes me weep every morning. I feel more and more how deep I rest in old-Jewish feeling, notwithstanding any modern intellect. And who hears me recite *Selichoth* will not understand if told that I am an admirer of Nietzsche. And indeed many a time I do not understand myself. But you do not need to worry about me getting excited too much. I have regained my tranquillity though at the expense of great physical suffering.

Dr. Fr[iedlaender] is perfectly correct when he describes Mr. Schiff's action as his obedience to the promptings of a sense of duty. Your arguments against it is a "Golus Argument." If Mr. Schiff is convinced that the Zionistic movement is harmful to the Sem[inary] and to Judaism, then it is his duty to combat against it even if the antisemites should make use of his weapons. Mr. Schiff may as well reply to you and your co-Zionists that you, with your demeaning the nationality of the country in which you lived, that you give the sharpest weapons to the antisemites.

The real tragic in the whole Schiff matter is that the Jews in America take their guidance on a question of prime importance for Jews and Judaism from a successful Wall Street man! Therein lies the great danger of specific American Judaism, that a handful of successful financeers and lawyers will become the master.

I rejoice with your Benjamin's presence in NY and only regret that I am not there.

I have a number of questions to put before you but as I am to be in NY before your answers could reach Europe, I will keep them for an oral conversation.

Wishing you pleasant holydays,

> I remain yours very
> sincerely,
>
> *Louis Ginzberg*

Amsterdam, September 20, 1907

Dear Miss Szold,

This is my last letter from Europe as I am to leave tomorrow for NY and I hope it will reach [you] before my arrival.

We passed the fastday very well and I am glad to inform you that my mother was permitted by the physician to fast and did it well. I attended services at the Russische Schule and I have no time to describe the effect the service had on me. Many impressions of my youth which became dim have been reawakened, and as I live now in the past, the day of affliction was a day of joy for me. But so was it for the old Jews who celebrated the fast day with *daven[ing]* [prayer].

I hope we will talk "the Schiff affair" over. I will say today only that I regret not to have attended the Zionist Congress, as my absence from the Congress might be misinterpreted—and this the more because Dr. Marx also was absent.[117] But what do I care what the fools will have to say about me?

With kind regards to you, your dear mother, and the Seltzers

I remain

Your

Louis Ginzberg

In spite of all my friendly calmness, I could not help feel warm through and through, when instead of a conventional gift, he gave me the first volume of his Haggadah, plus the conceited tale attached to it and his own mother's Techinnah.

There was some Genizah Studies work that summer, there no significance attached to that?—and some of our correspondence turned on that.

WORK, WALKS AND "LOVE-LOOKS"

When he came back, the dreadful accident had happened to Benjamin. The poor little fellow had just gone from the hospital to Baltimore. As soon as he arrived at his home, he telephoned that he was there, and could he come in the afternoon—it was the last day of the holidays. He came, and reduced as I was by the letter and anxiety of the last few weeks, I almost threw myself at him, all the time I sat shivering opposite to him. He questioned me about the accident, and when he noticed my reduced physical state, he began, "You see, you—" and broke off. He wanted to say, I think, that now I had a conception of grief, and how hard it is to suppress it. But he caught himself up, for he must have remembered that in all my letters, I had justified his sorrow, had even told him not to run away from it, but to indulge in it, as a tribute to the loved one—not to give way to mere physical ailments.

We walked and talked. I made him talk about his father and I do not think he realized how much he said, how freely he spoke. When he resumed his Tuesday lectures, which were to follow along the line of the Halakah lectures I had written out, he would tell me about them, insofar as they differed from the other course. He practically spent the whole of Tuesdays at our house, and I took that to be *ki tov* [for the good]. He came for dinner, stayed on until the four o'clock lecture, the interval usually being spent in the fall and early winter over the Legends and some letters of his, and then, in going out, he would say lightly: "I shall ring the bell at five, will you take a walk?" Did I ever refuse? And then he would come back for supper, and spent the evening, until I often sent him home.

He was much concerned at this time about his Yerushalmi work, which the printer could not be got to hasten. But I urged him to rid himself of the Genizah Studies. In December, I think—just a year ago—he followed my advice, and he would come two or three times a week, and would dictate, and I—I was happy to look up after his retreating figure as he walked up and down the room, or look at his dear face and eyes when he stood to the right of me thinking out some intricate point.

Before the Genizah evenings began, something else happened. One morning early he telephoned, could he see me for half an hour? Of course, he could! He brought me a German letter addressed to the Dr. Schechter as the President of the Seminary asking for an increase in salary. He asked me for advice upon every point, and then he asked me to translate it. Did that mean anything, I asked myself.[118]

And the same question I asked when in the middle of December on one of the Genizah evenings, a Saturday night, something of a different nature happened. For its significance, I must go back to the Tisha be-Ab I spoke of before. I wore a dress that evening with the short sleeves then fashionable, and as it was very warm, I did not put my gloves on. In the Elevated train, by the merest chance my bare arm touched his hand, and I observed how hastily he withdrew his hand. Thereafter, I was particularly careful never to come near him in that way. I guarded even against such chances as this had been. I remember even how I trembled inwardly, and if I had dared, would have withdrawn outwardly, when he would take my arm the following winter to steady me on the ice. I believe this fear of walking on ice, and the blindness in the dark, were the only ways in which I ever betrayed the physical weakness that might have made the appeal feminine to him. And God knows these were not coquetry. Of that charge, if charge it be, I am clear. I remember a walk down Broadway from Mrs. Davidson's, one Sunday afternoon, after having had dinner there—now I see how often people put us two together—I slipped and slid on the ice, whenever a patch of it came along, and always he helped me over it. Finally he took hold of my arm firmly, and firmly he held it even after the street was altogether free from ice, until we reached home. I set my teeth, lest I betray my inward tremors. It was a happy day, that, for he ended it with me, staying all evening, way beyond his usual bedtime.

But to return to what happened one Genizah evening. Some intricate statement had to be made. He dictated part English, part German, part Hebrew. Then I read, and the sentence was awry. It had to be done over, but how? As always when the style did not come out right, he stopped pacing up and down, came to the right side of the desk, so that I could study the profile I knew only too well, and scanned the paper on which I wrote. The time I speak of, he leaned over and put a detaining hand over my right hand holding the pen, and thus he kept it pinned down for five minutes. I sat with bated breath. To have withdrawn my hand would have obtruded his unconscious act upon him. I fairly shivered, but I thanked God, there no longer was any physical repulsion.

Did all the things mean anything? I continued to thunder no! at myself. They were accidents. He had tested my friendship and now I could be trusted with a secret—that was all there was about the letter, and as for the other—absentmindedness, which, to be sure, is not one of his traits—of his clear head.

But other signs appeared. On Saturdays, after the services, he no longer asked me in words, "Shall we walk?" He only put a question into his eyes, and I would answer with a nod. Often he was not close to me when question and answer passed—they would pass over heads and shoulders of persons standing between us as we crowded into the hall from the synagogue. Sometimes one or another person would walk down the street, and he would shake him off, and with an unmistakable air of relief begin the real conversation with me, when the other had left. And on our return, at the foot of the hill which I never let him mount with me, as he stretched out his hand for goodbye, a quick look—I cannot describe it—came into his eyes as he forced my gaze into his. Nor can I describe his manner when he came in on Tuesdays, or for that matter at other times, for last winter he invited himself to many meals at noon, always making a dear little apology to my mother. He always stopped on the rug in the reception room—it was not stopping, it was hesitating—caught my eye, wresting it away from the desk at which I would sit working, held my gaze, while a soft, half pleading, half apologetic light came into his eyes— a lovelight. The charm broke only when I rose and with trepidation held out my hand. And how often all year I saw the lovelight there! By this time we had accumulated a common fund of allusions, stories, incidents, opinions, prejudices—it needed but a word or a look to bring them up between us. As I sat at the table opposite to him, he would direct all his conversation to me, no matter whom he addressed—and the lovelight was there. If we sat together over a piece of work, and thanked be God, I caught his meaning almost before he had the sentence out, the lovelight look had passed from him to me.

That look whatever it was—and I was not the only one to notice it—weakened me. That does mean happiness, I said to myself. And my resistance diminished from day to day. Once, for no particular reason, I saw the inroads he had made into my fortress, built up by my years and the constant recollection of them on my part, and I sat down resolutely to drive him out. I reasoned with myself, that the death of his father had brought forth all the dependence of his nature, and he found me soothing and sympathetic. That was all. But I continued, you have allowed yourself to slip away from yourself. You must stop thinking of him! I wrote out for myself, on little slips of paper, Hebrew poems and prayers, which I carried with me wherever I went, and the minute he came into my mind on my morning walks with Creole[119] or while riding in the car, I whipped out the paper, and began to study by heart. While bathing and dressing, even at the synagogue, when I would think of him in spite of all I could do, I would recite the prayer by heart and at the same time pray, they would be an amulet to guard me against my passion.

But one day, it was unmistakable. I cried out, "The miracle has happened! He does not care how old I am! He loves me, he needs me! He loves me, as that woman poet happier in love than I shall ever be hereafter says, 'for nought, except for love's sake only.'" Not for a smile, or for a trick of speech or thought, but for myself, and in spite of my years. I could not mistake it any longer, I believed. Every word, every look made it evident. He might never marry me, but it was as he had written, he was content in his bachelorship, but he asked for my companionship. And as for me, what more did I want? Was I thinking of ease, of surcease from work, of the dignity of a professor's wife? I thought only of him, and of being with him and bring[ing] something to him.

Nothing definite had happened to bring conviction to my mind, but conviction was there at last, and at last—except for one attempt in August—I gave up self repression. I abandoned myself to my happiness. I was a queen, I trod on air, I sang within myself. If before, I could not sleep for longing, I now could not sleep for joy. And if I slept in the old sound way, I would awaken with a start to hug my joy. Every day confirmed his love to me. Formerly I had dreaded the days between Tuesday and Saturday, for I rarely saw him. Now he made excuses to come on Wednesday, because he worked all day at home. And he came in on Fridays often for dinner, and wrote his Shabbos letters here. And he came Saturday night, and Sunday afternoon and evening. More than that, he went nowhere else, not even to Dr. Marx's. And if he did not expect to be at the synagogue on Saturday, he always told me beforehand, as much as to say, we cannot have our walk. And if the weather threatened when we left the synagogue, he parted from me reluctantly, and sometimes he would even say, let us try. Once, I waited and waited for him, and something detained him, and for my shame I could wait no longer. I went home, feeling sore, as sore can be. I had just gotten my coat off, when the bell was rung six times, and I looked from the window, to find him beckoning to me in consternation. Of course, I flew down stairs.

Was I acting on insufficient grounds? Did I misinterpret? More was to come.

As the season wore on, and the weather became finer, our walks multiplied, and a feature that had been creeping into them became more and more frequent. There were long silences, irksome to neither of us. We would walk and talk, and talk on all sorts of subjects—how much there was, that I did not say, how much I laid up to tell him in some happy future when every conventional safeguard of sex would be broken down between us. And wonder of wonders, more and more this self-centered man took the talk into his hands, more and more he poured himself out to me on all sorts of subjects. Sometimes we walked and only he talked. Then, on the return, we would sit down on one of the benches at Riverside and sit silent for quarter house, half hours at a time. He would smoke, and both of us would look out over the water— and I looked beyond it to a more beautiful shore, a harbor I know my bark is never to reach. Occasionally, but with reluctance on my part—certainly, and I thought on his part, too, we would break the silence, to call attention to a boat, a light, a sound, a flash on the other side, a bird. The intimacy of these silences was to me the most eloquent testimony of his love for me. And finally, with a mighty effort, hardly able to control my voice, I would ask the time, and always it was high time to go home.

Once during the summer, on a Saturday evening, Rose Sommerfeld and Miss Eckstein came, and it had been agreed they would not come upstairs but merely ring the bell as a signal for a walk together. All the evening I palpitated. It was one of the two Saturdays on which, on account of the intense heat, he had not come to the synagogue, and therefore we had had no walk in the morning. Up to July 12th, we had gone and sat at Morningside Park, no matter how hot is was—more at his suggestion. I knew for a certainty he would come that evening, and I trembled lest I should have to go away with my announced visitors before my unannounced but as surely expected visitor came. When I ran down stairs in consequence of the summons, there he was, and I was content even though I had to let him walk with some of the others, while I devoted myself to the guests.

At ten o'clock we took Rose to the car, and then we returned with Thomas and Adele, whom we accompanied to their house. On bidding them good night, we turned eastward to my door, but suddenly—I do not remember articulate words, there was some sort of a murmur from both of us—with an impulse, we swung around westward and went to Riverside, and there we sat until midnight watching the yellow moon struggle through a heavy heat mist.

And what did this mean? Earlier, at the end of June I think, a memorial service was held for poor Alexander Cohen. Again it was a Saturday night, and we had had our walk in the morning. Neither of us had mentioned the evening. As I sat near the door, I suddenly felt my head drawn around, and I saw him enter. He went to the left side of the hall, I sat on the right. The service lasted until eleven. As we filed out, I was approached by two or three persons and detained on account of the memorial fund of which I had been made treasurer,[120] and then somebody wanted me to speak in public, which I refused, because I knew he hated women in public functions. (How often I refused for that reason!) Out of the corner of my eye I saw him go out of the door—he had shaken hands with me just before I was caught up by my various interlocutors. And out of the corner of my eye, I saw him turn back from the door, re-enter the hall, stand where he could catch my eye, and then one of those wonderful love-looks passed from him to me, and under the spell of his dear personality I nodded. It meant Riverside. To Riverside we went, he smoked two cigars that evening, and for once I did not remonstrate. I did not have possession of myself. I felt that with that look he had appropriated me wholly, and I had neither will nor wish of my own. I did not even, with my usual circumspection, keep tally of the time and when we rose to go it was 1:30. He teased me later about our having staid so late, and my heart was warmed by it. All the time we hardly spoke a word. What did it mean?

Another love-look! We had had an altercation with Anna, she had been unutterably disrespectful to my mother, and a parting seemed inevitable. The poor girl was distraught—so was I for that matter. On one of our June walks I told him about the trouble, as I told him everything, and say what he will, he was interested in all my tales. In spite of his mask of indifference—one of his little conceits that endeared him to me doubly—he would put all sorts of tell-tale questions to me. On this occasion he put in a word for Anna, and I returned that the operation, painful as it was, had to be performed for my mother's sake. A few days later, on a Saturday evening I told him that the differences had been allayed, and he asked, with a quick, surprised turn of the head toward me, "Who was the peacemaker!" I acknowledged myself the mediator, and a look beamed upon me, half admiration, half approval, and all love, that went to the very bottom of my heart, and made me sing paeans of joy and thanksgiving. If I had had any doubts, they were set at rest now, and the month that remained before his European trip was pure happiness.

As the days grew in length and as they waned in length, always he came, and when he parted with me at the door, he would ask, "Should I ring for you tomorrow evening?" What did it mean! What did it mean?

In May, he began to work at his so-called Introduction to the Genizah Studies. He insisted stoutly that it would not be more than ten or twelve printed pages, and I joked with him about his so-called "Appendix" of the summers before. How many such innocent little jokes there were between us, how many common recollections and allusions we had, that needed but a word, a look, a smile to bring up a whole train of thought! All that is dead now! The Introduction grew and grew under his fertile touch and I translated as fast almost as he wrote, getting up early, sitting up late to keep up with him. Once I took a day off for it, and he soothed my conscience by reminding me that the Publication Society still owed him for his having helped me with Helena Frank's Perez.

When the Introduction had lengthened out to about twenty pages of his closely written manuscript, he protested earnestly, he would not let me go on with it. Would I find a translator for him. Then I was bold enough to tell him he would make me unhappy if he took it from me. More I could not say, that almost choked me. The next evening the same protest was made, and then I was still more audacious, I told him, I felt that so long I had even a subordinate part in his work, I could keep his friendship, and I needed it. That was said just as he was parting from me after an evening at Riverside. There was no more protesting after that. Instead it was natural for him to tell me every evening, as soon as we turned our faces riverward, what he had written that day. Again and again he would say, I'll explain it all to you, and then it will be easier for you to translate. Or we would seek a bench near an electric lamp and he would read me his manuscript. I still feel the balmy, perfume-laden air of the June nights in my nostrils when I think of this, and yet it belongs to a past so dead that it lies upon my breast like a stone, and in truth, I ought to forget it, because I have no right to remember it and glory in it any more.

Such a hot summer as it was, and how I worked through May, June and July up to the 21st, when at last, it was finished notes and all. I refused all invitations to the country. I went on no excursions, I kept every minute for him—and I was happy, I even forgot my age and my fears. It seemed to me he, too, was not anxious to get away. Sometimes I thought it was because he was reluctant to go to Amsterdam where he had lived through such sadness the year before. But sometimes I timidly entertained the thought that he liked being with me, and rather welcomed the work that was his excuse for staying on in America, though his South African brother was urging him to make haste. Once I said—it was on one of those frequent occasions when I counted out, today four weeks you will be on the ocean, today three, today two—I can imagine how relieved you will feel when you stand on the vessel today two weeks, and tell yourself, "Then I am shaking off all this pother!" Little did I know how prophetic I was— that I too belonged to the shaken-off pother.[121]

Up to the very end he came daily. While Rachel was here, I said to him bluntly, he must not come. He did however, come a number of times, and always we remained in daily communication, so that he knew when she was away, at Mount Vernon, and then he was sure to be here. Shall I ever forget the last Sunday but one that we worked together? We were at the Seminary all day, and it was one of the hottest days I ever experienced. I was not up to the mark either, and several times I felt I was going to faint, especially when he insisted upon turning on the electric fan, for me, he said. And yet I could keep on, because I was working for him. The last Sunday *he* was sick, and we pegged away at the notes. On Monday he still was miserable, and I saw him only for a moment. If he was miserable, what was I? I never, from the first day I entered his class, could stand his not feeling well, and I always knew by a single look at him when he was not feeling well. His eyes were eloquent to me, and he was always surprised when I told him he had not slept. On Tuesday he was better, and we had a walk. Wednesday afternoon late, at about five o'clock, he came in to bid us, my mother and myself, good-bye. He had the manuscript of that precious Introduction with him, and from here he was going to the Post Office to register it. I said I would go with him. All the way over, I battled with my tears. After he had registered it, and in the presence of Max Radin, he handed me the receipt in an offhand, ownership-air manner, and said, "You'll take care of that." To me it meant, you are the custodian of that and more. How often he had implied the same all the winter, often with a lovable twinkle in his eye, when I had to get ink or other supplies from the lower part of the book closet, and my eyes would fall upon the two scrap books I had arranged for him, the one containing as many of his articles as I could get him to collect, the other a set of his encyclopedia articles, which I had lovingly straightened out from a huge crumpled mass of galley proof sent me the summer before. I would say, "Don't you want to take your scrapbooks with you?" And he would answer, "Not yet," as though he meant, the time will come, when they and I and you will have the same home, and it is of no use to move them separately. When he had let me buy these scrapbooks and with endless patience put them into order for him, and had not explicitly thanked me for it, I looked upon that insousiance as another pledging of our love. The two scrap books are still in my closet, the only one of his possessions still with me, and now I speculate how to get them to him "without compromising my dignity,"—an expression I have learned from others who call him the hardest names they can find.

At last Max Radin left, and I walked ten steps from the post office with him, and bade him a speechless farewell. He saw my trembling lips, my tearfilled eyes, but he said nothing, nothing. And I went home to weep, weep, weep, all night, and next morning. Thursday, I wept again over my work, again and again taking refuge in the bathroom where I could lock myself up, and weep and sob to my hearts content and unobserved. As always on Thursdays, I had to work in the little hall room. As I sat there in tears, the telephone bell rang, and my heart stood still, I felt it must be he. I flew to the telephone, and his voice came to me, telling me he called up, just as he was leaving, to speak one more word with me, and choked with tears, I could only say, "God bless you!" What did that mean? To me it meant that I was affianced to him, and I could not have been made unfaithful to my troth, if an angel, an Adonis, and a Rothschild combined had come to tempt me away. Almost at once I sat down, and wrote him a letter from out of the fulness of my heart—wrote of the beautiful summer I had had, and that all its beauty was due to him, wrote how I missed the personages of his Introduction, and wrote.—Oh, how I wish I had my letters to him back to see exactly how naked I made myself stand before him.

528 W. 123rd St. NY
July 26, 1908

Dear Dr. Ginzberg,

New York has only today consoled itself. From Thursday noon until Sunday morning the heavens dripped, and showered, and poured. The purpose of all the water that came down must have been to bemoan your going away. It certainly was not to give us relief, for the more it rained, the hotter it grew, and the more audacious the mosquito swarms became. This morning, at last, there was a semi-clearing, accompanied by cool, fresh breezes.

And as for me, I sorely miss Gal and Gak, and Shat and Shash, and Hag (with a dot) and Hag (without),[122] not to metion Albargeloni and Aaron of Lunel and Isaac, of the Or Zarua, and Rabbi Jehudai (with or without, as you like),[123] and life is dull without dear Rabbi Sherira and his Letters[124] and without Rabbi Hai and his garrulous Responsa.[125] My butter does not even come from Gischala[126] and I have received no news from the scholars of Kairwan.[127] And Riverside is wet, but not with the waters of the Hudson alone! So there was nothing to do but torture myself with Slouschz[128] and begin to make up my arrears in correspondence. This letter, however, I would inform you, is not arrears, this belongs to the avant-garde.

Life really has been very uneventful since your final telephone message, for which I want to thank you again, as I ought to thank you for all the pleasant hours you made for me this summer—I ought to thank you, but I won't.

There is not even a gleaning to send you from the Jewish papers, except that the Comment[129] had a brief notice on Professor Neumark's Judah ha-Levi, in which the point was made that it was a pity his friends did not prevent him from writing English before he could make himself understood in the language.[130]

At the Chautauqua a fool man got up and spoke in the strain of the other fool man Kuh, admonishing the Jews not to attract attention to themselves by loud manners, but to cultivate the social graces, and especially to refrain from building synagogues in the fashionable streets dear to the Gentiles, who are driven out by the religious assertiveness of the Jews. Fleischman is his name, and Buffalo his provenance.[131]

I hope the ocean has by this time exerted its usual magic influence upon you—putting you to sleep at night and keeping you soothed by day.

Sincerely yours,

Henrietta Szold

But do I need my letters for that purpose? Do I not know without them that I showed him all I was and had without keeping back anything, as I have never revealed myself to any being?—Or keeping back only these things that I reserved for the greater, the acknowledged intimacy of the day when he should tell me in words what his acts had long been proclaiming—that he loved me and needed me, if not as his wife, seeing my age, but as his lifelong companion.

The very next day his sister came to see me about securing her daughter a situation as stenographer. Her first word was reproachful surprise that I had not been at the dock to see her brother off—she had expected to speak to me there. So his family knew of the close relation between us! And her appeal to me for her daughter she based on the fact that she, too, was named Sophie like the other niece I was employing, and named so after the same grandmother!

Why should I pretend that this was the first intimation I had that his family knew of it. How often and how significantly his sister-in-law had spoken to me in the same strain. She would look me tenderly in the face, fixing me with her eyes, and say, "If only he would get married!" to which I opposed a strong silence. And did she not come, too, on the Sunday following his leaving for Europe, and talk to me of him only? And when I went to see her on the Jahrzeit, did she not express gratified surprise that I had remembered it? And yet a few weeks later she, too, could in cold blood, put a dagger into my heart.

Puzzling and Troubling Letters

I suffered much during the first few weeks of his absence. The pilot brought no card, the first letter, written on the vessel just before landing, was satisfactory as far as it went, but it was short.

on board the "C.F. Tiergen"
August 2, 1908

Dear Miss Szold,

We have traversed the Atlantic and are now nearing the Scandinavian peninsula hoping to stop at Christiansand this evening and then proceed to Christiania and Copenhagen.[132]

The sea was all the time through very smooth and calm, the weather however was not of the best kind. In the last week the temperature is not higher than 55 and rather chilly. I wished I were able to send you with my warm regards a little cold as you are certainly in need of it.

I have little to tell you about myself except that for the first time I had to pay my tribute to Neptune. But it was a light case of seasickness and of very short duration. The advantage of a small steamer is that you can afford to be humanitarian. There was not for a moment any necessity to wish the passengers to—as they were only few and well behaved. Prof. Bloomfield[133] introduced himself to me and we got on very nicely, discussing scientific questions and also the Jewish Problem the existence of which he was forced to admit.

I do not know yet whether I will disembark at Christiania or at Copenhagen as I am expecting information from my brother and from Elbogen and his party.

And how are you? I hoped to find a letter from you at my arrival in Amsterdam where I will hasten as soon as the Congress is over.

With kind regards to yourself, your dear mother, and the Seltzers

from

Louis Ginzberg

Then came only picture postals, two of them, one half by Dr. Friedlaender.[134] I had been writing two or three times a week.

> *528 W. 123rd Street*
> *New York, July 31, 1908*

Dear Dr. Ginzberg,

There are only a few minutes left before I must get ready for Shabbes, so that this will not be much more than a Gruss [greeting]. I have been rather lavish of time this week—partly I have been active, partly others have made me be, willy-nilly. My mother and myself spent the whole of Wednesday at Mount Vernon, with the Jastrows, leaving here at nine in the morning and not returning until half past ten at night. It happened to be one of the rare less hot (one cannot say cool) days we have had, and after a long, invigorating trolley ride, we sat on the porch lazily embroidering all day long. Embroidering—I haven't done it in I cannot begin to remember how many years, consequently I have not felt like a lady these many years. It is the most lady-like occupation, to put in stitch after stitch, with the most exquisite care of which one is capable.

I have had another revived sensation, given me by the book you lent me, Bernheim's *Geschichtswissenschaft*.[135] For fifteen years, ever since I became secretary of the Publication Society, I have not read a book—a real book that requires consecutive thinking. Last Saturday I tackled Bernheim, and when I became aware of its character, a feeling of terror seized me—perhaps I would now behold myself in all my mental nakedness, perhaps all the vapid newspaper reading I had done had incapacitated me for real reading. Well, I haven't been incapacitated, I actually can read, and I am really enjoying my tussle with Bernheim. It is he, however, who has made me realize how much of my time is dissipated in nothings. For three days my leisure was completely absorbed by people's coming in and spending the time in talkie-talkie. As you always say, they get no pleasure out of it, and you? So for three days I made no progress in Bernheim. Nevertheless, I am forging ahead.

One of the persons who came in—but I did not begrudge him the time—was Mr. Prokesch, to bid me farewell before he leaves for Europe. He had a very severe attack of his trouble, whatever it may be, and the physician ordered him to Karlsbad. He is leaving Mr. Rabinowitz to fill his position at the Protectory and me—to get out his Hebrew primer! You see how the Lord provides for me.[136]

Another person who came in—nor could I begrudge him the time, since it was on business—was a traveller returned from Europe instead of going there—Dr. Margolis, reporting himself ready and eager to begin the Bible work. He arrived at ten in the morning and at half past one he was at my house discussing ways and means. Such American hustling makes one understand why he says he feels as though he had come back to civilization! That feeling of his will not make him rise in *your* estimation.

A long Gruss, isn't it? But now it is time to stop, without telling you of the mosquito-ey walk on Riverside which I had with your sister-in-law and Sophie last Sunday. My mother has not yet succeeded in throwing off the last remnant of her cold, notwithstanding which she is working very hard in Anna's absence. Anna has had to leave temporarily on account of her sister-in-law's illness.

Sincerely yours,

Henrietta Szold

528 W. 123rd St.
New York, August 7, 1908

Dear Dr. Ginzberg,

I hope your trip is turning out to be as pleasant for you as it is educative, geographically speaking, for me. Your vessel was sighted from Butt of Lewis, and out my map came. I had never heard of this Scottish place before.[137] Then news came from Christiansand about it, and in due time from Copenhagen, which I had studied up before, as you know.

I don't know that I did anything more exciting than follow up your vessel all week. Anna is still away, and will be for another eight days, and although the chief burden falls upon my mother, enough odd jobs come my way to fill up the interstices of translating Slouschz—whom I like less and less, by the way, or is it his subject that displeases me? The Haskalah,[138] in some of its aspects, at least, is not much more heart-satisfying than the reform movement. It has one advantage, and that is a great one—a larger number of those interested in it, as compared with the followers of the reform leaders, knew the past and the documents of the past. Perhaps that makes their aberrations the less excusable, but at all events, it makes them personally more acceptable. In justice to Slouschz I ought to say that some of my own disgust is due to myself. I feel at every page that I do not know enough of his subject at first hand to do justice to it, nor does the French language form a sufficiently integral part of my organism to be a thoroughly live thing within me. Fortunately, there are only about thirty-five pages left for me to do in English. That, of course, does not count in my endless revisions, some of which I expect to save up until you come back to help me.

The weather continues horrid and the mosquitoes horrible. The only bearable day we have had fortunately fell on Tisha be-Ab, with the result, that I at least fasted so well that I am thinking seriously of eating only one meal a day. My work went wonderfully, I never translated so much French in one working day—no interruptions for breakfast and dinner, not to mention breakfast and dinner dishes in these Anna-less days. I came to the conclusion that eating and sleeping were great drawbacks to work. However, I hope *you* are eating a good deal and sleeping still more.

Bulletin

Riverside Drive

Business Prospects Rising!

Prosperity-Movement in Full Blast!

The *"Pearlmi"* Advertisement blazes
a shining path across the
Hudson
once more

Sincerely yours,

Henrietta Szold

---

528 W. 123rd St.
NY, Aug. 14, 1908

Dear Dr. Ginzberg,

This time it will really and truly be nothing more than a Shabbes-Gruss [Sabbath greeting] and a line to tell why such unusual brevity. Anna is not yet back, Shabbes is close, and many odds and ends remain to be done before it comes in at the end of an indescribably hot day, and, besides, there has not yet been a letter or anything from you. So I have neither time, nor brain, nor heart for writing.

I hope all goes well with you, and that you are having a happy, restful time.

Sincerely yours,

Henrietta Szold

---

528 W. 123rd St.
NY, Aug. 15, 1908

Dear Dr. Ginzberg,

This morning your letter written on board the steamer and your card mailed at Christiania reached me—at last! I had no right to expect anything sooner, and yet I did, and I was beginning to imagine all sorts of reasons for not hearing from you. This evening all the grievances of yesterday are removed. Anna will be here before the evening is over, a little breeze has sprung up giving us some relief, and your letter is here.

In spite of my ill humor yesterday and the pre-Shabbes jobs required of me, I finished Slouschz. This week I expect to spend revising the translation and, in particular, making sure that my retranslations of his French translations of Hebrew passages are not hopelessly distant from the original. The other task for the week will be reading the page proof of the Year Book, for the galleys are all back at the printer's. And then, do you know what is going to happen then? I shall be wishing impatiently for Legend material to work on.

The week has not been all work. Indeed, my mother and myself had a most enjoyable day at Long Branch with the Solises. We went down in the morning by the boat, the way we took together two years ago. Miss Solis . . .

August 16

Anna broke in on that sentence in semi-whirlwind fashion, and after she was through telling me of her down-town experiences, her disgust at ill-regulated conditions of living there, her brother's vain efforts and really extraordinary inducements to make her come to him permanently, her homesickness for one and all of us, and her joy at being back with us and in her own little room,—why, after that, there was nothing to do but go to bed. The little breeze of last night has persisted, and the morning is fresh and promises well for the day, a part of which we shall spend in Mount Vernon, to pay our farewell visit to the Jastrows, who go home in about ten days.

What I was going to say about Miss Solis[139] is that she had most carefully and thoughtfully planned out a whole day, with a view to enlightening my mother's ignorance of the Jersey coast. The automobile was kept in readiness all the time, and we were whirled, it seems to me, from end to end of Jersey. Incidentally, my own ignorance was enlightened, especially as to the beauty of Jersey's landscapes. We went through the Atlantic Highlands, and were charmed. I did not dare confess it, but the fast automobiling we did kept me in an uncomfortable humor. Emphatically, I am not fast. The day was perfect, however, up to the end, the very end. The sail up the superb harbor, with the red paper moon, as big as big can be, hanging low in the sky, with the old gentleman in it looking particularly jolly, in spite of a badly swollen face.

And the sleepy trolley ride was fine, and, above all, dropping into bed and into sleep simultaneously.

One of the incidents of the day was a ten minutes' visit to Judge Sulzberger, on his hotel porch—this at the instigation of old Miss Solis, who has the punctiliousness of the former generation, and insisted it was my duty to my "boss" (she did not use the inelegant expression). I was glad I did it. You never saw anyone so genuinely surprised as he was when the dowdy secretary stepped out of a Pierce-Arrow automobile on his porch at West End, and the surprise was allayed only when he discovered I was only spending the day. Of course, he sparkled during the ten minutes. He looks well, but nevertheless has the air of sitting around waiting for the hay fever.

No more space for the other happenings of the week!—I am not sorry Neptune exacts a tribute. Somebody must undertake the job of keeping you reasonably humble.—I hope you found your mother well, and that you yourself are in good condition. —My mother sends regards, also the Seltzers.

Sincerely yours,

Henrietta Szold

But when the second of the postals came I felt so deeply hurt, that I lost my assurance that he loved me, and I reverted to my former state of mind, and determined to repress my hopes and my love. For two weeks and a half, amid untold suffering, I refrained from writing to him. And by that time all was over for me! He had seen the girl, and practically sued for her and won her. While I was castigating myself, on August 21, he wrote me the first real letter from the leisure of Heringsdorf, and one sentence in it set my pulses flying. He knew that I had been much concerned about his having to fast twice in close succession, once on Tisha be-Ab, and again on the anniversary of his father's death. In this letter he thanked me for mine, and said, he believed he had fasted so well on Tisha be-Ab because he had had it that morning! What did that mean?

Seebad Heringsdorf,[140]
August 21, 1908

Dear Miss Szold,

The Congress[141] closed and I am glad of it. You know, "There is nothing so hard to show than too many pleasant days." The city of Copenhagen displayed such hospitality that the members of the Congress had hardly time to breathe. The municipality, the learned societies and the citizens entered into competition in entertaining their guests.

Of course, there is nothing absolute in this world, neither good [n]or evil, and the pleasure of the Congress members was partly marred by an accident of a very unpleasant character. Paul Haupt was the cause. At the second day of the Congress he repeated for the second time—the first in America, the second in Berlin—his lecture on the Aryan origin of Jesus. Although it is entirely indifferent to me who "*die Stammvater*" [progenitors] of Jesus were, I could not help to partake in this discussion, and this for the reason that the "*risshus*" [wickedness] was very much apparent. I began my remarks by saying: "The question about the race of Jesus does not interest me in the least—it is a topic largely for theologians and Antisemites—but I will remark that some of the geographical identifications on which Haupt has built up his theory of an unsemitic population in Galilee are false."[142] After I had finished, Dr. Yahuda,[143] an Oriental edition of Haupt, a mixture of humbug and arrogance, attacked Haupt in a very ungentlemanly manner, which really contributed to the sympathy which Haupt found among a number of non-Jewish members. Of the Congress I hope to write a few lines on the subject as soon as I return to America.

Your kind letters gave me great pleasure and I believe that I fasted on Tisha B'av so well because I had just in the morning of the fastday received your letter. My friends Dr. Chajes[144] and Mitternach forced me to go with them to Heringsdorf, a bathing place on the *Ostsee* [Baltic Sea], where I will stay for a week and then proceed by the way of Berlin and Leipsig to Amsterdam. Heringsdorf is a very beautiful quiet little place combining the sea with mountains, where one can walk for hours in quietude and solitude. Today I tried to take a cold seabath and if the result should be satisfactory, I shall repeat the experiment.

With kindest regards to yourself, your dear mother and the Seltzers

I am
Your

Louis Ginzberg

And the next day I had a picture postal from him with a map of the district of Heringsdorf, and he wrote that he was sending it so that I might locate him. What did that mean? I took it to mean but one thing, and henceforth I wrote him letters! Oh, how could he let me write them? He should have cabled to me for very pity! Every one of them, telling of my self repression, my joy, my need of his friendship, my happiness in being made the sharer of his intimate feelings even when they were harrowing, my delight when a letter of his came by the Mauritania, my hopes for the Minneapolis,[145] my concern about the report in the Jewish Chronicle about what he had said on the *Yerushalmi* manuscript at Copenhagen, and all my description of my walks in which I all but told him that they could not be perfect because he was not my companion, my prattle about all the incidents of my days—all this was written after he had pledged himself to another woman! Perhaps he was too much in love with her to read them? No, I haven't that refuge, for he answered some of them.

528 W. 123d St., NY
Sept. 1, 1908

Dear Dr. Ginzberg,

Mr. and Mrs. Diacritical Cowen[146] have just left and I breathe a sigh of relief. I have been on pins and needles all the time, wanting to acknowledge your Heringsdorf letter and the instructive Ostseecard, which came with the late afternoon mail, gratefully and without delay. Without delay, because they gave me the welcome opportunity to write to you again after two weeks and a half of self-repression. Gratefully— because I was glad to have a letter telling me something about yourself. Until today, I knew nothing about you since July 23, except that you had been seasick and you had made yourself agreeable to Dr. Bloomfield. Even now I do not know how to bridge over the gap from the boat to the Copenhagen congress. Did you meet your brother and your friends, and where, and did you take your Swedish trip, and how did you enjoy it? But you will tell me all that when you return. Having a letter reconciles me to waiting for the unrecorded parts of your journey, all the more as your letter contains so many indications of pleasure. Evidently, even the Congress was better worth going to than you had anticipated. I am glad that you took part in the Haupt debate, particularly glad that your malicious, emotional opening was followed by a scholarly criticism, and most glad of all that you mean to pursue the matter further. As for Yahuda, you know he is claimed as a particular friend by *your* friend Dr. Rosenau, who also claims Haupt in friendship—isn't that a fine triangular collocation? I have been wondering whether Dr. Rosenau was a witness of the mélée.

But what of your own paper at the Congress? Was it satisfactory to yourself? . . . Poor Itzkowski fainted (*choloshed,* I mean), I suppose, when you appeared in Berlin. And don't you think it's time our friend Horace Hart was heard from? I expected to have the proof by this time.

To-day I did the last of the Year Book proofs. The task was, of course, much smaller than under the other arrangement, but yet irksome. Indeed, the greater freedom of this summer has awakened the "natural man" in me. You would be amazed if I were to give you my own record of outings, at least half a dozen half-days in the country. One walk was particularly beautiful, and I hope you will let me show it to you some day. Miss Kahn—you remember the lady who was taking the summer courses at Columbia—wound up her New York stay by a week at our house, and, of course, it was incumbent upon me to show her the city—you know what a fine guide I make. It really was instructive for me—whether pleasant for my guest I cannot tell. One day I had an admirable lesson in geography, on the "Seeing New York" yacht, which takes you around the whole island of Manhattan. For instance, our Spuyten Duyvel walk is quite plain to me now. All this dissipation has had it effect. Sometimes I really do not want to work—I want only to get out, especially now when we are having charming cool weather. The most astonishing thing of all is going to happen at the end of this week, when I go on a four days' visit to a Baltimore friend of mine at Shelter Island, at the extreme eastern end of Long Island. I am told it is the most beautiful strip of seashore near New York. I hope all this will prove to my friends that I am not a monster.

Some of those friends are beginning to straggle back to the city. The Davidsons are here looking vastly improved, happy over their summer experiences, and happier still that they were successful in finding an apartment to suit them (on

134th Street) within twenty-four hours after their arrival. They have already moved into their new place.

With the return of the summer migrants my chances of becoming intelligent, which were fairly good these last two weeks, again vanish into thin air. Last Saturday afternoon might have been mid-winter, were one to judge by the number of visitors. Not a word could I read all day. Dr. Radin is back from the West, and his son Paul paid us a visit and gave us a very interesting account of his strange and varied experiences with the Winnebagoes.[147] And today we made the acquaintance of his fiancée, a Miss Robinson, a very attractive, interesting looking girl. And the Rabbis—Heaven save the mark!—who have transmigrated through our flat this summer, and stimulated all the latent pessimism in me! And what they stirred up, Zangwill kept boiling. He has delivered another of his speeches,[148] and its very excellence as a literary production brought out all the more glaringly its defects as a Jewish document. Then Perez[149] came,—at last I am reading his Hebrew stories which you gave me—and robbed me of my last bit of optimism on the subject of Jews and Judaism.

We are in a parlous state, there is no denying it. Commissioner Bingham has written an article in the North American Review on——I have forgotton the exact title.[150] At all events, it is on the subject of crime, especially juvenile crime, among the children of immigrants. Though he concerns himself mainly with the Italians, and pleads for a secret service police in order to reach their Mafias and Black Hands, he gives the Jews the first two pages, and makes preposterous, I am sure, undemonstrable, statements about the percentages of our crimes and criminals. But what can we say against it? We cannot go on forever banking upon our "glorious" past, and at present, qua Jews, we are doing very little constructive work, to hold up against disparaging assertions. When the Jews disgust one with their doings, one begins to appreciate what Zunz meant when he proclaimed the Science of Judaism the only refuge from the disappointments of Jewish life.[151] That is the reason, perhaps, you make me happy when you let me have a tiny, humble share in your work. I look back to those hot days spent over the Introduction with constantly increasing satisfaction. Even the hod carrier may feel he has a part in the finished monument. The scholar leads the life of peace—he walks, spiritually speaking, in Heringsdorf quiet all his days. And the modest translator is pleased to be permitted a glimpse of the charmed country. Of course, even there there are irruptions—Haupt and Rosenau.

You will be interested, I think, to hear that Jerome has been exonerated in connection with the Metropolitan Railway scandal.[152] Of course, you expected it, I know, in your *nil admirari*[153] way. The funny thing is that the reports censured his temperament, which leads him to do and say such things as bring suspicion down upon his aggressive, vituperous person. In the meantime, practically all transfers have been withdrawn. The worst blow has been inflicted at Fifty-ninth Street. Even there the privilege has been taken from the long-suffering New Yorkers, and in spite of Bloomingdale's strenuous opposition. Not only do they lose trade, but they will have to change their favorite advertisement all over the city as well as on the umbrellas the draymen use. As for myself, blunderer that I am about street cars and directions, I rarely escape paying a double fare these days.

And have you heard about Tels? Burnt to the ground! Only a few buildings remained to mark the spot where once it stood. Not a synagogue was saved. The bench upon which you sat and studied will never be marked with a tablet relating its distinction!

My mother, who is very well, and has been sharing all my walks and expeditions with the usual young enthusiasm, sends her kindest regards to you. And so do I, with the wish that you will continue to enjoy your vacation, plus seabaths.

Sincerely yours,

Henrietta Szold

---

528 W. 123d St. NY,
Sept. 11, 1908

Dear Dr. Ginzberg,

At last the proof of your Introduction has begun to arrive . . . I shall hold all the proof until you come back. But I shall read it as fast as it comes in, so that there may be no delay in getting it back to England when once you are here, as least so far as my end of the contract goes.

My visit to Shelter Island was a real holiday—a sweet do-nothing time. My hostess was ideal in that she was easy-going. I did as I liked, but I liked, in point of fact, all she provided for me—her children, her walks in the woods, her swimming and sailing, and her division of time, mainly between eating and sleeping. And the four days were just enough for that sort of vacation. I was not displeased to get back to my mother and my desk.

Since yesterday my brother-in-law, Mr. Levin, has been here, and he brought with him a big bunch of fine stories about Benjamin and the others—they came just in time to soothe away the memories of the day, for it was the anniversary of the dreadful accident. The physician seems to think that the arm will in time become right, though it will take years of care, and possibly repeated operations. All the work of an unhappy second!

At the same time there were other arrivals, the Schechters and the Marxs are back, and in general things are assuming a lively aspect. Everybody is looking well, even ruddy, and everybody seems particularly pleased with this summer's experiences. I hope you will come back with the same account of yourself.

In the last issue of the Jewish Chronicle,[154] there was some account of the Copenhagen meeting, and also an editorial in which particular mention is made of your part in the discussions of the lately-found manuscript of the Jerusalem Talmud. I was surprised to find that you had endorsed Ratner's view, apparently without reservations. Though I cannot recall a definite expression of opinion by you upon the subject, I somehow or other got the impression that you were not prepared to make a positive assertion one way or the other. The Chronicle takes your stand to be that of the Seminary as such, as though you had been the spokesman authorized as it were by the institution. I felt almost certain that that was not warranted by anything you said. I shall save the paper for you, so that you can see it, if you like, when you return.[155]

My mother, my sister, and Mr. Seltzer wish to be remembered to you kindly.

Sincerely yours,

Henrietta Szold

---

528 W. 123d St.
New York, Sept. 11, 1908

Dear Dr. Ginzberg,

I had just closed and stamped my other letter to you, when yours, the first one from Amsterdam, was handed to me. It is so full of yourself, so exactly the sort of letter one wants to receive from a friend at a great distance, that I weakly indulge my desire to reply at once. Judge now whether I consider myself a victim when you tell me of your intimate feeling on revisiting memory-hallowed spots. And since you are prompted to do it, I need not assure you that I can "*nach-fühlen*" [empathize with] what took possession of you as you approached Amsterdam. I may even say that I "*vorfühlte*" [anticipated your feelings]. All through the early part of the summer, it was my theory that you were content not to hasten to your beloved Europe but to linger here and work through those hot, hot days, because you half dreaded going back to the scene of your own suffering and another's a year ago. And yet, as you write, you owed it to your mother who mourns as well as to the father whom you mourn, and no less to yourself to go to Amsterdam during this vacation. In fact, you should consider yourself fortunate that circumstances favored you so that you could fulfil a *Pietäts* [reverent filial] duty. Some day I may tell you how may unhappy hours I endure because I cannot fulfil my duty of a similar nature.

From my other letter you have seen that Horace Hart, M.A., has sent proof of the Introduction to me . . .

I wish you felt that you or the Seminary could afford Drugulin.[156] . . . The real trouble lies in your awful fertility. If you were not as chuck full of material, which requires hundreds of pages to get itself said, you might venture upon Drugulin. Don't decide until you get back to America. Wait to talk it over with somebody here. Perhaps the funds will be forthcoming.

It does seem that work were crowding in upon you at a rapid rate, and I cannot promise to *lend* you any of my time. I can only give it to you outright when it can be transmitted into such work as I am able to do for you. In that form you know by this time, I hope, you can have it almost for the asking or without asking. No matter how you may feel about the amount of it, your friends cannot but be gratified that your ability is being recognized everywhere. As I wrote you recently, such a life as yours is the only sort worth living. Dr. Schechter has come to the same conclusion as Zunz.[157] Although he is full of praise of the character of the people he was thrown with this summer, he nevertheless has returned more pessimistic than ever regarding the future of American Judaism in general and the Seminary in particular. I was not able to console him. From day to day my feeling grows that we are defending a forlorn hope. What I wanted to tell you, however, was that after an outburst against things in general, during which he prognosticated the break-up of the Seminary after he was gone, he said that, seeing the futility of it all, he had made up his mind henceforth to husband his time and put as much of it as possible into the writing of books. I am afraid, however, that he will find it hard to undo the effects of his earlier policy. He has been drawn into too many practical schemes and affairs to be the master of his time or even of himself, the latter because he has engendered in himself the sort of appetite that grows with what it feeds upon.

Enough!—No, one thing more! I want to tell you that your letter, for which I want to thank you especially, brought you near in another sense. It came by the Lusitania[158] and was in my hands exactly one week after you wrote it.

With kind regards,

Henrietta Szold

September 13

On second thought I did not mail this long postscript to Friday's letter at once. The delay enables me to report to you that I saw your brother at the synagogue yesterday and Jesse and Charlie, the last a veritable Eiffel Tower. Mr. Breuer had donned his high hat, Dr. Schechter presided, the place was well-filled—it was evident that the Elul spirit was abroad in the land.[159]

H.S.

---

528 *W. 123rd St.*
New York, Sept. 15, 1908

Dear Dr. Ginzberg,

This note has the one purpose of wishing you happiness in the coming year—the happiness that springs from peace of mind and heart, from successful achievement in your chosen field, and from the happiness of all dear to you; and if you have any wishes beyond this, fulfilment to those, too.

I am writing this on my return from an hour's walk on Riverside. When I reached the river, the sun had already set, but a brilliant glow irradiated the sky, and it took the whole of the hour for it to die out. Meantime, the lights on the Jersey shore came up softly, one by one, and the stars, too, and a gentle breeze sprang up, that sent the dry leaves dancing along with me as they beat the ground rhythmically and melodiously. It was exquisite—exquisite with that early autumnal beauty—that is matchless all the year round! And then I ran home as fast as my feet would carry me, for you were not here to protect me from Anna's three-minutes-past-seven glower.[160]

My mother received your letter to her this morning, and I had mine written on the same date as hers last Friday, four days ago. I have been trying to decide all day long whether I like the Lusitania. It shortens one interval, but it may have the effect of lengthening the other—unless your next letter catches the Mauritania. I shall live in hopes.

With a *k'thivoh v'hathimoh tovoh*

Sincerely yours,

Henrietta Szold

[on bottom of letter from Sophie Szold, dated 16 September 1908:]

To-day the second batch of proof came to hand . . . they strike one as well done.—With kind regards.

528 W. 123rd St.
NY, September 20, 1908

Dear Dr. Ginzberg,

I am sending you the proof of the Appendix, which I received yesterday (with the Mauritania—but no letter!) . . .

Yesterday our services were rendered in full canonicals, Mr. Jacobson having gotten back from the mountains,[161] and as there was a Krulewitch Bar-Mizvah, the place was filled to overflowing. I came a little later than usual, having been detained by a friend from Baltimore, who dropped in unexpectedly, and I had to stand in the hall, with the plebs. For once I could sympathize with your little nephew's resentment. It was evident everywhere that the Selichoth season was upon us, and the holidays—both of which seasons will, I hope, fill you with satisfaction.

Sincerely yours,

Henrietta Szold

Meantime I received a book from Berlin, Delitzsch's *Jüdische Literatur,* for which I had expressed a wish one year and a half before. What did that mean? And what did the inscription on the fly leaf mean? It said in his usual handwriting of the bolder variety, "*Freundlichen Gruss aus Berlin*" [Friendly regards from Berlin], with the date August 28, 1908. Above this, in smaller, cramped handwriting, as though it had been put in as an afterthought, it says "*Seiner lieben Freundin, Frl. Henrietta Szold*" [his dear friend, Miss Henrietta Szold]. I kissed the inscription, I held the book close to me whenever I was unobserved. What I interpreted as an afterthought gave me most satisfaction. I had been in his thoughts to write an endearing word—he shrank from it—and finally he made a dash at it. Fool, fool! and fool again that I thought it meant something when he wrote "*lieben*" [dear] instead of "*hochgeschätzte*" [well esteemed or valued] he had until then applied to me. For on August 29th he saw the other woman at the synagogue, and I was banished from his heart, if ever I had entered it.

But this I was not to know until October 20th. Meantime I had three more letters from him. Those letters puzzle me and trouble me.

They may rob me some day of my ideal man. I cannot understand them. They are full of tenderness for me, full of apology that he had fallen short in friendship. Yet they were all written after he had seen the girl and made up his mind about her.

The first of them is dated September 4th, 1908 a Friday, one week after sending me the book with the blessed inscription. He starts out by saying that he was at last in Amsterdam, that he had lingered by the way because he feared to go to the place where he was painfully reminded of his loss the year before. It would have been better for him not to go to Europe—ah! if only he had not! Then he apologizes for the pain he is causing me in return for my letters, and he says he must speak to some one who understands him, and—of course I am the victim. These are his own expressions. The rest of the letter is about Dresden, and the printing affairs.

Amsterdam, September 4, 1908

Dear Miss Szold,

At last I am here. To tell the truth it took me several weeks to gather courage enough to visit Amsterdam, the place where at each corner I am reminded of a loss which I feel today as keenly as I did a year ago when it happened. I begin to believe that was not wise on my part to go to Europe this year. I did not enjoy travelling on account of my very nervous state from the moment I reached Europe. It is a very hard strain on my nerves to conceal all the time my inner feelings in presence of my poor mother and my sisters. On the other hand I see of course that is was my duty to be with my mother who as a daughter of martyrs and saints bears her loss with really Jewish resignation.

I know it is not kind of me to give you in return for your kind letters such pain as my letter will cause you. But I think it is absolutely necessary for me to speak about my present state of feeling to someone who understands me—and of course you are the victim. It is very depressing to know that my friendship brings little joy but much sorrow and pain to my friends.

On my way to Leipsig when I went to see Drugulin I shopped for some time in Dresden. It was a good idea on my part to have done it. The hours I spent in the picture galleries of Dresden were the few happy ones I enjoyed in the last weeks. It is strange that notwithstanding my strange anti-mythological and anti-Christian feelings I was able to enjoy the Jesus and Maria paintings of the Italian schools, while the Thorvalsen Museum in Copenhagen with all its treasures could not raise my enthusiasm.

My trip to Leipsig was without practical results. Drugulin asks about three times as much as Itzkowski . . .

I promised the editors of the Maimonides book to give them an essay on the commentators and expandery of the *Yad*.[162] I will have to borrow from you several hours for each day to be able to finish up all the work I have under my hands. But *qui vivera verra* [he who lives will see]!

Poor Creole went the way of all flesh. Do you know that at such occasions I am able to comprehend the fantastic doctrine of metempsychosis? The primitive man could not admit that the faithful companion of his joys and sorrows should entirely lose its individuality.

With kind regards,

Yours very truly,

Louis Ginzberg

The second of the three letters is dated September 15, a longer interval than usual. He begins by chiding me for the self repression I had exercised—he did not want to be the victim of my virtues. He complains of my having robbed him of the pleasure my letters give him and calls himself "the same old egotist." This makes him hark back to his former letter, in which also, he says, he was egotistic enough to cause me much pain. But strength failed him to control himself, and I and Dr. Marx were the only ones he could talk to, and again he says—I was the victim. Is there a double meaning intended in this use of victim as applied to me? Did he write me a Mishnah and expect me to supply the Gemoro? But to go on with the letter—he tried to keep this sickness of his a secret from me for nine months, and he broke down only when the crisis arrived, then he could no longer stand it, he spoke out to me. But he begs me not to worry, he is quite sure the crisis has passed, and he feels that he is gradually gaining control of himself. Oh God, *my* crisis has lasted four years, and where will it end! The rest is about the Copenhagen Congress and that he will sail on the Minneapolis and New Year's wishes. New Year came on September 26.

Amsterdam, September 15, 1908

Dear Miss Szold,

I must apologize to the post administration of the U.S.[163] for having accused it of inefficiency. I took it for granted that you had written some letters to my [me] but which were lost and of course I did not think of it to blame it on the Dutch post. Now I see by your letter of Sept. 1 that for two weeks and a half you exercised self-repression. Of course I do not deny that self-repression is a virtue but I fail to comprehend why I should be the victim of your virtues! I feel like picking a quarrel with you about it but I know that one needs two for a quarrel and it would by [be a] waste of time to try to get you a party to a quarrel. As I have to complain I can not even complain to you for having robbed me of the pleasures your letters give me and there is nothing left to me but to ask you to exercise self-restraint in some other way or on somebody else.

You see by it that I am still the mean old egotist. I do not care whether others will suffer by your virtues if I am spared. To be sure, I am ashamed of this egotism, but I can not help it. This was my feeling also in my last letter which undoubtedly caused you much pain but the strength failed me to control myself. There are only two persons, you and Dr. Marx, to whom I could tell the extreme agony which I suffer since my arrival here and you were the victim. The truth is that I tried to keep this, my sickness—I think this is the proper name—a secret from you the last nine months and I nearly succeeded till the crisis has arrived and then I could not longer show it. But I beg of you not to worry, I am quite sure that the crisis has passed and I feel now gradually that I am regaining hold of myself.

The Congress was a very pleasant affair, the pity is that you have for courtesy sake [to] listen to all kinds of nonsensical lectures. What I said about the Yerushalmi did not interest neither me nor others. For myself the lecture was superfluous as it is a matter which I had worked out since a very long time and there was not need to repeat it. Among the members of the Congress there was, with exception of Chajes, not one who could follow the discussion properly and I had talked the matter with Chajes for hours. Of course there was your friend Elkan Adler[164] who with the ignorance of an Englishman and the *hutzpah* of an American gave me—privately—the friendly advice not to commit myself as *he* is convinced that the entire Yerushalmi Kadoshim is a forgery. And do you know what I gave him as an answer? I said, "Dear Mr. Adler, there are so many important questions connected with the old Yerushalmi, that I would prefer discussing them with you before you begin the discussion in the new Yerushalmi." And he was silent.

By the way, I think Dr. Bloomfield has changed his good opinion he had of me. One evening he introduced me to my namesake, the *meshumod* [convert from Judaism to Christianity] Ginsberg and that old fool had nothing better to say to me than "Dear Dr., you have changed your name, you ought to spell it Guinsberg with an s and not with z" to which I replied: "There is no harm in changing a name as in my case a single letter only but I would not like to change myself for any consideration." Dr. Bloomfield reproached me later to have been rude to an old man and continued to say that he never would have believed me to be such a fanatic.[165]

Mr. Hart sent me the entire appendix and more than the half of the introduction with the promise to send the rest within a week . . .

I have booked for the tenth of October on the Minneapolis of the Transatlantic, sailing from London. As this letter will reach you for only a few days before *Rosh ha-Shonoh*, so let me wish you a very happy New Year and *k'thevoh v'hathimoh tovoh*.

With kind regards to yourself, your dear mother, and the Seltzers,

I am sincerely,

Your

Louis Ginzberg

The last letter has the date September 24. He thanks me in a Talmudic phrase for calling his attention to the way he had been misrepresented in the Jewish Chronicle as to his opinion on the new Yerushalmi manuscript, to this he devotes two pages. The third page and a few lines of the fourth he gives again to his abuse of my friendship. He again uses the expression victim, he again refers to my friendship for him (underscored), and again puts me on a level with Dr. Marx, and speaks of the cowardice of his action in not having spoken out, and then apologizes to me for having given an explanation to Dr. Marx and not to me, but that was not a lack of loyalty to me, it was because Dr. Marx had asked for an explanation.

Amsterdam, September 24, 1908

Dear Miss Szold,

The Talmudic saying "The wise is more than the prophet" may justly be applied to you. You divined my intention regarding the proof before you got my letter in which I expressed my opinion that it would be better to wait with the return of the proof till I am in New York. As a prophet, you are mostly concerned with the future and it does not matter whether your memory fails you concerning the past. Our arrangement made before my departure from NY was of an entirely different kind, but since it is now obsolete, I am not going to tell you how it really was.

Your gift of prophecy is evident in some other respects here. Of course I never said such a thing as the reporter of the Chronicle made me say. I took the trouble to go to the library and look up the Chronicle and all which I can say is that the reporter is an <u>English</u> fool. Never have I right if I refrain from having to do anything with the public. There is a congress of specialists. The most responsible Jewish paper sends its most qualified reporter—he is a B.A., M.A., and God knows all the *Shamoth Ha'kedoshim* [exalted titles][166] after his name!—to the Congress. He <u>is</u> present at my lecture and does not understand a word! What I said was that I have not doubt that Friedländer <u>made</u> use of a ms. and I added that I am also certain that he <u>doctored</u> his text and that therefore no final verdict can be given before the <u>ms.</u> is examined. Besides this I said that it seems to me that the ms. goes back to the <u>Geonic</u> and not Talmudic times and that therefore, though a Palestinian product, it is not free of Babylonian influences, as in pre-Geonic time in Babylonia, "the Pollution of the Land" were "<u>vorausgehend</u>" [widespread] even in Palestine. How a man could misunderstand me is a puzzle to me. You know I

am very proud of my gift to be able to explain a difficult problem and I am I sure did it in this case. Do you think it is worth
bothering about and ask the Chronicle to make amends? I am
quite sure that no amount of letters by me on this subject will
help me explain it to the readers of the Chronicle . . .[167]

In my last letter I apologized to you for having made you
a victim. Knowing of course your kindness and great friendship <u>for me</u>—you see, I am far from being modest—which
makes you delight in being a participant of my sufferings.
What I really ought to apologize to you for is that I did not
speak to you about my state of mind during my stay in NY.
What I felt here was only the climax to a slow never-ceasing
bleeding which I suffered for the last thirteen months. You
certainly have noticed that I hardly mentioned the name of
my father to you for many a month, fearing I would have to
confess to you my state of mind, and I fully believe that it
was a plain case of cowardice that I did not speak about.
Dr. Marx, who had noticed some strange thing about me,
insisted upon an explanation, which I could not withdraw
from him. I mention this fact that you may not misjudge me,
thinking I have spoken about my intimate feelings to somebody but not you.

As I wrote you in my last letter, the crisis has passed and
I am gradually becoming normal. I cannot describe to you
how fortunate it was for me to have spent some time on the
sea and along the sea. How can peace of mind fail to come in
view of the immensity, on the border of eternity, when one
cannot but feel that all things human are trivial and transient.

I think you are right when you say about S.[168] It is too late
for him to reform or rather he does not want at all to reform.
With him it is a matter of a transient mind when he despairs
of <u>his</u> Seminary and <u>his</u> Jewry. He was at first naive enough
to believe that a handful of bright lawyers and successful
financiers are sufficient to create a renaissance of Judaism,
and when <u>they</u> failed him he is in despair. <u>Great</u> changes are
created by <u>great</u> minds with the help of the <u>great</u> masses. One
has to work along the lines of great minds or he must come
in direct contact with the great masses. Hang the bourgusy!
[bourgeoisie] This is my view of life and I rejoice in reading
your letters, seeing that you are <u>now</u> of the same opinion.

I know that this poor letter of mine is a very shabby rec-ompensation for your three letters, but you may be assured that the wishes for the New Year accompanying it come from the depths of the heart of your

Louis Ginzberg

When I read this, my heart stood still—he was excusing himself for something that had not happened—He had never spoken to me so freely as he had during the last nine months. And as for putting Dr. Marx and me on the same level of friendship, that was not quite in accordance with facts, because he had sought me practically daily, and he had not been to see Dr. Marx for weeks and weeks at a time—so he had told me himself. Then he again assures me that the crisis has passed, and he is becomimg normal. It was fortunate, he said, that he had spent much time on the sea; it had quieted him.

I was disturbed, I did not understand, but all my queer feeling was dissolved in pure delight when I reached the last sentence at the very bottom of the fourth page—I remember every word—"I know that this poor letter of mine is a very shabby recompensation (I gloried even in the dear stammering English) for your three letters, but you may be assured that the wishes for the New Year accompanying it come from the depths of the heart of your ----------------." Then I was not wrong, then I interpreted it all correctly, I jubilated. That can mean but one thing—he loves me, I sang, and all that day and until two days before he came it continued to sing in me, and my heart swam. All year people had been telling me how well I looked, and how animated, and I hypocritically said it was due to having given up the Year Book drudgery. But I knew it was all due to my happiness through him. Those last two weeks before he came, I met no one who did not look me in the face astonished at the transformation. I must confess then whenever I re-read the letter and I used to read bits out of all he ever wrote me every day—the queerness of it struck me all over again. I did not like the third reference to me as a victim, I did not like its appearance, thirteen words even underscored in it—not his usual way—but that last paragraph, there was no mistaking it. And yet it was my hugest mistake. Four days after he wrote it to me, he was on his way to Berlin to say the binding word to the girl there, I cannot understand it—what does it mean?

I believe I have written before that those three letters evoked from me letters such as I have never written to any one. Why did he let me do it? Why was he so cruel? Was and am I such "a thing" that he need not have even compassion with me?

When I look back upon this past summer from July 23 until October 20, the picture I get of myself is always looking up the shipping news—first to follow his Danish steamer across, then to watch for the arrival of German and English vessels that might bring me a letter from him, and finally to keep the Minneapolis in sight by wireless and otherwise. And how I rejoiced when I could tell his family more accurately than they knew what the movements of the boat were! Morning and evening it was always the Minneapolis, and what leisure time I did not devote to it was put on the proof of the Introduction, and longing for another letter from him. Each time before when he had been in Europe he had written me before going on the steamer, and his last letter was dated quite two weeks before his sailing date. But looking my eyes out into the letter box brought none. By Saturday I was quite nervous about this but I sent my fears flying and my disappointment by such nonsense as that he was with his sister, that after the warmth of that last paragraph everything but *the* thing would be an anti-climax. *The* thing he did not care to write, so he wrote not at all.

528 W. 123rd St., NY
Sept. 29, 1908

Dear Dr. Ginzberg,

In a very little while, surely before I finish this letter, the above date will not be correct, for this time I am writing late at night. It suddenly occurred to me that it was my last chance to get a message to you before you sail. Indeed, I am doubtful whether this will reach you, as it will probably have to be forwarded to you to London. I fancy you are carrying out your plan of visiting your sister in Wales, and intend to leave Holland immediately after Yom Kippur. No matter! If only your vessel bears you safely and swiftly across the ocean, the good wishes this letter is intended to convey will be fulfilled, and these good wishes are cherished and now expressed, even if you never set eyes upon them.

The vessels of the line you sail on seem to take from nine to ten days to come. Accordingly, you ought to be here on Monday, October 19. Will you plunge right into proof reading? Mr. Hart has kept on steadily sending the slips, but the whole is not yet here. Dr. Marx expressed a wish to read the Introduction, and I am letting him have one set of the galleys for the purpose.

The holiday went off well enough. Mr. Jacobson was in good voice. There was a larger congregation than ever, and a more disorderly one, and the air was thick in spite of some improvement in the window arrangements, manipulated by Dr. Marx. But there was no sermon, though Dr. Schechter had threatened to give us one through Mr. Joffe.[169] He desisted only from fear lest he give you and Dr. Marx offense (he didn't mention Dr. Friedlaender or Dr. Davidson), and of course, he had no notion of asking either of you to preach, too. But he threatens that the Joffe sermon will come off if ever he wishes or has reason to take revenge on me.

As usual, there has been a Jewish summer sensation. Police Commissioner Bingham wrote an article in the North American Review on criminality in New York and charged the Jews with fifty percent of the crimes committed. Jews formed twenty-five percent of the population. He was particularly invidious in the expressions he used regarding the "Russian Hebrews." The downtown Jews were up in arms. Before twenty-four hours had passed, Bingham retracted in toto, saying he had the figures furnished him and had taken them on trust. The *Tageblatt*[170] accused the Gedolim [great ones] (Schiff et al, and the American Jewish Committee) of reprehensible indifference and inactivity, and Mr. Marshall is out with one of his letters, maintaining that the whole retraction was manipulated by the same Gedolim without fireworks and mass meetings, meaning backstairs diplomacy with Tammany Hall, of course. The whole occurrence has left a bad taste in our mouths, in spite of the handsome retraction. Fifty percent may be untrue, but some number or other *is* true, and we have so long posed as impossible angels that even twenty-five percent or ten percent does not suit our apologetic Golus palate. But I have no doubt we shall continue wanting not to know the truth, regardless of the fact that to find it out will not be a case of not letting sleeping dogs alone. They are aroused as it is, and we might as well have the benefit of the constructive work that may perhaps be done when once we do know what is happening to us. But constructive work is much more difficult than mass meetings and resolutions, and letters and editorials. Dr. Radin, of course, has been shouting himself hoarse, and Nissim Behar[171] has been gliding in and out more than ever, and the American Jewish Committee is more inscrutable and owl-like than ever.[172]

I hope you will have good company (i.e. no company) on the boat, and that you will rest up against all that awaits you in the way of work on this side.

Sincerely yours,

Henrietta Szold

A few days before he sailed, his sister-in-law came to see us. Of course, we spoke of him, and again as a hundred times before she ejaculated, "If only he'd get married," and then she told us how her little boy cried when he was told his uncle would marry and move away. But she had no mercy on me—she had known my doom for over four weeks, and loyalty to a stranger killed all womanly sympathy with one stricken as she knew I would be. My God! And she has so often told me about her love for her husband! I must be a graceless creature if they could use me so.

She said something else. At the time I smiled at its naïveté, with which, nevertheless, I sympathized. My mother was going on a visit to Baltimore the following Monday (October 12) and she said, "And you won't be here when he arrives!" To my shame I must confess the thought that went through my mind—"If she is not here, perhaps he will want to go to her with me, or perhaps we will summon her back!"

On Sunday, the last day of the holidays, I was at the Schechter's—, so were the Davidsons. I was actually *ausgelassen* [exuberant]. In less than two days my darling would be back! In the afternoon I went to see Ida Guggenheimer, and when I left there I could not bear to take a car. I wanted to walk on the lower promenade at Riverside—his promenade—and think of my darling at every familiar turn. It is impossible for me to recall now when the change came. But a change did come on that walk. I suddenly grew depressed and nervous and anxious. All my blitheness was gone—never to return. The dejection or whatever it was continued, and when the next morning at the breakfast table I had an unusually heavy mail and no letter from him, I was desolate. Worse was to come. There was a letter from Dr. Magnes an exuberantly happy letter, boyish, enthusiastic, just happy, in which he told me the secret of his marriage and asked me to rejoice with him. That letter nearly broke my heart. I sobbed and sobbed for an hour, saying again and again, "Never will I be so happy as that," and rebelling that forever appeals should be made to me for sympathy, and never did life bring me any joy of my own. The misery of that day! I had to go to the Seminary for something, and Dr. Marx asked me significantly if I were not going to the steamer that evening to meet him. I could only press out a no. He looked puzzled, and I knew what was in his mind.

"THE BLOW FELL": GINZBERG'S ENGAGEMENT TO ANOTHER WOMAN

Tuesday morning came. I felt cold but strangely composed. I did not dare go to the window to watch for him. I nailed myself to my desk. Half past twelve at last! The familiar ring—held just *so* long, and then he was in the hall, flushed, eager, excited, and I met him. He turned naturally toward my desk, I to our old stand. A few words passed between us, the aimless words one speaks after a long separation, because there is so much to say one cannot begin. Then—the blow fell! He said:

"Can we go into another room, I have something to tell you in private."

For one brief instant—it could not have been measured by any ordinary methods—my heartbeat went like a trip-hammer, my pulses beat, the blood rushed to my temples so that I could not see for dizziness. My happiness has come at last, all within me cried, sang, shouted, jubilated. The next instant, I was as cold as marble, for as quickly I realized that it was of some one else's happiness he was going to tell me. I led the way to the middle room, I opened the door and mutely bade him enter. I had no time to close the door, before he had pressed out:

"You will be surprised to hear that I am engaged!" "Engaged," I said simultaneously with him, I felt myself tottering. Fortunately, he turned his back upon me and walked a few steps further into the room up to the bureau, against which he leant. That gave me time to collect myself, and utter a prayer for strength, strength not to break down, but to keep calm.

"No, I am not surprised, I always had an idea you would come back some day engaged from Europe." I went on in an even tone, but I did not add: But that you would come back this time engaged, an angel could not have made me believe!

"A premonition, eh!" he went on, I thought slightly embarrassed, but that is not to be wondered at. One does not announce one's betrothal every day. "You know, I always do the unexpected (To *me* he says that? Does he mean to taunt me? I expected him to declare his love for me, therefore he affianced himself to another woman? The room whirled around me—I was afraid I would fall. At that time I thought God was merciful to me in giving me so much physical strength that it replaced spiritual strength. I no longer think so. Then and there I should have been permitted to make some sort of demonstration, and perhaps the explanation that would have had to follow, would have quieted me, and I would have been spared the slow torture, the living death I am now undergoing.) "You know I wrote you of the crisis I underwent when I reached Amsterdam?" (But, my God, he told me in his letter that that crisis was connected with his father, and now he connects it with his engagement!) "I had seen the girl in Berlin"—

"What is her name?" I asked.

"Adele Katzenstein. I went to the synagogue—you see what comes from being good—to meet a friend there, and I happened to look up to the women's gallery—I assure you it was not a frivolous thought that made me do it—and I saw a girl there, and I said to my friend, 'Rather a pretty girl,' and he assented, and told me he knew her, and that she was a fine girl. After the service I was introduced to her. By the merest chance I met her that afternoon again, and Monday evening I asked her whether she would be willing to go to America, and she said yes. Then came the crisis in Amsterdam."

(And then came that letter to me! With the rapidity of lightening I calculated that that Saturday—the day of my doom—was the day after he had sent me the book from Berlin with the inscription that had raised me to the seventh heaven, and that the letter he wrote after leaving the girl who would go to America with him after seeing him three times was the first one of the series in which he called me "victim." Was it possible that the crisis was chiefly connected with me? Was he making his conscience believe because he had not spoken even so binding a word to me as was the question about America asked of her, that he was more bound to her than a thousand acts of his publicly done bound him to me in the course of three years? And did he speak of crisis? A five day's crisis, to me who had been living a crisis for five years, and who may perhaps have to live a crisis all the rest of my life? Who, at all events, have been fighting for my sanity these eight weeks?)

Then he went on to tell me, that he wrote to the girl, which of course was objectionable.[173] But ridiculous! What had he to do with the father? The father objected to him, because he knew nothing about him. He would not give his consent until he had written to Mr. Felsenstein.[174] (Felsenstein! my God, a man—no I will say nothing about his character, perhaps he has retrieved himself since his Baltimore days. But Felsenstein give my darling a character [reference]! My darling, whose feet I would have been happy to kiss.) He told the father there was one man who could tell him all about himself— namely, himself. (Oh! I could not smile at his conceit—the conceit that endeared him to me in other days!) But he won, his fiancée he knew had had a hard time of it—in fact, she was not happy at home—a stepmother. The only thing he had inquired about was the family—that was the one thing he laid stress on—he found the escutcheon all that was desirable—a Frankfort family—you know, he said, I never cared for the South German Jews—these are extremely pious—so is my fiancée. She has the most beautiful eyes I have ever seen, a beautiful mouth, too, but not really beautiful, she is exactly as tall as I am, has a great deal of mother-wit, and the ordinary German education, and is very domestic, I am told.

As I remember, I interrupted the narrative once to press out with the greatest difficulty, though the words were sincere: "I hope you will be very, *very* happy." When I said that I thought I would be able to veil my broken heart forever. And once I interrupted facetiously: "Why didn't you send him the book on the family Ginzberg?" And I asked for her picture, which he showed me, telling me at that point that she was as tall as he was. By this time I thought I was safe, I was not prepared for the brutality with which fate—or must I say like my family, *he?*—treated me. He said: turning to me with a lively gesture very unusual with him:

"And do you know of whom I spoke to my fiancée? Only of you and your mother!"

Did he think that a compensation for my loss? I could not help clutching at my heart. Without the motion I would have screamed in agony. But *his* happiness, I kept repeating to myself, must not be marred, whatever happens to me! Ah! How I have marred it by this time, unless he is flint-hearted. Only a monster could bear my changed manner and appearance.

One incident of the conversation, I must go back to. I do not remember at what point it came in—but he recurred to his silence of the year before again, again he put me on a line with Dr. Marx, and again I did not say that he need not beg my pardon, because he had not been silent. I only said, that I did not resent his want of frankness, I only thought it was harmful to himself but that henceforth he would have someone to open himself out to. No, he said, he would probably not change in that respect. Oh, perhaps I should not have been so hypocritical, perhaps I should have said, you were frank enough with me! No husband could be more so with his wife. The thought passed through my mind, but as though I saw at once its only possible usefulness, I asked:

"Have you published your engagement?"

"We did not speak of it in Europe, because as a matter of form Felsenstein's letter had to be waited for. But I do not feel bound by that in America. I told everybody at the Seminary."

So, I was to have no respite—not a moment in which to accustom myself to the idea of giving him up forever. In fact, he had secured himself against protest on my part by telling me last of all in our circle. Or was it all passion for the girl, and the rest an accidental concatenation of circumstances? My, God, let me keep my ideal of him at least!

And not yet had the end come! As we turned to leave the room, he said, "I asked my fiancée to write to you, but she said, that was not proper. Is that true? Isn't it proper?"

"That is a matter of feeling," I said, and inwardly I added, "If you had asked me to write—or anything else perhaps even a criminal act—"!

"Will *you* write to *her?*"

I almost fainted, but it was *he* asking me to do something. Had I ever denied him any request in five years? The old habit was too strong. And, besides, perhaps if I wrote that letter, it would be the great renunciation that would help me keep my calm exterior. And I assented.

He went out, stopped to say that he would call for me to take a walk in the afternoon and I mechanically said, I would not be home until six, all the time wondering that I had been so deceived in his relation to me. If he wanted to take a walk with me on the first day after his return, engaged though he was, then it had all been cool friendship. And I braced up and said to myself again, "Very well, it shall be his conception—I was mistaken, he has done me no wrong." As he passed the kitchen door, he gaily said to Anna, in German,

"Well next Tuesday, prepare for me, I'll be here as usual!" So I was right, in our relations, as he conceived it, nothing had been changed. So must it be!

At the door I said, "When you come at six bring me Miss Katzenstein's address, and I shall write."—"Oh, I'll give you that now," and we turned back to my room and desk. If only I hadn't said that. It gave the opportunity for the cruellest thrust of all. As he started away a second time, I asked, "Shall I write German or English?" He said, "German, of course." "Then, you must look at the letter before I send it." We had reached the hall by this time, he had passed the curtain, and was opposite to the hat rack. Was there something in my voice that stirred his conscience or his memory?—for I was fast losing strength to keep up. Whatever it was, he turned around the least bit, and said "You *are* happy about this, aren't you?" And for the first time I faltered. "Ye-e-e-es!" I cannot recall what happened—how he went out. That last question had made my brain reel.

December 15, 1908

I interrupt the narration to record an incident of this day. When Sophie was ready to go home for dinner, she said, "I was told to ask for the books in which you pasted the clippings." Not a word of thanks—*never* a word of thanks for that labor of love, and no love in return either. But I did not have to "compromise my dignity," in giving up the books. Now all has gone to him of which he made me the custodian. His gifts and books and letters, I still have—*and* my memories. But alas! since last night my memories are no longer what they were. I am so afraid, he is not the ideal I worshipped. But of that in its due place.

I sat down to collect myself, I was cold as ice outward, inside I was consumed by heat and rebellion. I groaned. But I did not weep. I thought: Was I not of good family? Was I not domestic? Ah! but I was not twenty-two, I had no beautiful eyes, no beautiful mouth. Nor had I the surplus of femininity that enabled her to throw herself at him at the end of the third interview. I was only a woman who knew how to love and serve my beloved boundlessly, until my heart broke and my brain reeled. And because I had loved, I had been blind—I had been mistaken, he had never loved me. The last three letters in the same tone as the others prove it, the desire to resume his walks with me, also, he had never thought of me in that light, I was sexless to him. I had misinterpreted everything. But now, I would write to her, and with that letter I would put my past behind me, and be the friend to him he had thought me.

There were only a few minutes left before dinner, but I dashed off the letter, and then sat down and made a pretense at eating—practically nothing passed my lips for ten days, until I went to Baltimore. To Anna, who was alarmed at my small appetite, I merely said, "You know I am always too nervous to eat, when I am to speak in public"—for that afternoon I was to have half an hour talk before the Council of Jewish Women!

Immediately after dinner I copied the letter, because I wanted to keep a copy for myself. That letter! If the girl on the other side were a woman and not merely an undeveloped female, she would have read between the lines that a great renunciation had been made, an unwilling one and that a great wrong had been done. But—And he, too, he read the letter, and did he fail to understand? I re-read it a few days ago, and I wondered how I could have sent it.[175]

I dressed and went to the meeting. Everybody wanted to know why I was so pale. If they had put their fingers to my face, to my body, they would have shrunk back—a corpse! they would have exclaimed. But inside a big fire was drowning me. My brain was whirling. As I sat on the platform awaiting my turn, I was hardly conscious of what was happening to me and around me.

First Reactions: Horrors of the Night

December 16, 1908

The incident of yesterday rankles. Perhaps if I say one more word about it, I'll rid myself of it. He demanded them—or was it Sophie's awkwardness in delivering the message?—as though I were forcibly withholding property of his—as though I were keeping a pledge to testify against him. Does he realize that as mere property they are mine? If I were in a Rabelaisian humor, I'd send him a bill for the scrapbooks $2.00, labor employed, because in spite of night work, I was afraid I wouldn't have the Encyclopedia book done to give him a pleasure when he arrived, some $5.00, plus love untold, inspiring labor of unknown quantity. And to that I might add various items for typewriting, stationery bought for him and used only by him—did he not tell his niece only last spring, when the Introduction was on that she need not get paper for it, just to use mine?—and stamps. Some of the bills I still have. I put them with the letters simply because they complete the record of our intimacy.

And as for the books being a pledge—he had better destroy them before he brings his wife to preside over his affairs and belongings. They breathe on every page another woman's intense and encouraged love. And yet when I come to think of it, how little reward there is for an outsider of what I did—the translations I made do not bear my name, not even the private title page of the Halakah lectures proclaims my insensate devotion. And all the rest is like breath from the nostrils that has commingled with the universal air.

They say I spoke well—I never believe them, anyhow. All I did was with my outside brain. Only once while I was speaking, the dreadful thing faced me and outfaced me, and I had to clutch wildly at a thought until I rallied. There was some unpleasantness with Miss American, and then I was expected to talk social small talk to about two hundred women, and remember the names of half of them, whom I was supposed to have seen once before on a similar occasion. Can any one imagine the torture? Even I after two months cannot recall the feeling, I can recall the result. At last I got away—Miss Solis made me look at the vestry rooms of the synagogue—and then I chased, my teeth chattering, lest I miss my appointment with him. I was still dominated by him—I still did not realize that he was nothing to me, that I was nothing to him. I waited and waited, and he did not come. At last, feeling that I could not keep up any longer, I called up the familiar number. His sister-in-law answered—he was not at home yet—all his relatives were waiting for him—and what did I think of the news? It was fine, I said.—And how much she would love me—the girl—she knew all about me. This time I could not press out even a monosyllable, it was going beyond my endurance. And then the Parthian shot: I've known it long, but I couldn't tell you, could I?—No, of course not, I said, and hung up the receiver.

Knowing that he was not coming, I collapsed. My teeth chattered, one chill after another clutched my body, my senses left me. The telephone bell rang! It was he, saying he would not come. I returned, I only wanted him to see the letter. He said, "Oh, just send it off, your German is all right, there will be nothing to alter." How the little compliment would have elated me in other days! But, driven by a dark impulse that I understood only many weeks later, I insisted he should see it. Very well, he would call for me to walk the next afternoon, Wednesday. The impulse that made me insist was that if later I could not keep up the wretched mummery for which I then thought I had the physical and spiritual strength, he would know that I had not poisoned his fiancée's mind against him. The same undefined impulse made me give him the letter to mail. When he read it, a sort of quiet fell upon him, and he thanked me for it in a strained voice. What did it mean? O, I believe only that he cannot thank; it always chokes him, and he had to say something.

But I go back. After that second telephone conversation, I could only drag myself to bed, and Anna had to nurse me. The horrors of that night will never be told. In the morning his niece came, and said gleefully: "Now uncle has some one to dedicate his book to!" What! *my* book, I almost screamed out at her, the book that I have caressed and coaxed and petted and loved, because *he* wrote it—the book that I picked out of his close, cramped but beloved handwriting with toil and pain,—the book that is mine as much as it is his—and horror of horrors, the book that I must now work on daily for six or eight months more, eight hours a day, and work on it when love is gone out of it and must be banished out of me—that book is to be dedicated to another woman? I did not scream, but I died, and since then I have been dead—a dead packhorse. I wonder whether he remembers the incident I described to him *con amore* in one of the letters he received after he had decided to kick me out of his path—the angel-packhorse incident with Miss Adams?[176]

That Wednesday morning Dr. Schechter came about his Index.

AN OBJECT OF GOSSIP AND SYMPATHY

December 19, 1908

Today a year ago, that is the Saturday evening of Hanukah week, he came at sundown and we worked at the Genizah Studies until supper. Then I dressed and we went to the Seminary for the celebration of Dr. Schechter's sixtieth birthday. Before we went he told me one thing he was going to say. All evening I sat where I could see his face. When I left, he followed at once, and crossed the street with me to the house, and fairly besought—not with words, but in the manner I thought was meant for me alone, but was it?—fairly besought my judgment of what he had said in his address. And it had been fine! And I was happy. And a few weeks ago I could not go to a Seminary affair, because I could not dare to face him—perhaps my self-control would fail me, as it did yesterday when I had to leave the synagogue right after Rosh Hodesh Benshen [recital of the prayer for the upcoming Hebrew month]—"shame and disgrace" and "joy and delight," and "fulfil the wishes of our heart"—such expressions in the prayer reduced me to tears, I wish I had arrived at the stage at which I could say the whole phrase "fulfil the wishes of our heart unto good," putting the stress on "unto good," and feel that this terrible "shame and disgrace" had been put upon me "unto good."

Dr. Schechter had made the engagement with me on Monday. I was so demoralized that he said, "You do not seem well" and I returned, "I did not sleep very much last night." As if he regretted having opened the subject, he said "Neither did I, the first day of the Seminary is always exciting, and the engagement of Dr. Ginzberg — ——." "You are happy," I said, commanding my voice as best as I could, "that all your professors are married off now."

That was the first indication I had that my awful fate was known and talked of.

And now Adele came over, and I said, "The catastrophe has occurred." "Is Dr. Ginzberg engaged to be married?" she said. At once she insisted that I break with him. I refused.

Late in the afternoon he came. I handed him the letter to his fiancée. He read, and thanked me, neither of us made a pretense at scrutinizing the German style. Did he understand?

He put before me a white case—his gift from abroad, a personal ornament, a beautiful buckle, Copenhagen work. When I opened the box it was as though a nettle had stung me. A personal ornament! How could he bring such a gift to me, he an engaged man? And he had never done it before—always books, with the exception of the inkwell, which is as impersonal as books. And as an aftersound it echoed in my ear, "I bought it at Copenhagen." At Copenhagen! Before he saw the girl! So he had thought of me in more than a friendly way at that time? The friendship basis was a reconstruction of our intercourse after the event?

I refused the gift. I was surprised later when I thought it over that I had. I have been so unworldly all the way through. He opened his violet eyes wide, in innocent astonishment. So I was mistaken—he was guilty of no duplicity. He threatened to be offended—he did not understand what I meant, he said. And I kept quiet again, and again

I resolved it should be as he wished—we were friends and we had never been anything but friends.

We went for our walk. When we reached the corner, I realized that my strength would not hold out. My teeth were chattering, my lips were dry, my throat was closed so that I could not make a sound. And I said, "I think I had better not go walking, I—I—" "What *is* the matter with you?" he asked. And again I did not speak out. But inside I exulted—Adele was wrong, my ideal was saved, he was innocent, not calculating as she maintained. He promised to do the talking, and he urged me not to work so hard. We walked on down the familiar road, and as we walked I grew more and more composed. I was almost happy—I would have been happy, if I had not been so weak that every now and then I had to stop to rest and catch my breath. And then the horror of it rushed over me—I was permitting myself to love a man who was as much as married to another woman. And what would happen if I went on with him on his own terms of friendship, doing for him as I had done, and letting him come and take me on walks? I would go on loving him. I would be wicked, dishonest. Or would my feelings change to calm friendliness? Yes, they would, they must.

When we reached the house, I expected him to go on home, and I said a word about the buckle—I hoped he would not think I didn't like it, but I never cared to have such gifts given to me—I would take it if he insisted. He assented silently, as though the matter did not concern him, but he did not go home and I was constrained to ask him in for supper. He accepted exactly as in the old days. While we sat there, Adele came, and she congratulated him, and he told her "his future wife" bore her name, and he admired her new hat, and gave her a Dutch plaque.

He stayed all evening. We spoke of history and equally remote subjects.

As he left, at about half past ten, Anna came in and I said, "Anna, Dr. Ginzberg hat sich in Europa verlobt" [Anna, Dr. Ginzberg became engaged in Europe]. And she said she had heard it from Dr. Marx's servant, and added that she had nearly fainted when it was told to her. So she had expected something else!

I did not see him again until Saturday at the synagogue. Weeks before Mrs. Davidson had invited me to dine with her on that Saturday. I had refused, because I had counted out that he would be here, it would be his first Saturday at home. But then I reconsidered, I should not be able to have a walk with him at any rate, he would want to go right home with his people that first Saturday. So I told her a week after I refused, I would accept.

That morning at the synagogue was a trial. I could not breathe. My chest heaved and heaved, and still the breath would not come. Florence Robosin watched me, and wanted to take me out, and Dr. Schechter shook his head in despair, and then averted it, apparently unable to bear the sight of my distress. At the end of the service, I joined Mr. Davidson, and hoped to get out without speaking to him. Can any one imagine my consternation when I found that he was to be the guest of the Davidson's as well? Can my agony be imagined during the dinner? And when the time came to leave—Adele had joined us meanwhile—he said as that other time, "I will go with you." Another proof that nothing had changed. We walked along Riverside home. I expiated all my sins on that walk.

On Tuesday he came for dinner. I sat at the head of the table speechless. I do not remember what happened between dinner and his going to the Seminary, except that he arranged to ring the bell in the old way to summon me for a walk, at five o'clock. I took the walk—the same experience as before—agony and peace and horror at myself. This time he did not come in for supper, and I bade him good-bye before going to Baltimore on the following Friday. He said he would see me again the next day, after a faculty meeting at the Seminary. I would not be at home on Wednesday, I had an engagement. Ah! But in the old days, I would have flown to the telephone and called the engagement off. This evidence in my own favor I must render—from the moment I knew him not to be mine, I sternly repressed all my secret indulgences with regard to him. I mean all these that required actual locomotion, that were subject to inhibition by an act of the will. I have never gone to the window to watch him go to and from the Seminary at his well-known (to me) lecture hours, hiding behind the sash, waiting to see whether his eyes would wander upward, as they always did—not once have I been guilty of this. I have not once since the fateful day read his letters, the letters that used to accompany me on all my trips, even my day trips to Philadelphia, the letters that I read at least once a day formerly. True, there is not so much self-abnegation there as may seem at first sight. I know them by heart, every word. On one of our walks he said of something "as I wrote to you," but he hadn't written it, and I said so. He disputed it, and I was silent, because the only retort I had would have been, "I remember every word you ever wrote to me—you cannot tell me what is in your letters and what is not."

But unhappily thoughts and tears are not to be inhibited, and thoughts of him and tears of longing for him have not ceased as yet. I feel like an adulteress.

In Baltimore bitterness and self-pity overwhelmed me. I was sick. My physique, even *my* physique, could not stand the strain any more. I had intended to speak to my mother when I got to Baltimore. But I could not. I was afraid I would not meet with sympathy, for in all those years she had not betrayed by a twitch of the eyelids that she noticed what was going on in her daughter. She would probably think it ridiculous, the whole affair, on account of my age. Or was it only because she is really, as my sisters say, "a married nun," so reticent and pure that she never will touch upon sacred concerns? Besides, among her papers in her room, I saw an envelope in his handwriting, and it sealed my mouth every time I opened it to speak. I had written the news to her in a simple sentence, the very day it came to me, simply, "Dr. G. has announced his engagement with a lady in Berlin." When I found after some days that she had not congratulated him, I urged her to do it. I wanted to clinch the thing for myself in every possible way. She, too, was to commit herself in writing, as I had in writing to his fiancée.

Only once during the Baltimore stay, did I see an opening for talk. Dr. Benderly asked about the engagement, and wanted to know whether it was an old flame, and I replied, "No, he saw the girl accidently in the gallery at the synagogue, and was practically engaged after the third meeting two days later." My mother exclaimed and gasped. But I could not take the opportunity. If I spoke, it would be as with Adele—opprobrium was his lot if there was sympathy for me. I could bear that as little as I could bear lack of sympathy with myself.

Even that dreadful visit came to an end. We stopped at Philadelphia on our way back—torture, for the engagement was discussed. We reached New York, Thursday evening, November 5. On Saturday Alice Seligsberg[177] came to go to the synagogue. That gave me the opportunity to slip away without seeing him after the service. In the afternoon he came to pay his respects to my mother—my mother whom he had always loved, and on that love I had built hopes. As my father loved my mother's mother, so he loved my mother. If he loved her, was it not because he saw me in her?

His manner was exactly as always. If it was calculated, it was the most wonderful acting that has ever been done. But they cannot make me believe it was designingly as before in order to deceive me into believing that he had not loved me, that he had not known that I loved him—in short, there had been nothing between us. He complained that I had gone off without him after the services. Again he proposed a walk, and I went with him, and was convinced anew that I was walking on ice. Something had to be done, but what? A question I have even now not been able to answer.

The following Monday morning I went to the Seminary to look up references for Slouschz. As I left, he joined me, and we arranged to meet there in the afternoon and fix up the proof of the Geonic Responsa and the Introduction, which reminds me to say that on the various walks we took, he consulted me, as usual, about the books, and took my advise—exactly as before. It was decided to make two separate books.—As we came out of the Seminary, he espied my mother down the street, and I walked with him to meet her. On the way I said, "I think I am now able to control myself, I have been struggling day and night, and I feel I have conquered." "Oh," he said, callously if not mockingly, "I hope you don't think it necessary to restrain yourself in my presence." I felt as though I had been dealt a stunning blow. At all events, the result was that I did not control myself that afternoon, as though that was not enough, Adele came over to the Seminary and tried to get me away. As I worked there with him until supper time, the tears would roll down my cheeks. He came with me for supper. We worked after supper until ten, and he asked me to take a walk. I did. The usual consequences—a heavenly, hellish peace stole over me.

Tuesday: he came for dinner, and between dinner and his lecture, I believe we worked. Or was that the time he went off at once to see Mr. Ehrlich[178] at the hospital? With the evening mail, on that day, came his fiancée's reply. I read it and passed it to Mamma to read. She read it, looked up with astonishment, and said "I do not understand!"—"There are many things I do not understand," I returned.

I have been so utterly and abjectly miserable since the twentieth day of October until this twenty-first day of December—my luckless birthday anniversary—when I am writing this sentence that I do not see how I can distinguish degrees of misery. But it does seem to me that I reached the very nadir that evening after receiving his fiancée's letter, and I felt that I must have sympathy, or the knowledge that I deserved no sympathy. The one would soothe, the other perhaps bring me to my senses. The only person I had spoken to all those

Henrietta Szold in adolescence, 1877. *Courtesy of the Jewish Historical Society of Maryland*

Henrietta Szold with her parents, Rabbi Benjamin Szold and Sophie Szold, in Berkeley Springs, W. Va., 1897. *Courtesy of the Jewish Historical Society of Maryland*

The five Szold sisters, 1888. Left to right: Henrietta, Bertha, Rachel, Adele, and Sadie. *Courtesy of the Jewish Historical Society of Maryland*

Scholars and Zionist leaders at Tannersville, N.Y., 1906. Seated, left to right: Louis Ginzberg, Judah Magnes, Solomon Schechter, Samson Benderly, Henry Malter. Top row, left to right: Z. H. Bernstein, Alexander Marx, Norman Cowen, Max Schloessinger, A. E. Lubarsky. *Courtesy of the Library of the Jewish Theological Seminary of America*

	Times Absent	Progress	General Remarks
Bila	10		
Barron	3		Gentlemanly all the year throu...
~~Abraham (—)~~			
Basel	36		
Blechman	6		Has done fine work
Dobrin	26		
Egelson	13		
(~~Dino Friedman~~)			
Ginzler	9		
Hirshman	6		
Hirsch	6		
Hirsh	31		
Kohn	26		
Lublensky	19		
Melamed	4		Has done very finely
Botorul	4		
Rabinowitz (E.N.)	0		
~~Rosenthal~~			
Rosinger	0		
Rubenovitz (H.H.)	16		
Schwartz	29		
Szold (Miss)	6		
Tintner	22		

"Dr. Joffe's Report, 1905–06," listing students enrolled at the Jewish Theological Seminary. *Courtesy of JTSP, General Files, box 13*

JTS students and faculty, ca. 1909. The faculty, in the second row, is flanked by a student at each end. Faculty from left to right: Mordecai M. Kaplan, Joshua Joffe, Louis Ginzberg, Solomon Schechter, Israel Friedlaender, Alexander Marx, Israel Davidson. *Courtesy of the Ratner Center for the Study of Conservative Judaism, Jewish Theological Seminary of America*

JTS building, 123rd St., 1903–30. *Courtesy of the Library of the Jewish Theological Seminary of America*

Henrietta Szold in Riverside Park, where she walked with Louis Ginzberg, 1907. *Courtesy of the Jewish Historical Society of Maryland*

Ceramic inkwell, a gift from Louis Ginzberg to Henrietta Szold, 1905.
Courtesy of the Jewish Historical Society of Maryland

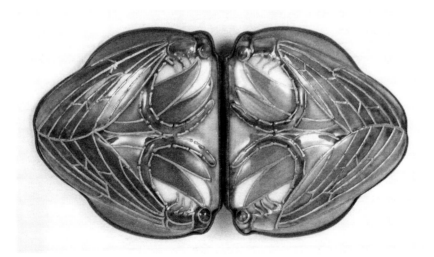

The belt buckle that Louis Ginzberg gave to Henrietta Szold upon his
return from Europe, where he became engaged to marry Adele
Katzenstein, 1908. *Courtesy of the Jewish Historical Society of Maryland*

Engagement photo of Louis Ginzberg and Adele Katzenstein, shown to Szold after Ginzberg's return from Europe in 1908. *Courtesy of the Jewish Publication Society*

Philanthropist Jacob Schiff, whose anti-Zionist statements were severely criticized in the Szold-Ginzberg correspondence. *Courtesy of the Philadelphia Jewish Archives Center*

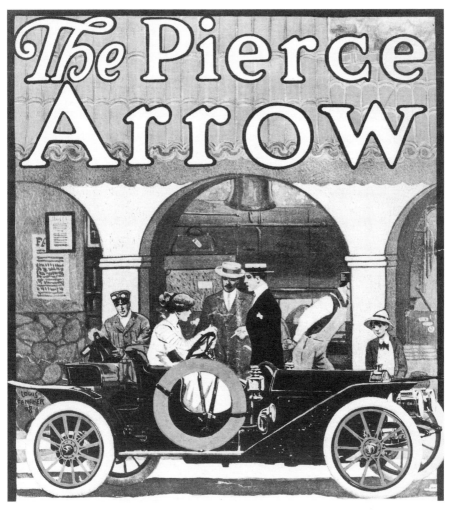

Poster ad for Pierce-Arrow automobile, 1909. "One of the incidents of the day was a ten minutes' visit to Judge Sulzberger . . . I was glad that I did it. You never saw anyone so genuinely surprised as he was when the dowdy secretary stepped out of a Pierce-Arrow automobile" (Szold to Ginzberg, 22 July 1908).

Riverside Drive and Grant's Tomb, frequently traversed by Ginzberg and Szold, 1905–08. *Courtesy of the Mel Scult collection*

HIS ACTIVITY BEING SOMEWHAT RESTRICTED

HE VOLUNTARILY WITHDREW

In 1907 the Szold-Ginzberg correspondence dwelled at length upon efforts of the Hebrew Union College administration to muzzle and ultimately dismiss three Zionist professors. Bible professor Max Margolis, caricatured here, resigned from the faculty after a rebuke by President Kaufmann Kohler for preaching a Zionist sermon in the college chapel. *Cartoon by Maurice Chessler in the* Jewish Comment (Baltimore), *courtesy of Baltimore Hebrew University*

Banquet in honor of Solomon Schechter, 1910. Head table: Solomon and Mathilda Schechter, Jacob Schiff, Louis Marshall. In front of head table: Judah Magnes, Mordecai and Lena Kaplan. Henrietta Szold is seated near the front, in a dark dress with a white collar. Louis Ginzberg and his wife Adele were placed at the far left of the table next to hers, to her considerable consternation. *Courtesy of the Philadelphia Jewish Archives Center*

Board of the first JPS English Translation of the Bible, held at JTS. Left to right: Samuel Schulman, David Philipson, Max L. Margolis, Solomon Schechter, Kaufmann Kohler, unknown man, Cyrus Adler. *Courtesy of the Philadelphia Jewish Archives Center*

JPS Jewish Classics Committee. Seated: F. de Sola Mendes, Mayer Sulzberger, Kaufmann Kohler, Cyrus Adler, David Philipson, Samuel Schulman. Standing: Louis Ginzberg, Jacob Z. Lauterbach, Henry Malter, Alexander Marx, Israel Friedlaender, H. G. Enelow. *Courtesy of the Philadelphia Jewish Archives Center*

Portrait of Mayer Sulzberger, head of the JPS Publications
Committee and Henrietta's boss. *Courtesy of the Philadelphia
Jewish Archives Center*

three weeks was Adele, and she was too sympathetic to be entirely helpful—too antagonistic to him. She had liked him, or rather tolerated him only for my sake; and besides, she had known all my tremors for years. My mother had always loved him—I would speak to her. So I did that night when we were quite ready for bed, in bed, in fact, all the lights turned out. I began with a reference to the letter, I had not gone far in my confessions, my early course of rigid self-restraint, and my nine months tumultuous happiness, when she interrupted me, to tell me of her own grief for my sake—what a shock the news had been to her in Baltimore. How all day Yom Kippur she had thanked God for the late happiness that was coming to me, how she had planned to live with Rachel for a year after my marriage, how she had even thought out a way of distinguishing Louis Levin from him. For a brief moment, it was as though the whole burden were lifted from me—the burden of humiliation and of a loveless future. If my pure, unworldly mother exonerated me of folly, exonerated me, too, as she did of unwomanliness, if she had noted his love-looks, his devotion, I could not be the despicable creature I had been thinking myself. And she had loved him, and he had loved her. She wanted still to think well of him.

But the surcease did not last long. Satan himself must have whispered to me that it was my own mother who was sympathizing with me. A mother would naturally see things through her child's eyes. No, I was not yet justified, I was not in any way helped to an understanding of the horrible fate that had befallen me. Besides, I felt stripped bare. For my mother I allowed all my precious, guarded secrets to pass my lips. To her I told all my signs and tokens, all at least that I had considered signs and tokens. I opened every fold in my heart, and I felt as though I had put him up as a target.

And so it was, Adele continued her cry of "Break with him totally," and my mother began to criticize him unmercifully. All day long I had to beseech her not to give him cavalier treatment. There was an explanation of what he had done to me. He was incapable of a base act. Love had enthralled him—he had not been master of himself. It had so captured him that he did not remember his relation to me. The new love was so different from the old, if ever it had existed, that he no longer put them in the same category. We went through all his acts since his return, and they interpreted every one as a coldly calculated act, part of a plan to make me believe there had been nothing but friendship before. I always insisted that there was a possibility that he was wholly innocent, that what seemed calculation was perfectly natural.

On the Thursday following he came in the evening to finish the proof of the Introduction. We did finish. I showed him the letter I had received from his fiancée. It contained two messages for him: I was to ask for their joint picture, she had sent him a copy for me. My God! All these hot summer days and nights, from May until July 21, while I worked at the Introduction, I tried to get up enough boldness to ask for a reward—his picture, to have by me while he was away in Europe. But he gave me one word of praise—that I had rendered well in English an explanation showing the difference of conception between the Jerusalem and Babylonian Talmud, and I said to myself, "Reward enough! He has never said so much to you in praise of work done for him, ask for no more." And I let him go without making the request that had hovered on my lips for years. How near I came to making it one evening at his house when his sister-in-law showed me several of his pictures! Perhaps if I had let myself go, he would have known my state of mind and heart and—— However, I did not ask for the picture, then either, at his fiancée's bidding. Of such self-abnegation I was not capable.

The second request in the letter was that I was to see that "her *Schatzilein*" [darling][179] did not work so hard. I call upon your name again, my God! was that not more than flesh could stand? to make such an appeal to me who had saved him all manner of drudgery, proof-reading, letter-writing, the necessity for writing in a strange language, for nearly four years! I was still to slave for him and also for her?

He read the letter, and—this is the only bit of malice that I have to record about myself, in this whole dreadful business, so help me God!—and I watched his face while he read it. Even this one indulgence failed of result. His face wore a mask. I do not know whether it pleased or displeased him. I only know this, that according to Mrs. Marx's account, he was very insistent about seeing his fiancée's letter to her, and she was so ashamed of it that she refused to show it to him. *She* could afford to be generous, she was not bleeding from a thousand crucifixions. It is only proper that I should add that Mrs. Marx told me that a subsequent letter was more decent.

When he finished reading the letter, I said, in reference to what she wrote, that she had been afraid of the learned woman her "*Schatzilein*" told her about, but that my letter had dispelled her fears—with reference to this I said: "So all you could tell your fiancée about me was that I am a learned woman? You know that that is not true. You know that you do not consider me one, and you know that I do not consider myself learned"—"That depends upon the point of view," he replied.—"But you did not tell her that I am a woman with red blood running in my veins?"—Coldly: "I would say the same again, what I did say."

And yet, when the proof was finished at about 9:30, he asked me to take a walk with him, I wonder whether the psychologists will ever invent an instrument to measure the effort I made, to say: "I cannot—I have struggled—and cannot control myself......" He looked at me with wide-eyed surprise. His eyes were void of understanding. He is innocent! He is innocent! went through me like a Hallelujah. And for a moment I believed that all was not irretrievably lost—that I could be the friend he wanted me to be.

He left at once, and I realized again that I had been too happy while he was near me. A break was absolutely necessary, to save myself from wickedness. Someday I would surely strain him to me and beg him to give up the other woman.

On Saturday after the service, I walked with Mamma toward Morningside Park. He and Sophie overtook us. I paired off with Sophie, and left him to Mamma. At 116th Street, the sound of his voice had become too much for me, and I turned back. In the afternoon we went to see him—Mamma had promised to give him her congratulations in his own house, and we both had a Bar-Miztvah visit to pay to his sister-in-law, one of her sons had become Bar-Miztvah during my trip to Baltimore. He spoke to me about his book—some typographical device for his lists. Their picture was passed around—I did not have to look at it, Sophie had been kind enough to show it to me before at my house. I almost choked all the time I sat there. When we rose to go, he said he would walk with us, he was going to visit the Schechters, I did not speak a word to him all the way over.

On Monday at noon he telephoned, wanting to know about some manuscript of the Legends, I had it, I said, and he came for it. At the same time I gave him the holiday lecture, pointing out to him that one set was corrected and furnished with the Hebrew citations, but not the other four, and he said with the old manner, "O, don't bother about the rest!"—"I do not intend to, I assure you," I did have the gumption to eject. Did he really think I would continue to work for him?

Then he said, "By the way, I won't come on Tuesdays any more, I have made a change about the afternoon lectures, they are later, and I can go home for dinner." So he does understand, I thought. I called my mother, and told her of the new arrangement, and he added, with the jocose manner, affectionate and deferential at the same time, that he had always adopted toward her, "Yes, you will miss our little talk!"—How right he was in his conceit, the loss is all on my side. Then I asked how Mr. Ehrlich[180] was getting on, and he said, "If you want to go to see him, I shall be glad to take you. Do you want to go?"—"perhaps?" Did he still fail to understand. Was this still a part of the plan? Or was it innocence or the conscienceness of having nothing to reproach himself with?

Tuesday afternoon I met him going to the Seminary at the same hour at which his lectures had always taken place. It may be that he went an hour earlier to look up some references. Or if not, the acted lie was justifiable. But why, then, pretend innocence? Why not talk out to me?

The following Saturday Melvin Krulewitzsch's Bar-Miztvah was celebrated. The crowd did me the service of not bringing me face to face with him. But by that time I was so reduced in body that standing on my feet was pain, and all self-control had vanished. Louis Levin was here, and again I went outside for sympathy. I got it from him in full measure, I was getting it from my mother, from Adele, from Thomas. Each new person helped me for a few hours. My self-respect would be restored temporarily. And at that time it was my self-respect that was suffering intensely, for day by day it appeared that all tongues around and at a distance were wagging—not ill-naturedly, but still I was being talked about—Henrietta Szold, the daughter of her father, who would turn in his grave if he knew how his child had been spurned, was in everybody's mouth. She was an object of pity! Connected with a love affair! All these years it had never occurred to me that people were noticing. Nobody had ever so much as attempted to tease me. And now!

Louis talked to me, and showed me over again all Adele had said—but I was not satisfied. They were my people, they loved me, they saw my unhappiness minute by minute, and they accepted my interpretation of acts and facts. Since I had spoken to my mother, I had felt that I would have to go to an outsider—Dr. Marx, the friend with whom he had so emphatically coupled me in those last letters, the person with whom he had associated most intimately, always excepting myself. To what had I sunk, if I could consider the idea of opening my sanctuary, despoiled though it was, to an outsider? For a week I struggled. Then fate decided. Dr. and Mrs. Marx came to see us on Sunday, November 29, and as they left they asked me to take a walk with them the next day. I consented. The next day I spent in weeping—working at his book with the tears streaming down incessantly. By the late afternoon—it was three weeks ago today—I was incapable of thought. I was a mass of bruised spirit, and started from the house to tell the Marxes I would not go with them. They insisted, and I yielded, because I was weak in body and mind, only promising myself I would not speak a word.

DECEPTION OR SELF-DECEPTION?

December 24, 1908

Somehow or other I cannot finish this record. Instead of getting accustomed to the new order of my life, I grow more and more puzzled, more and more sore. I am stronger physically than I was, but less strong from day to day spiritually. Today I was overwhelmed by the tragedy of it—that a friendship such as ours was, over and above my love (and his?), should be ruptured completely. I am not too proud to write down that I still miss him every minute of the day and night. And he? Apparently, he goes on serenely without thought of me.

Today I translated this sentence in the Legends: "No matter how great one's grief is over the death of a dear one, at the end of a year one responds to consolation." But the disappearance of a living man leaves one inconsolable.—And he has disappeared from my life living. I wonder whether he notices how many many things in the story of Jacob and Joseph are applicable to my state—only he does not know my state and he does not care.

To go on again—after I had walked some distance along the path in Morningside Park that we took every Saturday, I could not stand it any more, and I wanted to run away, but they insisted I should stay, and then I could not hold in any longer, and I spoke, and I told everything. But before I had gone beyond the first few sentences, Dr. Marx told me that he was as much puzzled as I, that he could only suspect some mysterious explanation, though not the notion of it, that he had supposed that I had refused him until I began to speak, that he had expected the engagement with me to be announced two years ago, that he had even told him before leaving for Tannersville in 1906 that he could certainly expect to hear from him as soon as the thing happened—that—well, I cannot set down all he said, but what he said was enough to show me that there was no necessity for me to reveal my secret joys and hopes and signs—what the outside world had seen was enough to justify my fond expectations. Only I had not nursed fond expectations until the merely conventional "attentions," had developed into what I took to be manifestations of real and deep feeling. I have spoken again and again to the Marxes, I have gone over the whole ground with them, always begging them to give me the outsider's, the outside friend's, *his* friend's interpretation, always begging them to keep up their friendship with him. They have sometimes succeeded in restoring my self-respect. They have been fair to him, though they do not see him in the same ideal light as I do, but they condemn him utterly, chiefly because he gives no account of himself to his friends and to me. They do not know him. Once he has set his face forward, he never looks back. He looks at a thing from all sides, he makes up his clear mind upon it, and then he does not reprieve.

At about that time I began to be much troubled about the proof from Oxford. I wanted to finish that for him. Had he received it? Everybody said I was not to bother about it. But how could I let my darling worry with all those petty details? I saw him at the synagogue on the following Saturday, December 5, and although I had torn up two letters during the week asking him to be sure to let me have the proof, I could not help saying it to him when he came up to me with a little scared look on his face, and bade me Good Shabbes. He had not received the proof, but he had received a letter, and he would send me the proof when it came. Will he?

That scared look! I know it so well. His face used to wear it whenever he met me, as though he wanted to propitiate me. Then a year ago when my happiness began, it changed into that something indescribable upon which I based all my happiness. It was all propitiation then, all entreaty, all love in short. But it seems I was mistaken.

On that Saturday something dreadful happened. Besides speaking of the proof, I told him I would send him some chapters of the Legends with queries. "Please to look through them and return them to me for the printer." That it should come to this! And a few days ago I did send him the manuscript by express, with dozens and dozens of queries written out, and a formal secretarial letter. I contrast that with the Tuesdays when he sat at my desk and we wrote over the mss. together, and——I weep.

The dreadful thing that happened was that almost at the end of our forced conversation, Mamma appeared, he stepped towards her with something of the old assured manner—the manner of the man who knows he is regarded with the kindly eye of friendship, and in spite of my pleadings, my command, my tears, my mother eyed him coldly, and stretched out two fingers and drew herself up. And a look came into his eyes of the hunted animal. I see it before me all the time. Or is that, too my imagination like all the rest? I do not think he cares whether I suffer or not—he probably thinks that loyalty to the woman to whom he gave his word does not permit him to care, but he did love my mother, and she wounded him. That, I believe, ended all there was between us, even the coldest of friendly feelings.

My next contact with him came on December 15, when he sent that brutal message asking for the clipping books. On the previous Saturday he was not at the synagogue. And last Saturday, December 19, my feelings became so vehement that I had to leave before the services were over.

This week has been particularly hard. It is vacation week, and during vacation he used to spend days with me, and walk with me. Tomorrow it will be a year that we went to the Hall of Fame together. He came for dinner, brought Mamma a bouquet of flowers for her birthday, went with us on our expedition, came back with us, we worked Genizah, he staid for supper, and so late after that I had to send him home. This year I might as well be in my grave for all that life means for me. It is all dull, colorless, toneless. Nothing means anything. I think of him all day long, I need him, I continue to save up thoughts and incidents for him, and *he* might as well be dead—never will he hear them. Oh, if only it had been possible for me to keep his friendship! If only that first day I had not been as strong as I was, or if only I had been stronger afterwards. But it was impossible. Even when I spoke to him at the synagogue about his proofs and the Legends, even then a feeling of peace and happiness took possession of me. If I had associated with him on the terms he seems to have proposed, I would have been wicked, and lost the last vestige of my self-respect. No, it was impossible.

Reconsiderations: "Dark Chronicle of a Broken Heart"

Tokens of Love and Servility

What have I learnt by putting down all this history, all my feelings, my bitterness, my happiness, my joys and my sorrows? What has it revealed about myself? Nothing new—only that I loved, and alas! still love him passionately, to the point of adoration, that he was and in spite of all they say in detraction of him is still my ideal; that I lavished myself upon him with the reckless generosity of love, never counting the cost, never harboring a worldly thought, never stopping to ask what the world was saying or thinking; that I stripped myself bare of all reserve before him, I stood naked spiritually; that it made me blissfully happy to do it all. O that I could do it now and always! What I gave him was virgin love, my first love, and coming so late in my life it was love strengthened and chastened by a rich experience of sorrow and manifold happenings and varied circumstance,—love to which knowledge and the discipline of practical life was made subservient so that it might serve the loved one all the better—love that knew but one object, the man loved. I did not ask for marriage, I did not ask for release from drudgery, I asked only to be permitted to serve still more, and asked in exchange only companionship. And what did this strong, virgin, disinterested love of mine, of which a maiden in the flush of youth need not be ashamed, what did it bring me? No "attentions"—no flowers, no candies, no theatre, none of the gallantries other women carry off as trophies. Books he brought me—Perez, Jehudah Halevi, the Hebrew book of legends, Morpurjo, the Jalkut, his Haggada, a copy of all he published, all these with treasured inscriptions, except the Jalkut and some of his lectures, Delitzsch's with the treacherous inscription, and his mother's Techinnah—gifts he brought me from abroad, the inkwell and the Copenhagen buckle, he once bought me a Megillah downtown for a penny. But my two treasures were the veil knotted by him, and the little pasteboard medicine box in which he brought me a remedy for a cold which he discovered me to have one Saturday morning when he hastened over to find out why I had not been at the synagogue. How happy I was at his concern, his wide-eyed alarm! Over and above this he awakened my womanhood to consciousness. From him, because I loved him and because at last I thought he loved me, I learnt the mystery of sex, supplementing the knowledge about it which he had given me of it as my teacher in the Talmud. All that came from him. Before I was as ignorant of these realities as a girl of sixteen.

I have memories—bitter sweet, wholly sweet,—and wholly bitter memories. He occasionally looked up references for me, he helped me with the article on *Weiberliteratur* [(Jewish) women's (liturgical) literature], he read the Slouschz proof this fall, after his return, when I thought I could keep up the pitiful mummery, he used to take my watch to the jewelers whenever it needed repairing. He walked and talked with me. He made me believe he loved me. He made me supremely happy for a brief space. He gave me everything—and nothing, for now I must doubt the reality of the happiness. It was either deception or self-deception. In either case it has crumbled into dust and ashes, and the residue is unhappiness.

How much happiness he gave me I can now recall only in a shadowy way, only a reflex of it comes back to me. I sometimes think myself walking by his side, and I feel it. I remember how I trembled toward him, when he came this fall, and I know how happy he made me. But what is present to my mind now is my unhappiness, my tragedy. I wonder whether he can conceive of the feeling with which I work over his book seven hours a day, six days of the week? I wonder whether he knows that he has made of me the sort of "poor thing" that woman was whom we met crying aloud on the street when he took me to the Friedlaender dinner last February. We both shuddered. Would he shudder now if he saw how my tears and sobs have come unbidden day and night, in secret and in public, these last ten weeks? Does he realize that I am still stunned and dazed? That for weeks I could not find my way on the most familiar streets? That I could not detect glaring errors in proof? That I left the gas burning in unused rooms? That all my practical sense deserted me? Does he know that minute by minute I groan because I am a jilted spurned woman, an Agunah?

I called my love disinterested. To be honest, I sometimes craved a tangible reward for my devotion. I do not remember whether I mentioned it before, that all the time I was at work at the Introduction this summer, I was nerving myself up to the point of asking for his picture, and I desisted because he praised a sentence in my translation. And when the Introduction (which is no more an Introduction than the Appendix we joked about is an Appendix) was done, I did timidly suggest that we have a celebration, but it was shortly before his going to Europe, and he was not very well, and it was hot, besides, so he said, "Wait till the book is quite done, and then we'll have a big celebration." Now it will never come, after five years' work! And what had I not planned when the Legends came out completed! And now they are to be dedicated to the other woman. And once he was going to take me to New Haven by boat on a day's excursion. He was sick that day, and we could not go. So do all my little rewards vanish into thin air! But I have the memory of work and walks with him, and not even he can rob me of that. Whatever he did or did not, he made me happy, and for that I must thank him forever! But again the question comes, was it happiness?

Did he love me? It seems that I cannot find many things to enumerate that would indicate that I was in his heart. My signs and tokens seem to be impalpable for the most part. He sought my society for three years, always more and more, the last six months practically daily. We never discussed love, certainly not our love, or must I say *my* love? It may be that I was entirely mistaken. Perhaps it was all only what he wanted me on his return this fall to think it—only friendship. I dare not say, it seems, that he loved me. At all events, if he did, he loved the girl in Berlin at once, spontaneously, and much more than he loved me. He rushed to her, he did not stop to weigh and calculate as to youth or age. If the thing I thought a sign of love was such, then he sent it to me one day, and he saw the girl the next, was infatuated by her, and my fate was sealed. At best I had but unlocked his heart, as Louis said, for her to walk in and take possession of the kingdom I could not conquer. He had the right to prefer her to me and act accordingly. He had not bound himself to me by an explicit word, only by those thousand intangible threads that may possibly not be what I thought them, what outsiders thought them.

But if it was not love, what *was* that change of manner that came about a year ago? When he gave himself to me with such unreserve, looked at me so warmly, sought me, spoke spontaneously, discussed all his affairs with me, came to me daily. What did it mean if it was not love? Why was he willing to take from me material as well as spiritual goods without as much as thanking me, as though there were no mine and thine between us? When the change of manner came, I was older than before—he was not deceived as to that. He had then been associating with me intimately for three years. If ever, he should then have been sure he wanted me either as his wedded wife or his lifelong unwedded companion. And what did the daily visits mean, if not love? And the silent sittings at Riverside?

No, it could not have been love. Otherwise he would have declared himself before he went to Europe, and not left me behind in the misery he saw me in at the Postoffice. Did he mean to say the word on his return, that would give me the right to minister to him or make me his life companion? Only he saw the girl, and the old love seemed none? I accept that. Only if that is the case, what becomes of his definition of happiness? Did he not have a duty toward me after all those years? Had he a right to such complete oblivion of me? Or was his love so great that he cast his definition of happiness as duty performed to the four winds? Surely *I* ought to understand that and many other inconsistencies in the name and for the sake of love. Or does his conception of duty vary with his convenience and desire of the moment? That does not comport with my knowledge of his character and principles.

But in respect to what has happened since his return, and the backward light it may throw upon the whole past, in respect to his innocence as it were, in respect to his remaining my beau ideal, the important thing is not whether he loved me and now loves someone else more but whether he knew that I loved him.

Was it possible not to know it? Until Dr. Marx assured me of the contrary, I thought I was constantly screaming it from the housetops. Dr. Marx says that the impression made upon the outsider was that he was following me up, and that I was not giving him much encouragement that for this reason he thought I had rejected him when he made a proposal, to me, as he felt he must have done. It is possible, then, that he, too, did not know—that I hid my love from him!

It is true he could not know, for instance, that I never separated myself from his letters, that I read in them daily, that I took them with me even if I went on a day's trip, that when a new one came, I kissed the signature, and wore it next to my heart, until the fear possessed me it might be discovered, or I took it to bed with me, and would get up in the middle of the night and put it into my desk, lest someone see it in the morning, and that I preserved every scrap of paper he ever addressed to me. Nor could I have expected him to deduce from so many heterogeneous items spread over so long a period, that in the last three years I was out but four times when he came or telephoned—that I arranged my whole life, down to the smallest details, with reference to him. If he telephoned, and made a claim upon my time, I gave it, no matter to whom I had pledged it before, or rather, I avoided making engagements until I knew what he might want, or I canceled engagements as soon as I found out they interfered with his plans. Nor could he have noticed that I denied him only one request in all that time—he asked me not to go to Philadelphia to a meeting when I had a cold. And yet, why shouldn't he have noticed my uniform complaisance with his wishes? But he could not know that sometimes when he telephoned in the evening that he had received proof, could he come with it, I would get up out of bed and dress by the time he walked from his house to ours. He could not know that I always saw to it that on Tuesdays the dinners were arranged with a view to his predilections that I always saved my portion of his favorite dishes as his second [helping], that for looking at him, I could not eat. But he should have noticed that when he suffered with thirst after our walks, I always saved my glass of phosphate, when no one else was by, for him, though I myself was parched. He could not divine that when he called the Legends "our" book, my heart almost jumped out of my breast with joy, and yet it seems to me he might have read it in my eyes. He could not know that when I sustained money losses, about which I told him freely and unreservedly, my chief regret was that my dear little Litwack's Babylonian and Palestinian trip would not be so comfortable as it might otherwise have been, for a dollar saved had no value in my sight except inasmuch as it would serve the purpose of taking him where he so often said he wanted to go. He could not know that last Pesah a year ago, when he came down from his seat in the synagogue, and went for a

Mahzor [High Holiday Prayerbook], and told Sidney Breuer to give it to me, I was almost delirious with delight. But on the other hand, did it not mean something on his part that he did it? He could not know that last January when he was at Adele's house one afternoon in honor of Miriam Schaar and Alice Bernheim, I arranged it so that when we walked to Riverside, he would be at the side of the young girls, and that I sang Hosannahs when, a few hundred steps down the Drive, he deliberately left them and came to my side. How well I remember our conversation then—about happiness, and I said I could imagine a mother happy though she sat by the coffin of her child— she at least had had a child! Or in the summer when we, Mamma, Rachel, he, and I, went to the Jersey side and took the trolley, I manoeuvred [sic] that he should be seated next to Rachel as the guest, and always he was with me, he could not know that I was in a beatific state. But why did he always gravitate toward me? Had it no meaning? Or could he have known that other time on the Jersey shore, with Mamma and myself, that it gave me a thrill of delight when he drew my shawl from his pocket as it grew cool, and with his dear eyes insisted that I put it on. Always the language of the eyes! He surely could not know that when his people spoke of moving to a house in our neighborhood, I trembled lest the change make his Tuesday dinners with us superfluous, and while I was trembling because he might withdraw himself a little, he was already lost to me forever, he was engaged to another, and I suspect the moving project was abandoned on account of these very relations into which he had newly entered. Or could I have expected him to know how jubilant I was when his South African relatives sailed, on a Saturday, and we discovered he would have to eat his Shabbes dinner alone, and we carried him off to our home from the synagogue for dinner and a nap. He cannot know that if I was called to the telephone while he sat beside me at the desk, I would touch his hat hanging on the rack in the hall outside, because I could not, dared not touch his hand and tell him how I loved him. He does not know that the veil he tied, the box in which he brought me medicine, were my treasures. He does not know how assiduously I collected statistics of happy marriages between younger men and older women. Nor does he suspect how many favorable cases he himself contributed to my not inconsiderable list. He does not know that before he returned from Europe this fall, I could not enjoy the charms of the autumn without a pang, because he was not with me, and how I praised God because I saw that the beauty of the season was lingering on and I might yet have the opportunity to take him to one of the places we had discovered during the summer and about which I had written to him. He does not know how the spring sunshine, the budding trees, the falling leaves, the rain, the stars, the new moon, the full moon, the mute benches on Riverside, the stones and bricks of this neighborhood, how they all cry out to me his name, and only his name. One of my letters in which I described a solitary walk on Riverside should have given him an inkling, however. Or our walk in the rain at Spuyten-Duyvil this spring should have told him something, if he had had a heart for me. That walk was typical of my luck when it comes to pleasure and reward, even of the simplest. After many plans and attempts, we had at last got off for a country walk that afternoon. But it was hot, a storm came up, and I suffered, because I was afraid he was not comfortable. I brought him home early, and nursed him, and he spent the rest of the afternoon and evening with me. Could I expect him to know my feelings, seeing that I carefully suppressed all expressions of them, when so far back as the summer of 1906, we went to Riverside on a Saturday afternoon with the Marxes, and they rose to go, and I said we will go with you, and he said almost petulantly, and masterfully, No, we'll stay—and we staid. Naturally, then, Dr. Marx must have thought he had a claim upon me, or meant soon to make it. And what about dropping Dr. Marx and Dr. Malter at corners? Nor could he have known that all through his year of mourning, when I knew that he had to get up early in the dark and the cold, I would get up too in sympathy. And as for keeping his father's Jahrzeit, even if his sister-in-law had written to him of it, it would have made no difference, by that time he had won the girl in Berlin. But should he not have known that my sympathy with him was always active—that I was almost sick when I knew him to be sick, for did he not, dozens of times tell me, and several times write me not to worry that he would be all right? I could not expect him to know that all the work I had in connection with the Year Book and Directory, seemed glorified to me because he interested himself in my struggle with the problem of describing Orthodoxy and Reform for the Census Bureau.

But was it possible for me to feel so intensely, and not let any of it penetrate to him? If he could not know the facts which stimulated my love, were there not a thousand others, impalpable in part, indescribable in part, that should have told him of my worship? Does he not remember when I told him I believed he could do anything he wanted to do? How he laughed and cast a sidelong glance at me. Is it the habit of women to write men such letters as I wrote him unless they love? Certainly, I never wrote such to any one else. One day he came into my room, and he saw the copy of Dr. Schechter's Studies lying on my table, which Dobsevage[1] had had bound for me specially. He admired it, and I said quickly, "It is yours." Does one do such things ordinarily? Does he remember how this summer I made him take off his coat, and how I carried it and his hat for him through the Drive, so that he might have a comfortable smoke in spite of the heat? Have I ever done that, or thought of doing it, for another man? Now that all is over between us, I am ashamed of my servility. At the time it was a joy and natural. Does he remember how day after day this summer I tried to make him comfortable the minute he came in by giving him a glass of lemonade which I myself prepared, because it was a joy to do it for him? Does he remember the very last day before he left for Europe, how I asked him with my eyes—he had taught me that language—whether he would have some, and how he answered with his eyes? Did he not notice that in spite of my poor memory, I never forgot his likes and dislikes—riding backward in the car, and things like that? Poor memory! I must apologize to my maker, for having always called the memory He gave me poor. This record shows—and how much more I might have put down!—that I must only know where to write a fact, not in my brain, but in my heart, and my memory is as tenacious as his own wonderful apparatus.

Did He Ever Love Me?

December 30, 1908

Two little incidents: We were told that Miss Silbert had married Dr. Danziger, and had been deserted by him.—The man I found for Miss Silbert's sake, and hated for his sake. And now I class Dr. G.[2] with him,—he deserted me in absolutely the same sense as his enemy who tried to vilify his character, deserted Miss Silbert, I cannot recede from my position that before God I was his affianced wife.

Yesterday, by the merest chance, it was mentioned in my presence that Rabbi Mayer of Kansas City, his first friend in America, to whose planning it was due that he ever came here, married a woman fifteen years his senior, and they are happy. Is it possible, that he alone, he, my ideal, could not rise above a convention? I thought him built on the largest lines possible.

Above all is it the practice of ordinary friends, men or women, to enter into the work of others as I entered into his? To stay up until all hours of the night and morning to do his work, and spare him all drudgery? He put me on a level with Dr. Marx in his last three letters. Would Dr. Marx do such services? Or even approximately such services? He once told me of some one, a man, who had loved him devotedly, more, he thought, than any one had ever loved him. I remember I said inwardly, but since then some one has loved you more, whatever may have been or not been before. Would he have entered so sympathetically into every thought and discovery of his? Does he not remember that I once wrote to him, if he would but take the trouble to explain a little bit, I could follow him in any work he did? And I can flatter myself that he never needed to explain much, and that not because my knowledge is great or my wit keen, but because my heart was entirely his.

And it is not as though I had been a woman of leisure. These years since I have known him have been crowded with work almost beyond endurance. Yet *his* work was not allowed to suffer. When he had lectures to deliver, I always asked him to let me have them at least two or three weeks ahead for translation. But he usually brought them to me piecemeal, beginning about two days before the date of delivery, and I would sit up night after night, and count it joy. Did he not know it was love that sustained me? I once heard him say that there is no love in modern times as there once was. I almost cried out, and asked him to put me to the test. I am ashamed to say that crime itself would not have been a deterrent. I admit that after his engagement I failed on the test. In his Legends, he tells again and again of Rachel's nobility—who from love of her husband permitted him to take her handmaid to wife—gave him her handmaid herself, and that she was rewarded for her self-abnegation. But what of Rachel's relation to Leah? And at least she had a claim upon Jacob equal to the claim of the two others. I have only memories. And he tells of Tamar, who proclaims herself ready to perish in the flames rather than betray Judah. And I could not hide my grief and humiliation from him and from the world—I could not say unfalteringly that I was happy because he was happy with and through another woman. I tried and I failed, and he probably thinks it is resentment if I am and show myself to be crushed, and not intense love and fear of becoming wicked and dishonorable if I continued to be on the terms of friendship which he tacitly proposed to me on his return. Is my modern love, then, less, than the ancient?—I cannot conceive it possible that he should not have known that I was madly in love with him. But if he loved me once, and only loves her more now, or if he merely knew I loved him, how can his actions on his return be explained? How could he permit me to write the letters, the glowing letters, I wrote at the last, encouraged by his final telephone message, encouraged especially by his telling me that he had fasted so well because he had my letter in the morning? How could he write to me in the strain he did after his engagement? Was that merely an overflow from the feeling aroused by another? Why did he come back and at once announce his engagement publicly? Why didn't he tell me first, and let me get accustomed to the idea? Why did he engage himself at once? Why didn't he come back and gradually estrange himself from me? One must be off with the old love before one is on with the new. There was no need for hurrying the announcement here, it was announced in Berlin fully four weeks later. If he knew I loved him, why did he tell me he always did the unexpected thing? Why did he ask me whether I was happy over his engagement? Why above all things, was he so cruel as to ask me to write the letter to her? Did he want me to commit myself, and did he know that a wish expressed by him was an elementary law of my nature? If he knew my passion for him, how could he come back and manifest a desire to continue in the old ways that meant life to me—the walks, the discussions, the meetings after service on Saturday? Did he count on my heroism? What right had he to count on it? Or is he himself not capable of the modern love that is as intense as the ancient, and therefore does not realize what he has done to me and asked of me? The insistent question is, why did he engage himself in such haste? Why could he not correspond with the girl, and give me time to adjust myself to the new order? Did he think I was not large-hearted enough to yield to a greater passion than the one I inspired? Then I could have found a basis for the friendship I need and crave even now, and all the time. Did he feel that he must get rid of me summarily? Was he afraid that the girl in Berlin would not be true to him unless he clinched the matter at once? Is that the sort of wife he wants?

I must assume, then, that he never loved me in the least, and moreover, he had no inkling of my love for him. First and last, it was cool friendship. But if it was that, his actions since his return, or rather since his engagement are still inexplicable. Why was he at such pains in his last three letters to class me with Dr. Marx? Why did he call me a victim? Why did he connect the crisis in the early days of his visit in Amsterdam with his father in his letter, but with his engagement in his talk with me? Why does he not now, or why did he not, as soon as he saw my distress, seek to have an explanation with me, and tell me he wanted my friendship, and had always wanted it, that there had been never any idea of love in his mind, that he regretted it if his acts had been deceptive—but friends we must remain. Would that have been disloyal to the girl in Berlin? I think not. And it would have been far different from the tacit, almost debasing offer of friendship he made me on his return. Why was he so brutal about telling me I need not restrain my feelings in his presence? Why so brutal about demanding the book of clippings? If our relation was mere friendship, then all I did for him required him to come to me and thank me in retrospect—for the letters I wrote for him, the translations I made for him, the clippings I pasted up for him, the lectures I wrote out for him, all the hours and hours and hours I spent in what was joy then, and turns out now to have been only drudgery. Then, it seems, he was neither lover nor friend to me. It passeth my understanding.

Except that I have spoken to Dr. Marx, I have not considered the outside world in all this. But since his return the outside world has insisted upon making itself heard—as to him and as to me. As to me— I know now from a hundred sources that the world, my friends, and strangers in the neighborhood, either expected my engagement to him these two years, or concluded he would not marry, but secure the continuance of my companionship. I was and am unworldly enough not to consider the outside world. But had he a right to disregard the fact that he was putting me into people's mouths? Should he not have withdrawn himself from me, if he had no intentions of devoting himself to me, instead of becoming more and more intimate? Is he unworldly too? Perhaps, but also he is clear-sighted. And also he knows how Judaism condemns the man who puts another to shame publicly. And was he not nailing me to the pillory when he proclaimed to all who had eyes to see, up to July 23 when he left the city, This is the only person, this woman, with whom I care to spend a single moment of my leisure, and returned on October 20, and proclaimed as loudly, I have spurned this woman? Must not the world think that he found a shameful thing in me? It was not an old sweetheart he went back to. It was a girl he had seen only three times, after he had the closest association with me for nearly four years. Had a right to put me in a position in which I have become an object of pity, as well as self-pity? Is there any room left then for respect and self-respect?

As for him, people say many many things that break my heart all the more. Do they run him down in order to console me? Then they do not understand my great love for him—I loved him the man and him the ideal. If he went away from me because he loved another woman it was my duty to crush the love for the man in me, but there would not be any wrong in continuing to love the ideal—that would have been friendship. They condemn him—before me, but what would they say to him?—for "paying me attentions" if he had no "intentions." They condemn him for having "exploited" me. They condemn him as a conceited man who was flattered by my friendship, so conceited that he thought I would conquer my love and remain his useful friend. They interpret all the things in his letters after his engagement, all his acts since his return, as refined calculation. He announced his engagement here, they say, so suddenly, so as to give me no time to think, but merely accept his terms. I refuse these explanations—they do not comport with what I know about him by reason of my intimate association with him.

I have an explanation of his conduct—only it does not comport with his character as I know it either, because it assumes that he so is a passionate man, and I know him to be the most self-controlled and in the best sense of the word self-sufficient man in the world. Two cases occurred this summer of men making hasty marriages after they had had plenty of time to make the same marriages in leisure and with dignity. The incidents were discussed in his presence. He was unsparing in his ridicule, and that attitude was of a piece with his whole *Lebensanschauung* [outlook on life]. And yet the only explanation that is at all satisfactory requires me to say that I was mistaken in this fundamental respect. My explanation is that he did love me, and that he knew I loved him, and he meant to be my life companion with or without marriage. That was the status up to August 29, when he saw the girl in the women's gallery of the synagogue. Then a passion seized him, and he said: "The other was not love. I was mistaken in my own feelings." And straightaway he began to adjust the whole of the past to the new conditions. The first thing he must have concluded was that he had been equally mistaken about my feelings toward him. And once he made the readjustment, he mechanically went on doing in respect to me what he had done before—he wrote, he let me write, he came back and took walks, he even expected me to be happy at the very moment when he was twisting a dagger around in my poor little loving, unheroic heart of flesh and blood. The only role I had played was that my ministrations had unlocked his heart, opened it for another to take possession. Or, perhaps, he was particularly in need of love, those last days of August, I was not there, a pretty young girl was, he said those words about America, and he was bound, so that he could not awaken any more and see things as before. This would explain the overflow of feeling in his last letters, it would explain his putting me on a level with Dr. Marx. The only thing that remained was for me to accept the readjustment, and alas! that I could not do.

My friends will not accept the explanation. They say that the one thing that not even he could forget, not even a man caught in the whirl of passion, was that for two years he had proclaimed to the world that I was his choice. And above all things, they reproach him with the manner of engaging himself, almost with undignified haste, to a girl after associating with me for four years.

But should I not understand and sympathize with him in love? I whose whole misfortune comes from love?

This, however, I see, unworldly as I am. Even if I could have controlled my feelings in his presence, even if I could have pretended to cool friendship, and associated with him without becoming an adulteress, respect for the world demanded the break with him that is killing me.

There are many things in the matter that puzzle me, and that go round and round in my head even while I translate four thousand words a day in his book—I am puzzled by his change of manner toward me a year ago. I had not grown younger, so he must have made up his mind that my age was outbalanced by my qualities of mind and heart—and my devotion to him. If he made up his mind to that, and there is no other way of explaining the peculiarity of his change of manner, and he thereby broke down in so reserved a person as I always have been, the last barriers, and tempted me to show him all there was in me, to reveal to him my inmost thoughts on men and things, why did he not declare himself before he left for Europe? Why did he then write as he did, and call forth such letters as I wrote him? Why did he connect the crisis in Amsterdam with his father once, and later with indecision about his engagement? Was that the time, when in spite of passion for the girl, he saw my relation to him clearly again? And when he deliberately cast me aside? But if he deliberately cast me aside, why did he permit an overflow of feeling to creep into his letters to me? Why did he write at all? Why did he announce his engagement last of all to me, if he cast me aside deliberately? A deliberate act implied knowledge of my feelings. Why did he not tell it to me first, and wait to announce it here when it was announced in Berlin, and so give me time. Why indeed did he engage himself before seeing me? Would the girl not have waited? Is that the sort of girl he has preferred to me and my unquestioning patient love? Why did he say he had done the unexpected? Why did he ask me to write to the girl, though the girl wrote to Mrs. Marx of her own accord. In my case she had not found it seemly to make the advances. But if he is innocent of all this, and I was not cast aside, why does he not or did he not, make an effort to retain my friendship?

These are the things that puzzle me. But I must admit that there are some that ought to puzzle him, if, indeed, he ever allows a thought to stray in the direction of my unhappiness. He can charge me with several hypocrisies: I often told him I was happy to be allowed to help him because it kept me in vital connection with Jewish work. It was the truth, too, and the other truth, that it kept me in connection with him. I dared put into words only once, this summer when I was working on the Introduction, when I told him I must do it or be unhappy, because it was the only way I could keep close to him. But in how many acts did I express the larger part of this truth!

My other hypocrisy is connected with the engagement. He may justly ask why I did not face him at once with my outraged feelings, why did I wish him happiness with my supplanter, why did I write the letter to his fiancée—did he read that letter only with his eyes or with his mind as well?—Why did I do the extreme thing of advertising in words if not in manner that I was happy in his happiness?

I wonder whether he would understand it if I told him. I do want him to be happy, and one of my greatest sources of unhappiness now is that I was not strong enough to continue as I—began—that my body was too weak to carry out the resolve of my soul as I stood next to him and heard the story of his love. O! how I prayed for strength to hide all my misery from him! It was impossible. He quotes a sentence in the Legends, that he who begins a good deed and fails in carrying it to completion, brings misfortune upon himself. I wish I could make him understand how much of my unhappiness is expressed there. My only consolation is that in his serenity he is not in the least disturbed by what I feel and by what people say.

But if he puts a thought upon this miserable business, I have no doubt my poor little hypocrisies will rise to his mind as indictments, for, it seems, I have nothing to hope for for myself in his former feeling for me, and nothing to hope for for myself in his clear-mindedness. He has cast me out of his life. He is serene and happy, I am disturbed and miserable. I need him every day, every moment. O how many have been the beautiful days this beautiful fall when, in other circumstances, we would have enjoyed God's earth together, and God's creatures in each other. And I do not dare go out in the sunshine, I can only go after darkness has fallen, because I must cry and sob whenever I am not working hard. I am sure he does not miss me! I still value his good opinion, I want him to know that my conduct is not dictated merely by wounded pride—though some of it is—but chiefly by disappointed love. I would like him to know—O what would I not like him to know—that everything is sealed up in me, that I still treasure up things and thoughts to discuss only with him, and he never comes, that I think of him all day long and all night, but it's no use!

I know only too well what he would say if he read this record—"Fool, Ridiculous!" Perhaps he would even call me by that dreadful word "*Gouvernantenseele*" [soul of a governess or school marm]. Or perhaps he even thinks of me at all, as a designing old woman, like the Zuleika of his Legends. But he cannot, cannot, if he remembers a single one of our precious Riverside walks. Or perhaps he compares me with the fresh young girl he is to marry, and he shudders. But in justice he should tell himself that he has added twenty years to mine, by the disappointment he caused me.

There is but one thing that might possibly, relieve my pangs and give me a small measure of peace—a frank talk with him. I long thought that I would have a talk with him as soon as I should have sufficient control over my tears and my voice, and my feelings. That time has been long in coming, but I now see that even when I am perfectly calm I may not resort to that opiate. I know it to be his principle not to look back with vain regrets and reproaches once he has set his face forward. He feels certain that at every moment in life he acts with due deliberation, weighing circumstances and arguments to the best of his ability, and more no man can do. That is the reason I said he was not a passionate man. But I have known principles to break down at crucial moments with the strongest of men and women. Especially principles connected with marriage and love can be undermined easily. Knowing him as I did, I should have said that it was impossible for him to contract an engagement as he contracted his. In fact, my knowledge of his character has nothing to do with my surprise, I have but to remember a clearly enunciated principle, enunciated as I said, on two definite occasions only this past summer. And yet he betrothed himself in haste.—I thought I would seek the explanation when he came to me with the Introduction proof. But he will never come with it, though he said he would!

Now even though his principle is not to repine, who knows whether a word I might say to him if we had an explanation would not rise up sometime and come between him and his wife, and make him unhappy. Perhaps it would stalk like a ghost between them at the moment when their marriage is consummated, and the peace of husband and wife is sacred! So long as I do not speak, the matter may be vague, clear as his mind is. I am so unhappy, that I can bear the loss of this possible surcease from pain too. And indeed what could I gain? The elementary fact is that I have lost him, and he is lost to me no matter which of my doubts he sets at rest. The only thing I could hope for is that he would give me an explanation of his conduct that would enable me to hurl a denial at his detractors.—As it is, he is slipping away from me as an ideal.

As I said, the elementary fact is that I have lost him as lover and as friend. I have had a hard life, my sister says a colorless life. Suddenly a light and a joy shone in upon it, and I looked into the future gratefully and buoyantly. Some Satan came and dashed the cup of happiness from my lips, and placed then a bitter draught, which I am draining slowly, drop by drop. Perhaps, if I did not have his book to work at, I could recover more quickly. But as I write, on this last evening of the year 1908, the year of my greatest happiness and at the same time my greatest unhappiness, I cannot but feel that though I may recover outwardly, my life is done. I shall probably go on working because I have disciplined myself to that all the days of my life. I shall probably learn to eat and sleep normally again, I shall probably cease to weep in every unobserved moment, I shall probably laugh without a pain, I shall probably even lose that sore heavy feeling on the left side of my chest—Strangers and even friends will cease to notice that something is wrong with me—I tell them unruly nerves, because it is not proper to say a broken heart. All this will happen, but I doubt whether I shall ever be the same as I was—was even before I knew and loved him. Before, I was unconscious of my womanhood and the happiness of love, he made me conscious of both, and now I am conscious only of loss of love and perhaps even of self-respecting womanhood. Thus must I thank him, even while I try and am unable to hate him. God bless him and the other woman, and God help me!

December 31, 1908.

RAINY TUESDAYS

Tuesday, January 5, 1909

A rainy Tuesday! I wonder whether he remembers how glad I used to be when the weather was bad on Tuesdays, it made his coming here for lunch seem worth while, I used to say, from his point of view. Always, always I thought of his greatness and superiority, and my little worth—and now I can only think of the wrong he has done me—how he has murdered me. And how I still love him and need him! These last few days have been nothing but bitter tears. A true Agunah he has made of me! Does it ever strike him that way, or does he think only of his right to assert his youth and its claims and the youth of the woman he has chosen above me and my sorrow?—It matters not whether the sun shines or the rain falls. It is always he of whom I think—and the thought is always pain. Pain all these wonderfully fine days we have had this fall and winter brought me, because in other days they would have meant walks on Riverside and happiness. Pain a rainy day brings me, because in other days he would have been at my side by my desk. It is all pain and darkness and void. And day by day, I translate his book! And he does not bring me the proof of that on which I worked for five years. Fool, fool!

So many things come back to me—I think about it all enough to make everything come back, to be sure. Today I remember his indignation whenever the matter of my mother's treatment by the congregation[3] came up. And yet there is nothing in the history of our family that can rank beside that except his treatment of me, and my mother herself puts it above the other in baseness and cruelty.—He once wrote to me that I was neither a Jew nor an American, in that I did not know how to guard my own interests. But never was I so guileless as with him. Alas! alas! If I write in this way, I am on the road to losing my ideal. If only I lose my love for him and return to a normal state. Perhaps I will wake up one morning cured of my infatuation and my sorrow. At present I cannot yet believe him capable of what they say he has done to me. He is not calculating. Something happened—I don't know what, and I was wiped out of his memory and his heart.

LOVING NOT WISELY BUT TOO WELL

January 7, 1909

After several—I don't know how many—wakeful nights, with pain from abscesses in my ear (that tells the tale of these last four months, and the ravages of sorrow on my physique) and still greater pain at my heart, I am having a comparatively quiet day, and on quiet days I see only his side—he could not marry one at my age and to ask him to remain unmarried, my companion, is to expect the superhuman of flesh and blood. And when I see his side, I am grieved that I should have inflicted pain upon him, for, however callous he may have made himself by now, at first he must have felt keenly this one aspect of our ruptured relations—that he had told his fiancée of our friendship. When he told me he had spoken of me—and her letter proves it—he looked at me warmly and gratefully, but also I must confess to the joy of his detractors, he spoke in a tone of voice as though he expected *me* to be grateful for his generosity in so speaking and thinking of me in the flush of his young love. But God knows how hard I tried to accept and live up to his view. I could not! And then there always remains his public acts toward me, designating me as the chosen one before the eyes of all! And there always remains his inevitable knowledge of my love for him, which should have made him come back unengaged to give me time to recover. And there remain all the other things, that I cannot banish from my mind. And even on my quiet days, I can find no balm. And on my quiet days, I miss his companionship more than ever. What shall I do to cure myself?

I have been two days without "copy" from him to translate. Does he realize now that I am not so slow as he always thought me—as he taunted me with being? Would it be a satisfaction to know his thought on this subject? No! Nothing is a satisfaction, if I cannot have his love in return for mine. There is no getting away from that elemental principle—how elemental my ruined soul testifies, I am like the earthquake-devastated region of Messina and Reggio. Oughtn't that *Massenunglueck* [mass disaster] make me forget my personal unhappiness?—

Suppose I had accepted his tacitly offered new (or according to him old) relation, how would or could he have lived up to its terms? Suppose this would have happened again as it happened last year; I waited around for him on a Saturday after the services—it was a beautiful day, I waited, and waited, and he did not come.—He had gone up to the library. In dejection I went on home, and slowly removed my wraps and even my gloves, not yet my hat, when the signal of six bells was given violently. I went to the window, and there he stood his face all puckered up with consternation, his child-eyes troubled, until I nodded, and flew down. Could he still be in consternation and trouble. Was that all friendship? Would he, could he come after me if the circumstances were repeated. I am as far as ever I was from understanding.

Last night I thought out one explanation, as unsatisfactory as the rest. The girl is young, he was truly attracted to her when he first saw her, he met her, and his evident admiration called forth all the coquetry of her nature, she exercised it upon him, and for once losing his habitual control over himself he did something, what I do not know, which was even more significant than the question about America. In Amsterdam the thing assumed big proportions. My age was against me at any rate, and he adjusted matters so in his mind that he made good the flagrant act whatever it was. Not a very flattering explanation to my ideal man! And what becomes of the flagrancy of his two years' public "attentions" to me. No! the explanation does not explain.

Mrs. Grundy,[4] the world, convention, spoke to me today through the mouth of Anna. She said, she did not understand how it was possible for an intelligent person like myself to "go on" with a man for so many years and not make sure of the sincerity of his intentions. She does not understand—and she is right not to want to understand—the coupling of intelligence with unworldliness. But my unworldliness is no sufficient excuse. There are other ways of doing besides sending one's brother to a man and bluntly finding out his intentions. In the summer of 1906 when the incident with the Marx's occurred (he insisted upon staying alone with me), when he chose to go down to Long Branch with me, when he wrote me from Tannersville about his walks and added that he would rather be taking them on Riverside, when he telephoned twice in one day whether I had returned from Maine—when so many other things happened, I should gradually have withdrawn from him. That would have been properly feminine, a proper concession to a proper convention. Only it seems I am too much of a woman, a loving trustful woman ever to be feminine.

But if I did not do that, why didn't I cry out when he had done the unexpected? when he connected that crisis of his with the girl and no longer with the father? when he said he had spoken of me to her? when he asked me to write to her? when he asked me whether I was happy about his engagement? when he gave me the buckle? when he asked me what was the matter with me? when he said I need not restrain myself in his presence? when finally, I told him I could not control myself sufficiently to take walks with him? I have only one reply: I loved not wisely but too well.

He himself, with all his scorn for which the world says, calls me a "fool" now for my unworldliness, I am sure I should have known that unless the word is spoken, a man will not hold himself bound. He once wrote me I was neither American nor a Jew, I did not know how to take care of myself.

He and Mrs. Grundy and Anna are right. Convention is historical, organized common sense, handed down for the safeguarding of those laboring under strong emotion. My love seems to have passed all bounds—or my trustfulness.

January 8, 1909

I have not shed a tear for twenty-four hours. Have I conquered myself? The long continued period of quiet seems to be due to the absence of his book from my desk—I have had no copy from him for three days—and the consequent absence of his niece from the type-writer desk outside. How can they let that child continue to come here? I ought to be flattered by their confidence in my generosity—I am sure I treat her with the same gentleness and consideration and forbearance as before, but consciously and intentionally not with the same affability. But how could they be sure I would not in my passion fly out against her?

At first, as I said, the inward calm made me see only his side, but as calm does not yet mean cessation of thought on the one subject—it is not absent from my mind a second—I have reached a clearer view of the situation as a whole. Those last three letters of his are plain now. They protest too much—too much on the subject of his egotism, too much on my having been victimized, too much on the character of my friendship as compared with Dr. Marx's, too much as to the "greatness" of my friendship for him. I felt all that dimly when I received them. But I did not have the commentary at hand. Now I am absolutely certain that up to the morning of August 29 he did love me, and he did know my strong love for him, and he did expect either to marry me or be my life companion unmarried. Then the inexplicable something happened—either a stronger love overwhelmed him or he distinctly made up his mind he must rid himself of the incubus of my age. The letters were a reconstruction of our past relations, a warning finger held up to me not to make any claim upon him, or I would suffer, for his course was determined upon—to be followed kindly if I was amenable, cruelly if I showed myself a "fool." I am absolutely certain now that is what happened. It shatters my ideal, but alas! not yet my love. Someday I may be able to explain to myself why my love persists.—This I know—he was not even a true friend, for he never took the trouble to find out the largeness of my nature, else he would have come back, and told me of his greater love, in confidence that I would set him free, and remain his friend, besides. I must conclude that he, too, is unhappy now, for his definition of happiness is duty performed, and I insist his duty lay with me—in spite of his not having "spoken" to me, I was his affianced wife before God and man. But man does not live by definitions alone, and so he probably is happy. May he remain so!

As for myself—I certainly have not lived by definitions. I believe I have done my duty day by day. Long I believed that duty would fill out my whole life. I did not say to myself I would or would not marry. I just lived as best I knew how to live. Then love did unexpectedly come, and it became my joyous duty to serve love's God, or a perfidious fate, forbid me to serve love any longer, and I can only hope I may become sane enough again to accept the decree with resignation and trustfulness—the same trustfulness with which I entertained love—and in righteousness, too, banishing love because it has become unholy now that he is to marry another woman.

Notwithstanding all this, or probably on account of all this, I am an unhappy, heartbroken woman.

"NO WAY OUT OF THE DARK"

Saturday, January 9, 1909

Saturday is the very worst day of the week now—because it was, with the exception of Tuesday, the happiest before. On the Sabbath I realize how the whole current of my being set toward him. All the calm of which I boasted a day or two ago, vanished when the Sabbath approached, and today I have been as uncontrolled as ever. Was it because he sent me fresh "copy" for his book? At all events, I could not trust myself to go to the synagogue, and I have quite made up my mind to stop going to the Seminary altogether, and find another place of worship, for his sake as well as mine.

But now I find that whether I am calm or perturbed, I feel that he wronged me cruelly. He owed me a duty, from which only I could absolve him, and I cannot help feeling that if he had kept his duty in mind while he was abroad, he would not have wanted to be absolved when he returned to me. Am I overrating myself?

To-day I suffered not only though realizing the loss of his companionship, but also the old sorrow for him came back—perhaps my rupture with him *does* hurt him a little, and so my life is marred, and what should be the happiest time of his life is not so perfect as it should be, all because I was not strong enough to bear in silence and apparent unconcern what I must bear at any rate. I hope, since he has thrown me over and has been guilty of a cruel wrong, he is at least reaping the benefits of what I cannot but look upon as an aberration in one so good, noble and gentle as I know him to be, and never gives me a thought.

January 10, 1909

Yesterday someone spoke of the marriage of Julius Pels to Hannie Neuman, and said that in congratulating him, she had added: I congratulate you particularly upon having married the girl you "went with" so many years. Two things I learned: That it seems to be a common thing among men to throw the girls over in whom they long encourage hope and love—another one of my unworldly ignorances it appears; and that an ordinary average business man showed more instinct for honorable conduct than my ideal man of culture and scholarship and high principle. The curious thing is that he is not unconnected in my mind with Julius Pels. He came over from Europe with his brother, at all events we had a supercilious conversation about the family. So in this record it has come out that I cannot classify him with his friend who could brave a convention, nor with the average businessman who was true to the woman he had spoken to in the acts of years—not a young woman, either; and I have, God forgive me, classified him only with the scoundrel who vilified him and whom I abhor.

Yesterday evening I went to a dramatic reading "Votes for Women." One of the motives was the life of a wronged woman, and her coming face to face with the man in her case. Her sadness had driven her into public work, and she is in a degree solaced. Why can I not find solace in work? Because I am not young, and am not taking up work as a new thing and a refuge? Because I have worked so many years? Or because I am condemned to work at *his* book, the once well-beloved? Or because he wronged my spiritual part entirely? Whatever is is, I see no way out of the dark into the light.

January 11, 1909

Yesterday someone spoke of having found it difficult to secure European passage for June and July, so many persons had already engaged it. The thought it awakened in my mind was not the prompting to seek a place for myself for the European trip which everybody says I ought to take as soon as his book is off my hands (and heart!), but only that he was probably one of those hastening to obtain a cabin that he might be on the other side in good time for his marriage. Since then, all evening and all night, envy and jealousy have had possession of me. That is what he has made of me—an Agunah filled with sobs and tears, and a receptacle for vices and vicious thoughts that never before had lodgement in my mind. O, if only I had never seen him—the darling of my heart!

January 19, 1909

Such wretched days and nights—as there have been since I boasted of calm! I do not know why the shame, and the humiliation and the pity of it have overwhelmed me anew and with all their original force. I still hope against hope that when this book is done I shall recover. But how many weary months of work there still are upon the book that once was my joy, and held promise of endless joy. My mother still harps upon the plan of moving away from this neighborhood. I haven't seen him for a month of days living here when I saw him daily. So there isn't much in that, I see him all the time at any rate. If I only had pride! But all I have is love, and love increases misery.

This is the supposition of one of my sleepless nights! Suppose the case had been reversed. Suppose he had returned from Europe to find me engaged to another man. The world would have condemned me utterly, despised me, and he?—He would have been full of scorn, but probably he wouldn't have cared. The real supposition is that he never loved me enough even to care whether I suffer or not. But why was he so needlessly cruel? Why for instance did he write in one of those last letters that I had no right to deprive him of my letters, knowing, as I did, they gave him pleasure? And the letter I wrote him in reply! I was so secure then in his feeling for me! God forgive him for that! He once said to me, long, long ago, that women forgive, perhaps, forget never. I do not forgive, because in my eyes my darling is still right no matter what he did—he has some good and all sufficing reason for it, because he is incapable of baseness. But if only I could forget.

To-day I suddenly had the picture of him as he looked—I don't know how long ago it is, it must be four years this May—when he came up hastily one Monday morning, and said with a dear little important air, that he had something to tell me. He had been in Philadelphia the day before, and he had made Judge Sulzberger understand that I needed clerical assistance, and he even threatened to withdraw his book unless I were given it, on the plea that it would not get done and therefore he would not continue to work at it. I remember that, angry as I was at the Society—for granting me through an outsider what had always been refused me, and rather churlishly at that, my chest became too narrow for my proudly swelling heart. It fairly ached—and now it aches all the time, and now I have but the one thought, to get rid of his book—the book I always feared would get done, or might get done, before he settled things with me, and then I would have to drift away from him. Things are settled! But what did his interference in my affairs mean? He who abstains so vigorously from meddling? And he was willing to say, almost directly, to an outsider like Judge Sulzberger, For that woman I change all my tactics and reserves?

Also it came back to my mind today, that during that dreadful interview on October 20, when he told me minutely about his engagement, he told me of Dr. Friedlaender's surprise at his betrothal, attributing it to his former stubbornly avowed preference for a bachelor's estate, I was told subsequently that the surprise was due not to the fact of the engagement, but to the girl's being in Berlin, instead of her being the woman in New York whom he had so long designated publicly as the wife of his choice. The story implies sympathy for me, and yet I cannot glow in it. To think that my darling made himself ridiculous before me by his misinterpretation of an emotion awakened by him, he who despises folly of every kind. Of the imputation of unrighteous conduct I do not speak. That hurts me doubly, for his sake and for mine, alas for mine! That imputation carries with it the blankness of despair in which I now spend my days and nights.

January 20, 1909

Today it is three months! I read yesterday that one of Ibsen's heroines, Hjordis in "The Warriors at Helgeland" says, "I have been homeless in the world from the day that you took another to wife. Ill was that deed of yours . . . When a man does that deed . . . he wastes two lives." The man she loved in generosity gave her to a friend who loved her. She finds out that the generous one loved her too.[5] In my case there was no generosity, not even confidence in my generosity, and I have no assurance from his lips that he loved me. But he has wasted my life—one life at least, and that he had no right to do, even to save his own, after four years of public proclamation of his attachment to me.

It is just about a year ago, when he had to undergo treatment for nose trouble, and again and again when he returned from the doctor's exhausted he came to us before going to the lecture, and asked for a glass of milk, and let me help him re-pack his nostril. What did it mean? Was that not equal to a lip-assurance of his love?

It seems I am one of the Asra that die when they love. But there are various ways of dying. At present my body lives on, but my soul and my heart and my brain are dead. And sometimes dreadful thoughts take hold of me about the life and death of my body. God help me!

He was not so wise as I thought him—there *is* love nowadays as there was love in the olden time. Unfortunately, I must illustrate it to myself, and at a time of life when no recovery seems possible.

ADVICE FROM SCHECHTER AND MARX

January 21, 1909

Yesterday the thing came to pass which I had been saying to myself should never happen—I had a talk with Dr. Schechter about my sorrow. But it came about naturally, and he was so gentle, so restrained, so wholly the sage, and not the impulsive prejudiced man, that I do not regret it. He told me not to stay away from the synagogue and not to leave New York, but to resume my relations with him. The last I cannot, unless there is some sort of explanation and he is hard as flint. Dr. Schechter says, I must forget what was a dreadful episode in my life, which I brought down upon myself because I was an innocent baby in worldly things, because I was too great an idealist, because I had no *Menschenkenntnis* [knowledge of human nature]. As though my love had anything to do with *Menschenkenntnis*. He spoke of his great scholarship, he even found an excuse for him, that his mother had wished him to do what he did. But I know that the excuse cannot hold water.—I know it, because I know that *"er sich nichts sagen laesst"* [He didn't want to be told by anyone], and I know it because I know the circumstances. He did not see his mother between August 28 & 29, and his mother did not know the girl. Finally Dr. Schechter said, it must be a consolation to me that I was avenged and he did the wrong. No, a thousand times no! I want my happiness back, not a self-righteous feeling. And his having done a wrong has not yet made me miss his companionship. I want him!

And, again, he like all the others assured me there was no humiliation to me, that all who know were on my side, Ergo they condemn him, my darling. And what do they know of my inward shame, that he who knows every fibre of my being as I have never shown myself to any other person, should have taken up with the first girl he met, after four years of intimate association with me. How can I have any self respect after that? And the public shame is greater than they know. And that he should have thought I had so little pride that I would continue to pretend friendship!

At last Dr. Schechter gave me two books of the *Weiberliteratur* and said he had made up his mind to furnish me with all, and I must work at that, that I must hurry and finish the Legends. Ah, but he does not know that the impetus to the *Weiberliteratur* came from him, too. He will be with me in its pages, as he is in the pages of the Legends. I asked Dr. Schechter whether intellectual pabulum could satisfy a heart-hunger, I know that it cannot.

But Dr. Schechter was kind, kind especially as he said little against him.

Things still continue to come back. Today I recalled the letter in which he gave me a gentle chiding for not wanting to share my troubles with him. That was while his father was ill. Oh, I am sure I could have made him happy, and he—what he could have made out of my life! Why, why, why?

January 22, 1909

A calmer day today, I did not have any work to do on his book and his niece was not here. Calm it was, but not without its shock of memory, and filled with thought of him. In the middle of the day, I told my mother that I was so much more composed than I had been all week and on my way from her room to my desk, the mail was handed to me. It contained the last issue of the *Revue des Études Juives,* which I always passed on to him. By the negatives in my life now, I see how full of positive contact it was with him before. And he feels none of that? Can that be possible?—I am not going to risk my new-found peace by going to the synagogue to-morrow.

January 23, 1909

I asked Dr. Marx whether to accept Dr. Schechter's advice to resume friendly relations with him; he advises against it with great decision. Also I asked him whether I should send the *Revue* to him, also, no. Whereupon he told me he had once asked him from whom he received the *Revue,* and he had answered evasively. That Dr. Marx said, showed his sense of guilt about his relation to me. Possibly, but also it may show the sensitiveness of the lover, who does not reveal to all the world all threads of his relation to the beloved. But in this case neither interpretation helps me—the event proves that he did not love me, and if our relation was the friendship he wanted me to believe it, then he was not generous, and my ideal crumbles more and more into dust!

Nevertheless, Dr. Marx knew he received it from me. He once saw my name on a copy. Dr. Marx says my whole misfortune is that I idealized a human being. He said fault, not misfortune. In any other person, it would be an amiable fault, contributing to her happiness. But in me in whom the last touch of *chen* [grace] was forgotten, it means an added source of unhappiness.—He has been with me all day!

PHANTASMAGORIA AND SELF-PITY

January 25, 1909

Yesterday at the meeting of the Publication Committee they discussed the Movement Series, and the additional subject of Rabbinism was suggested. When a writer was sought, he, it was agreed, was the only unexceptionable candidate, only, as the chairman said, the Society could not be turned into a "Ginzberg Publication Society,"—they had already a number of books contracted for with him. How my eyes used to swim in unshed tears of joy when such things were said, and how I used to have a struggle with my acute conscience, and finally tell him after all—reveal to him the secrets of the Society which thumbscrews could not wring from me otherwise. It is true, it seems what I have always said, my love for him could make me commit crimes. And now! My heart gave three or four heavy thumps—that is the way, I imagine, death must supervene after long pain and exhaustion—and the emotion was due to the mere fact that his name was mentioned in my presence, not to the *Shevah* [praise] attached to it—I am schooling myself to indifference! Indifference? It is acute indifference.

I remembered yesterday a conversation I had with him last summer on one of our walks by Riverside—the air was perfume-laden by the spring. The closing sentence was, "You know, I don't really know much about women." Perhaps he really does not know enough to have realized what he was doing to me when he *made* me love him, and when he then cast me off like an old shoe.

Lately, I have again and again been possessed by a sense of unreality about the whole thing—it is too monstrous for it to have happened. I get the feeling that I used to have in my childhood, when I was to have my picture taken, and the photographer put my head in a vise to keep it still. I think it can't be I, and it could not have come to pass, and when an artificial calm envelops me, suddenly a set of circumstances comes about which recalls an atmosphere of the happier days, and the pain is there in full force. That is what happened last night. As I was crossing the ferry, though it was foggy, wet-cold, and disagreeable, the mere standing near the gate while the guard was putting it down as we touched the slip, brought back the last time he brought me home from the Jersey shore then with my mother. We had been at Englewood. The night was starry, perfect, and he stood near me, he had sought the place next to me, and there was an air of ownership about him that I thought was unmistakable. And I was but six weeks younger then than on August 29, when he threw me over on account of my age. Or am I entirely mistaken? Is he innocent? Did *my* love create the whole phantasmagoria of *his* love? But is it possible he didn't know even so much about women that he innocently exposed me to three years of gossip? And he the most clear-minded of men! How hard it is for my ideal to die, only now I am convinced that the death of my ideal does not mean death to my love, I love him, him as he is, with all his faults.

Yesterday, I was thrilled by the newspaper account of how 1650 passengers of two ocean steamers in collision in the fog, the Republic and the Florida, were rescued by the intervention of the Marconi wireless. It summoned the ambulance of the deep seas—four ocean liners went steaming around looking for the victims. The picture of that rescue brought tears to my eyes. And then I continued to weep, because I could not discuss it with him. At least I must be grateful that my poor old battered heart can thrill with any emotion beside disappointment and hopeless love.[6]

January 26.

I realize more and more the mediocrity of my character,—my virtues are too small, my faults are too small, for full, deep-breathed living. The self-discipline that enabled me to control myself when the blow first fell counts against me, in another person it would have made for heroism, or, at least serenity. In me, it merely prevented the outbreak that might have cleared the atmosphere, but it caused this lingering, paralyzing pain with its progressive deadening of all my energies, perceptions, and interests. If I had cried out wildly, when he told me the fact, when he said he had done the unexpected, when he reported how he had referred the father of the girl to himself as the only man to tell him about himself, from him he would learn all the truth; when he connected the "crisis" with his engagement instead of the memory of his father; when he brought up again the equality between Dr. Marx and myself, when he told me he had spoken to the girl only of me, expecting me to be grateful for that crumb from the table of the gods, when he asked me to write to her, when he asked me whether I was happy about his engagement, when he gave me the belt buckle, when he asked me what *was* the matter with me, when he told me not to put any restraint upon myself in his presence, when he read her letter—if I had cried out at any time before we kept apart and began to avoid each other, the passion I would have displayed would have been reprehensible, perhaps from a philosopher's point of view, but my moral and physical sanity and balance would not have been unhinged for so many months. It was either—or, and I did both. If I repressed myself at first, I should have kept my peace forever, if I had stormed and raged at once, the rupture would have been justified.

I am a poor weak vessel, and my weakness is not amiable. If I could now only resign myself to my loveless fate, if every day did not bring me a reminder of my unselfishness toward him, my self-sacrifice where he was concerned, so that the self-pity might cease!

Self-pity! Today will be a long pull at his book—going over his corrections of the chapter on Joseph, when I must rub, rub out, his pencil marks in reply to my queries, which he used to answer standing by my desk. Today is Tuesday, too. And mechanical difficulties are arising as to his two volumes, in their relation to each other. I have a solution, but I cannot propose it to him, because it involves one step of friendly advice which I am not permitted to offer.

I wish I could stop writing down my thoughts. It is no relief to me any more, but I must repress myself with my family now. They do not understand why I go on sorrowing. Even they do not realize the measure of my love for him, and the measure of my sense of loss. Such a life as I am leading is no life. And so I resort to pen and paper in the hope of finding them opiates.

January 28, 1909

I go back to this diary as if it were an opiate. But in reality nothing deadens my pain. And I have nothing new to write. During my surplus hours last night it came back to me forcefully, that there was barely an interval of six weeks between his leaving me, with a thousand assurances of his love, and his engagement to the other woman. Six weeks! No, one night passed between his sending me the book and his determination to cast me aside. He treated me as a woman of the street, for he came back fresh from his engagement and proposed to take up the relation with me where he had dropped it, and no matter how he had forced himself into regarding it, he knew how I regarded it—to me it was love. And so he prostituted those four years of my devotion and of his in my eyes.

And perhaps he is right—perhaps I am nothing but a woman of the street seeing that my love for him persists. He has written me three business letters this week about his book, and cold as they are, the mere contact with his living personality through them fresh from his hand thrilled me. And they are silent witnesses against him. In spite of the errors in English, the vigorous use he makes of our language testifies to all I have been to him—he never could have written these without me. And still, or because of this, he does not need me.

January 26, 1909

Dear Miss Szold,

Replying to your letter of yesterday, I beg to inform you that *under no consideration* I would consent to the plan of mutilation decided upon by the Chairman of the Publication Committee of the Jewish Publication Society. I consider it under the dignity of a scholar to discuss such a suggestion and will only add that there will be *no first and third volume of the Legends* if the Jewish Publication Society is to carry out its plan and in due time I shall announce in the press that I was forced by the policy of your Society to give up continuation of the Legends.

I still believe that if you can make your printer work with more speed, the first volume of the Legends could be out in April. But this has nothing to do *with my determination never to allow* the publication of the second volume before the first and you would confer a great favor upon me if you would inform the Chairman of the Society of this my determination as soon as it will be convenient to you.

Very truly yours,

Louis Ginzberg[7]

January 29, 1909

Yesterday I went through our hall toward the entrance door, and a rush of feeling overcame me. When I analyzed it, it was a memory of something that came back to me for the first time since the current of my life has been changed. Over and over again, all last year, he would shake hands with me twice when he went away, if there was anyone else there, and sometimes when there wasn't. He would bid me goodbye, go out to my mother, take leave of her, and when I accompanied him to the door, halfway down, he would turn and again extend his hand, as though mine was to be the last contact. And yet, in spite of all these tokens, it is becoming clear to me that he only "loved" me, he was not "in love" with me. I was and am both. As for him and the girl on the other side, they are only "in love" with each other. I do not doubt that love will come, too, perhaps has come to him by reason of my protesting unhappiness. It was because he only loved me that he could go on from day to day without saying one word to bind himself, and also go on from day to day filling each with binding acts. But did he not see how cruelly he was wronging me in not crying a halt?

The other day I heard that he had asked Dr. Schechter's permission to dedicate the Genezah Studies to him, and I cannot rejoice that my and his joint work is approaching completion. Was I nothing more than an amanuensis in that? I wonder whether anyone is doing the Index for him that was still left for me to do? If he had only waited this one year, until all our common work was off! I think I could have stood it better.

February 1, 1909

This week-end has been as sorrowful for me as all the others. I dread the coming of the Sabbath! Friday evening suddenly a hitherto unremembered phrase from his letter of September 4 came back into my mind: "It is distressing to me to think that my friendship brings only sorrow and pain to my friends," or words to that effect. I think I must be very close to the words he uses. That is the way he ends the paragraph about feeling the necessity to tell me about his perturbed state of mind—the first time he calls me "victim."

Half a dozen persons—the Marxes, the Schechters, Adele, and Mrs. Davidson, to the last of whom I was forced to speak about it because I had repulsed her sympathy rudely—have said to me that they had never trusted him because he was "a man that did not talk"—"*verschlossen*" [closed up] the Germans call it. But he wasn't toward me! He said himself in that terrible half hour when he announced his betrothal to me, that he would probably not confide in his wife either—then I enjoyed more of his spiritual self than she will!

I also recalled something he said to me on one of the walks we had together since he returned an engaged man. It was altogether unprovoked. Nothing I said called it forth, nothing in the nature of the conversation. He said suddenly, "It was useless for us to take so much trouble about the title of the 'Legends;' the Rabbinical portion will never be written now"—as though to say, "So long as I had in mind making you my companion, I entertained the idea of a book in which you would help me as an equal almost," though he had never said definitely before, that he would do it when I would ply him with questions—no, not ply, but suggest it playfully. I wonder whether my interpretation is correct. Was he constantly at that time putting aside things as belonging to another life, as I was? The difference being that he was having joyous compensations of his own choosing, and I was weighted down with the sorrows of an Agunah!

Mrs. Malter arrived from Europe and I went to see her on Saturday. A double trial! She is young, handsome, happy in her husband and child, and the sight of her aroused the ugly jealousy that now has a place in my heart. But chiefly I could not but remember, how she and Dr. Malter, when writing to me, had never failed to mention him to me. My mouth was closed as with a screw all the time I sat there. Oh how he has humiliated me!

Out of this last humiliation the resolve has grown to have a talk with him. The fear of coming between him and his wife is futile. My silence has been as eloquent as speech, and neither silence nor speech will intrude itself between him, who is happy and cock-sure of his rightness, and her who is in love with love and will be happy and will in turn also love him, though love him as I did and do she never will. No woman who has ever written a letter like hers to me, even in her youth, can develop into a loveress like myself. Perhaps, though, I am mistaken.

I shall write to him to-night I think to come here Thursday night, and I shall write for what purpose. Perhaps he will refuse! And in truth I do not know what I expect to get from the talk. If he puts up a good defense, my ideal will be re-erected—and my love pangs redoubled. And if he does not, I will be where I am. In some occult way, I am hoping, it will restore my mental balance. There was always peace for me in his society.

I am told that the page proof of the Introduction has arrived, and he said they had done it so well, there was nothing for him to bother about—he wants to assure himself he can do without me even for such externals. He need not trouble himself, I know he can. I never fooled myself on that subject. But I should like to read it and make sure it needs no more revision, Oh how much love there is in these papers, besides the scholarship the world will see! Did he write the two papers? And what of the Indexes? What a fool I am!

CONFRONTING GINZBERG WITH HER LOVE

February 2, 1909

Today I decided to have a talk with him, and I have just had Adele mail my note to him. It reads:

"Dear Dr. Ginzberg:

I feel there are some matters in regard to our past relations that I would like to talk to you about. I hope you can come to see me Thursday evening of this week at about eight o'clock. In case this time does not suit you, will you let me know when you can come? Truly yours."—

I am prepared for the worst—that he will refuse to come, or that he will even disregard it and make no reply at all. That, however, may cure me of my insanity, I do not know what I expect to gain by this interview. I believe I am so low that I want one more talk with him—I cannot bear the idea of having parted with him petulantly without a rational explanation of my conduct. I wonder whether I shall have sufficient composure to tell him all I want him to know. Since I have made up my mind to speak to him, I have been calmer than since the thing happened. Will the calmness hold out until Thursday?

February 3, 1909

He had replied that he will come. I am still calm. Is it because I am going to see him and talk to him?

His reply consists of two lines at the end of a half-page business letter about the Legends: "Complying with your wish I will call on you tomorrow (Thursday) about 8 p.m."

February 5, 1909

He came, and we had a talk that lasted two hours and a half. I cannot set it down consecutively. The result is that I have my ideal back and my pangs *are* redoubled. He never had any feeling but friendship for me, he never suspected that my feelings were anything else but friendly toward him. I asked him about various expressions I had used in my letters and my conversation, extravagant expressions, and he said he knew that our friendship was extraordinary and that my nature was extraordinary. All the circumstances which the others explained as calculated acting, he simply shrugged his shoulders about. They were to him as I said they might be—perfectly natural friendliness. The comparisons with Dr. Marx he was not aware of. He still considered me his best friend, and for his part he could resume our association where we had left off. He realized now, in the light of later events, that he had done wrong in taking so much from me, in absorbing me, but it had never entered his mind that it was open to misconstruction. If he had found me engaged on his return, even if he had come back unengaged, he would have rejoiced if only the man of my choice had pleased him, and he would have expected me to continue associating with him. As for his own engagement, he thought no one with the exception of his mother, would have been so happy about it as myself, and he looked forward to closer association with me after his marriage, on the same terms as before.

I spoke freely, I told him about my feelings, the various manifestations of them toward him, of what I had interpreted as signs of his love, I told him about the views of the world, about Mamma, and Dr. Marx,—he was panoplied in his rectitude and in his happiness. I told him why I had finally broken off associating with him—I had been too happy with him. I did not tell him half of which I might have told him. Once he interrupted me to say that if I cared to tell all the signs and tokens, he had no objection. But did I think it served a purpose? For him my assertion that I loved him was enough, and I had to believe that whatever he was, he was not a blackguard, who would willingly injure a woman privately and publicly.

Towards the middle of the conversation he said that a practical problem had arisen. His fiancée had written several times to inquire why I had not replied to her letter. He had at first said nothing. Then he had written that apparently it was my opinion the relation could not continue as it had been now he was to be married, and she had expressed sorrow that I should think her so selfish.

At another point, he said that until I showed him his fiancée's letter, and did not ask for the picture she mentioned in it, which she had sent for me—the only one she had sent except the one for him, he did not understand what was the matter with me. As for my being a learned woman, what he had told her was that I was the only person who understood him.

I do not remember whether it was then or another time that he confessed the question of his relation to me had come up between him and his fiancée. He said he had considered it his duty to tell her at once about me. I asked why? His answer amounted to a mental shrug of the shoulders. And she had asked, whether there was nothing more between us, and he had called her a child, I wanted to know whether that question had not made him think back and see our relation in my light too. No!—To show me how innocent he was, he said he had received one of my letters in Berlin on Yom Kippur. All day he could not open it. In the evening on the return from the synagogue, he snatched a bite, and said before he ate he must read the letter from his best friend!

I asked what was I to do? Resume relations with him knowing that I love him still? He said I was to consider only myself. I was the only sufferer, he was not suffering. He would write nothing of it to his fiancée. I agreed. I reiterated that I missed him all the time, that I had been bottled up these three months, I had spoken to no one. He returned, he had neither. But I said the difference is that you did not miss it. He could not say that he had not. But it was evident either that he was careful or happy.

He is happy, he is in love with her, and the woman who marries him is lucky, and I alas! am not the lucky woman.

The one thing he could not reply to was his having associated with me while deserting Dr. Marx.

I asked him why, if it was all friendship with him, he had not come back and helped me out of my distress. He said, he had no right to assume that his conjecture as to the cause of my avoiding him etc. was correct. If he had come and spoken to me, and had been wrong!

His main argument against the world's taking my view of the situation was that the Davidsons had invited us together the first Sabbath after his return, and they were not barbarians, and Dr. Davidson had known him since his being in this country.

As for the age question he said it was ridiculous, it would not have entered his mind not to marry me on that account.

When he left, he said, it was with the understanding that as far as he was concerned he was my friend as he always had been, and had the same feeling for me as before.

I asked him about the letter I had written to his fiancée, how he could let me send it, how she failed to see its real meaning. He had seen nothing amiss in it. As for my writing it, he said he did not consider it hypocrisy on my part, he said he would have done it in the same circumstances.

All this is put down higgledy-piggledy. But I cannot remember how it went, and this morning I am crushed. If fate had only been kinder!

On going out he expressed his confidence that I was strong enough morally to get over it. He was not afraid to associate with me even if I had that feeling in my heart for him—he was sure of me. I am not sure of myself by any manner of means.

There was much, much more, but I cannot recall it to put it down.

I must put the thing out of my mind and my heart. I must not talk about it any more. But I must think how to act for his sake and for her sake too. She knows by this time.

As things come back to me I shall write them down. I asked him whether he classified my working for him with what I did for others.

He said, by no means. He knows it was different, he knew my friendship for him was a thing apart, but friendship it nevertheless was.

I asked him also whether he was not struck by my manner the day he came in and saw Dr. Schechter's book in a fine binding, and when he admired it, I said instantaneously, it is yours. He acknowledged that he had felt uncomfortable.

I told him I did not understand how with my overpowering feeling for him it had failed to penetrate to him.

It remains true, I do not understand! And it remains true, I am an unhappy, broken-hearted woman, and what have I lost or rather failed to gain, for it seems I never possessed him, is a jewel beyond compare. And he is so clear-sighted and he did not understand what was going on inside of me.

At some point or other he said his not understanding may have been due to his being associated so little with women. That tallies with what he told me one evening last summer.

He said I would get over it. I demurred, and asked how he would feel if his fiancée were taken from him by another man. That was different he said, there was reciprocal affection. But I insisted, what of the four years in which I had thought my feelings were reciprocated.

He maintained he had used equally extravagant expressions in his letters to me. Yes, I said, and I interpreted them in my way.

February 6, 1909

One of the questions he asked me was whether he seemed embarrassed when he announced his engagement to me, and I said yes. This record testifies to it that his question did not suggest the opinion to me. I wrote in my account that perhaps his air of embarrassment was due to the natural hesitation one feels in telling of an unusual personal occurrence. But now as I think back, it was more, the embarrassment manifested itself in an over-exuberance of spirits, not in hesitation. But over-exuberance also may be natural, and may be natural precisely in a person of his restrained temperament.

At one point he unemphatically acknowledged himself wrong in having permitted me to do for him, in having allowed things to go in such a way that I saw and spoke to only him. His voice was perfectly even, and then he went on "And for that I must apologize to you" as though he had stepped upon my dress instead of my heart. On the whole his manner during the interview was not unkind, but it was far from comforting, there was not a suggestion even of the tenderness of the warm friendship he protested for me. That may have been wisdom and design. He may have found that an approach thereto would but add to my misery. But on the other hand, was it necessary to say such a thing as this? I told him how I had looked forward to a celebration over the Introduction, now it had been frustrated, and as for the celebration over the Legends! And he said: "It has turned into a legend too." He might have suppressed that.

Several times he uttered his Y a t-t-t, to indicate that a human being must resign himself to the inevitable. How I used to love the peculiar exclamation, which is habitual with him.

If he thinks his fiancée is a child, he is mistaken.

February 7.

Her penetration in asking whether there was nothing more between us, me and him, than mere friendship, shows worldly wisdom beyond her years, and can spring only from a few "experiences" of her own. *I* would not have asked the question. But on the other hand, I would not have engaged myself even to him after three conversations, and some persons may call that experience and worldly wisdom on my part. I hope she will not pursue the subject farther.

He says that he is sure his fiancée would not object to his continuing the intimacy with me on the old footing. I think he is mistaken in that, too. At all events, I told him I would not have permitted it if the positions had been reversed.

They do seem to be in love with each other. As he left, he said coldly, that I would get over it. I asked him how he would feel if his fiancée were taken from him by another man. He returned with belligerent animation, that was different, there had been reciprocal affection. And I said, I had thought for four years there had been reciprocal affection between us.

Perhaps there is more to her than I expect, perhaps she is a better woman than I am now showing myself to be.

After all it is a flimsy excuse which he offers as to not having come, in the consciousness of the friendly nature of his feelings always for me, and helped me out of my distress. Suppose it had turned out that his conjecture as to the cause was wrong, suppose I had repulsed him! It would have been one sacrifice of dignity for my numberless ones of time, effort plus dignity.

It is curious how a person as innocent as I believe myself to be has been hounded by fate. He believes the world, our world, sides with him. Nobody moves muscle to disabuse him. Dr. Schechter congratulates himself that when he announced his engagement, he had enough restraint not to burst out with my name. Also Dr. Friedlaender, Dr. Marx spoke only in a veiled way in 1906, about wanting to hear of our engagement. He seems not to have understood. Dr. Malter, of course, is not in a position to speak. Apparently his sister-in-law has not opened *her* mouth. I told him how she had tortured me with her exclamations, "If he only would marry!" And he laughed and said, that that was what she said to everybody. Did she say it with the same significant look? I wonder whether she would be honest enough to tell the truth.—I mean the truth as to how his conduct struck her and all outsiders. And so he is panoplied and fortified, within and without. Yesterday, my mother tells me, he was "called up" for the *Shirah*[8] at the synagogue. How proud I was of the same distinction accorded to him last year! And now it adds to my soreness.

I told Dr. Schechter the result of my interview with him. He first said he was sorry I had written, then he was glad I had done it. He advises aloofness, but a visit to his wife when she comes.

Adele has confessed that she cut him. That is the reason he said, my future conduct was a matter for me to decide upon with my family. She and Thomas do not believe his explanation, nor does Mamma, nor does Dr. Schechter.

I do. He did not love me. Impossible as it is to understand it, I *will* to believe that he even did not know that I loved him madly— how could he escape the knowledge,—because he is as he himself says, not a blackguard. My God, all those looks meant nothing! I *will* believe him in spite of the testimony of my senses and my inner sense. I told him the conversation with him had saved my ideal. And so it shall be. Now it only remains for me to find a modus vivendi. I am still under obligations to speak to Dr. Marx once more, and then I shall settle that once for all, as to him and as to her.

In a half hour I go to the funeral of Dr. Radin. I wish I were in his place. I have no desire to live without my darling. The real question is, not whether I have the desire, but the ability. God help me!

One of the things I asked him was, had he not noticed at the Post Office when I bade him good-bye that I was ready to faint. Yes, he had seen I was much affected.

And what had he thought of my letter in which I put him next to my father. He said, yes, I know whatever that may mean. And what of that one, in which I had blessed the Mauritania for bringing me his letter so soon. Extravagant language, he had called it. But why did I use extravagant language? And after his telephoning, I had written how beautiful the summer had been through him, and how I missed Hag and Chag etc. (meaning that I missed him). A mental shrug of the shoulders was all the answer to that.

And then I told him how in spite of all I had much to thank him for—the awakening of my womanhood, the understanding of the mystical, cosmical relations of the sexes (he nodded his head, as though I in turn had opened up that vista to him, but he was not generous enough to say so), stimulating intercourse, and in short, I humiliated myself, as Adele would say. Was it fair after such a pouring out, even if he was engaged to another woman, seeing, besides, that he had been, to say the least, heedless in calling forth all the affections in my being, that he should now in going away, say, "O, you'll get over this! Are you perhaps working too hard? Sometimes these things are physical!" In the first place he knew how hard I was working at his book, in the second place, had I not said that I could understand some of his difficulties because I knew what it was to be in love. Could he not have imitated me? Could he not have suppressed his diagnosis? Or did he want to let me know that he considered me a "woman"?

Once in the course of the interview, when I asked him whether he thought my willingness to do for him was comparable with my relations to others, he said, no, he never put himself in a class with others, he considered himself extraordinary, and he considered me extraordinary. Did he think that would help me? If only he had considered me an ordinary woman with a great capacity for love, whose heart would be broken by such conduct as his!

Adele is right, if friendship meant so much to him, why did he not secure me as a lifelong friend. Marriage can offer nothing better, so long as there is not physical repulsion, and that there was not.

I saw him this morning at the funeral of Dr. Radin, and I suffered renewed pangs. What shall I do? I hope Dr. Marx will speak to me soon. Perhaps I will quiet down then. I cannot say I have great hopes.

Sophie got a semi-permanent position. She wants to work for me in the evening. It is not a practicable plan—fortunately.

CONFIDING IN MARX; RECONSIDERING GINZBERG

February 8, 1909

Last evening I reported my interview with him to Dr. Marx. I did it minutely, not as to Dr. Schechter by way of summary. I wanted to get Dr. Marx's impression, and I wanted to clarify my own. Dr. Marx calls him still, in the light of my narrative, which I am conscious of not having colored, sensual, selfish, ungenerous and conceited. He advises as modus vivendi natural intercourse with him *and* no attitude at present towards his future wife, but whatever I do to have only one consideration—myself. On the point of sensuality, he told me several things that I must put down. He said that to call our relation "friendship" in contradistinction to "love" was a juggling with words. Real love was sublimated friendship, which tallies with Adele's remark that such friendship as ours was, justified, demanded marriage. Furthermore, Dr. Marx said, he had it from an older man that I ought to congratulate myself on an escape. If he had married me, the catastrophe would have happened afterwards. And, he went on to say, an older man of varied experience sometimes saw clearly into these things. I was so bold to ask who the man was, and he mentioned Mr. Lubarsky's name. I do not think I have set it down before that Mr. L. called him a "hog," a "*Schwein*," when he heard of his engagement. Dr. Marx went on to say that Mr. L. had talked it over with Dr. Radin, and they had agreed that I had been saved from a greater misfortune than has befallen. Perhaps, but even now I am willing to take the risks. Something corroborative does, however, come back to my mind. On the walk down to the dock when he went to Europe in 1907, we spoke of Ruth Schechter's engagement to a man she had not seen since she was eleven years old. And I said that although I was certain she would be happy, I thought in general it was a dangerous experiment—that the senses had a word to say in such matters, too. I remember now that he gave unusually vigorous assent, and for a moment I was mastered by the impulse to explain to him that I meant the eyes wanted to see and the ears to hear, not senses in the connotation of tickling sensuality. But I refrained.

So Dr. Radin knew of it, too. He said not a word, of course, he must have known. Did he not go with us, my mother and myself, to see Dr. Radin. I do not remember how long ago, I think it is now two years? He had asked us to take him along when he heard us arrange to go. I felt like an "engaged couple" then, and a little uncomfortable at that. Two significant incidents connected with that visit come back to me. There were two seats in the Elevated, and with the excellent heart-memory I have, I signed to him to take the seat looking forward because I remembered from long before, he could not bear to ride backward. And on our way back, I insisted upon his not going home with us, but taking the subway direct to his house. I should not have been so "un-young-ladyfied," . . . . considerate. He might have realized then that I was an ordinary woman with a capacity for love that transcends friendship.

Dr. Radin had my strict notions on the subject of the relation of the sexes. He condoned no laxity.

As for my interview with Dr. Marx, it did me a world of good. The ice crust around my heart melted for the first time since many a day, and I slept well almost all night. This morning I still feel the good effects, though there is an occasional twinge in the heart region, and I think my prime handwriting today as compared with yesterday shows that I am more vigorous. It was agreed between Dr. Marx and myself the matter would not be mentioned again, unless he spoke with him—which now is not at all likely. He knows that I made Dr. Marx my confidant, I even told him that Dr. Marx knew of the interview with him, he has seen Dr. Marx half a dozen times since, and he has not spoken—he never will—he believes himself innocent, or his detractors would say, wants to act as though he believed himself innocent.

My feeling about the interview now is: He is hard towards me in order to be loyal to his fiancée, he is too self-righteous, he calls it objective, he was not generous, he made it appear that he was capable of the highest sort of friendship and I was not; he was not humane in putting my excitement down to physical weakness, though I revealed my heart history of four years. He should have permitted himself to speak more warmly of his fault in the matter—his having absorbed me so completely, instead of "apologizing" and saying that he was not a blackguard, and he did not like to see any one—(not me)—suffer.

My explanation is that he is deeply in love, he does not dare be gentle with me ever, for fear on the one hand, of softening me still more, and on the other hand, giving color to his fiancée's suspicions as to our past relations. He was in a difficult position. But I did not put him into it. I gave him a chance for weeks to come to me, and say I had misinterpreted friendship, and I gave him another chance at the beginning of our interview, when I asked him whether he was under any misapprehension as to the purpose of my having [him] come to me. He took neither. He hardened himself toward me—he gave me no help in my distress.

In spite of all this, I hold with my former opinion of him. He may be a faultier, frailer man than I thought him—but he is still the man I love. I believe him that he did not love me—one of the signs is that he has given up all that valetudinarianism in which I am afraid my pampering way with him encouraged him; from the first day of his return he was vigorous in manner. Hard as it is to understand, I am going to try to believe that he did not realize my distracted love for him. But I shall put him out of my heart, and out of my thoughts, and out of my life, insofar as it is possible to eradicate those four years in which he constituted the warp and woof of my existence. I shall set my face forward, and act naturally—as naturally as I can—and let circumstances do the rest. As for his fiancée, she does not now exist for me, no matter what her young agonies may be. The future must take care of itself. God help me to carry out this plan of action.

This morning I blotted the above with a thump to express finality. I thought I would not add anything for a long time. But the memories keep coming, and I want to rid myself of all of them. This thing that I am going to write of now has been in my mind all along, but I always forgot to put it down. I wrote of the lovelight in his eyes whenever he looked at me from his return from Europe in 1907,—or rather a little while after his return, for I remember that it was not there when he visited me on the day of his return—until his leaving for Europe in 1908. In spite of the eager flush on his cheeks when he announced his engagement, the light had gone out of his eyes when he spoke to me after his return, and it never came back. His eyes were innocent but not illuminated. This is not self-deception. I can attach the recognition of the change to a particular incident. That Monday after my return from Baltimore when he worked with me at the Seminary, he casually picked up a book at the Library and saw that he was taken to task by the author for poor Latinity in his *Haggada der Kirchenväter*.[9] He took it good-humoredly, and told me about it with laughter in his eyes, and yet it was not as before. In those other days, he looked me in the eyes until there was a response in mine. Now there was laughter, but not a quest for sympathy. Did that look of former days belong to the paraphernalia of friendship? If so why did it not survive his engagement? And so it was all the three weeks of my pathetic struggle to maintain a friendly footing—his eyes were dull, expressionless. Oh, I am sure he loved me. My "will to believe" is weakening. And I must believe in him in order to believe in myself, for I have merged myself in him altogether. I cannot understand, and I never will be able to understand what happened.

QUESTIONING THE FRIENDSHIP

February 9, 1909

What the world saw! Have I put down before that Mrs. Marx told me that in 1907, when he was in Berlin, and much with them after his father's death, she prevented her mother from arranging for him to meet an "eligible young lady" who would have been a very fine mate for him? Mrs. Marx implored her mother to desist, saying "*Ich habe meine guten Gründe*" [I have my good reasons].

What he and I knew: It was that hot long Sunday, when I was miserably sick, the twelfth day before his leaving for Europe last summer, 1908, which was spent at the Seminary at work on his "Introduction" from 8:30 in the morning, until 6:30 in the evening. When we returned for supper, we found Fannie Kahn here. He washed up, so did I, not having the time to change my dress. After supper a walk to Riverside was proposed for our visitor's sake. He stuck to my side, and Mamma *had* to take charge of Fannie. As we sat in the park, I could do no more than address a few occasional words to her on my right, because he on my left claimed my attention in his compelling way. When we started home, to escort Fannie, again he was at my side. On the way I said, "How is it about letters this summer? Am I to write to you?"—"Of course you are, what a question!"—"I always feel queer about writing to you. I know you dislike writing and receiving letters."—"It depends upon to whom and from whom."—I was elated, and six weeks later he had forgotten me. And now he can have the cruelty, when I pour out my wounded woman's soul to him, under the most humiliating circumstances, to ask me whether my grief has not a physical cause. He of all men should know my inner strength. It never gave way under the stress of work for him joyously done.

Adele says she must cut a man who engages himself in the frivolous way in which he did. What is his mysterious power over me that

I do not cry out against him when he is so cruel to me, that I cannot see the baseness everyone else points out to me in him [?] I cannot understand his power, and I cannot understand his action.

I was quiet yesterday externally, I did not speak of him. I thought I should be able to refrain from writing about him. But I will permit myself this outlet for the feelings I may no longer speak of to any one, until I have set down all my memories, at least all such as are tangible enough to be put into words. After all my happiness in the past and my sorrow now are due to an impalpable something that entered the atmosphere in which I lived, and the impalpable something was radiated from his dear personality.

He said in our recent interview, he knew me to be an extraordinary woman. Does extraordinary mean to rise above human feeling? It means to be intensely human, it means to raise ordinary feelings to an extraordinary plane. And in that respect I am extraordinary. My love for him was not an everyday affair, though he has prostituted it to the level of an "affair."

It comes back to me that years ago, in 1905, we, he, Adele and I, had a discussion about a related question. He said he did not understand a purpose of the play Adele had written and the attitude of her heroine, why an intellectual woman should crave approval. We two women cried against what he said, I in pain, because even then I felt that he never gave me the little caresses, for what I did for him, the little praise I craved. As we went on from month to month I didn't care so much whether he stroked me down, because there was the life prize before me—he made me feel that he needed me, that was more than caress, and petting and praise. And still how happy I was when he gave me approval last spring for that Yerushalmi—Babli-comparison! Perhaps it is true, he does not understand women. And the other night, when I told him that I had relinquished my desire for a picture of his, because of his praise, was I mistaken in thinking he was a little startled out of his forced coldness? O, I don't know! It may be that I have been subtler than the facts warranted all along.

February 10, 1909

The "atmosphere" came back to me yesterday in such a way as to overwhelm me with longing, doubt and grief. I was reading the Sunday paper, and I suddenly had the picture of myself clipping two columns from it with a description of walks in the neighborhood, and then showing it to him. He took it, and asked me to let him have it, and thereafter until he left for Europe he would draw it from his vest pocket or inside coat pocket from time to time, and with a quick warm look at me study it. The result was only one actual walk—the one to Spuyten-Duyvil when we saw the red-bird flash in and out, and he made me climb through that dreadful unlady-like thicket comrade-fashion (will he ask her to do such things?), and we stood in the door frame of a cottage while the rainstorm came down. But even if there were no other walks, his manner whenever he drew the clipping out and sent me one of his looks!

He was always willing to draw upon my wonderful physical strength, and yet he could venture to say to me the other day that my present distress was physical, and that I would get over it—he who knows how tenaciously I cling to dear memories! No, there was not even real friendship on his side. Else he could not have said, with an air of magnanimity, that he for his part was leaving me with the understanding that he could resume our relations when I had broken them off. He implied that my conduct had not been magnanimous. It was the demi-god air that I love in him, to be sure. But I realize now that he is a fallible human being, whose frailty has caused me a terrible sorrow. Take this! He said he would have rejoiced if on his return he had found me engaged to a man of whom he could approve. If he were not too sure of himself, he would realize that his conduct would have made such a consummation impossible, even if I had been the youngest and fairest of women, because for four years he had been shouting from the housetops, "Beware, transgressors, keep off, this woman is mine!" No one would have dared approach me. In his supercilious disdain of the world (and in my humble disregard of all but my own darling), he did me irreparable mischief, if, indeed, it be true that he never loved me, that he did not know that I loved him.

How much finer it would have been, if even after my public exhibition of my grief, he had taken the opportunity of our recent interview to confess freely, to plead infatuation with the girl in Berlin, to throw himself upon my mercy. *I*, in my great love, would have understood his love, and I need not now be eating out my heart for both the loss of his love and his friendship, and for the loss of my ideal, my demi-god. If only all these revelations about his character and his fallible mentality would uproot my love for him from my heart.

Yesterday I removed the inkwell from my desk which he gave me in the fall of 1905 on his return from Europe. I have no hope that the removal of a physical reminder will help me cast him out of my memory. It was Tuesday, and I wanted to do something forceful on that beloved day. That is the trouble, the days, the minutes themselves, are eloquent of him.

He twice said he felt uncomfortable, when I insisted upon giving him Dr. Schechter's book, and again upon carrying his coat. That was not the question. Did he know what it meant on my part? For that after all is the important question—did he know that I loved him to distraction? If he did, and he felt "uncomfortable," or in other words, did not love me, why did he continue more and more to seek me? And why did he come back as he did, and ask me whether I was happy over his engagement? This is the important question, and it is the aspect of the case which continues to trouble me. No amount of willing to believe his statement that he thought my actions were dictated by pure "friendship" can make me overcome my torturing doubts. But why do I not disbelieve and cast love for him out of my heart? Why do I go on missing him sorely—I mean sorely in its literal sense.

Friendship? If he had seen me associate in the same way, or approximately the same way, with three or four other persons, with one other person, he might have called our relation mere friendship. But, of course, he is entrenched on all sides. If I hold that up to him, he will say that he is not like any others, and that at once any relation to him must assume a different character from a similar relation to another person. A human being so sure of himself will never realize how cruelly he has wronged another. And still I love him and miss him minute by minute.

Today is Wednesday. It has been raining all day, and now, late in the afternoon, the sun has come out. In the old days he would have pretended he had something to look up at the Seminary, and would have come over here for a walk, or for supper and the evening. And all this is over, and I cannot understand why and how it came about.

February 11, 1909

He emitted almost a snort when I recalled to his mind how often his sister-in-law had said to me, significantly, "If he'd only get married," maintaining that it was a constant exclamation with her, and could not be addressed as testimony to the world's vein of our relations. Either he did not ask her about it, or she lied to him. It was a constant cry with her, but did she always accompany it with a significant look at the person addressed, and did she always say significantly,

"I will never forgive my brother-in-law, if I hear of his engagement first from someone else, he must tell me himself before anyone else does," as much as to say, "If you ever are engaged to him I don't want report to bring me the news, for I know it is imminent."

THE BREACH OF PROMISE INSINUATION

February 12, 1909

Today it is six years since I met him for the first time, and since I have loved him. Yesterday something came to my knowledge that makes me believe almost that the tense of "have loved" is not correct. I think the spell is broken. I must introduce another strand in my narration of my poor battered heart.

A series of inner circumstances compelled me to speak to Mrs. Davidson about my troubles. I think it must be two weeks ago when I did it. The fact which gave him so much comfort as an argument, that the Davidsons, no barbarians, as he said, had invited us both together on the Saturday after his return, that same fact had naturally been rankling in me all these months. I felt that they sided with him—that they justified his act on account of my age. Therefore I repulsed all of Mrs. Davidson's gentle advances brusquely and once I went so far as to say, when she asked me to walk with her, that I was not in a companionable mood, and preferred not to inflict myself upon anyone. My conduct towards her was atrocious, impardonable, and of course I regretted it, and at once tried to make up for it, by going for a walk with her. On that walk I wept and wept and spoke lugubriously on every subject that came up. But I said nothing of my real trouble. Soon I agreed to take another walk, and then I spoke out. Unfortunately, she had sympathy—and revelations. Dr. Davidson who, as he boasted, had known him since he was in America, had a terrible grievance against him. He, Dr. Davidson, was practically engaged to a girl, and he, my hero, came between them, and separated them, according to Mrs. Davidson's account, for the pure pleasure of making mischief. And the mischief was done. The engagement was dissolved, and the experience threw Dr. Davidson into a seven years' nervous state.

At the time I did not put this down here, because it seemed to me irrelevant, and it rested upon a wife's sole testimony. It naturally flashed across my mind during our interview of a week ago when he typified the outside world's attitude, by that taken by the Davidson's.

No one has been so bitter in denouncing him as they have been. Mrs. Davidson can see no good in him in any respect except his scholarship which remains unassailed.

Mrs. Davidson urged me strongly to have a talk with him, and her arguments fell in with the temper I was in. It was the Tuesday succeeding my talk with her that I wrote to him to come here.

Yesterday Mrs. Davidson visited me, and I told her the upshot of my talk with him.

Thereupon she told me that a little while ago, the following incident occurred in the Seminary Library. He received a notice from a lawyer announcing his having taken an office, or something to that effect, and he said to Dr. Marx and Dr. Davidson, "I wonder why he sends it to me. Perhaps he thinks I have a breach of promise suit on hand."

That ought to kill all feeling for him in me. If it does not, then love is an even more mysterious passion than I knew. The occurrence shows that Adele is right, in his associations with us he was raised beyond his ordinary spiritual plane, it was a strain for him to associate with us, and I add that as we brought out the best in him, so these recent events are bringing out his worst side.

My explanation of his remark is not that he actually believes me capable of suing him, but that he said the thing in a spirit of bravado, he dared himself to see whether his daily associates would move a muscle. He wanted to know what his status with them was, whether they would venture to say anything to him, or whether they would be afraid, as he always told me people were. They were afraid! Perhaps he thinks I am "afraid" to bring a breach of promise suit case against him. Yes, "afraid" of smirching myself, but afraid of him? If I had been, I would not have courted the interview of a week ago.

Mrs. Davidson deplored the fact that I had made a confidant of Dr. Marx. She does not trust him. It appears he has not treated Dr. Davidson well. The Davidsons altogether feel sore about the Seminary people. With my newborn worldly wisdom, I began to suspect Mrs. D's report. Accordingly, in the evening, at Dr. Schechter's Lincoln lecture,[10] when we met again, after she had completed her information, at my request, by telling me that this innuendo against me had been thrown out today a week ago, that is, the morning after my great-hearted talk with him, I approached Dr. Marx without delay, and asked him about it. He admitted it had happened, he was sure, it had happened longer ago than last Friday, however. It is unspeakably ugly at any time, but if it happened last Friday it is the vilest thing I have ever heard of. Dr. Marx vouchsafed one piece of information— that since my talk with him, his manner with his friends is less unstrained, almost lighthearted, Dr. Marx does not understand why the interview with me produced the result. I do. So long as I did not speak, he did not know what I had been doing, how I had been "poisoning" the hearts of his friends against him. In my talk with him, he found out, because I told him frankly, that I had spoken to Dr. Marx, and that Dr. Marx knew I was speaking to him then. And yet Dr. Marx said nothing to him! Now he was sure that his position was secure. He knows that Dr. Marx knows, and Dr. Marx knows that he knows, and so it goes on, and respectability at the Seminary is safeguarded, because no one will scandalize the rest. It is all natural. The Don Quixotes are not running loose to right the wrongs of a single defenseless woman.

For instance, Mrs. Davidson prides herself on this! He, it seems, is having difficulties about some things connected with his book. He has something to translate, an article Mrs. Davidson says, but I suppose it is the preface either to the Genizah Studies or the Yerushalmi, and when he heard that Dr. Davidson had an English article to translate into German, he offered to make an exchange. He would do Dr. Davidson's, if Dr. Davidson did his. But Dr. Davidson declined, having found out that the foreign magazine would take his article untranslated. Then he approached Dr. Davidson about the Index to the English part of the Genizah Studies—the Index I had looked forward to making as perfect as ever Index had been compiled. He asked him to do the Index, and Dr. Davidson refused on the plea of no time. Then he asked him to show him how to make an Index. Dr. Davidson did. He went home and tried, and got impatient, because, of course, indexing is not an occult art. Again he applied to Dr. Davidson, and asked him whether he knew any one who could do it for him. Of course, Dr. Davidson thought of me, but equally of course, he repressed my name. And he, as though regretting that he had put the dangerous question, exclaimed, in gratitude that the feared and perhaps hated name had not escaped his lips, "You're a good fellow! I'll give you a book!" And Dr. and Mrs. Davidson are congratulating themselves that he exercised such wise self restraint!

Of course, it must be remembered that I am accepting Mrs. Davidson's psychologizing. The book, Dr. Marx tells me, will appear without an Index. So he misses his "intellectual mistress!"

Another incident Mrs. Davidson told me. Weeks ago this was—he complained of not sleeping well, and especially that night he had not slept well. And Dr. Davidson said banteringly, "You must have a guilty conscience!" And he started and said, "Why, what do you know about me?" Again I depend on my informant.

I repeat so often that I am accepting other people's judgment, because I am completely bewildered, by the revelation of human character this terrible experience has brought to me. Until now everybody agreed with me in extolling him to the skies, no one breathed a word against him. Now no one has a good word to say for him. And I am conscious of not evoking the bad opinions. I plead with everybody to tell me his side. I feel enmeshed in a net of selfishness. One speaks against the other, and warns me against everyone else. Whom shall I trust? I must depend upon myself. If God will only give me strength! If Dr. Marx has reported to him all I said, so much the better! But I know that they all take good care not to speak to him, not to let an eyelid flutter. And he—he takes good care not to speak, because he is not able to calculate what the conversation will lead to, no matter how it is begun.

The Lincoln lecture last night was a trial. When I entered the room—how its crowded condition reminded me of the Alexander Cohn memorial service, after which he affianced himself to me as I thought!—there was no room except on the last bench, and I came to sit behind his sister-in-law and Sophie. I bowed. Sophie came and told me how she dislikes her present position. But she shall never come back to me. When his sister-in-law left she looked at me pleadingly, for a word, a glance, but I was obdurate. The Lord only knows how it goes against the grain with me, but I cannot act hypocritically any more.

Also I met Miss Kussy there, and I recalled her story—how she poured out to me the indignity put upon her by a Baltimorean, and appealed to me, a comparative stranger, to know whether she had been unwomanly. So mine is but the eternally feminine lot and feeling. And that Baltimorean! Would I have ever thought of coupling the two names together—his and my darling's. And his treatment of me—well, it is useless!

Suppose he had made that poor joke about a breach of promise suit under other circumstances! Dr. Marx went home and told his wife. And Dr. Davidson went home and told his wife, and he would have come here and told—*his* wife, his "spiritual mistress," his "friend!"

He feels comfortable with Dr. Marx, because I exercised magnanimous self restraint and did not tell him how completely he professes to be on my side. I said only the one sentence—"He said he could not understand." At first, he misunderstood and took the object of the verb to be "me"—instead of "you." After all, nothing makes any difference—not his feeling toward me, not his relation to his friends who are ostensibly mine—the main thing is that my heart has been bruised, shocked, battered, broken—that I am left stripped of love and regard for an ideal—and from that I must try to recover, if recovery is possible.

I have re-read what I wrote today. Am I dropping into self-righteousness? I speak of my doubt of all to whom I have spoken about this, of their prudent self-restraint, of my utter contempt for him. Am I blameless in the matter? Am I sincere toward all?" From such faults do I then choose one!"

I search my heart, I cannot find untruth there. I do not believe myself indispensable to him, I acknowledge that he has been, and for all I know, in spite of these revelations about his character, still is indispensable to me. But I believe myself to have been magnanimous, single-minded, pure—my devotion in the past, and each step in my conduct, from the writing of the letter to her to his interview with me and all that I said to him, I know to be absolutely devoid of an arrière-pensée [ulterior motive]. I want to steer clear of priggish self-righteousness—objectively he calls it—but I hope that the consciousness I have of having acted truthfully and even nobly, will restore my soul to tranquility and enable me to behave with dignity henceforth.

DREAM TWINS

February 14, 1909

Another talk with Dr. Schechter à propos of my having gone elsewhere for services, not to the Synagogue at the Seminary. I had fully intended to resume my normal Sabbath routine yesterday, but I was thrown out of gear by the "breach of promise suit" insinuation. Dr. Schechter admonished me impressively that if I went on I would wreck two innocent lives—mine and the girl's in Berlin. As for him, he said nothing about him, and he refused to believe the vulgarity he committed in the "breach of promise" innuendo, I sent him to Dr. Marx, I am merciless now, because I am fighting for my honor, which his conduct has besmirched—my honor and my reputation for common sense. I have to tell the signs and tokens he gave me, and put it to others whether I was a fool for interpreting them as I did.

The girl is innocent, yes, but not so innocent as it would seem. She gave herself up to him after three interviews, she suspected there was more in his relation to me than he told, she now questions my aloofness. Take it as I will, I am the only innocent in the matter—innocent, trustful, and suffering. If I have come between him and her he can but ascribe it to his arrogance, his unpardonable certainty of his own rightness in all things, which he displayed when he told the father there was but one man who could give information about himself—namely, himself! And then the father applied to Felsenstein!

He said to me that he was not a blackguard, nor is he, but the dastardly wrong he did me in the blackguardly act of an otherwise honorable man—blackguardism nated [?] by selfishness, self-sufficiency, and arrogance.

I have it set down before, that my mind rarely dwelt upon the thought of my marriage with him. I was happy as things were, and I was content to leave the future to him—content because I was happy and because I had unquestioning confidence in his rectitude and wisdom—a subconscious confidence, I never said as much to myself. But occasionally the thought would come to my mind that he might want to marry me, and then I would pray God would put it into his heart to do so soon, that I might surely bear him children, and then my mind would wander further, and I would pray that if marriage came into his purpose so late that I could bear only one. God would let me bear a pair of twins—a boy and a girl—that nothing might mar the perfection of his human experiences. And how happy I would have been to be educator of his children! Such depths did he stir in me, and such depths must now settle back into dark quietude. Can they expect that to happen in a jiffy? It is true I must consider him and the other one, but after all I am only a frail woman, I have never boasted of heroic qualities.

I have travelled so far from my attitude on the first pages of this diary, I have put down so many things derogatory to him who was my idol and ideal, that I have the courage to write an indictment against him that has been uttered a number of times by Anna. She says his character, its ungenerosity, appeared to her in the fact that he did not offer her so much as a penny's worth in recognition of the many services and attentions she was called upon to pay him on his frequent visits and at the frequent meals he took with us—though he went so far as to ask her to go for cigars for him, promising her jocularly a wedding present for it when she got married. She says, this attitude of his always stirred her gall, and if she always appeared considerate of him it was because she saw I loved him—he says he never saw it—and because I had once vehemently told her, she might talk against whom she pleased, but not against him. She is a girl of excellent judgment and perhaps she has hit upon a significant trait—but—

I feel that Mrs. Davidson is wrong—I trust Dr. Marx's sympathy, and Dr. Schechter's. They are not going to do anything quixotic for my sake, but they honestly condemn him. Perhaps even if he were boldly to challenge them and ask them for their opinion of our mutual relations, they would hold back, would hem and haw, or would even say they had had no thoughts on the subject. It is not easy to hurl the truth at one's close associates, especially if one must consider a larger cause, as, in this case, the Seminary. His scholarship is an invaluable asset—for its sake they must and will put up with much. But they are sincere in denouncing his conduct. This denunciation does not make me happy, does not even diminish my unhappiness. I would rather be wholly unhappy in my loss, and have the consciousness that the jewel I lost was exactly as precious as I always thought it. All it does is to reassure me on my own sanity.

During the past night, I was desperately sick, my whole system gave way, no doubt on account of the inner excitement under which I have been laboring since Thursday, since I heard the "breach of promise" innuendo. My love for him dies so hard. It was a bitter pill, this realization that he has not even "friendship" for me, not even decent regard for the "self-sacrificing" person he took me to be, but it will have wholesome effect.

If I had had a brother, he would have been horsewhipped for that. As it is, I suffer.

CLOSURE ON THE "LEGENDS" AND "GEONICA"

February 16, 1909

After two comparatively quiet days, I am again very much excited, and the cause of my excitement makes me realize that I must permit myself to have as few relations with him as possible. I must act in pure self-defense, no matter what effect my acts have upon him or her or anyone. I had a letter from him to-day, a business letter, in reply to one of mine, urging him to let me have "copy." He writes: "I understand that Moses is not to form a part of the first volume and I do not understand why you are waiting for it so anxiously"—that after I told him in our interview that work at his book was hourly crucifixious, and asked him to go on with it consecutively, as I did not know whether I would have the strength ever to resume it if he stopped it now. Does he want more humiliation to make him understand? I have been disposed to chide myself and call it pettiness, this insistence that the book shall be finished now. But it is a necessity if it is to be done by me. The Lord only knows what grief and shame I am laying up for myself by the letter I purpose [propose] to write, in which I shall say that I shall have to ask the Publication Society to relieve me of the translation, indexing, and even proof-reading, unless it is finished by the middle of July. The Society may refuse, and then the humiliation, for, of course, I cannot sacrifice my position. If I disregard such prudential possibilities, it ought to be evident to myself that I am but taking a life-saving measure. If ever he felt any friendship for me, or if he appreciated mine, could he insist upon driving me to these extreme steps? Must he have everything said to him in so many words? Has he no mercy in his make-up? And so my heart has been as heavy as a stone today, and as sore as an open wound after I had thought I had made myself unfeeling in the matter. I believe now there is a good deal of *Weltschmerz* mixed in with my personal sorrow—that such a human relation as ours was, apparently full of grace and sympathy on the intellectual and the social side, should have been ruptured and the rupture should be attended by such ugly manifestations of character all around. Doubtless he will think my insistent letter an ugly manifestation of my character—that I should hound him when he should be enjoying his young happiness undisturbed. Oh but they neither of them seem young to me—they both seem so calculating, so cold, so worldly-wise—all to murder my soul. Perhaps there is not an iota of right on my side. But if she suspected there was more between him and me than he was in such inexplicable hurry to disclose to her, why was she willing to publish her engagement?—an engagement entered into after she had seen him three times? It is Tuesday today, a rainy Tuesday, perhaps that accounts for my renewed tears.

February 22, 1909

If I did not know that there have been days of undiminished pain and torture and longing for his companionship such as he gave me particularly freely a year ago, I would congratulate myself upon not having written anything in this diary for nearly a week. In the business letter of a week ago he also asked me whether he was to read the proof piece-meal as I sent it to him, chapter by chapter, or might he wait until the book, Vol. I of his "Legends" was set up entirely. He preferred the latter, strangely enough, as hitherto he had always desired to have it in bits, so that the printer and myself had concocted a plan to accommodate him without inconveniencing the printer. So I wrote

> *"If the literary and scholarly interests of your book can be served best by your reading the proof after the whole volume is set up, it will have to be done in that way, though it is a somewhat slower way from the printer's point of view. I realize that yours is the surest method of guarding against repetitions and discrepancies, and I am content to leave the matter to your judgment, confident that you will give due heed to all considerations involved.*
>
> *My reason for urging you to send me the chapter on "Moses" and the material for the third volume is that, unless the Legends are out of my hands—translating, indexing, proofreading and all—by the middle of July, the rest of the work cannot be done by me, but must be done by someone else. If it is an indifferent matter to you whether or not the same hand manipulates what remains of your book, there is no hurry. It is conceivable to me however, that the handling of your book by a new person, not acquainted with your plan, may be so objectionable to you as to make a sacrifice of present comfort seem preferable, if only you are made aware of the alternative betimes."*

Dr. Marx, Thomas and Adele, all objected to the gentle, reasoning tone. Dr. Marx was particularly insistent that I should leave in a paragraph I had written mildly taunting him with the boast he had always made that he could easily keep me supplied with "copy"—that I was not able to keep pace with him. But I know him better than they do. He is still the darling of my soul, whose one aberration I do not understand. What has happened since his return is only a mistaken way of insisting that there had been no aberration. And I was right—he returned the proof promptly by chapters. As to the other subject, he has not yet replied.

I was just beginning to recover from the acute excitement into which his letter had thrown me, I even went to the Synagogue on Saturday—to be sure it was not a test, he was not there—when another letter came today, about the "Geonic Responsa." It is strange that I should not be able to conquer my grief when every day reveals a new and intimate contact between us. "The Geonic Responsa"—that book of his was with me five times 360 days, 1800 days—And how I labored on it last spring and summer! And how I loved Hag and Chag, Shaz and Shat, Gak and all the rest! And how I discussed that Introduction with him point by point walking along redolent Riverside! God forgive him and help me! And now he writes:

[February 21, 1909]

"I have finished my preface to 'the Geonica' (a new title for it?) And I would like to ask you whether you have any objection to my reference to your kind assistance without which this book would never have been published in English. I do not think I have any right not to mention it, on the other hand I have no right to mention your name in connection with this book without asking your permission!"

I have written an answer refusing permission. I shall not dispatch it until tomorrow. I am not actuated by pettiness, nor by the desire to prevent him from ridding himself of obligation to me, by a public acknowledgement of it. How disagreeable the thought must be to him that he ever accepted a favor from me! Long ago, it must be all of five years, I remember walking up Riverside Drive between him and Dr. Marx, and his saying emphatically that he would not accept favors from certain persons because they expected returns without end, but he would accept them from us two. And now he must say to himself I expected not returns and acknowledgements without end, but one great return. If he does, he misjudges me. Not once did I think of a return, I knew only the joy of saving him drudgery. He speaks of "kind assistance"—"insane devotion" would be nearer the truth.

I do not see how I can do anything but refuse to have my name mentioned in his book. In the first place, if it is to be mentioned at all, it ought to be on the title page as translator. In the preface should be acknowledgement of my labor as proof-reader. But he did not let me see the last proof of the Introduction, he did not let me do the Index. If without my "kind assistance" the book could not have been published in English, and if his feeling of friendship for me was so great that he could resume our former relations even now after my confession of love, why did he not come to me with the proof and, acknowledging his indebtedness to me, seek to soothe me in my distress and find out its cause? Why didn't he take the opportunity I offered him in our interview of a little more than two weeks ago, when I began our talk by asking him whether he was under any mis-apprehension as to why I had asked him to come, and he said, in cow-ardly fashion, he had no notion of what I wanted? Although later on he admitted that he knew what was in my mind the evening I showed him his fiancée's letter to me, and he tested me by waiting to see whether I should ask for his picture and hers as she bade me? Why didn't he take the opportunity I offered him again in the interview, when I asked him why he had not come to me with the proof and made that the occasion for telling me I was mistaken; he had not loved me nor known I had loved him? His answer then was, would I believe the proof had arrived only the Saturday before? And I asked whether he had intended sending it to me, and he answered in the negative, whereupon I insisted that in that case its late arrival had nothing to do with his implied repudiation of my reproach.

No, I cannot let my name appear in one of his books. I worked at them with the feeling that corresponded to the world's interpretation of his public conduct toward me, his daily association with me and exclusive absorption of my time. I was not his employee, I was his helpmate. If he cast me off at the end of four years, he will have to take the consequence of his deed. If he could not meet me in manly fashion and confess his love for another, and ask me to release him because he realized that his feeling for me was not the best love of which he was capable, and so give me a chance to change my feeling into friendship, instead of murdering my soul and humiliating me, he will have to bear the burden of his obligation to me. I owe it to myself not to run counter to convention now. If my name were to appear, it would be an acknowledgement that ours had been a mere literary friendship.

And who knows whether it is not better also for the sake of his wife. He thinks her nobler hearted and unselfish. If she loves him, she will not care to see my name in his books, knowing as she now does what she suspected before.

Perhaps he, too, now that he has the consciousness of having wanted to do me justice, will feel relieved not to have his name cou-pled with mine in any way.

He and she are uncertain quantities, however. What is certain and constant is my own suffering—in soul and substance. I suffer, no one can know to what extent, because I must seek ways and means of disavowing my four years relation with him, and again as innumerable times before for other reasons. I cannot avow myself to be the conscientious workman and earn my reward as such. Take the money value of which I did for him and translate it into terms of satisfaction of the craftsman. I am never permitted any assets—therein he is like the Publication Society and all other for whom I have sacrificed time, effort, and self. Is that again priggish self-righteousness?

February 23, 1909

I kept the letter by me for twenty-four hours, until I felt so sore that what little judgment I had had was lost in pain and stupor, so I decided to let it go as the expression of Adele's clearer view. Nothing matters at any rate. I hope he is so happy that he does not care what I do—I suppose he doesn't. This is how I wrote:

> "*I appreciate the motive that prompted your letter of February 21, but all things considered—the change in our personal relations, the fact that I was not afforded an opportunity of seeing the last proofs, etc., and the other fact that you always regarded most of the work as being of subordinate importance—it seems advisable to me not to make mention in the preface to 'The Geonic Responsa' of my share in your volume.*"

My eyes are so sore from crying that they are like my judgment—veiled, warped and dim. It is best, after all, I think to cut every thread, and be it of the slightest, that connects me with him, now and forevermore. Those prostituted years of mine, when I lived for him and, apparently, was used by him must be covered with darkness now and in [the] future.

UNLOCKING HIS HEART, INCREASING HIS SALARY

February 24, 1909

I have been far from happy today over yesterday's repudiation of him and the past five years. And still I feel more strongly than I did when I dispatched the letter that every memorial of that time of "happiness turned into shame" must be—has better be—extirpated. Of course, I am again the sufferer. It is true as he said in our recent talk—*he* is not suffering, his *fiancée* is not suffering, *I* am suffering. I have again given silently of my blood, my time, my disciplined ability without any return in money, recognition, or love—again as hundreds of times before. Only all those other times, love would have meant as little to me as money now. As I unlocked his heart, humanized it, for her occupancy of it, so I unlocked the stores of his beautiful knowledge to the English-speaking world, and I myself had to bid him throw the key away. Dr. Schechter told me the other day that when he asked for an increase of salary, in the letter I edited and translated for him, the directors of the Seminary had been disinclined to grant it, because, unlike the others, he was not married, and Dr. Schechter had urged it, saying, he knew for a certainty, he meant to get married—of course, he meant to me. At the same time Dr. Schechter said he knew I had had a hand in the letter of application, and that had strengthened his feeling that after all his doubts, something would still come of his close association with me. So I have smoothed the way in material respects too. I am nothing but a lifeless instrument of such malleable material that it took what shape he would in his hand, and—so he says at least—he never suspected that there was a delicately attuned soul within upon which he might have played all his life and found it responsive to every mood, intellectual, emotional and social.

In our talk he said he knew what was wrong only on the day I showed him her letter, three weeks and two days after he told me of his engagement. How was it that after the second day, when I had him read my luckless letter to her, he did not once mention his fiancée to me, and only once spoke of her in my presence, when my mother asked him about her?

I had promised myself, as so often before, that I would add nothing but actual happenings to this dark chronicle of a broken heart, but I must break the promise. Someday when I am stronger than today, I must put down more than I did about our interview. I feel that it has possibilities of fortitude, if I can make my impressions less evanescent than they are so long as they are derived from spoken and thought words, instead of written words. But not today!

"Psychologic Analysis"

February 28, 1909

I went to the synagogue at the Seminary yesterday—and misbehaved. As soon as he entered, my breathing became heavy, everything swam before me, the back of my head hammered, at one point I could not stand on my feet. The sermon nearly killed me—the new preacher used the Song of Songs allegory for the relation of Israel to God with all its bridal imagery until I thought I should scream out. Several times I was on the point of taking to flight, but I held on, and was rewarded by growing quieter as the service approached its end. I am determined to go every week, and force myself back into normal ways. I do not know myself to be the same person I used to be. Why have I lost all power of self-control, all pride? Why do I acknowledge before all that have eyes to see that I depend upon him alone?

And he? He wore an indifferent look, but he could not have been comfortable. What can he do? The situation is as trying for him as it is painful for me. I do not in the least think that I am interfering with his happiness about his engagement, or that he feels the wrong he did me to the extent of confessing it even to himself in his most silent communings. Perhaps I but serve as a foil to the girl who writes him serene or fun-bubbling letters—once I could write such to him, too. Yes, I know that he is not joyous over the end of our relation, both because the relation *did* mean much to him and because the present situation is vulgar. I am more and more sure that he was carried away by a sudden infatuation, and accustomed all his life to doing only the right by instinct, by training, by character, he could not conceive that in this instance he had been capable of wrong when he gave way to the new feeling and followed it to the extreme to which it led him. Then he built up his logical fortifications retrospectively—he had never uttered a binding word to me, it was evident our relation had not meant anything but friendship, for how could he have gone four years without saying something? (As for acts, they were open to various interpretations, and probably I too, had interpreted them lightly. But if I had not, I would be sensible and say he had not bound himself, heroic and say I must accept the inevitable, and proud and say the world must not know.) To save appearances, I would continue the relation in a way sufficiently resembling its former character to deceive me and him and the world as to what had actually been. All this was not conscious calculation, it gradually built itself up in him, and became a part of his moral and mental background, and the readjusting structure once finished, he could not remember that things had ever been different. If he now says he never loved me, never knew that I loved him, he tells a subjective truth, not objective as he flatters himself. He actually does not recollect what happened during those four years of intimacy with me, his happiness through his fiancée helps him to forget still more effectively, and my thwarting him at every turn must naturally change any surviving good feeling into actual resentment and contempt for me. He cannot now conceive, probably, that he once thought well of me and my character—Alas for human relations!—I of whom he said that I understood him better than anyone else ever had—said so to his fiancée!

I wish I could rest satisfied with this psychologic analysis, but at once all sorts of searching questions arise like accusing spectres. Why, for instance, did he tell me, when he announced his engagement to me, joyously that he had spoken only of me to his fiancée, as though to convey that he had described my ways and character enthusiastically, and in my interview with him he said, he had considered it his *duty* to tell his fiancée at once after their engagement about his relation to me. Why duty if there was nothing more between us than friendship?

And I gave him abundant chances to speak openly. During all these three weeks while we were associating on his own terms, he did not help me out of my distress. If he was conscious of [innocence], why did the friend not help the friend? Instead of which, he told me in our interview that he did not realize which was actually wrong with me until I responded to his test—I did not ask for the photograph offered to me by his fiancée. Nevertheless, instead of speaking then frankly and consolingly, he asked me to take a walk with him after we finished our work. Would he have spoken on that walk? If he had any such intention, he should have said to me, when I refused because I could not control myself, that it was that he wanted me to speak about. And then three months passed, and he did not seek me to help me. And again I gave him the chance in the way I opened the interview with him. I said: You are under no misapprehension as to why I asked you to come here?—I have not the slightest notion what you want of me, he returned. Was that ingenious, after I had written, I wanted to speak of our past relations?—And then I went on: During the last three months I have been living in a state of constant perplexity, I do not understand what has happened, but you have meant too much in my life for me to let you go out petulantly. I must try to have an explanation from you. All these years, I have been putting but one construction upon our relations, and so sure was I that this construction was yours, too, that when you came here the day you returned from Europe, flushed and eager, I thought for an infinitesimal moment of time, that you had come to tell me in words what I thought your act had meant. Why didn't he interrupt me half a dozen times during this speech and throw himself upon my mercy? Instead, he uttered an impatient exclamation, and said, no such idea had ever entered his mind.

Such confessions as I made during that interview! I cannot recognize myself in them, either. I told him how perfect he was in my eyes, that he was my ideal—and he said he certainly was not perfect, but also he was not a blackguard. And then when I poured out all to him, he could ask the question, had I never had such a relation with other men before? Had he ever noticed any, I should have asked him. Is it possible to have such relations more than once in one's lifetime? In my present state I cannot conceive it possible. All other men seem to me like sawdust stuffed into coat, vest and trousers, next to him. It is true what he says—he cannot be classified with any one else. And it is true, I do understand him better than any one else. But why did he not secure for himself the person who understood him so well? If he had seen with what sang-froid I rejected a proposal of marriage last Tuesday, he would know how little I care for marriage per se. And was it not so with all my suitors of my younger days, too? Did one of them make my heart beat? Have I regretted one of them?

But that N.B. of last Tuesday said a true thing—he spoke his "lively admiration" for me, for my abilities and character, but he thought I lacked one thing, joy, and that he could give me. I do lack joy, I am only a phantom, but there is only one who can make me live, and he will have none of me.

I said to him in the interview that I wished I could hate him, and he replied with a platitude, hatred cures nothing.

When I charged him with not having come to my rescue, he reminded me of the letter of a friend of his which he carried about with him unopened for four years and then took back to Europe and gave to the friend unread, because he knew it contained a quarrel. But that may have been a righteous quarrel on his side, and I can see right only on my side in this case of ours.

These platitudes—sometimes I think now that I am appointed as the instrument to make the period of his engagement less happy than it should be, that I meant to drive him into unworthy silence, unworthy posing with his friends because he was so much in the habit of talking cynically about marriage, and his "immunity" from the feeling that leads to marriage.

That proof of his innocence which he adduced—that he went away from the table at the breaking of the long fast of Atonement in order, as he told everybody, to read a letter from his best friend which he had had to leave unopened all day—that has been bothering me. Is it a proof of innocence? My letters last summer, under his encouraging "friendship," grew warmer and warmer, as the summer wore on. Must he not have feared that one might come in which I would be carried away to use expressions which would make it impossible to cling to his policy of readjustment which ignored all but "friendship" between us. Such fear would not long permit him to carry a letter from me around unopened for twelve hours, let alone four years. He was at such pains too, when he came back to tell me he had received *all* my letters. That he told me on the day (Wednesday) after his return, also à propos of nothing at all.

There I am back again at my fine-spun detective searchings. No explanation explains—I love him, that is the whole matter, I admire him in spite of all they and I say, what he has done, as I see it, does not comport with the man I "understood," the mystery will remain unsolved, and I will apparently remain unhappy.

But I am going to pull myself together. I am physically much stronger in spite of the testimony of yesterday's breakdown at the synagogue, I can eat oranges again and peel them as I used to peel them for him day after day when he came here. I can break eggs without a pang of recollection that that, too was a service I had constantly done for him. My hair has begun to wave again—all these months I was so lifeless that it hung down straight as an Indian's. Perhaps all these outward signs betoken a spiritual regeneration.

If only he were not so hard toward me! He has not yet replied whether he will finish the "Legends" or let them go over so that the work would pass the mid-July limit which I set in my letter to him. And it does seem to me, that when I refused to grant permission to him to discharge his obligation to me in the matter of "The Geonic Responsa," he might have written me a note, telling me what my "kind assistance" had meant—that he appreciated it—that it was not quite of the subordinate importance he had called it in the happier days when I had compensations for the low estimate he put on my devoted work. Well it is appointed and ordained that I shall reap nothing but tares and tears, and the Lord knows that my sowing was not in joy.[11]

Possibly he thinks me as hard as I think him. I wish I knew his side! Oh how glad I would be to forgive, to be friends with him after a frank explanation. I need him! Does he think me ungenerous? Would he, if he had heard my first and all my subsequent conversations with Dr. Marx? My first word was to say that he had not acted dishonorably, that he had never uttered a word of binding character.

And from that time on, I have never left him undefended when his detractors spoke. But too often I had to say I did not understand when I was confronted by facts.

And that is the end of the matter—I do not understand him, I do not understand what happened, I do not understand the persistence of my love for him.

FRIENDSHIP, PRIDE, SCHOLARSHIP, AND SENSUALITY

March 2, 1909

Since last night my heart has been tied up in a harder knot than ever—it is all pain and soreness, and all on account of the recurrence of a bit of "atmosphere." Almost immediately after we sat down to the table for supper, there was a ring at the door bell, and it happened to be very much like his—the bell held down firmly for a more appreciable time than most people keep it pressed and then let go with decision. And I was flooded and overwhelmed by the old feeling, as when it used to happen. I followed his steps from landing to landing, and then trembled during the interval between the second ring, at the upper door, and his appearing near the hat rack in the hall, looking in upon us in the dining room, with the air of apprehension and appeal and apology, affected by the man oversure of a cordial welcome. Then we all would welcome him and move up a bit to make room for him, and I—I was supremely happy, for it meant an evening with him here or a walk at Riverside, and happily I broke his eggs for him and peeled his orange, and fetched the matches for his cigar. And he—he looked content with the radiance in his eyes that was never there for others. And yet he says it all meant nothing—but friendship.

And did he look at others with such infectious warmth when, for instance they did a little act of bonhomie such as my picking out a stout rubber band for his packages, to give to his little nephew? I cannot believe it—or does particular "friendship" of men for women manifest itself thus, and not particular friendship for men? Then particular friendship should never exist between men and women.

This morning it came to me with a rush, that his actions since his return have not been those of a man easy in his mind about what he has done, even accepting his statement about his feeling of "friendship" for me. Calm friendship would not have tolerated the harsh pride he showed toward me. He did nothing, it is true, to bring about a rupture, he would probably even say that he came back prepared magnanimously to give me all he had given before—but was he prepared to give, did he give? Did he not return making a renewed draft upon my intellectual and my emotional sympathy? He continued to let me work for him, he asked me to welcome his fiancée and be happy in his happiness. Did he try to rouse me out of my apathy, stupor, and distress? Was not my state such as to awaken questioning in the mind of a stranger, let alone of one who had known me sprightly, alert, energetic, helpful and happy? Did he sacrifice an iota of pride? Is that the equality of friendship for which he once plead in a letter to me, when, he maintained, I was too feminine in that I was willing to take upon myself his troubles, but apologized for giving him an inkling of mine? Until now the balance of credit for magnanimity was on his side in my books—I thought his tacit offer of friendship meant everything, and that I was petty not to have accepted it with candor and joy. But I am beginning to see that he did nothing, nothing. Why does it take me so long to see the obvious? Because I love him in spite of all—I am only a "thing" in relation to him, worse than an *Agunah*. A deserted wife has her children and her legitimized right to mourn and sorrow, I must hide my grief, must pretend my heart is light, and I may not even acknowledge before the world the children of the intellect which his "intellectual mistress" bore him.

If I could only look down to the bottom of his soul and his heart, and see whether I really have been forced into the background by a new love, but that the old love was a reality, not a phantasmagoria of my weak brain, I could regain a measure of self-respect—I would not feel like the "fools" he despises—and I could manage to overcome the feeling that I have lost the respect of others. But so long as he does not acknowledge his act a defection, I cannot cure myself, because I do not trust my interpretation of which my senses perceived and my mind recorded.

I suppose all this renewed turmoil is to be ascribed to the simple fact that he returned the galley proof of "Abraham" last evening, and there are many changes which need discussion, and the discussing must be done by post. And today is a rainy Tuesday!

March 9, 1909

"These days of Purim" have been anything but days of feasting and joy and "sending of gifts from friend to friend." Alas! the friend who never failed me with his offering of friendship at this season has been repudiated by me—had to be repudiated by me because he stood neither the test of lover nor the test of a friend. The pangs of memory were intensified by my physical condition. I have been suffering with an ulcerated sore tooth for two weeks, the cause of which the dentist, without any suggestion from me, put down to systemic degeneracy. And on Saturday, he must needs poke into my letter box on his way to the synagogue, an addition to "Joseph," and his "short" preface of 2000 words, ending with perfunctory thanks to me. They will not appear in my translation. Why doesn't he send all such missives by mail? Does he want to pretend that he is willing to risk meeting me face to face? Why then, did he deliberately turn back to the platform on Saturday night after the reading of the *Megillah* (my reading of it was tearful—has one ever heard of weeping over the *Megillah?*), when he had descended, but suddenly realized that unimpeded progress on my part and his would bring us together face to face at the door, as it always did in the happy old days? Is all this aristocratic?

And Purim itself I had to spend at a Publication Committee meeting in Philadelphia, at which his book was again discussed at length. It was decided to publish it in four volumes. This makes my present labor lighter. The first volume runs to Jacob now, and that is almost all set up. Nevertheless I had a talk with Judge Sulzberger, and told him that I must have a six month's vacation, and also that I would refuse to do the last volume of his book unless it could be done at this sitting as it were.

That burns the last bridge connecting me with the happy shore, and when he hears of it [Szold's translation of the final volume of the *Legends*], he will set it down to malice, and not to self defense. I feel that I am growing quieter or deader, and I have hopes that when this book is out of my hands I shall be able to control myself.

At the same meeting [with Sulzberger] it was brought out that in the text of Dr. Margolis's commentary on Micah, three words had been omitted, and the Chairman rebuked me. It was not fair to hold me responsible, especially after I had been rebuked with equal vigor all these years for concerning myself with matters in proof reading that belonged to the author. But suppose I had told him that when I had to read that proof I could not find my way in the most familiar parts of New York, that I was insane and sick? Not to mention that, as always, I was under double pressure, other people had delayed doing their duty by the proof. I was told to hurry, and at the same time had 8000 words of translation to do of his book, the book of the man who was driving me to insanity. So there is my first flagrant failure as an editor to be set to his account. He has ruined me in every relation in life.

I have heard much talk about his sensual nature—I do not believe it. He is no more sensual than the normal human should be. That he was carried away by a merely physical infatuation, that in the first moment of complete infatuation he permitted himself a liberty with the girl which he did not confess to me—a kiss or caress or something—seems certain to me, and his sense of honor then led to his betraying me. All that I can forgive if it is true to fact. But why not treat me frankly and considerately afterwards? Why act so that I had to break down before the world and lose my respect for my own intelligence? Why use so many subterfuges, followed up by wholesale denial? Is that aristocracy? Is it aristocracy now for him to keep proudly silent towards all his friends? Is it even the consciousness of innocence? Is it not the wicked stubbornness of the man who deems himself infallible?

If he were a sensual man, what would have kept him with me for years? During that time he could not have had any associations with other women. There was no time left for it, he was with me too much. And such contact as he had with young girls under my eyes was of the most incidental sort. Would a sensual man have been satisfied to be with me? And yet I cannot now understand what *did* keep him by me. It was not any intellectual attraction, that I would have had for *him* as little as a sensual attraction. Then it must have been a quality of intellectual sympathy which could exercise all the charm it had because on the side of the senses there was at least no physical repulsion. But why did that not suffice him, if he craved it for a period of four years?

How mistaken I was about Dr. Schechter. I always felt that he would not be pleased if it came to pass that he married me. Instead of which I now hear that he says that if he had married me, the successorship to the presidency of the Seminary would have been settled so far as he was concerned—he as my husband would have been his choice. But not as things are now. With me he would have trusted him fully, without me and after his treatment of me, he trusts him not at all. Mamma said the same—not only has he lost you, he has lost the presidency of the Seminary, she said that first night when I spoke to her.

And yet he will make his way to it or to some other high position by the sheer force of his lucid, powerful intellect. And say what they will, his character, too, is great. He has made a mistake in my case—I cannot yet account for it, I probably shall never be able to account for it. But when his life comes to be summed up, this act of his, whatever it was—for it was only a single act which he tried to justify and fit naturally into the scheme of my life and his by artificial and little noble means—will be seen to have been but a scratch upon the surface. I looked at him furtively during the Megillah reading the other night—he remains my hero, my ideal, my darling, and I am a vessel full of envy of her whom he has chosen instead of me to wear upon his bosom. But that one act—that looking up to the women's gallery was all it brought in its train, that calling me into a closed room to tell me what he had told openly to a dozen persons across the street, and all the juggling with words, the petty prevarication, the cruel disregard of the distress of one whom he avowed his best friend—how little it comports with his definition of duty and of aristocratic conduct.

It is another rainy Tuesday!

As I went to put this sheet back into the drawer dedicated to my poor memorabilia of him, my eye was caught by the one-cent Megillah he bought for me four years ago downtown on the East Side. I had said most casually in his hearing that I was going there to hear the Megillah read, and in a moment he asked to be allowed to go with me. Why? What was the attraction about going with me? And afterwards we ate in a dingy little restaurant, in an upstairs room. How excited I was that evening and how happy! And how excited I was this Purim and how unhappy! The first Purim in five on which I did not receive a *Mish'loah Manot*[12] from him! And how it enraged me to hear that he had read the Megillah in private to Mrs. Marx. If she denounces him as she does, how can she let him perform a religious function for her? I must get accustomed to the idea that their life will flow on smoothly, that his and hers will flow on brilliantly, and that mine is wrecked—mine alone. If only I can grow quiet!

TRANSCENDING FRIENDSHIP?

March 11, 1909

Every day some one fact or aspect or occurrence takes possession of my mind and makes me "*grübel*" [ponder, brood]. Yesterday, all day it was the haste with which he announced his engagement here, the apparent calculation with which he made me the last to hear of it, his telling it to me behind closed doors as a "private" matter, though the street was speaking of it, the fact that the engagement was announced in Berlin almost five weeks later so that there was no necessity for hurry here—all this stared at me and I could not believe in his innocence.

This morning I awoke with an unknotted heart, and I said to myself gaily, that the presence of spring in the air would cure me—I would think of him as the man I had loved through no fault of mine, no fault of his, when suddenly all my peace of mind was destroyed by the recollection of a bit of conversation which I have not recorded here. On the second day of his return, the Wednesday when I showed him my letter to her and he brought me the tell-tale buckle, he also gave me an invitation from his sister-in-law, to have supper with them the following Saturday night, and almost before I could decline, certainly before I gave a reason, he said, "I told my sister-in-law you would not come," and I corroborated him, "I go to a Publication meeting in Philadelphia on Sunday, and I do not care to be late on Saturday."

Why did he know beforehand that I would not come? So, it appears, the old relation was untenable in his opinion, too? He knew it was not possible for me to come to him and his people, unless the relation transcended friendship. And the sister-in-law? The Marxes may be right and the Davidson's, who excuse her, because they are sure that like themselves she thought I had refused him. But the main point is that he realized the situation he had put me in. Whether he had loved me or not, whether I had loved him or not, in no circumstances could such a friendship as ours continue after his betrothal to another no matter how magnanimous he might represent her to be, let alone as the circumstances actually were. That realization was logically connected with the feeling of duty he told me about, that had prompted him to tell her at once after their engagement about his relation to me—the relation as he then chose to conceive it. What was it that could make my darling act so dishonorably? So cruelly to one who had shown him that she lived only to make him comfortable and happy? It passes my understanding. I understand it less and less as the days go by, less and less as I grow calmer.

March 13.

I went to the synagogue, and choked and gagged and dropped tears in my book, but I conquered myself sufficiently to stay until the services were over. In the hall I met him face to face. We both nodded imperceptibly. He looks well, happy, complacent, not a sign to show that he feels he has anything to reproach himself with.

What would not leave me today was something he said in the interview with him three or four weeks ago. I recalled to him how when I had maneuvered that he was to walk with Miriam, it had taken him only a few minutes to stray back to me, and how that had settled it in my mind that he wanted me. He replied: "I do not deny it that I find more pleasure in conversing with you than with a girl like your cousin"—and yet he had chosen for his wife, if I may judge by her letter, a girl who cannot touch the hem of Miriam's garment—a young girl who has in no way reached maturity either of heart or head. Somewhere then, there is insincerity toward me, either in repudiating the thought of comparing me with Miriam or in repudiating me. It is maddening—this not being able to hold on to my ideal. I was a fool to believe him my lover. I was a bigger fool, it seems, to believe him an ideal, big man. To cease to believe the latter is to deal my better self a crushing blow. It means that I must eliminate from my memory all that was beautiful during the last five years of my life.

March 14, 1909

In one of the last few letters I wrote to him, one of those in which I abandoned myself to my phantom, illusory happiness—it must have been the last or the last but one—I reassured him upon the subject that seemed to give him pain—that he made a victim of me in making me a participant of his troubles. I said that he forced me to tell him what his friendship meant to me—friendship. I meant in my sense, not in his limited juggling sense. I reminded him that I had once told him that all idealism had gone out of my life with my father. That I continued was no longer true. He had it brought back in a great measure. I maintained many friendly relations, relations, too, with women whose circle of experience must needs be larger and perhaps deeper than my own, because they were married and had children. But in all of these I felt, in all modesty, that I was giving at least as much as I was receiving. Only with him it was not so. He gave me, I said, so much, much more than I could return. Was that the letter he received on Yom Kippur? The letter the reading of which in impatient haste was to prove his innocence?

Now, alas, my feeling is that I gave all and what I thought I was receiving, was not given, was not there to be given, I counted it, attributed to him. In his interview with me, he made it appear that only he had been capable of magnanimous friendship (instead of selfish love), he made it appear that the girl, too, was magnanimous, or would be magnanimous in permitting me to associate with him as before, only I was petty and mean minded. When he wrote in one of his letters, the one in which so many words were underscored, of my *great* friendship for him, was he magnanimous in thus preparing me for his treachery? No, he has been neither aristocratic, nor honorable, nor magnanimous, nor anything but selfish and self-righteous in this matter. He has with all his might and main banished the least promptings of conscience and memory—he is complacently sure that my unhappiness is my folly and not his worry. And he has his life before him, this experience might chasten him. For me it holds nothing but bitterness, because he has ended my life. Am I self-righteous too?

And I compared him with my dear father. Now I am almost—God forgive me—tempted to say *lehabdil*.[13] And yet his children will see in him what I saw in him and what I saw in my father. It is providential that time grows moss. If it would only grow over my keen memory.

NY, March 21, 1909

Dr. Louis Ginzberg
60 W. 115th St.
New York City

Dear Dr. Ginzberg,

Under separate cover I am sending you two sets of the galley proof to "The Legends of the Jews," together with your original. Kindly return the latter and the marked set of the former at your earliest convenience.

I would request you to state in the Preface that there are passages scattered throughout the book that were not translated for it, but were taken from secondary English sources; that some of these have been slighty modified in diction to bring them into accord with the general style of your book; and that the sources will be duly acknowledged in their proper places in the Notes.

At various times in the past you asked me to take down memoranda for your preface. One of these is a caution to the reader to use the book in connection with the corresponding Biblical narratives, which could not be woven in for lack of space.

Another memorandum I give you now, though it cannot be used in the preface to the present volume. But, as it appears from your letter of March 16, that the fourth volume of your book will not be handled by me, it may be well for you to keep it on file yourself, namely that the Bible references are to the Hebrew Bible, and when the Vulgate verses are different, they appear, in addition, in square brackets.

And the last memorandum was that a list of abbreviations was to be made out of the works frequently referred to in the Notes, and these abbreviations were to be used consistently throughout.

In accordance with your letter of March 16, I beg you will send me German copy for the third volume as fast as you finish it.

Yours truly,

Henrietta Szold

March 22.

To-day a week ago I had a business letter from him, and it gave me such keen suffering that I had not had the heart even to confide my feelings about it to this paper. Apparently, it was a reply to my letter of more than a month ago, in which I told him, in answer to his question about my urgency, that unless his book was in my hands by the middle of July, someone else would have to finish it, I would not. Apparently—for he did not have the courtesy to refer to it. He said that he had six weeks before him in which to work at the book and he would send it to me piecemeal, and then he goes on "I want to call your attention to the fact that if I would not read the proof for the second volume before I leave for Europe, about the middle of May, I will not be able to do it till the end of October." He "goes me one better" so to say and he "rubs it in." But he is mistaken—I am fighting for my bare physical life, and am fighting for it from a sense of duty, not because I value it any longer.

Is his hardness intentional, to show me he never cared for me? Is his discourtesy awkwardness? Or is the whole procedure the outflow of traits of character that I wilfully overlooked in the old happy days when he showed me only his *chen* [charm]? It is of a piece with his action toward his Berlin landlady, of which he boasted so often, and with his keeping that letter unopened for four years of which he reminded me again on the evening of our interview, and with his article on Dr. Rosenau. Now it is turned against me, whatever *it* may be.

In our interview that evening he said that he placed love high, but also he placed friendship high—so high that he considered it a betrayal of friendship to "thank" me when I spent nights and nights toiling for him. If that is betrayal of friendship, what name is one to give to his having let me go on suffering for months without helping me out of my distress, and when I—magnanimously, I believe—asked him to come and speak to me, pretend that he did not divine the nature of what I wanted to say to him? What made him refer to his own magnanimity and his fiancée's, in contrast to my low conception of friendship, as he implied. Was that friendship or was it self-righteous pride?—aristocracy, he calls it? How could he say that he could resume our relations where I broke them off, when he could not even conquer this pride of his sufficiently to come to me and give me the chance at an explanation? Is it aristocracy not to tell the truth—and did he tell the truth when he said—not that he did not love me, I am now willing to concede that—but that he did not know that I loved him? Is it aristocracy to have made it appear before the world for four years that I was the woman of his choice? Is it aristocracy to have selected a wife as he did?

Am I self-righteous?

Why did he ask me whether I had never had such a relation to other men as I had had to him? Did he mean to imply that I was accustomed to being jilted? That I throw myself at men as they come along? And why, on the other hand, did he ask me whether he appeared embarrassed when he told me of his engagement?

My impulse all week was not to let my name go on the title page of the "Legends," but Mamma and Louis and Dr. Schechter and Dr. Marx think otherwise. And in all my soreness I glimmeringly feel that they are right. It makes it more impersonal than to set people guessing who the translator is, and then wondering why my name was withheld. But, of course, I will not permit the words of thanks to the translator he has put into the Preface. In the first place, I am too "aristocratic" to translate them. In the second place—that I need not specify.

I myself have been saying all along that if he had offered to put my name on the title page of the "Geonica" as translator, that I would have accepted. But I could not permit "kind assistance" in the preface, especially as he had not the "magnanimity"—nor the "aristocratic" insight to let me know the exact form his acknowledgement would take, nor had he the "friendship" to write afterwards that at least he would express his obligation to me privately. That is vulgar pride.

Am I self-righteous? And do I pity myself too much? Heaven knows I *have* been going around with a chip on my shoulder for many years. But it is not without reason. The trustfulness that worked my undoing with him, has made my unhappiness in my relation to the Publication Society. My character is at fault, but the fault is such that it does not exonerate the other party in either case. In a more fortunate woman, it would have been accounted a grace of character, a womanly trait. In me it means ruin.

How much I continue to hear against his character? *"Verlogen"* [mendacious] they call him. They say they had buried all the tales they had heard about his early days, but his treatment of me has brought them back into the foreground of their memory. So I am his evil genius! I do not care what these tales are, I do not believe them. He acted dishonorably toward me, but it was the one dishonorable act of a high-minded man, whom I shall continue to love to the end. And he will hold his own, too. He and she will live a triumphant life and the others will again forget the apocryphal tales, and I, too, will become apocryphal with the rest. They even now associate with him normally again. As usual he will go to the Marxes for the second Seder evening, while I am wondering where to hide myself during Passover. They will forget, he and she will be happy—and I am a wreck.

To-day it came back to me how the air between us had tingled whenever I asked him, as I often did, to bring me the articles of dramatic criticism which he had written when he was a young man in Germany. I believe they were in Europe. Was that "tingling friendship?" But he did not remember it! My infatuation for him has sharpened all my faculties, his infatuation seems to have dulled his. I understand no phase of the situation—I understand less and less as time goes on. They say that he had no connections with Berlin Jews in his student days!

He has dedicated his "Legends" to his brother.

A QUESTION OF PIQUE

April 1, 1909

Sometimes now, I feel as though he were well pleased that I had not been heroic—it was disagreeable at first, my not falling in with his plan of readjustment, but once my behavior forced the breach he congratulates himself, he need never speak to his wife about me.[14] Present intimacies will never form cross-references to the greater intimacy of the past, for consciously or unconsciously he took good care that my name should not stare at my "successor," from the many many objects and acts with which it was identified. Why, he cannot touch a piece of paper without having it called to his mind that it was I that supplied him with it. He cannot do anything that should not remind him of me, and always of me serving him. And yet he says he did not know I loved him, and he has the hardihood to say he did not love me while acknowledging that he took largely of my substance and all of my soul life! I wonder whether the ache will ever cease!

I spoke to Dr. Davidson last Monday. How bitterly he denounces his character—his ruthless selfishness, manifesting itself in spiritual as well as in material concerns. And he hints darkly at so much more than he tells. He will speak out if I ask him to, but I don't want to know anymore. I know now that I shall love him if he is a villain—I always knew the strength of my love transcending even respect. Why did I see nothing of all the selfishness they speak about? Did I really raise him to his highest level? And did he throw me over on that account, it was too uncomfortable? Am I self-righteous again?

Oh! if I could only know the truth—know exactly what did happen! I would still be unhappy, unhappy because I miss companionship with him, but I would not be crushed, unable to regain a hold upon my personality. And I never will know the truth—he alone might have told it, and by this time he has so overlaid it with prevarications if he is guilty of a dishonorable act or with resentment toward me if he is innocent, that he, too, has forgotten it.

Pique, he said, at his not having told me first about his engagement, he thought it was, when I asked him how he had accounted for my changed manner, until he tested me by waiting to see whether I would ask for his picture and hers as she bade me do in the letter I gave him to read. Was not he rather the piqued one when he read the sort of letter, the "*Backfisch*" [adolescent] letter, she wrote to me? And did he really think that for three weeks I would gasp for breath, as he saw me do whenever he was with me, from pique? And did he really think that the woman of the calibre he knew me to be from four years observation would be "piqued?" No more than he actually thought she would bring a breach of promise suit. Is "pique" only an un-English awkwardness? Or is the whole thing as lame as I now find all the rest of what he said and did in this matter? Did he judge me by himself and think me as little genuine during those four years as he himself had been? O how I have lost an ideal!

And if it was "pique" shouldn't the "friend," in his great "friend-ship," "innocence," and "objectivity," have tried to talk me out of my distress into a semblance at least of my former gentleness and complaisance and tranquility? Or would that not have been "aristocratic?"

Objectivity! That is the word he used the evening of our interview. He insisted upon his innocence, he knew he was innocent, and had given me no reason for believing my feelings toward him to be reciprocated—he knew it because he could view the situation with objectivity. And yet he was my "friend" whose "friendship" was so great that he considered it a betrayal to "thank" me when I worked myself to death for him! And yet he could tell me with his next breath that he was in love with the girl in Berlin! Objectivity in spite of great friendship and great love!

I wish I were out and out insane, unless insane people suffer. Then I may as well be as I am.

GALLEY PROOFS AND "WEDDING TRIPS"

April 21, 1909

Yesterday it was six months since he came and told me of his betrothal to another, it was a rainy Tuesday again—and a letter came from him. On my return from Baltimore, after spending the Passover holidays there, I thought I was proof even against such a combination. I came back feeling that I had regained some of my personality. My family had petted me into it, dear Rachel had even come all the way from Madison to help them do it. After my address to the Federation of Charities and again after my address before the Council, there had been so much praise, so many demonstrations of joy and pleasure at my being a Baltimorean, so much adulation and kind speech as to my appearance, my manner, my voice, my language, my ideas, that for once I permitted praise to enter my soul and give me consolation which I needed so sorely. The minute I stepped into New York, I knew that it was self-deception—my nature was the same, it craved realities, not childish concessions. Yet I kept brave. I behaved with self-respect at the synagogue on Saturday. But on Sunday when I began to work at his book, I realized how little reserve bravery I had stored up. Before I left for Baltimore I had sent him the galley proof of "Joseph," adding the request that if there was any "front matter" to the second volume, of which "Joseph" would form the first chapter, to send it to me now. He returned the proof Saturday evening with a note saying he could not write his preface to the second volume until the whole was in type. Thereupon I wrote to him:

> "*In view of the fact that your withholding copy for over two months and your tacit refusal to accept my time limit, the middle of July, have made it impossible for me to read the proof of this volume to the end, I would request you to stretch a point and furnish me with the front matter, so that at least the translation, if not the proof-reading of the volume, may be done uniformly. If you cannot grant this concession, there I herewith make the formal request that my connection with the second volume whatever it may turn out to be, shall be explicitly and impersonally stated in your preface, wherever it is written and by whomever translated.*"

It was to this that the answer came yesterday:

> "*I am trying to get the chapter on Moses all done before I leave for Europe but I doubt whether I will succeed. In all events I will have the greater part of it ready before my departure and I hope that you will not on account of a few pages make me and the Jewish Pub. Soc. look for an other translator.*"

I wonder whether he understands my psychology sufficiently to realize that what keeps me excited is the fear that he will put me in such a position that his book will have to be done by someone else, and not done so carefully as I can do it, or at least so consistently and uniformly as I can. Rachel and Mamma noticed my excitement and there was a scene, Mamma threatening to write a brusque letter to him. They certainly do not understand! They think it resentment on my part, and on his, and I know it to be love on mine, unwounded love, the more wounded as I must wound the loved one, and know at the same time that he, too, thinks it resentment, Mamma's threat drove me wild, she had written her letter out and showed it to me. So I wrote as my feelings dictated—a private letter—this one:

> "*In reply to a paragraph in your business letter of April 18 to me, I want to say that your desire to have me finish the translation of the "Legends" cannot possibly be so great as mine. My literary conscience is very sensitive upon the subject, and for this reason, as well as for the sake of other days, it would be lasting pain to me to mutilate your book, as it is pain to have to resign the fourth volume to other hands. That is why I have been urging you so persistently all along to go on with the work. If my act in setting a time-limit seems*

to belie these regrets, it is because I am driven to measures of self-preservation. My strength is giving out under the strain of emotion. Can't you understand that it has been hourly torture, as I told you when I spoke to you last, for me to occupy myself with your book? For the first time in my life I must give up work and seek forgetfulness and restoration. If I have your book on my mind, and if I must resume it and relations with you on my return, even if only business relations, my efforts to regain physical strength and peace of mind will have been vain. I appeal to you to make a desperate exertion to get the third (seemed it should have been) volume done even to the reading of proof. I go so far as to ask a sacrifice of you. Give me a fair chance to get your book off my hands now, and there may be a possibility for me to recover to a normal attitude towards life."

That was last night, and a sleepless night followed. This morning my feelings are divided. Perhaps I should not have written as I felt—it may excite even him, cold and self-controlled as he is. Or if I wrote, I should have written more. I should have told him what pain I suffer whenever I remember—and when I do not remember?—that he did not give me the opportunity to put the last touches to his Geonic book. He knows my literary, even scholarly sensitiveness if not for myself, then for him—has he really forgotten, how I would sit for hours and re-read dozens of pages to find a little inconsistency that had struck him? and how I would not let him undergo the same drudgery?—and he could not bend his pride sufficiently to come and ask me,—say that he knew my magnanimity, that even in the changed circumstances I would want to complete five years' work. I should have told him in the letter, how everybody has been urging me for five months to drop his book like a hot coal. And I should have appealed to him by the memory of the friendship he professes for me, the friendship which he said he could resume, the friendship he placed so high, the friendship so great that he could thank me for nothing I did for him. I should have appealed to him the memory of all the service I did for him, the sleep I lost in his service, the insane devotion I manifested only a year ago when I began to translate his Introduction. He can afford to sacrifice some of the hours he will have with the worldly woman in Berlin—he will have a whole lifetime with her. And I have given him my life and my soul without a return.

Day before yesterday I received word that the Publication Society had granted me a six months' leave of absence, my salary to be paid as usual. And I am going to go to Europe in order to recover my poise there. My wedding trip while my darling is being married to another! Is it only sadness or is it age, too, that prevents me from rejoicing in the opportunity that would make others go wild with delight? He has made me sad and old and indifferent and unenergetic. Sometimes, in other days, the thought would surprise me that he would take me to Europe and show me the Old World treasures, and I would feel hot with pleasure and ashamed. The shame is all that is left.

He ought to remember that he failed to furnish me with copy regularly. And I wonder whether he recalls his frequent boast that he could keep me supplied with matter—I was so much slower than he. Of course, he has gotten ahead of me now, but that is because I read the proof of his book a dozen times to make sure that *his* book was as perfect as I could make it.

This morning it came back to me that in one of his letters last summer he wrote that he regretted he had gone to Europe that year. But he was not truthful then either, for as I remember it was the letter of September 4, and on August 31 he had asked the girl whether she would go to America. What does it all mean? His character as I knew it, his actions, his double-meaning words. I cannot understand it!

TORTURE TO CONTINUE, TORTURE TO GIVE IT UP

April 23.

In my talk with him, when he said that he had thought his betrothal would only serve to make our relations, our intimacy, he said, closer, that he had thought no one in the world, except perhaps his mother, would rejoice more in his happiness, I asked him whether he thought his fiancée, under the circumstances, would want our intimacy to continue. He responded by praising her magnanimity. I confessed to having none such—that I would not sanction it if the case were reversed. I questioned further, whether he himself, knowing my feelings (which he protested he had not known the state of before!!), would want to see me daily, etc. And he said, Why not? Again, I returned that I for my part could not trust myself—I would do something wicked if I gave myself the opportunity of being with him as before. He laughed a laugh of confidence—it was meant as an expression of that boundless friendship he professed for me!—and said "I am willing to trust you." "But I cannot trust myself," I said.

He simply is undeveloped on the emotional side—he does not know what love is. I knew it always, even when I had not experienced it, that is even before I met him. Because I denied the power of love and my capacity for it, I could not make up my mind to enter the marriage relation all the times it was proposed to me. But how much better it would have been for me if I had—how much less unhappy my life would have been, even if not happy. Yes, it is true what I said before, he is "in love" with the girl in Berlin, but of love neither of them has an inkling. They will doubtless lead a sober, humdrum, Philistine existence, with thrills of joy when their children are born, and perhaps other thrills of which I have no knowledge, incidental to marriage, and the world will call them happy, and they will be satisfied with themselves and with each other. And the world and they will be right. Creatures like myself are all wrong, therefore all unhappy. And they think that a trip to Europe will restore me! It may calm me, and dull me, but I am incurable. The wound may heal, but the cicatrice will remain forever.

April 25, 1909

I have his answer. It is the gentlest utterance that came from him since his last European letter—he himself, the self I knew and loved and still love, wrote it. He cannot finish before he goes to Europe, whither he must sail not later than May 12, for reasons which he does not care to explain to me (!! as though he needed to!). Of course, he says, he is willing to read the proof and pass on it during his stay in Europe. Of course, it is not true, because in his other letter he wrote very blatantly that what was not put before him by the middle of May he would not look at until the end of October. He gives me his address in Amsterdam, the same as last year, a fact which, naturally, he does not mention. His last sentence is: "If you would ask my advice, I would ask you to stop working at my book *immediately*. You certainly have no obligation in the matter neither to the J.P. Society nor to me."

[text of the full letter:]

> *Jewish Theological Seminary*
> *531–535 West 123rd St.*
> *New York City*
>
> *April 23, 1909*

Your desire to get the third volume done can not be greater than mine, yet I regret to say that I hardly believe I will succeed in getting it finished. For reasons which I do not care to explain to you I must leave for Europe not later than May twelfth and I do not see how I shall manage to complete the work in such a short time. Of course I am willing to read the proof and pass on it during my stay in Europe. My address will be 24 Swammerdam Street, Amsterdam. If you would ask my advice, I would advise you to stop working on my book *immediately*. You certainly have no obligation in this matter neither to the J.P. Society nor to me.

Very truly yours,

Louis Ginzberg

He does not understand either—it is torture to work at his book, but torture also to contemplate giving it up to some one else. Alas, I have not yet learnt that he does not read my love between the lines of his book. And he does not know my character. Give up work entrusted to me because it is hard to do, and when giving it up means the risk of spoiling a beloved man's book!? And it is getting harder every day. Today I realized that I have not the same facility as formerly in reading his dear crabbed handwriting. Has it gotten worse, does he want to try me, or am I losing the clairvoyance of love now that I know that I was the victim of long deception or self-deception?

This afternoon the old torturing doubts returned again for the thousandth time. I saw only his side, I saw myself an old scheming woman throwing myself at him, giving love when there could be no possibility of a return of it on his part, and then making a vulgar scene and causing him, if not unhappiness, at least discomfort. I went on a walk, there was glorious April sunshine, but a high wind was blowing. Something in the air brought back to me two years ago, when he was preparing to go to Europe, and it had already been arranged that I was to walk down to the steamer with him. It was so vivid, that I felt the same clutching at the heart as then when I could not grasp the idea that I was to be separated from him for over five months. And now I have not associated with him practically nine months. I survive, but in what shape! Suddenly I caught sight from my seat in the Elevated of a tree that blooms now, with a greenish, yellow blossom, and suddenly my memories crystallized. On a Friday afternoon in April two years ago, it was just so sunny, and so windy, and the same trees were in bloom. I can count out the date. He left on a Saturday, the last Saturday in April, April 27, so that Friday that comes back to me was April 19. He must have come over for lunch that day. Yes, I remember, it rained, and as so often when it rained, he telephoned whether he might have lunch with us. Then it cleared, and I said I'd have to go to the milliner's for my spring hat. Adele was to go with me, and Thomas joined her. At once he said he would walk along, and we walked together down Broadway to 81st Street. It was blowing hard, for when I reached the milliner's I had to comb my hair which was dishevelled by the wind. In the course of the work, it was the following Friday when he took leave of Mamma, in the very room in which he afterwards killed me by announcing his engagement, he asked me whether I had gotten my hat, and whether I'd wear it the next day to the steamer. Yes, I would provided it did not rain. How his question made my heart beat!

The next morning when I called for him, his sister-in-law looked at the bobbing red roses on my hat and said, "Now I understand why my brother-in-law asked me a question. He wanted to know whether rain would hurt a spring hat. I know now he was thinking of yours." And I felt hot all over,—and happy. Those warm feelings have been coming back to me so often these last few days. I feel his eyes resting on me again and again. And he says there was nothing between us! Rachel says what made her certain that there was an understanding between us was that at the synagogue he never took his eyes from me, and she even thought it must be annoying to me, because of its indicating that he was far from being absorbed in his religious devotion. I knew he often looked at me when I sat opposite to him, and if I had not known it, his present manner of studiously avoiding a look in my direction, of averting his eyes hastily when they happen to fall upon me, would recall it to me by contrast. Today it occurred to me that his prevarications during our interview were so uneven. Why did he feel compelled to acknowledge that he had noticed my three-day's distress two years ago after he told me of his contemplated five months' absence? It was a matter of two years and he might have denied it, seeing that his notice and his recollection of it are indictments—they prove that he knew the state of my feelings toward him. That he did not deny having noticed my distress at the post office last 22nd of July I can understand. It was too recent, and had been too palpable—I actually wept before him. Why did I not that day throw myself upon his mercy and beg him not to leave me without giving me some assurance that he would return as he went? What would he have said? That he did not care for me? Perhaps—probably—but at least he would not have been able to humiliate me before myself on his return by telling me he did not know I had loved him, and I would not have written to him this summer, and would not have been taken unaware and broken down before him and the world with no prospect of gathering my bits together again.

Dr. Friedman was here this evening. I wonder whether he remembers how I used to grow eloquent about my darling's achievements and abilities? Did he notice my silence upon what was once my favorite topic with him, favorite because he shared my estimate of his attainment and his capacity? Is there anything or anyone that does not bring back my loss to me? Perhaps Europe with all its new sights will remove him from my mind. And from my, heart, too?

THE IDEAL BEGINS TO TOTTER

April 26, 1909

What need could there have been for me to ask a direct question at the post office on July 22nd? Did I not have my answer three or four weeks earlier, when he found the Introduction was growing very long, and he asked me to find a translator for him, that he could not impose the big task upon me. And I told him how unhappy it would make me to have him withdraw it from me? And the next evening when he brought the subject up again, I spoke even more plainly and said, I must do those things for him for they kept me in connection with him, I feared he would drift away from our friendship if I did not. If he had loved me, he would have spoken then, I cannot remember what I thought at the time. Probably what I had been thinking all along when he failed to speak though his actions were becoming more and more pronounced,—that until he had been in Europe again and had completed the year of mourning for his father, he did not want to put his thoughts on other matters. I felt all summer that he was going on the short European trip to settle an epoch in his life, and then he would return and start out anew with me. An honorable man would have gone home the evening I spoke so plainly and written me a note to say that our relations must be more sober if they were to continue at all, or he would have insisted upon taking the work away from me instead of coming day after day and discussing it point by point with me. Is he really so materialistic that he wanted me to do the work and save him the money?

Mamma says that my obvious grief at the post office determined him to come back from Europe engaged to a young girl so as to shake me off. I will not believe it. He did not love me, that is evident. He is "in love" with the girl, and he counted on my physical and spiritual strength not to betray my feelings when he returned. But why did he know me so little after four years of intimacy? Why not treat me with frankness?

Now I mistrust him all around. When he advises my giving up the work at his book immediately, is it because he fears, after my high strung letter to him, that I will break down utterly, and he will be pointed at with scorn? He knows men well, he knows that if his associates do not see me in distress, his path will be smooth with them. And in spite of all he used to tell me about not caring for people, it is evident that now, when he is about to bring a wife over, he does care. Otherwise, why should he have so insisted upon everybody's writing to her? That was not his usual way—to ask for favors of that sort. This after all is the worst feature—that I have lost my ideal, and with it I have lost all that four, nay now it is five years of life stood for.

If I can hold on to the feeling I have this morning, that he acted dishonorably toward me, that I was not a fool, but responded naturally to a feeling which he professed in acts, then perhaps Europe *can* cure me. At all events, my European trip is so timed that he and she will establish themselves here in their and my circle without my pale dejected countenance as a sentinel, and when I return I may find definitely that it is no longer my circle, that her charm has conquered it and justified him. And then I will yield the ground and begin all over again.

I keep on woefully not understanding him. Even if the fear is at the bottom of his heart that I may break down completely and be a constant reproach to him, he will know how to transform it to his advantage. He will scratch it and kill it by the argument that he never uttered a word that plainly meant that he loved me or that he recognized my love for him, and therefore I am an inexpressible fool for having acted as I did. I wonder whether this subterfuge actually gives him comfort. If it does, then he is in no sense the man I took him to be every day for four years, and I ought to console myself for the loss of his companionship. But is the explanation of his conduct so crude, so blatant as all that? And so I go on circling round in the contracted cage life has put me in.

Just now the telephone bell rang. It was Mr. Dobsevage to tell me he had received a note from him asking that a copy of the first volume of the "Legends" be bound up for him this week. Her birthday, I suppose!

Thus I am tortured by having to maintain business relations with him. I cannot be a woman, being a Secretary—not even an unhappy woman with grief kept sacred. If I have been undignified in my sorrow and misfortune it is not altogether the fault of my character.

April 27

What a day I had yesterday! I was like a tigress, all on account of the unknown girl's unknown birthday. I cursed her, and him, and myself. My excitement grew to the point at which I found it impossible to decipher his handwriting. It is getting harder and harder for me to do the translation. Almost I believe I shall have to accept his advice and give up his book. I hope not. Not because I still have any love for it, but because I want to rehabilitate my character in my own eyes. They all call me self-indulgent now.

An element in my excitement is his way of addressing questions and demands to me through Mr. Dobsevage. Have I not shown him the way? I write him a business letter. Why can't he imitate me?

I wonder what would have happened if that girl had not been at the synagogue that morning when he looked up in the women's gallery? Would he have "fallen in love" with the woman who happened to occupy the same place, only in order to rid himself of me? So little do I believe in his being "in love." Of course, he will now show the world, to spite me, what a devoted husband he can be to a girl whom he "picked up."

It is all an enigma to me. How could he go to the Marxes for Seder when he knew from me that Dr. Marx disapproved of his conduct toward me and had told me so? At least he should have sought to find out from Dr. Marx how far his disapproval goes. Of course, I know he is defiant, in the first place he cares for no one's opinion, and the fact that Dr. Marx invited him was sufficient proof that the disapproval was only skin-deep.

I wonder what it is that keeps on feeding my excitement. I believe it is simply the fact that having his handwriting constantly before me I am kept as constantly in mind of the unlimited amount of myself that I gave him. If my name were attached to everything I did for him, what a charnel house he would have to bring his wife to. It would stare at her from every corner. But I was so large-hearted that I never put my name to anything, not even that book of Dr. Schechter's, and he will take good care never to tell her of my character as he knew it in those days. If he speaks of me, it will be as a designing woman. I ought to rest satisfied with one huge grudging admission made by him. When I asked him whether he realized that he had absorbed me and my time completely—that I had associated with no other person, he said, Yes, he realized it now, and for that he must apologize. Thus, he admitted my whole charge, in general and in particulars. A man of thirty-five who does that means something or he is a knave. He may be a knave, and yet I have been a fool, and I am a fool. If only his wedding day were over! I am afraid of it and of myself.

Adele says that that last letter of his is the only thing she has seen from him that has a true ring—the one in which he advises my giving up his book immediately. I am becoming more clearsighted than she is, or more warped. I detect lack of sympathy only. He says, "You certainly have no obligation in the matter to the J.P. Society nor to me." He knows that past relations are an obligation for me, not to mention literary considerations, and Jewish sympathy for Jewish scholarship. So the expression is another piece of bravado—he does not care whether I do it or not. Or he reduces "obligation" to money relations and he knows how little they count with me. True sympathy would have made him write very differently. He should have acknowledged my right feeling in the matter, and regretted that circumstances made my task so difficult. But that would have involved a confession of wrongdoing on his part, and never will he make that. And I believe that in the back of his head is the unacknowledged thought that after I come back, the J.P.S. will force me to do the work after all, or my feelings will have been reduced to indifference. I anticipate neither contingency—alas, that the latter should seem so impossible to me.

Many years ago—he had manifested his "friendship" for me by accepting only a few services from me, two or three translations etc.—so that we were not yet very "great" friends—I met him at the Schechters and when I entered they were teasing him about writing the article on Kissing for the Jewish Encyclopedia. In the conversation that ensued he spoke enthusiastically of the chaste ways among the Jews, and he instanced the fact that he had never seen his mother and father, a very devoted couple, kissing each other, whatever they may have done in the privacy of their chamber. And he is to marry a girl who gave herself to him after the third meeting, and who writes to me, an utter stranger, about her "Schatzelein." So it was all platitudes—all that he told me of his admiration for Rabbinical Ethics! And I took him to be the embodiment of the noblest sayings by the noblest men! It cannot be that I was so utterly mistaken all those years. It must be that—I do not know what. Today is the second anniversary of my walk to the dock with him.

April 28.

How was it possible for him to say after he knew my true feelings for him—which he avowed he had never suspected before—that his fiancée would not object to a continuation of our intimacy? So long as they were what he says he thought they were, he could have said it, but once he knew the truth, he should not have gone back to the old relation and possibilities even as a supposition. The truth probably is he would not have objected to a restoration of the forms of intimacy in order that the real state of affairs might not be revealed to her too glaringly. That is what he counted upon when he engaged himself and pooh-poohed the idea to her that there was more between us; that is what he expected of my heroism, that is what lingered in his mind, so firmly had it been established then as the course of things would take, as the best solution of the vulgar difficulty in which my strong feelings had placed him. If he is an aristocrat, as he always boasted, how the vulgarity of the present situation must cut him to the quick, as it does me, who am a poor suffering democrat. I cannot help or extenuate. It was his sin in the first place that brought it upon him—his sin in making me love him, in absorbing my being, though he apparently had no notion of taking the consequences—and then his fault—his fault in not facing me honorably and truthfully.

I remember that for a time I thought he was relieved that the breach had come about, it would save him from reproaches and suspicions from his girl-wife, to which such intimacy as ours might have exposed him. But, of course, such intimacy as was ours, and as he says he could have kept up under the changed conditions, is an impossibility under the changed conditions. It would have dissolved itself even if I had been a heroine. What he dreaded was just the sort of breach that the strength of my love brought about. My present explanation is correcter. He was willing to resume relations with me in order that they might die out naturally under her eyes, and her suspicions be allayed, and the people around not talk.

But if it is true that he actually could have kept up the intimacy, and if he was speaking the truth when he replied that he could even after my revelations as to myself in relation to him, and chucked aside my fears that I could not remain a righteous pure woman if I met him constantly in the old way—if that was real and not a platitude, then he does not know love, he neither loves the girl he is going to marry, nor does he understand my love.

April 30

Yesterday was an inclement day. It started with sunshine, then came snow, hail, thunder, and lightening and volumes of rain, and all the time it was nippingly cold. Everybody exclaimed against such near-May weather. I seemed to be the only one with a memory from which its regularity might be inferred, and I did not speak of my memory. Last year the day like it came not on April 29 and a Thursday, but on May 1, and a Friday. It was the day of poor Alexander Cohn's funeral. The rain came down in sheets, and everybody prevented him from going to the funeral, which took place at midday.

How I suffered that day! In addition to having my heart wring for the poor mother of Cohn and all the rest. I was sore because I saw his pale face, drawn with emotion—he sat behind me on the other side of the room, and I could watch him out of the corner of my eye. After the services were over, I walked halfway down the block with the cortège, and returning I met him and a single word and a glance from me made him come to our house for dinner, and he stayed on in the afternoon lingering over the "Legends," writing his Shabbes letters, and—what an appalling memory I have!—that stiff letter to Itzkowski, which I begged him to modify—in vain. I wondered at his willingness to write so harshly, especially as he had been so softened a couple of hours before, and especially to a man for whom he pretended to have consideration on account of some slight connection with his father. I wonder still, more than ever now that that hardness, that callousness, that insistence upon the righteousness of his own ways has put a dagger into my heart and left it there for every occurrence, daily and hourly to give it a twist, and keep the wound bleeding. He stayed on until it was nearly Shabbos, and he had to hasten away to get ready for it.

And one short year later!? Last evening Judge Sulzberger lectured at the Seminary, I went from a sense of duty, he, too, I suppose. As luck would have it, I turned my head as he took his seat, two or three benches directly behind me. So I knew he was there, and where he was, and I was disquieted all evening, after having boasted a couple of hours before, that the soreness had several times that day lifted from my heart. After the lecture was over, I rose, and turned to go. He was already standing up, squarely planted with his back to me, and he hastened out and went into the office to avoid me. That is what one short but bitter year can produce.

He told me twice that he knew nothing of women. I was so meek, submissive, and idolatrous with him that I did not retort either time that I knew as little of men probably. Evidently he thinks me shameless else he would not have asked me whether I had not had such relations with other men as with him. He, a man of thirty-five, knew [this] woman well enough, if he did not know women. I realize that since I have been translating the "Legends" relating to the Patriarchs. I was the innocent one, not he. And as for me, if I knew men and men or not, I did know truth, honor, affection, devotion. Apparently he did not, and hence my unhappiness.

Shall I go on forever writing a backward calendar, and a commentary upon his life and sayings? Heaven help me!

I wonder, too, whether any of these reminiscences come back to him, not as a pang, that is not what I mean. I only wonder whether they recur to his wonderful memory, so much more perfect than mine. Or is it all a matter of heart and not of memory? It must be, else he would not continue to send me his manuscript or the papers that I kept him supplied with, because he liked it. Fool, fool, fool!

THE JOINT PICTURE

May 4, 1909

He passed me just now, on the other side of the street. He kept his eyes fixedly ahead and did not greet me. It is the only way.

The evening of our interview he said he did not know what was wrong until I handed him his fiancée's letter to read and I did not ask for the picture she told me to ask for—the only one, he added, she had sent except the one for him. The term she used was that probably their joint picture had meantime reached me, if not, I was to *"reklamier"* [claim] it from the *Herr Professorlein* [little Professor]. Obviously, he had had it some days. Why had he not brought it to me? Had he been afraid? Did he suspect? Let me see, can I reckon it out still when that picture arrived? I must have seen it soon after its arrival. Sophie brought it here one afternoon, when she came over with "copy" from him, I think. I remember I had told her in the morning she need not make the trip specially. But she came, because, she said, she was going to see Mrs. Marx, and timidly, she added, might she show me the picture she had of her uncle's fiancée? When was that? I saw it at his house again on Saturday, November 14th, but that was after he saw the letter. No, I cannot fix the time of Sophie's showing it to me. But it was before he saw the letter. So he might have brought it to me before. He saw the letter on November 12, and he had been here on Tuesday, November 10, and Monday, November 9, and Saturday, November 7. I had returned from Baltimore on Thursday, November 5. I have a feeling that Sophie showed it to me before I went to Baltimore, which was on October 30. I have that feeling, because as the scene comes back to me, my mother forms no part of it, not even the consciousness of her presence in the house. If it had been the same week of his seeing her letter I would have spoken to her about it.

I am again doing the detective service that robs me of sleep and even the artificial calm I have attained to. But I wish I could fix that date. It would demonstrate lack of truth in me particular at least. And I must know the truth about his untruthfulness or the reverse to re-establish myself in my own eyes.

More and more the feeling grows that Sophie brought the picture before I went to Baltimore. I have it! It was the day before I left for Baltimore, because I was so annoyed, knowing that Sophie had an appointment with Mrs. Marx, that I was not permitted to see her, I mean Mrs. Marx, when I called to bid her good-bye. If I am right, he had the picture on October 29. He had not given it to me on November 12th, two weeks later. In the meantime he had seen me on Saturday, November 7, Monday, November 9, Tuesday, November 10, always by appointment. So he knew he would see me. Why didn't he bring it to me? Because he realized. He did not have to wait to apply the test, as he said. Did he use "test" accurately? Then he would have been telling the truth as I see it. It would have meant that the explanation for my conduct had been buzzing in his mind. My not asking for the photograph was the clinching test. But in that case what did his direct answer to my question mean? I had asked him, "What did you think was the matter with me all those weeks? Had you no suspicion?"—"I had no idea," he said, "until you gave me my fiancée's letter. Then I made the photograph my test."

Why am I so anxious to establish his untruthfulness? Because it pleases me to show him up a liar? Far from it. That cuts to the quick. But I must act in self-defense. I must do what I can to prove to myself that I was not a fool—that there was a reason for my frightful collapse—that I may again respect myself. If he did not give me the picture all that time, then he knew what was happening inside of me, and he knew because he was in the best position of anyone in the world to know it. Or is there a loophole for him even now? Did he

287

withhold it because, knowing my state of mind and heart, he did not want to hurt me? That would be compatible with innocence on his part, and leave my fooldom where it was before. Mere knowing the reason of my breakdown is not evidence of the guilt of having caused it. The man on the street might also have divined the cause of my grief, and yet he was not responsible for it. Nothing favors anything! If only I could get back my old trust in him! I would be a fool, and would have been a fool, and I would be unhappy, but my darling and my hero would be my ideal still.

REPERCUSSIONS IN SCHOLARLY CIRCLES

May 5.

Today I started from a drowse into which I had fallen over "Philo" on account of too little sleep during the night, and I realized that I had been dreaming of him—I had seen him look white, pained, suffering, his eyelids irritated as they always were when he was not well, he looked as though he were about to faint, as he did that Tisha-be-Ab evening when I had to take him home. And seeing him in that plight, I stretched my hands out to him. Before he could respond, I started up. It is not the first dream-vision of the sort I have had of him. This one, I suppose, is due to the occurrence between him and Dr. Marx and Dr. Davidson of which Dr. Marx told me last evening as having happened during the day. I cannot set it down yet because I do not get it quite straight. Some time, I suppose, I'll hear more about it, and without asking, too, I know enough, however to understand that it may be an explanation of the grave expression, grave even for him, which his countenance wore yesterday when he passed me so stolidly.

May 7, 1909

The reccurrence that Dr. Marx alluded to is a dreadful thing—dreadful for him and more dreadful for me. Mrs. Davidson of her own accord told me all about it. She started off by saying Dr. Schechter had risen in her estimation by what he had done in connection with the Jewish Quarterly Review, and she seemed surprised I did not know about it. A meeting, it appears, was held to determine in whose hands the editorial management was to be. I cannot make out who was present at that meeting. At all events after it he took Dr. Davidson aside, and complained he had not been treated properly, that he was at least as great a scholar as Dr. Schechter and perhaps the greatest scholar in America, and yet Dr. Schechter had declined to let him have a place on the editorial board. It seems, he continued, they have a grudge against me, and I don't know why. Dr. Davidson spoke up, and said, "I am not a fool, and you are not an ass, don't tell me you don't know what the grudge is,"—"No, I haven't an idea"—he insisted. I know the tone of voice, I know the wide open innocent eyes, it is but a repetition of what he said to me in the last conversation in here. Oh, I understand! He cannot, he does not recede from the position he once took. Alas! that he ever took it.

I do not get a clear idea of the Jewish Quarterly Review business. I can only make out that the old antagonism between him and Dr. Schechter has been increased on account of what happened with me. He put a convenient handle in the grasp of all who cared to have one against him. And to think that my darling, my peerless darling, should go about claiming recognition for his obvious superiority. I have no doubt he thinks I am doing underhand work against him. If he does, he does not understand me in the least. Any harm that comes to him hurts me a thousandfold. All I want is him, and his humiliation does not give him back to me. If it did, perhaps I would use even the underhand methods my soul has never known—I need and want him so badly. She said in her letter, he would make a *"ganze Person"* [complete person] of her. I am beginning to have respect for that chit of a girl—that is what he made of me and now!

Altogether Mrs. Davidson upset me about him. She says he is seeking them—seeking everybody's company about the Seminary. She says he makes a point of running after her on Saturday and greeting her—does it ostentatiously—he, who never was dependent upon others, who was proudly independent. I do not wonder—he cannot expose her to what he can stand. Oh that I should have brought all this misery and ugliness down upon him. But is it my fault? Shouldn't he blame himself? If he only had been truthful and loyal to the friendship at least which he professed for me.

For no reason I must set down here what I heard about Mania Wilbushewitz.[15]

FOUR BOOKS IN ONE YEAR

May 8, 1909

I didn't know it was still possible for me to suffer as I did today. I thought I had used up my capacity in that respect. This morning I walked toward Riverside with Louis and Harriet,[16] and near the end of our block I came face to face with him, and he deliberately turned at a sharp angle and crossed over to the other side. So that is my farewell view of him—Wednesday he sails on *my* wedding-trip!

Obviously he intends to cut me thereafter. He did it last Tuesday and today. And obviously he does it in consequence of that Jewish Quarterly business, of which I am as innocent as a new born baby, as dear little Harriet herself. I wish I could be told that story straight. Up to this time, it appears he still respected me, now he believes I am wicked. God knows that I am not so far as he is concerned—only wretchedly unhappy, only loving him still as though there were hope for me, only missing him all the time, night and day. If only I were dead and gone!

At last I am reconciled to the European trip. It will remove me from his path from now until January. By that time it will be practically eighteen months that I shall not have spoken to him. That ought to wipe him out of my heart, if such a thing is possible!

Mrs. Benchmiel was here yesterday. I had a most interesting conversation with her about her industrial classes, about Palestine, about my own attitude toward Judaism as a religion, about women and men and the eternal mystery of their relation to each other (how I quailed when she described her relation to her husband—exactly what mine might have been if——), and finally about Miss Wilbushewitz and her marriage. She is married to a certain Shochat, a laborer in the colonies, in the last stages of tuberculosis, ten years younger than herself. She is very happy, and very submissive even to the opinion of her husband who is not her equal in any intellectual respect. They all shrug their shoulders, that this magnificent creature, perfect in physique, an Amazon in strength, masculine in mind, should have thrown herself away, as they call it. I can understand it all! The world does not understand her and my kind—*he* certainly did not understand my kind.[17]

I wish I had been in Europe and were back again, and could face him and her calmly, and could resume the ordinary business of living life. Meantime there is still a three month pull at his book before me.

In three different places in the American Hebrew this week, mention is made of the fact that he has four books issuing from the presses this month! The Legends, two volumes of Geonica, and the Yerushalmi Fragments book. Much is made of the fact that three of them go to enrich Jewish literature in the English language. Nothing was said of the poor broken-hearted interpreter, who put them into English, and did it so lovingly for the sake of the writer and for the sake of the Jewishness of the subjects—she even loved the Geonic Responsa, the driest of dry subjects, for the two sakes.

"I MUST LIVE! I MUST LIVE!"

May 9, 1909

It recurs to my mind that Dr. Marx spoke the other evening, when he alluded to the talk Dr. Davidson had with him, of his ingratitude to Dr. Schechter, who had secured the money for his various books—he had barely thanked him. I know how to take these things as his due if I do not know it who should? He took more than money from me without thanks, without return of any kind except the things that I *made* a return from him in the crucible of my love—he took time, energy, brain effort, soul effort, everything I was capable of, everything I could save by social, physical, emotional self-abnegation. But does he not realize that it is his ingratitude that is setting Dr. S. against him and not I.

I walked with Louis on the lower Riverside Drive yesterday, and at a certain spot the memory that came back to me was that he "boasted" to me over and over again that he had not been in Dr. Marx's house for over two months. Yet he compared Dr. Marx's friendship with mine,—me whom he saw daily during that time, and several times a week all day! And to think that he who was so proud of his independence and so self-sufficient in his isolation is now charged with trying to curry favor with his associates socially! Not even the rudiments of all this untruthfulness in act and word and character were visible to me before. Is my vision distorted now?

Yesterday the third gentlemen appeared since I have been in New York who thought me worthy of desiring to make me his second or third wife! It seems I can please only the broken down, the weary, the helpless. And it seems that the one in all the world that attracted me with a thousand charms lacked truth and honor.

I keep on torturing myself, by saying, if we were still on the old terms such and such would happen now—he would ask me to walk with him in this beautiful weather, I would show him this letter, I would discuss this book or occurrence with him, he would come and play with Harriet. I would tell him the thought that has come into my mind—as though it were my fault we were no longer on the old terms. Suppose I had succeeded in being as heroic as I tried to be those first three weeks, and as, apparently, he had reckoned upon my being, could he have continued to come day after day, coming early and staying late, eating four, five and six, and more meals a week with us, waiting for me always and everywhere? He did say to me, that he had expected our intimacy to be increased by his engagement and marriage. But that is preposterous—not such intimacy as ours was.

Two of the notices in the American Hebrew were from the hand of Dr. Jacobs[18]—not the first indication that has come to me, that he has attached himself to the men for whom he always professed little respect. He after all has to seek to replace the external services I did him as to English, and the man who is reported not to have been overwise in sex matters is the one towards whom he must gravitate. Thus we both deteriorate because of his lack of truthfulness. Or is it because of my misunderstanding hugely?

May 10, 1909

Other women have suffered as I am suffering, and so far as I know they have not suffered so obviously—the world has not known so much about it, and they have not obtruded their suffering upon the cause of it as I have. Why? Am I more self-indulgent than others? I have not been so the rest of the years of my life. But other women, all that I have known, once they have realized the wicked treatment accorded them, have been able to cut loose from the cause, the men. In my case, partly on account of his deliberate action, partly on account of circumstances, that was impossible. The circumstances are summed up in work on his book. And as for him, he wanted to make me believe and perhaps himself believes that his betrothal was not a break. How many women, for instance, were placed in such a position that as they sat at the head of their own table, the table at which he had enjoyed hospitality innumerable times, unselfish, uncalculating hospitality, he, the one who had inflicted the mortal injury, should say to one's sister, "My future wife bears the same name as you"—say it joyously, triumphantly. In all other cases, the man would not have put the wronged woman in the position of having him at the table. Such things robbed me of the strength to dissemble—and there were so many of such things! And if he suffers under my behavior, I can only see it in the light of a boomerang.

I wonder whether he has enough imagination to realize what it means for a person like myself to have to say every morning on rising: "I must live! I must live!"

May 11, 1909

Again and again I am overwhelmed by the monstrous unreality (because untruth) of what has happened, and then I feel as though I would go insane. Then something fortunately recurs to my mind to bring back the "atmosphere" of those other days, and I regain a sense of reality. He sails tomorrow, and he will not bid me farewell, unless his ostentatious crossing over to the other side of the street without a greeting when he met me face to face last Saturday can be construed as an eternal farewell. In other days? When he went in 1907, on his last Tuesday with us I remember, my mother and myself lamented that it would be the last dinner he'd have with us. "Don't cry," he said, "I will come Thursday again, if you want me," Want him? I remember Mrs. Antonia Oppenheim was here at that dinner, and I refused to go out with her, because he stayed on with me. And yet he says there was nothing in the old relation that he could not go on with and intensify as a man engaged to another woman! And again he came in on Friday, to bid us a final, final farewell! And then I walked down to the steamer with him, and told him how unhappy I'd be if he permitted himself to be persuaded to remain in Europe. It is unreal, after all. But the unreality lies in his untruthfulness, not in my folly. My folly was sad but justified by his actions.

"THE CAD!"

May 12, 1909

He sailed today, I do not even know on what steamer. I might have trusted myself to find out. I need not have feared that I would have followed up this steamer as I did his various movements last year. I have been perfectly honorable in such matters. I have never since Oct. 20 watched for him at the window as I used to, nor done anything I need be ashamed of. Since I know him to have sailed, I have been remarkably quiet. I seem to feel that the irrevocable step is near.

He is to marry in London, because not being an American citizen he cannot marry in Berlin. How irregular it all seems.

Yesterday I broke down at Mrs. Friedlaender's. They feel strongly with me. Mrs. F. has no respect for the girl's precipitate engagement, she appreciates the obstacles presented by my age, she condemns him as all the rest do—and do now in particularly unmeasured terms—she told me how she and Dr. F. felt when he crossed over the street from the Seminary on Oct. 20 to tell me of his engagement—Dr. F. clenched his fist and said to his wife who happened to be there, "The cad!" It still hurts me unspeakably to hear him run down. Everybody does it—only to me? No, Mrs. Marx is sincere, so is Mrs. Davidson, so is Mrs. Fried- laender, so are the Schechter's. I have no reason to doubt any one. And Mrs. Marx was anxious to speak to him about me and present my point of view—show him that it is feeling, not resentment. But her husband would not let her. It is just as well! Dr. M. cannot get back on to the old footing with him. And they tell me that it was he himself who urged the insertion in the American Hebrew of the notice about his books. Then all he told me about his indifference was not true! No, his whole character has changed under this trial—this vulgar display of feeling. Oh, if I only had been as strong, at least physically, as he reckoned upon my being. I pretend to myself that I do not care whether he judges me correctly. But I do. If Mrs. M. could have seen her way very clear to speaking to him, and a modus vivendi (instead of moriendi)[19] had been agreed upon, I would have been happy enough as things go now— happy, because further misunderstandings might have been avoided. It is good, very good, that I go away. Mrs. Marx says her relatives speak well of her beauty and "*Nettheit,*" [amiability]. She will make her way with everybody, through youth and mother wit, and conquer his place back for him. It does not really matter about me. As I cannot go through life with him, it matters little how I go without him. God bless him! as I told him when he last went to Europe, my own then.

The Girl in London

May 13, 1909

Mrs. Marx says that the American Hebrew business went this way. Dr. M. teased him about it, and he said (how well I know the man- ner!) that he had said something to Jacobs about it in fun, and Jacobs had taken him up seriously. But from Dr. Jacobs it appeared later that he had actually put down the titles of the books on paper. On the other hand, I know how anxious the hunted journalist is to have a bit of news and a succulent paragraph for his editorial. Still it is not the man I knew.

Mrs. Marx says also that her feeling is that his marriage is bravado—he wanted to show that he, too, could marry a young and beautiful girl, like the other professors, younger and more beautiful, in fact, than their wives, and a European girl at that. It is what Adele said at the first. When she said it I dissented violently, when Mrs. M.

said it, I simply did not assent. That is the saddest part of all the sad business, that we have lost respect for each other. My love, I must accept, was not reciprocated. But he respected me and I idolized and reverenced him.

As for that being the motive for his marriage in general or to this girl in particular, it is nonsensical. Marrying a European is no great distinction. The others have been married some time. Why does he attempt to outdo them only now? No, he is truly in love with her. If he had wanted to marry, merely marry, he would not have stuck to my side. If he had wanted to marry a European as such he had plenty of chances on his former trips. No, he loves this particular young, beautiful, domestic, witty, sprightly, Berlin girl.

Mrs. Friedlaender said all of her own accord that I had done more for him than ever any wife she had seen or heard of. But that does not help me, either, the more fool I! No matter which way I turn, I remain unhappy.

But I am strangely quiet—with the quiet of a churchyard inside of myself. I have been trying to remember in vain whether I used to live in this doggedly sullen fashion before he came into my life. Perhaps this, too, will pass as the violence of my grief has passed, and leave me serene, and with that true resignation that is called being "at peace."

"At peace" I surely am not. Underneath the quiet, I am conscious of the girl in London who *does* know with what vessel he has sailed, who watches the wireless reports as I did last year, who knows exactly how many hours that steamer will take, as I knew it of his returning steamer last year—last year when he hastened to me to murder my best self.

I cannot understand why Dr. Marx, knowing that he knew that he (Dr. Marx) knew my view of the situation did not speak to him frankly, so that their relation would have been straightened out. It would, of course, have reacted on mine, too. But that is not what I am thinking of. In spite of all men may say, I a woman have much more "eye to eye" view of what friendship is. Now the time has passed forever. Once he is married the old tales may not be raked up. However, things will adjust themselves with all (except me) during my absence in Europe. But how I hate that European project!

May 14, 1909

Yesterday I had a day of agony, because nothing came from him for the "Legends," neither additional copy nor the page proof of "Joseph." I thought he was carrying his resentment over my fancied intrigue so far as to refuse to let me go on with his book. At last it came. But it turns out that "Moses" is not half done, and now it will be this way. I shall be the translator of Vol. I and Vol. III complete. Vol. II of Joseph, The Testaments of the Sons of Jacob (The Fathers of the Tribes, and Job) and half of Moses. I wonder who will do the rest.[20]

When I went over the notes and remarks on the page proof in his handwriting, I felt completely at peace—I felt as though he had asked my forgiveness, I felt as though it were again July 22, 1908—which it can never again be—nor can I ever again be what I then was, and alas! he can never again be what he was then, neither in my eyes nor in the eyes of his world here, nor, I fancy, in his own eyes. What is he thinking of these long days on the ocean?

Today the feeling of peace continues. Is it because he is gone, and is this the beginning of tranquility for me, to be completed by the eight months' separation made by his journey and mine? Or is it a lurking hope that the girl has heard and will have none of him. O but she will! She is already in London waiting for him. Have none of him?! Mrs. Marx revealed in the course of her conversation that though she had written but twice, she had received five missives from her. But to me to whom she would not write in the first place she refused to write a second time though she wondered at my not having replied to a letter that required no reply. To Mrs. Marx she could make the advances, and yet again make the advances. I had to humiliate myself. Such was *her* wish and *his*. And I, in all my fondness and respect for him, did it! There can be no doubt she knows she is building her happiness on the ruins of another woman's happiness. And could I take him back if she cast him off? Alas, alas! that I should want to.

Yet,—calm as I am, I see the wrong he did me clearly as never before. It was monstrous! If ever he feels himself walking on Riverside with me, it must come home to him.—Or standing at my desk—or reading a letter of mine in which I tell him of the work I am trying to save him—or—or—a thousand acts!

Mrs. Marx also says they have an idea he will try to get away from here. I was afraid of that right at the first, and begged Dr. Marx for that reason to continue on the old footing with him. But he cannot so easily give up a secure position now [that] he has a wife to take care of. And my European trip will solve the problem. It is intended that I shall be the victim and not he. I sent him proof today with many suggestions for changes in arrangement. Should that not convince him that I am true as steel in all his concerns? Have I harmed him with the Society? Did I not plead for the first volume instead of the third as the first to appear?[21] Did I not slave all winter that it could so appear? He ought to know after four years—he ought to know from the way I spoke that evening in February, the last time probably that I shall have spoken to him on earth. Is that possible?

MORE FACULTY REACTIONS

May 16, 1909

The leisure of the Sabbath put the Davidson incident before me clearly. He had been banking on the Davidson's and their act in inviting us together to their home that first dreadful Saturday as his apologists and representatives of the world and the attitude of the world. From this point of view represented by them and their act I had not a leg to stand on with my charges against him. Now, suddenly, Dr. Davidson rises up as the only one to hurl an accusation against him, even if veiled. He comes to the conclusion that I have poisoned the minds of his friends against him. Have I been so wicked? Have I not pleaded with them to remain on the old terms with him, to disregard me and my agony, since it would not help me to see him unhappy? Or did words have no effect in the presence of such abject misery as was depicted in my face and manner? Could I have helped these physical and mental disturbances in me brought by his untruth? No, that was elemental. Am I again dropping into self-righteousness?

Of course, he cannot know that the Davidson's have been kicking themselves all these months for their childish behavior. He cannot know that they like everybody else thought he had offered himself to me, and I had refused him. But why does he not remember the wrong of a similar nature once done by him to Dr. Davidson? Why did he have to wait for Dr. D. to turn against him? Why did he not speak to Dr. Marx the morning after our interview, when he knew that Dr. M. knew? Why, indeed, did he not speak openly to Dr. Davidson?

The end is that he cuts me. As I said before, it is fated that I shall be the sufferer alone. So be it.

What I cannot understand is how a man in love fails to have sufficient imagination to realize the pangs of disappointed love. If he really loves the girl, how could he have treated me as he did—as a mere "thing?"

Yesterday I read the review of the books in several "Nations," and I came across two novels, one called "The Spell," the other "David Bran," by Morley Roberts, based on the love of one man for two women, the two women of different types. Was that his attitude? And did he expect me to accept the situation in the spirit of Patriarchal times, and did he expect me, an articulate, conscious woman of modern times, to accept it tacitly? Is that what he expected from his "best friend" "who understood him as none other ever had?" And now we are enemies, and totally misunderstand each other.[22]

Mrs. Marx questioned the other day, why it was that he had not named her father[23] as reference when his future father-in-law wanted one? But he mentioned no one in his pride. The question and its implication would be justified if he had mentioned another.

Mrs. Marx also says that if her husband had had an idea that he never offered himself to me, he would have made him understand as long ago as 1906 that he had no right to go on with me as he did—to accept from me what he accepted. But I think Dr. M. is mistaken. He could not have summoned enough courage to tackle so delicate a subject with a man so difficult a subject. An open plain conversation would have been impossible, and as for hints, he did hint to him before he went to Tannersville that summer that he expected to hear the news as soon as "it" happened. I repeat it once more—I was foredoomed to the fate I am suffering. Nothing could have saved me but worldliness, and that I did not possess.

This is the way a notice reads in one of the papers: Dr. Louis Ginzberg of the faculty of the Jewish Theological Seminary is the author of four volumes that will issue from the press during the month of May. One of these is the "Legends of the Jews," which the Publication Society is about to send out. Having accomplished this much, Dr. Ginzberg is going to Europe to get married—

but not to the woman to whom he owes it—to whose unselfish work he owes it—that three of those four books appear in English, and in good form! The woman whom he jilted, spurned, left an "Agunah," after he had made her believe for four years that she was the only woman in the world to him.

RIVERSIDE MEMORIES, PRESENT REALITIES

June 2, 1909

On the day of my last writing in this journal a revelation was made to me that was so shocking, so revolutionizing of my whole inner world that I have not had the courage to put down my thoughts on paper. They are more orderly now. I feel as though I had attained to full maturity at last, the maturity that should have been my heritage a quarter of a century ago.

Before I put down what has made an epoch in my thinking about him and many other things, I will write out other thoughts that have come to me. Perhaps the other will be the last I shall ever say on the subject close to me.

During these two weeks came *Shabuot*.[24] *Shabuot* last year—how happy I was! That was the day I heard him read the Haftarah for the first time, and when we took our walk, he told me that the first chapter of Ezekiel was traditionally assigned to a great scholar. And the next day, the second day when he told me he would not walk with me for he wanted to pay Mamma a formal visit after her return from Baltimore, and at my suggestion he paid it to her in Morningside Park, I walked with his sister-in-law and told her how much she had missed in not having heard him read the Haftarah, that it had been "*betamt*" [tasteful] as everything was that he did. Did she notice the joyous catch in my voice? Did she? and then ask me whether his engagement to another girl was not fine? And on that second day, how angry he had been at Mr. Breuer for not having saved our seats for Mamma and myself. And his wrath pleased me to the point of making my eyes swim with happiness. Such a fool as I was! And how we walked through that blooming, steaming, fragrant park! And how painful that delicious fragrance is to me this year! These soft May and June evenings, drive me wild with their reminiscences. His Introduction, Riverside—Riverside! The other evening Miss Solis called for me with an automobile, and she suggested Riverside. I did not object, because sooner or later I would have had to see again the lights upon the river that shone upon him and me together, breathe in again the perfume-laden air, hear again the murmur of the idlers whose throng we joined so often together. We rode up and down, and as luck would have it—it was the first evening of the illumination of Palisade Park. More lights—cast into the shadows of my inner consciousness! The extinguishing of those Palisade lights had always been our signal for home-going—with a sigh from me. And the ferry glided across the stream with the same unearthly beauty as though I were still there to look upon it with lovelit eyes!

These two weeks and more, when I have had to think each day that it may be his wedding day, I have again and again tried to believe that he was telling the truth when he said he did not have a notion that I loved him. But I could not, I cannot. I recall the voice in which he said to me that February evening of our last interview, "Oh! You'll get over this!" and I realize that his manner was that of a person who says aloud mechanically what he has said to himself again and again. It was the evidence of the struggle he had had in making up his mind to give me up—not a struggle because he cared for me, but a struggle because he feared the very thing that has happened—that I would not be heroic. And in the course of the struggle, he repeated to himself again and again, "Oh she will get over it!" And perhaps—I am sure—he added, "And if she does not, and shows disappointment or resentment, all the worse for her. I am panoplied, with a young wife, her overflowing happiness, my happiness, my rights as a comparatively young man, and my consciousness that I have never said anything binding. Besides the world will be on my side. No one expects a man like me, or ever expected me to marry that old woman!" Only in the last he was mistaken.

He knew I loved him! Does he remember the letter I wrote him on Ereb Rosh ha-Shonoh. It seems to me it was the last letter I wrote him to Europe. I wrote it in the morning, and then I left it open, and told him I was going to leave it open, for the purpose of adding a line just before going to the synagogue, so that the last thing I did in the year might be connected with him. And what I wrote was the Hebrew wish, that the old year with its inflictions might pass, and the new year with its blessings enter triumphantly.[25] Alas! I did not know one great affliction the old year had brought me, and I did not know that the new year would almost be the death of me. But he—did he not know that the woman who wrote thus was in love with him? And on his return, he did not know that the marble statue that he dragged with him to Riverside, that sat opposite to him at the Davidson's, that shivered wrapped in a shawl—warm-blooded creature that I had always been—in the corner of the sofa, and on all these occasions spoke only when absolutely forced to do it—he did not know that it was the withdrawal of all hope from me, withdrawn by him, that had turned me into stone? Can I believe that?

That Sunday, May 16 of which I mean to write in the end, was important to me in another way. While I was out learning an elemental fact, his sister-in-law visited Mrs. Marx and spoke to her, and wept. She sides with me. Every day when Sophie went home from here, she wept with her mother, and they did not know what to do about Sophie's coming here. They were afraid of hurting me still more if she withdrew. She, however, had not thought, as the others did, that he had asked me to marry him and that I had refused. She said, that no matter how beautiful the girl he marries is, no matter how attractive, it will not be the same as if he had married me. And, finally she confessed that she had made an attempt to speak to him about the sorry business, and he had said, "Mind your own business!"

Is that a confession of wrong-doing on his part? Not at all. To his view all these late demonstrations must necessarily seem artificial. When he arrived everybody was happy. No one mentioned me; no one expressed astonishment. His sister-in-law had known of his new love for six weeks. Had she written to him, You have imposed silence upon me, but there is one person who must be told? No, she had actually taunted me with my disappointed love. Why did she come here! Why did she ask me to rejoice? So it was only after my breakdown that everybody turned against him. Must he not disbelieve in their sincerity, and ascribe their belated attitude to false sympathy with a woman who imagines herself injured? And yet it would not have hurt his dignity to protest his innocence, if he had felt innocent.

Mrs. Marx was very circumspect, and told her nothing I had confided to her, except the fact that I had confided. The same sort of circumspection everybody exercised from the first. They are all acting in good faith, I am sure, but it's queer, the way they act. I was careful not to reproach Mrs. M. even when she told me that she had given an evasive answer when his sister-in-law asked directly whether I had ever had an explanation with him.

I wish she would speak to me—I should like to get at her psychology.

And now! No I cannot write it tonight, I am too tired. I shall try tomorrow or the next day. Or perhaps I'll wait until I have done translating "Moses."—On Monday I told Judge Sulzberger plainly again that I would not finish the second volume as copy had not been left with me. Dr. Adler was by. They both obviously understood the reason, but Judge Sulzberger refused to assent at once. He would have to let it sink into his mind and think about it. It is a dreadful business!

Get over it? Yes, I will—as a man lives on with a wound from which the missile that has produced it has never been removed, and everybody that passes and everything that happens, knocks against the protruding handle of the dagger, and gives it a painful wrench. The air that comes in through the window now, soft as June can make it, yet has power enough to twist it until the pain makes me cry out aloud.

THE HASTY MARRIAGE

June 3, 1909

Just now I was told that his marriage took place on May 23, before *Shabuot*, on the third day, and the second day after his arrival in London. He had known the woman who is now his wife from Aug. 29–Aug. 31, 1908, from Sept. 28 to Oct. 7, 1908, and from May 21 to May 23, 1909—seen her, I mean—about fifteen days in all!!! And not one person of the Seminary circle knew the day of his wedding. But I am not through with him yet—I mean so far as this record is concerned. I must still put down what is in my mind. Not today, though.

July 21, 1909

To-morrow it will be a year since I last saw him while under the impression that I was to him what he was to me. The next day it will be a year since he sailed for Europe on that fatal trip—a year since he called me up on the telephone and told me he wanted to speak to me once more before he sailed, as he stood with his grip in his hand. To-morrow it will be a year since he saw the tears streaming down my cheeks as I bade him farewell at the post office—I did not look upon it as a humiliation then that I should weep, but in the light of all the humiliation he has put upon me since then publicly and privately, it, too, was a humiliation—I cannot yet free myself of that feeling of degradation. It has been nearly seven weeks since I wrote in this journal—inside of myself nothing has changed. Outwardly I have been completing all arrangements for the European flight,[26] inwardly I have been weeping,—I miss him, I long for him. I dare not think that he is with another woman—her husband. And the woman! The tale of that marriage is extraordinary. He writes apologies to his friends for not having told them that his marriage was to take place immediately after his arrival. He says he did not know it himself. Is that another untruth, another lie? From other sources comes the information that she had made all the arrangements most circumspectly, so that if his vessel should be delayed, the whole thing could be shifted forward a day. Did she fear, did he fear, that I would break up the quiet of their happiness at the end? Was she afraid he would escape her, this man whom she had ensnared with her wiles? Or did he ask her to make all the arrangements? And now denies his part in them—having made them because he did not want his antagonistic friends to have any part, a forced part, in his joy, and willing to tell a falsehood, one falsehood added to the many he has told, in order to shield himself. It does not sound like the proud man I knew and loved—and still love. He abandoned me as one abandons a prostitute, and he married as one goes to a prostitute.

But all this is fencing with myself. I began to write with the intention of setting down what I promised to set down, but it is still hard. And yet it must come out of me before I go away to Europe to forget this episode in my life.

THE ULTIMATE REVELATION

On May 16, I went to see the Gottheils[27] before they left for Europe and the East, and I then met the Schechters and the Friedlaenders. We left together, and Mrs. Friedlaender walked with me. She insisted that I must look upon the relation as having been fine while it lasted and not speak, as I always do, of four prostituted years. She went on to urge that I must feel what she said was true, that while he was at my side he had lived his very best years, such as he had never had before, such as he would never have again. I demurred violently—he did not need me in any sense of the word—the world would see what he could and would produce. But, she said, I do not mean intellectually, I mean morally. I looked at her in astonishment. "You know he led a loose life in his Berlin days, and even later." I could not take in the idea, I asked, do you mean in sexual relations, I asked after several vain attempts to get at her meaning—Do you mean that he had relations with women? "Oh," she said, "unfortunately they have peculiar notions in Germany on the subject. They are not really considered women."

White slave traffic! He one of those for whom it is carried on!

I was silent after that. She left us. I had to go in to the Schechters to meet Mr. Lewin-Epstein about my Palestinian trip. He did not come at once. Mrs. S. beguiled the time with all sorts of small talk. I could not keep my mind on it. Finally, I burst out with a question, "When you called him sensual, what did you mean?"—for she had over and over again told me that the whole explanation of the occurrence was his sensual nature, and would go on to give me instances of how he had acted towards Ruth, so that Ruth, a mere child, had been afraid to be alone with him—he had touched her, and drawn her towards him. But I had attached little value to these evidences, they meant nothing to me. No more did Dr. Marx's calling him sensual mean anything to me. It had to be said bluntly, as Mrs. Friedlaender said it, for me to understand—only I do not yet understand. Mrs. S. replied—"I meant exactly that." Again I asked, "Did you mean that he was in the habit of maintaining impure relations with women?" "Oh," she said, "they are not women, they are *Frauenzimmer* [literally "women of the chamber"], and such relations are as necessary to some men, and as natural as eating, drinking and sleeping."

My darling! He—I refused to believe! How I had been vexed with Adele in her probation officer days—when she would tell before him all about her terrible experiences in connection with the white slave traffic. He never replied, never asked questions, he would have a far away look in his eyes; and when the conversation was changed—generally I did it artificially and forcibly—he would bring his eyes—those innocent baby eyes of his—back as it were with a sigh of relief. I thought it was prim-mindedness, and if they are right, it was a sense of guilt because he had profited by the pernicious trade.

Need I say that once the poison was injected into my mind, it worked there incessantly, and I had no peace. One thing after another came to make the dreadful knowledge sink into my mind. As luck would have it two terrible books fell into my hands at that time. "*Der Heilige Skarabaens,*" by Else Jerusalem, dealing with brutal frankness with the white slave traffic and the attitude of men towards the women that adopt the trade, and "*Das Hohe Lied,*" by Sudermann, an artistic but dreadful presentation of masculine sex consciousness and feminine sex ignorance, and perdition in consequence of ignorance. He would have condemned them as literature—he called "*Das Tagebuch einer Verlorenen*" a pathological investigation.[28] But as for me, suddenly life, the world, literature, my whole past was illumined. I understood as I had not understood before—or rather I understood what it was that I had not understood. The object of my not-understanding had at least defined itself—defined itself to me who had had such painful difficulty in translating certain passages in his "Legends." He again—it is he again that has made me see clearly—that is why I miss him, through him all things became clear to me.

But I am not the important factor—he is! and he! Can it be true that he led a sensual life? I asked Dr. Marx about it—he says positively, the charge is true so far as his early years are concerned, and he says Dr. Davidson maintains that it continued true even in America. In America? While he associated with me? Impossible! for he spent all his leisure time with me. I have spoken to no one else about it, and I never will. But Dr. Davidson of his own accord said something to me. I tried to excuse him—sorry excuse!—by saying that my theory about his engagement was that the girl is a coquette, she drew him on, until he did something compromising, I do not know what, perhaps kissed her, and he felt bound. Dr. D. sniffed—"Not the first girl he kissed!"

And since then I have been collecting little straws in spite of myself. One day I was walking with him in Morningside Park, and in the heat of discussion I rested my hands on my breast. Quickly he looked around at me, and with his eyes directed towards my hands as they lay on my bosom he flushed. He had a habit of flushing. And I loved it. Sometimes when he was unexpectedly called to the Torah, the red blood would surge to the roots of his hair at his forehead and on the back of his neck. I asked Adele casually whether she thought him a sensual man, and demanded evidence when she replied affirmatively. She reminded me how once she had stepped into the manuscript room of the Seminary, dressed in fluffy, snowy white, and how he had flushed. I remembered the incident, first because it had made me jealous of her youth that could evoke such pleasurable feeling in him, and second, because I cherished it as proof of his sensitive nature—not his sensual nature.

"The Cosmical Mystery of Sex"

But I cannot understand! He hated exploiting of all sorts—he would not buy cigars at the United Cigar Stores Company's stores on that account. To be sure, they all turn upon me and say that he exploited me intellectually—as I myself say, I was his intellectual mistress. Unconsciously, it seems, I arrived at a knowledge of him borne out by the facts of his early life. And they go on to say that they are sorry for his wife—I did not understand what they meant— what dreadful thing they meant—that he would "use" her as had "used" the women in the public brothels he is said to have frequented. But they are wrong. Even if the reports about his youthful sins are trustworthy, by now he has conquered himself—perhaps Mrs. Friedlaender is partly right. I helped him conquer himself, and he may have left me because he knew his original nature and throws safeguards about his acquired self-control. For self-control he has in all other respects, and even self-restraint, as in eating, and if he is not, as he always asserted, aristocratic, his asserting it shows that he values aristocracy, and sensuality certainly is not aristocratic. As I said, he throws safeguards around his acquired self-control, and if it is true that I helped him acquire it, he yet is right in discerning that I could not help him as his wife in maintaining it, if his nature is sensual and if sensual men are as they are described by the authors of "*Das Tagebuch einer Verlorenen,*" and "*Der heilige Skarabaens*" (a beastly book!) and "*Das Hohe Lied.*" If these things are true, then I see that though his action toward me was neither honorable nor kind, it was prudent. He ate of the tree of knowledge and he was clearsighted. I understand his action through a bigger thing that I do not understand—the whole sex relation. I understand at least that I, old as I am and constituted as I am, would not have satisfied his nature. Dr. Radin and Mr. Lubarsky were right—I could not have made him happy, he would have sought other women, bought them as before, and my work—if Mrs. Friedlaender is right—would have been in vain. Sorry satisfaction, to have purged him for another woman! And I, fool that I was, thought that I noticed assent in his manner, when I confessed to him in our interviews in February, that through him I had learnt the cosmical mystery of sex! No, I alone was the learner—I learnt not only cosmical mysteries, but also the earthly and the earthy mysteries—he from me only self-control, if that. He learn[ed] the mystery of sex from me—he who once told me in the days way back, when he was relating to me how various people had tried to urge him into marrying, and I asked whether he was really opposed on principle to marriage, that there were some people who did not need that relation. I did not understand, but I asked no more. Evidently he wanted me to infer that he was one of those who did not, from the physical point of view, need marriage—that he was one of those who according to Maimonides may keep away from marriage, as all those should who are not drawn into it in order to keep themselves from debauchery—only now do I understand this attitude expressed by Maimonides. And yet, while he was asking me tacitly to draw this inference, he had the consciousness that he had indulged himself illegitimately, that he was not one of those of whom it would be said, as of Jacob (his Legends!) that he had been permitted to enjoy a foretaste of the future life where there is no evil inclination, that it would not be said of him as of one of Jacob's sons (his Legends!) that he had never "known" any woman save his wife. My God! perhaps there is now somewhere in the world, as a result of his licentious indulgences, a daughter of his verging on womanhood, and her mother cannot protect her from men with passions like his, or a son with his brilliant, clear mind, and his mother is not able to have it developed as his mind is! When such thoughts come to me, I am almost crazy, and I rejoice that I made him suffer the scorn of his friends by my inability to hide my grief—I avenged the poor white slaves he nefariously used. The intellectual mistress whom he cast away when he had exploited her sufficiently, avenged those poor mute things that perish in the dark.

He is an enigma to me. What need had he to tell me that he had never known women, and therefore, perhaps he had been led to do me the wrong I attributed to him—that it was an unwitting wrong. But if the reports his friends give of him are true, he knew women much more intimately than he had a right to. Is it because he was aware of these shadows in his past that he dared ask me whether I had not had such relations with other men as I had had with him? Is it because he is sensual that he shrank from physical contact with me that Tisha-be-Ab evening? He did not trust himself? And yet is it possible that he is so sensual—he who could speak to me as he did about the relation of parents to their first born that never-to-be-forgotten evening in Morningside Park? On the other hand, was it to excuse himself that he always asserted so vigorously the superiority of intellect to character—the rarity of the one compensating for the value of the other? Did he mean to imply that possession of intellect granted license? And if he had eaten of the tree of knowledge, he that knew Rabbinical literature so well with all its adjurations against sexual immorality, why did he, knowing also his uncontrollable nature, not yield to his father's solicitations and get married, and keep himself pure? Did he suffer in conscience when he wrote his Legends, with all their allusions to the vexed subject, which is not so modern as they would have us believe nowadays—those old Rabbis assigned a properly important place to it? Those Rabbis seem to have realized what apparently is fundamental in the thing, that though love fills out a woman's whole life, and is only an aside with man, the aberrations from love affect man's character radically. And is it possible that Dr. Wise's repudiation of him as professor of the Hebrew Union College had something to do with his reputation at Berlin, where they say, he, curiously enough, had no associations with any of the Jewish scholars.

I am glad I did not write about this at once. I can see more clearly than I could when this last, most serious assault was made upon the man who had been my irreproachable hero, the darling of my heart in whom I had never seen the scintilla of a fault. Alas! the February interview left him stripped of the ideality, the perfection in which I had clothed him—he was not even truthful towards me in that talk, as, indeed, he had acted a lie towards me either since nine months ago on his return, or during the four years preceding Oct. 20, 1908, or August 29, 1908.

And yet, and yet, I cannot believe him actually wicked. Or, rather, if he was led away by the thoughtlessness of youth, he had departed from his crookedness. He had become true to his better self, and not merely through me, but through that same better self. I have no right to condemn him for the sins of his youth. And from that point of view his marriage with the other one is right. That chit of a girl is more powerful than I am to be a true helpmeet to him. If Mrs. Friedlaender is at all right, it is only to this extent, that I put him on the narrow path, only the woman he has married, who seems to have appealed to the remnants of sensuality in him—he thinks it is true love—can keep down that sensuality. It is true. I unlocked his heart, she took possession of it. He cannot be so sensual as they say, else he could not have associated with me so intimately, and gotten satisfaction out of the association. I must say *L'Tovah* [It is for the good].

I say it with my intellect, my logic. But what does my heart say? That I love him, love him, love him! That I would have forgiven every frailty of youth, if he had but confessed it, and not pretended to righteousness, and not indulged in it again to escape from me! That, because I love him, I cannot forgive the cruel wrong he did me—the humiliation he put upon me—the callousness with which he allowed me to go on seeing him—the coldness with which he could assert ignorance of my feelings—with which he told me he was not suffering,—with which he could lie about my relation and Dr. Marx's to him—with which he could say that he had expected to be more intimate with me after his marriage than ever he had been before—with which he could console me that I would get over it. Get over it! Yes, the world knows all such things, and it agrees with him. I will get over it, it says. But who will give me back those nine months—only those nine months—of agony, of not living, who will restore to me those four years? Who will compensate me only for that one moment at the

Seminary commencements when his books were praised, the books translated, or for the moment when those books were sent to me, and not by him, but by the Seminary? Who will repay me for the torture I endure when people pity me, when for pity of me some of the members of the Publication Committee and the Board of Trustees sent me a check for $500 for my European trip, my honeymoon, as they might have sent me for my wedding with him? Who will repay me for all that? And for the envy and jealousy when I see a happy wife, a happy mother? Get over it! Does he know what the phrase means? Does he know what love is, what a broken heart and spirit are?

Why was he so intimate with me all these years? Because he did not know the ways of women! Because he thought me too old to entertain love? Or too self sacrificing ever to obtrude myself? These last four days a new thought entered my mind—he intended actually never to marry, and so long as he did not marry, his relation to me, the older woman, was legitimate. Then he fell in love—actually fell in love, and all was forgotten. Yes, all was forgotten for the moment. But could he continue to forget for six or eight weeks? Did he continue to forget when he saw me break down, but did not ask a question of the friend he had extolled to his friends! My explanation may explain his act in enjoying himself, it does not explain his conduct from Oct. 20, 1908 to May 12, 1909.

In ten days I sail for Europe. Perhaps after all, I will recover my balance there. At least he will recover his place here, and she will make hers. In any event, I must, I must remember that he is a married man, that my passion for him is as illegitimate as was his debauchery if indeed, that ever existed. I must forget him!

I add to the record the letter I once wrote, at the beginning of my passion for him, when he had done nothing to make me believe it was reciprocated, though he had done much to awaken and encourage it, as a reply to an imaginary letter of his. It was prophetic. Why did I ever recede from the position I took then? Why did I ever forget my age? Oh, I am not all wrong—he made me forget it—made me by seeking me day after day. And now I sit here like the woman of Madison Cawein's poem, which I copied out at the same time as I wrote the letter, to strengthen the rebuke I administered to myself. But who could have withstood four years of such association as ours was? Yesterday we had a letter from Miriam telling of her engagement to Dr. Schloessinger, and a few days ago I heard of Dr. Benderly's marriage to Miss Miller. Happiness for all except me!

The Solitary[29]

Upon the mossed rock by the spring
    She sits, forgetful of her pail,
Lost in remote remembering
    Of that which may no more avail.

Her thin, pale hair is dimly dressed
    Above a brow lined deep with care,
The color of a leaf long pressed,
    A faded leaf that once was fair.

You may not know her from the stone
    So still she sits who does not stir,
Thinking of this one thing alone—
    The love that never came to her.

RENUNCIATION[30]

July, 1905

Dear Friend,

I have been sitting with your precious letter in my hand all day long. I cannot delay longer—I must make the reply that is my own death warrant. Heaven help me! I feel I am going to be un-Jewish, unwomanly. Perhaps before I reach the point of returning the treasure of love your letter gives me, my unreserve will have forfeited it. But I cannot otherwise— I cannot be prudent and restrained. I must once before I renounce pour out my heart to you. And, indeed, what harm can there be? You must know all. In these hard months of my solitary struggle with myself, I must have betrayed myself to your clear vision over and over again by my very efforts to exercise self-control. You must have divined it, that I was tranquil only when I was near you, one of the slight services my powers can accomplish; only when you permitted me to do something for you, that at all other times I was restless, disturbed, unable to do the tasks I set myself, and which never before had found me distracted. Why, then, should I refrain from telling you in explicit words that my whole happiness lies with you—that you are the first to give my soul its woman's heritage, a soul that up to the time it was awakened by you—Oh! so many wearily happy months ago—had known only filial passion. You guess all the rest, all I have suffered to pretend indifference to you, all I would suffer to win you and hold you forever. You remember my definition of woman's love—the opportunity for self-effacement. Your favorite Zarathustra expresses what I mean: "*Das Glück des Mannes heist, Ich will; das Glueck des Weibes heisst, Er will*" [A man's luck is his own desire; a woman's, her husband's desire].

Yet there remains a good deal to be said; and it is hard, bitter to say it, but it is better I send it across the waste of waters. Then when you come back, I shall be fortified to look you in the eyes without flinching.

Somebody has sinned, or I should not have been exposed to the temptation of loving you—loving?—of adoring you—and you would have been spared the disharmony of being loved by me. Either I sinned against myself, or others sinned against me. Certainly it is not in nature that my spring-time should come when the lines in my face are hard and set, when my hair is whitening—it has grown much whiter since you went away, from my intense sorrowful thinking of you. But whoever sinned, one sin is not expiated by another. And I should be committing a grave sin against you, your young manhood, your high scholarship and ideals and gifts and prospects, were I to hang myself as a millstone about your neck. When you went away I wept and wept and prayed that this one time yet you might come back to me heart-free, so that I might have a space to grow accustomed to the idea that you would belong to some other woman. And then I grew bolder—I prayed for what has happened—I prayed that you would learn to love me. Happened, do I say? How we delight in deceiving ourselves! It has happened only because you guessed at the tumult in my soul and because you are chivalrous. For how can one like you spontaneously love one like me?

But whatever wild idea came into my disordered head and heart, I never lost sight of this one—that in the end I should have to practice renunciation, a more absolute self-effacement than even my definition of a woman's love calls for. I dare exercise no claim upon you. You belong to a happy, sprightly young creature, one that has not known the heat and burden of life, who will not so much give you intellectual sympathy—you do not need it, your penetrating, sane, unclouded mind suffices unto itself— as she will give you warmth and color to glorify your life. With me you would walk in the gray shadow of sorrows.

Only one thing I ask of you, my dear friend. Do not think it easy for me to give you up. If you could see what I see before me now: my own future dark as night, cold as death. I can never go back to the ignorance of my passionless days. You have made me to eat of the fruit of the tree of knowledge, and my eyes have been opened—only to behold my own misery, only to pity my past self which was so stupid, to pity my future self which is doomed to unhappiness. And yet I kiss your hand for the fruit it gave me to taste of, for I still may love you, worship you, only I may not purchase my happiness with yours. And so I hug my misery; it is at least a pale similitude of the happiness I know exists for another.

I give you back then what you offer me, I shall bear my lot bravely. You will see how I shall control myself though my heart break. And if my strength gives out, I shall go away from where you are, and shall thank you evermore for the moment's glimpse of genuine living which you in the richness of your ample nature granted me—shall thank you for the happy "might have been." God bless you and that other one!

EPILOGUE

Writing a Life Before Living It

One of fifteen articles composed by Henrietta Szold for the *Jewish Encyclopedia* was entitled "Herz, Henriette." The author was named after this woman, whose life span (1764–1847) was remarkably similar to her own (1860–1945). The two women shared more than longevity and lives divided between two centuries. Insofar as Henrietta Szold displayed both a refined Victorian sensibility and a high regard for twentieth-century science and pragmatism, she replicated her namesake's embrace of eighteenth-century reason and nineteenth-century romanticism. Szold wrote that Henriette Herz inherited intellectual ability from her physician father and "energy and philanthropic spirit" from her mother, obvious parallels to her own situation. Like Szold, moreover, Herz was an educator, a minor writer, and a translator in command of several languages.[1] But the resemblance was far from complete. Henriette Herz was not only accomplished but beautiful as well. She was also a married woman. Szold welcomed Jewish intellectuals into her home, but the important men who flocked to Herz's salon were the lights of Gentile society. They convinced her to convert to Christianity after her husband's death. There was one uncanny parallel between the men in the lives of the two women. Henriette Herz received Frederich Schleiermacher, a seminal Protestant thinker, in her home, where she taught him Italian. Their social circle buzzed with rumors about their friendship which, Szold assures, was purely platonic. More information about the relationship is, however, unavailable. Herz destroyed her correspondence, but Szold and Ginzberg saved the letters they exchanged.

According to William Thackery, "To love and win is the best thing; to love and lose the next best." Without doubt, marriage to Ginzberg would have fulfilled Szold's deepest aspirations. This is not to say, however, that her life would have been richer without their friendship. In life we seldom achieve "the best thing," but we may be better served by "the next best" than by nothing at all. Examination of Szold's life after 1909 demonstrates that her passion yielded advantages almost commensurate with the costs. The Ginzberg correspondence foreshadowed Szold's future, calling to mind the words of feminist literary critic Carolyn Heilbrun: "(A) woman may write her own life in advance of living it, unconsciously and without recognizing or naming the process."[2] The epistolary interchange with Ginzberg illuminated the path that Henrietta Szold would negotiate during her very active later years.

The letters indicate unhappiness with her position at the Jewish Publication Society. As early as 1905 Szold had confessed to Rabbi Bernard Felsenthal, an old family friend and Zionist associate:

> *Secretaries of Jewish Publication Societies who must get out Jewish Year Books in time for the fall holidays do not have vacations. I have scarcely stirred from behind my desk, and do not intend to go out of town.*[3]

Every summer, as seminary and Zionist associates left New York for more comfortable or stimulating locales, Szold felt obligated to continue working in her sweltering apartment. She waited two years before finally speaking up for herself. To Ginzberg she reported:

> *I had a long and satisfactory talk with Mayer Sulzberger. I told him many a thing I kept bottled up within me for years. The upshot was that, he said, he saw no reason why I should not have a 14 weeks' holiday next year.*

In response, Ginzberg offered encouragement, even as he pointed to her responsibility to herself.

> *You ought to have your work and duties exactly defined. If the JPS expects you to be ein mädchen fuer alles—secretary, translator, author and collector of statistics, then let them look for somebody else.*

With relief and embarrassment Szold acknowledged the correctness of his analysis, admitting a vulnerability that bordered on masochism.

> *I am almost entirely to blame. When . . . I look back upon the years of my secretaryship, I realize that I actually usurped duties. I now enjoy the logical return: the Committee has no confidence in me, only the confidence one places in a upper, well-tried loyal servant with a* Bedientenseele *[soul of a servant].*

These words invite the reader to distinguish between Szold's passion and the genuine friendship she shared with Ginzberg. As the object of her affection, Ginzberg caused Szold terrible suffering, but as a friend and confidant, he gave her valuable advice and support, and provided the courage to consider terminating her association with the JPS: "A little more initiative, a little confidence that I can make a modest place for myself in some other position, and I'll cease to be their secretary."

This exchange reveals something about Ginzberg as well. Like the protagonist in Cynthia Ozick's "Envy, or Yiddish in America," Ginzberg depended on an English translator to bring his thoughts before an American audience. It is likely that the benevolence displayed in his letters is evidence of a need for Szold's ministrations nearly as pressing as her passion for him.[4]

There was the additional factor that the writer and the translator were of opposite sexes, a fact infrequently noted in the correspondence. In their discussions of Szold's position at the JPS, Ginzberg's *ein mädchen fuer alles* is the closest he came to acknowledging the gender-based source of her exploitation. Turning his statement on its head, she acknowledged personal responsibility for her own subordination:

> *I wonder how much of it is due to the goading of others, how much to overwrought nerves—thoroughly feminine reasons, I hear you generalize, feminine lack of independence and feminine unsteadiness.*

Women in Judaism

As these exchanges stirred Szold's feminist sensibilites, they prompted her to reexamine the role of Jewish women in the home, the synagogue, and the public arena. She had publicly considered the first issue in 1893, delivering a lecture at the World's Parliament of

Religions held at the Chicago World's Fair that endorsed the traditional Jewish household. In answer to the published question "What Has Judaism Done for Women?" Szold settled on the biblical matriarchs as prototypes of all Jewish women. Content to function in a separate sphere from the men, she asserted, they were nevertheless religious models whose piety and purity strengthened Jewish life. The fact that in all ages, including the present, women's role has been essentially supportive and domestic gave her no pause.[5]

When this lecture was delivered, Szold still resided in a parental home that provided a satisfying emotional environment. A few months after delivering the Chicago address, however, Szold left Baltimore to work at the Publication Society. A response to a questionnaire of 1897 indicated her early views on the subject of "Women in the Synagogue."

> By occupying the pulpit only when her knowledge of the law, history, and literature of Judaism is masterful, and her natural gift so extraordinary as to forbid hesitation, though even then it were the part of wisdom not to make a profession of public preaching and teaching, the old Jewish rule of not holding women responsible for religious duties performed at definite times having a deep-seated rational basis and wide applicability.

This statement was uncharacteristically ungrammatical and painfully equivocal. Szold accepted halakhically imposed strictures on the sexes: women were exempt from certain ritual obligations, and so were barred from the rabbinate. And yet she began her response by acknowledging the capacity of women to be superior scholars, the most important qualification for the rabbinic post. The fact that she did not spell out these distinctions clearly indicates to me a subliminal uncertainty on the subject.

In the same article Szold also opposed the common practice of staffing Sabbath schools with female volunteers. Teachers, she insisted, should be paid professionals. This statement foreshadowed her later concern with the role of women in the workplace, personalized in the letters to Ginzberg and reinforced by his friendly advice. Both of them knew that she was exploited. Not only did the Publication Society pay her far too little for work that was actually the nuts and bolts of the operation; her superiors wielded much more power, setting general policies. Their job was to select the books to issue, much less difficult work than Szold's day-to-day administrative, editorial, and translation duties, and decidedly more glamorous. Their official titles—Mayer

Sulzberger, as chairman of the Publication Committee and George Dobsevage as secretary of the Society (not just one committee) entitled them to most of the credit for the Publication Society's success.

Ginzberg sympathized with her plight, respecting her intellect even as he expected her to remain behind the scenes. Although he discouraged her from speaking in public, he sanctioned her scholarly efforts. He found and turned over to her a series of *tehines*, Yiddish language supplicatory prayers which addressed women's concerns; they were composed expressly for (and sometimes by) Ashkenazic women over a period of three hundred and fifty years. The result was an article, entitled "What Our Grandmothers Read," published in 1907. Written for a popular audience, it helped open a new field of scholarship. Szold took the research techniques of her seminary professors in investigating rabbinic texts and applied them to the *tehines*. She described each piece, analyzed it, then placed it in its historical setting. So impressed was Solomon Schechter that he suggested a full-blown monograph.[6] Upon returning from Europe that fall, Ginzberg brought her his own mother's collection of *tehines*. Szold certainly appreciated the gesture and probably entertained the prospect of continuing the research. At the same time, however, she advanced beyond scholarship and began to view the *tehines* in the light of her own spirituality. To Ginzberg she lamented the personal irrelevance of these prayers for an unmarried woman:

> *But do not speak to me of the progressiveness of Judaism! Why isn't there one* Techinnah *in all the books to fit my modern case— not one to raise up the spirit of a so-called emancipated woman, Heaven save the mark! To be sure, I don't know myself what I am to look for in the prayer-book—what I am to thank [God] for? Have I escaped a danger, or a responsibility—or my own folly?*

Maternal and Paternal Imperatives

If the letters to Ginzberg were a necessary first step in Szold's pursuit of vocational autonomy and religious fulfillment, they also provided an opportunity for an airing of her Zionist concerns. Most of the articles that she clipped from the Anglo-Jewish press and enclosed with her Europe-bound letters dealt with Zionism, directly or obliquely, and Zionist issues at home and abroad pervaded the extensive correspondence of 1907. Her fondest dream, she confided to Ginzberg, was to attend a Zionist Congress in Europe.

Studying these letters led me to reexamine the prevailing theory about Ginzberg's role in Szold's life. Irving Fineman, an important Szold biographer, asserts that the Ginzberg episode was a major turning point in her life. Virtually all his successors have agreed, and rightly so. Still, I would argue with Fineman's key assumption. He divides Henrietta Szold's life into three segments: "Her Father's Daughter"; "The Turn," subtitled "Trial and Transfiguration"; and "Her Mother's Daughter." The three titles encapsulate Fineman's gendered thesis: Before the Ginzberg "trial," Szold was totally absorbed in her father's world of Jewish letters, as indicated by her early forays into Jewish journalism and her career at the Jewish Publication Society. The "transfiguration" took place in the wake of Ginzberg's rejection. Szold abandoned the "masculine" life of the mind. Instead, she concentrated on "feminine," "practical" pursuits: medical, health, and social welfare projects in Palestine.

In my opinion, Fineman creates a false dichotomy. In her young years in Baltimore, Henrietta engaged in traditionally feminine pursuits at the piano, in the sewing room, and in the family garden. At the height of her "intellectual" life in New York she sustained a meticulously bourgeois apartment and relaxed on a relative's porch "lazily embroidering." Measuring herself against Ginzberg's fiancée in the "Meditation," she inquired rhetorically, "Was I not domestic?"[7] By the same token, were the Fineman thesis correct, then Szold's life after the "transfiguration" would have found her absorbed in practical endeavors to the exclusion of intellectual activity. The facts do not conform to this theory. I maintain that this woman always lived suspended between paternal and maternal imperatives.

According to Fineman, Szold's involvement in Zionism during the summer of 1907 was a mere ploy "to divert her mind" during Ginzberg's European sojourn. Along the same line, Eli Ginzberg's apologetic review of "an exceptional friendship" maintained that his father "deepened (Szold's) perceptions and understanding of the essential role of Zion in the long span of Jewish history."[8] Adele Ginzberg—who no doubt held Szold responsible for her own initially awkward position in the seminary circle—spoke only partly in jest when she claimed credit for Hadassah's creation.[9] Like Fineman, she implied that Szold, disappointed in love, turned to Zionism. Or, as one wag put it, "Love builds mountains; unrequited love sets hospitals on mountains."

Practical Idealism

The depression suffered after the Ginzberg rejection did render Szold helpless to change her situation for some time. Indirectly, though, the crisis precipitated the next step in her evolving Zionist development. Judge Sulzberger had not honored the promise to grant her a vacation in 1908. The following year, in an effort to comfort her after Ginzberg's marriage, the Publication Society granted a six months' paid leave for a trip to Europe plus additional funds to visit Palestine. In the old-new land unsanitary conditions and primitive medical care deeply troubled Henrietta Szold and her mother, who accompanied her. Sophie Szold advised her daughter to take on "practical work in Palestine."[10]

In the prevailing Szold myth, the very sight of young children blinded with trachoma and other preventable and reparable calamities triggered an epiphany. This, however, was not the case; neither the travel experience nor her mother's recommendation produced instant "transfiguration." When the two women returned to New York early in 1910 Henrietta's depression had lifted sufficiently to allow for public addresses, now delivered freely, without concern for Ginzberg's disapproval. Many lectures reviewed the Palestinian experience. Szold described the beauty of the land and its human and natural variety and waxed eloquent over its potential for the regeneration of religion, the resurgence of Jewish national feeling, and what she called "the conquest of Jewish culture."[11] This was the vocabulary of cultural or spiritual Zionism, which she had embraced early in life. As a charter member of Baltimore's proto-Zionist *Shavei Zion* and *Hevrat Zion* societies, she had been an early follower of Ahad Ha-am, and one of his first English-language translators.[12] What initially attracted Szold to Zionism was its potential for reviving the spirit of Judaism, a central motive in Ahad Ha-am's writings. In 1899 she verbalized this sentiment in a letter to Stephen Wise:

> It (Zionism) is the only living thing in the Judaism of to-day. Reform and Orthodox squabbles, public Seders and Synods, and all the rest of the palaver, is on dead issues.[13]

Reinforcing her early Zionism after the move to New York was friendship with Judah Magnes and Israel Friedlaender, America's most prominent cultural Zionists. A letter to Friedlaender and his wife in 1906 proclaimed "Ahad Ha-am remains our one strong-hold!"[14] To cherish this conviction was not to denigrate Herzl. Like Ahad Ha-am's European followers Chaim Weizmann and Leo Motzkin, American supporters of the Zionist philosopher did not share their mentor's distrust of political Zionism.[15] Friedlaender, for example, demonstrated his regard for Herzl by sending Szold a copy of Herzl's portrait a few months after the Zionist leader's untimely death in July 1904.[16] Furthermore, on some matters, Szold and Herzl were kindred spirits who envisioned an "Oldnewland" grounded in humanistic as well as Jewish values. Szold's eulogy of Herzl delivered the Zionist leader into the camp of the "practical" Zionists. Resolving that

> . . . *the cause, the idea, abideth forever. Upon us, now that the leader is no more, it is doubly incumbent to labor for the hoped-for consummation,*

she portrayed Theodore Herzl as a "practical idealist."[17]

Szold had pondered education, culture, and Zionism in the Ginzberg correspondence. After 1910, these issues occupied the center of her life. While retaining her position at the Publication Society, she took on additional responsibilities. She joined the New York Kehillah, presided over by Magnes, and became secretary of its education committee, headed by Friedlaender.[18] Chosen honorary secretary of the Federation of American Zionists in 1910, she organized its records and restructured its finances. Her original motive was to banish thoughts of Louis and Adele Ginzberg, who frequently crossed her path. Adding additional chores to an already overextended schedule, she hoped, would make her "hard and practical and drive out sentiment and grief."[19]

Judging the task of "cleaning up other people's Augean stables . . . too far removed from Jewish ideal hopes to be a solace,"[20] Szold next turned to a man whose interests were far removed from those of Ginzberg. In 1910 Aaron Aaronsohn, the discoverer of wild Emmer wheat in the Galilee, was in the United States, conferring with American agricultural experts. Szold and the young scientist became personal friends. A hallmark of cultural Zionism was its embrace of scientific and technological advances alongside literary and artistic development. Szold greatly admired Aaronsohn's ability to advance Zionism through astute application of modern science. With the aid of American Jewish leaders he established the Agricultural Experimental Station at Athlit, near Haifa, where he pursued his scientific research. Szold accepted the position of secretary of the organization. As usual she was the only woman on the board.[21]

A New Direction

In 1911 Henrietta Szold underwent surgery, most likely a hysterectomy. Her thoughts turned away from the Ginzbergs, new parents of a baby boy. Szold's eyes also gave her trouble; she was forced to limit her reading time. This provided an opportunity for prolonged self-examination. Now she focused on her whole self: physical, intellectual, and emotional. A year before she had acknowledged culpability for her willing subservience to Ginzberg with a biblical phrase: "I did not keep my own vineyard."[22] Now resolving self-cultivation, she reconsidered ideas and sentiments articulated in letters to Ginzberg and reintegrated them. The result was a stronger personality and a tougher mind. Pondering the recent past, she admitted to Alice Seligsberg:

> The elation produced by the European trip was illusory. I was trying all these three years to "bluff" myself—first recreation was what was needed to restore me to sanity, and then hard work, but the body rebelled as the soul had before.[23]

During that interval Szold composed another journal. Like the "Meditation on Lost Love," it noted every painful encounter with Ginzberg and/or his wife, and discussed efforts of the seminary circle to maintain separate social contact with each of the parties. Some bordered on French farce, as the time when Adele Ginzberg was hastily shunted into an inner room when Szold appeared at a professor's door; others were cause for humiliation, as the occasion when an invitation from the Malters was rescinded after they discovered that the Ginzbergs were scheduled for the same evening.[24] Unlike the "Meditation," however, the later journal pursued no explicit healing purpose and dealt with other issues in her life. During this period Szold found solace in family and women friends; Seligsberg proved the soulmate to whom she particularly unburdened herself.[25] Undoubtedly, the passage of time also helped heal the wound. The letter to Seligsberg continued:

> I am determined now to blot out some of the passages of the past and leap into a new existence as soon as the elasticity of the body at least is restored.

Founding Hadassah

Six months later, in February 1912, Szold's recovery was sufficient to allow her to take on the project that would secure international renown: the founding of Hadassah. We have seen how confidentialities disclosed to Ginzberg raised consciousness of her own passivity and prompted a reconsideration of Jewish women's domestic, religious, and professional functions. Also under scrutiny was the question of female participation in public life; Ginzberg's disapproval of women speaking in public has already been noted. Following Heilbrun, I will argue that after 1912 Szold assumed an activist position, recasting her life to conform to aspirations suggested or implied in the Ginzberg correspondence.

Because the moral and cognitive framework of the early twentieth century thwarted feminine ambition, Szold had previously operated as an implementer of other people's plans. No longer a facilitator of men's work, she now became a leader among women. Control of a national organization cultivated latent talents as an administrator and a decision maker. Unconsciously, the Hadassah president forswore the "Renunciation" composed in 1905 and reiterated at the close of the "Meditation" in 1909. Then, shamelessly, she had coveted "wifely love" as "the opportunity for self-effacement," and quoted Nietzsche to the effect that "man's luck is his own desire; a woman's, her husband's desire." Now, husbandless and self-reliant, she would exercise her own desire and earn her own luck by applying lessons from the past to her own life and an organization that raised female confidence and encouraged female assertiveness. From Israel Friedlaender she solicited a biblical verse for the Hadassah motto. Whether Friedlaender intended to suggest Szold's personal predicament or not, "The Healing of the Daughter of My People"[26] was a wise choice, for in healing others, Szold herself was healed.

Following European precedent, American Zionist officials downplayed the value of a national women's Zionist organization. Early Zionist thinkers, decrying the supposedly passive "feminine" role of Jews in society, declared manliness to be a Zionist virtue. Max Nordau's call for *Muskeljudentum*, a "muscular Jewry," implied an unrectifiably inferior role for women in the movement.[27] Even after Hadassah figured prominently on the American scene, language with a palpable masculine bias persisted; the ZOA waved the banner of "Men, Money, Discipline!"

Hadassah's disciplined fund-raising success did not alter the masculinist vocabulary, but it certainly changed Zionist realities. Initially, Louis Lipsky, president of the Federation of American Zionists, tried to subsume Hadassah under that organization. Szold and her lieutenants declined the offer. The women's attachment to Zionism and willingness to toil for its realization, they insisted, was equal to that of the men. They were no longer willing to confine their efforts to "woman's work": selling small items and preparing dinners for men engaged in weighty discussion. Moving in from the margins, they funded projects of their own. To confirm Zionist credentials, they dispatched a portion of Hadassah dues to the FAZ, and each member contributed a $1 shekel to the World Zionist movement.

Beyond Zionism, Hadassah's self-definition as the Women's Zionist Organization of America advanced American Jewish women's associations in general. Hadassah was not a ladies' society, not a women's club, not the female auxiliary of a male Zionist "*shul.*" Hadassah was born an independent affiliate within the general Zionist movement and would struggle to remain so until it secured sovereignty in the mid-1930s.[28]

Historian Melvin Urofsky attributes Louis Brandeis's successful refashioning of American Zionism in 1914 (two years after the founding of Hadassah) to his legitimation of the movement in American terms.[29] Szold's choice of specific "enterprises" performed the same task for Jewish women. Adopting forms from American women's clubs—e.g., parliamentary procedure and a rational dues structure—Szold filled the new organization with Zionist content. But it was a personal Zionism, grounded in cultural Zionism yet responding to her experience as a woman in a man's world and her subservience to Sulzberger and Ginzberg. Zionist ideologues had romanticized rural cooperativism and Szold herself greatly admired the cooperative and collective villages. It was her heightened awareness of the oppression of women in the cities of Palestine that determined Hadassah's first projects—a district visiting nurse system, medical clinics, milk stations, midwifery training—and benefited urban women and children.

Dual Objectives

Years later a German Zionist publication accused Szold of refusal to distinguish between practical work in Palestine and Zionist work in America.[30] In truth, duality of purpose was no failing, but rather the substance, strength, and originality of Szold's vision. A "practical idealist" like the Herzl of her eulogy, Szold conceived a program that was both pragmatic and idealistic. The invitation announcing Hadassah's founding meeting in February 1912 read: "to promote Jewish institutions and enterprises in Palestine and to foster Zionist ideals in America." During the 1920s two mottos headed the organization's stationery: "Object in America: to foster Zionist ideals, to make Zionist propaganda"; "Object in Palestine: to maintain Hadassah Medical Organization, formerly American Zionist Medical Unit." On Hadassah's twenty-fifth anniversary Szold summarized the founding members' enduring "purpose" as "the healing of the daughter of their people, physically in Palestine, spiritually in America."[31]

Szold's Zionist colleague Israel Friedlaender defined the relative merits of America and Palestine as "solutions" to what was known as "the Jewish Question." America, he proclaimed, relieves the material problems of the Jews, but only Palestine could alleviate their spiritual distress.[32] Dexterously, Szold turned Friedlaender's thesis on its head, matching it to an American and feminine reality of her own making. Hadassah's educational program was intended to satisfy the spiritual requirements of American Jewish women, stimulating their Jewish national consciousness, proving their worth as thinkers and doers. At the same time, the organization's fund-raising projects would improve physical conditions in the *yishuv*.

A follower of Ahad Ha-am, Szold, like Friedlaender, did not ascribe equal valence to the two objectives; she always considered the spiritual enterprise superior to the material one, both in Palestine and America. That Hadassah's goal of healing American women's spiritual malaise prevailed over the satisfaction of physical needs of Palestinian Jews was best expressed in her pithy declaration at the Hadassah Subconvention of 1918: "Where money goes, the heart follows."[33] In her value system, Hadassah's medical and public health projects were practical means to spiritual ends. Szold's 1937 address before the Peel Commission recalled a personal history of forty years of Zionism, "reached not by the road of Anti-Semitism, not by the road that looked to Palestine as the refuge of the Jews, but by the road that leads to Palestine as the refuge of Judaism."[34]

Spiritual or cultural Zionism stood upon the premise that modification of the Jewish condition must proceed from change in the inner world of the Jew. For Ahad Ha-am's American partisans, education was the fundamental vehicle of transformation, "the decisive

Zionist act."[35] In that sense Szold's labors for the JPS and the Kehillah Education Committee as well as her public lectures were Zionistic. In Hadassah she found a new agent of Zionist—and Jewish— reconditioning, not of members alone, but also of their husbands and children. In her words, "We need Zionism as much as those Jews do who need a physical home."[36] Here the dual objectives coalesced. Contemporary scholars Ellen Umansky and Allon Gal noted that Hadassah programs such as aid to the poor and sick and medical education reflected Szold's personal religious and moral convictions.[37] Gal, however, erred when he credited Louis D. Brandeis with influence on Szold's social thinking. In the judge, four years her senior, she ascertained "a prophetic spark,"[38] and she cheered when he wrested the Zionist helm from Lipsky in 1914. But the advanced social ideas that she shared with Brandeis were nurtured in a common matrix: Central European parents who cherished democracy with the ardor of new converts and the Progressive movement of their younger days. When it came to Zionism, it was Szold who sent manuscripts on the subject of Palestine to Brandeis. It is unclear whether he consulted them, but he did turn to other cultural Zionists such as Friedlaender and Eliyahu Lewin-Epstein for enlightenment on Zionist theory and the current conditions of European Jews.[39]

Szold imparted Zionist ideology and accomplishment to Hadassah members by means of classes and books. A new publication fulfilled an old Zionist dream. Between 1905 and 1908 Szold, along with Friedlaender and Friedenwald, had collected articles intended for publication in a "Zionist Handbook." Some were published, but inadequate funding rendered the project, as envisioned, impossible.[40] When Hadassah was expanding into a national organization, Szold enlisted the aid of bosom pal Alice Seligsberg and Jessie Sampter, a new friend. Seligsberg and Sampter, like Szold, were high-minded unmarried women and devoted champions of learning, justice, and universal peace; unlike her, they were so assimilated as to have previously considered personal faiths outside of Judaism. By force of a growing personal charisma Szold convinced them of the validity of Zionism. At her suggestion, Seligsberg and Sampter attended classes taught by Mordecai M. Kaplan, principal of the JTS Teacher's Institute, and enjoyed informal Saturday afternoon discussion sessions in Kaplan's home. At first all three women accumulated "folder propaganda" to disseminate to Hadassah chapters. During the war years Sampter took on two formidable tasks: the creation of a "School of

Zionism" and the composition of three progressively more detailed Zionist manuals. Only then was the Zionist educational project initiated with Friedlaender and Friedenwald accomplished, and by women rather than the customary cluster of men plus Szold as token female.[41]

Soon after restructuring Hadassah, Szold met the challenge of Jews who were willing to support public health services and social welfare in Palestine but unsympathetic to primary principles of national regeneration and a restored Jewish culture. When asked whether to admit non-Zionist women into the Philadelphia chapter, Szold remonstrated:

> I ought to warn you against this non-Zionistic trend. It would be a mistake for us Zionists to let our fine idea become colorless . . . Unless we insist upon the Zionist coloring, the result will be degeneration into flabby philanthropism.[42]

Nevertheless, because she could not afford to relinquish any aid, Szold found a way to accept their help. Hadassah welcomed all contributions, whether motivated by firm national feeling or "flabby philanthropism," but women who did not espouse Zionism were tagged associate members and carefully differentiated from active, committed Zionists. For the Lipsky group this was proof of Hadassah's weak Zionist credentials. To dispel this impression, Hadassah abolished associate membership in 1916. Nevertheless, the sewing circles continued, neutral ground where Zionist and non-Zionist women, working together, outfitted indigent Palestinian women and children in new clothing. (In the years to follow, older Hadassah women would continue the sewing circles, while younger ones would opt for the more sophisticated fund-raising activities and/or educational programs.[43])

Toward Personal and Organizational Autonomy

It was at this juncture that Szold was finally able to realize the dream confided in Ginzberg and resign from the JPS. During the summer of 1915 several prominent, well-to-do, and generous Zionists awarded Henrietta with a lifetime annuity. So strong was her hunger for independence—from the benefactors whom she admired and even from the official Zionist movement—that she hesitated to accept it. Only after receiving assurance that the stipend carried no strings did she agree.[44] Never again would she be beholden to others a livelihood; now she could perform Zionist work in total self-sufficiency.

World War I spelled an end to the FAZ, but not to the question of Hadassah's autonomy. The Balfour Declaration of 1917 conferred international recognition upon Palestine as the Jewish national home. In the flush of excitement which followed, Hadassah acquiesced to submergence into the new Zionist Organization of America. Of the ZOA's constituent departments, only one was headed by a female, Henrietta Szold herself, chosen secretary of the department of education. On paper, Hadassah was reduced to a shadow. The last issue of the *Hadassah Bulletin* was published in March 1918. The American Zionist Medical Unit, Hadassah's primary project, now functioned under ZOA administration. But soon disenchantment set in. The ZOA's plan of determining constituencies by geographical districts rather than group interest proved unsatisfactory to Hadassah members. The women continued to identify themselves as Hadassahites rather than undifferentiated Zionists. As Rose Jacobs, a future Hadassah president, pointed out, they looked to Szold for guidance, and she continued to unite them by force of her personal charisma.[45] Hadassah chapters multiplied; in 1920 Szold crowed: "The Sections absolutely refuse to go out of existence!"[46] The following year witnessed publication of the first *Hadassah News Letter*. By the end of 1921, the women's organization, ten thousand strong, had regained a semi-autonomous position.[47]

Still, the ZOA's stance toward the women's organization remained antagonistic. Hadassah's male critics vilified the women's Zionist organization for promoting what political scientist Yonathan Shapiro would later designate "Palestinianism,"[48] its meaning close to Szold's "flabby philanthropism." They denigrated the organization as a mere collection agency for medical, public health, and welfare services in Palestine. All through the 1920s they scoffed at Hadassah's specified projects as "Diaper Zionism," fit only for dim-witted women incapable of higher conceptualization. As contemporary scholar Michael Berkowitz points out, it was a peculiarly perverse criticism, in light of Hadassah's fine educational programs, intended, we might add, to create Zionists. The ZOA's educational efforts, by contrast, were minimalist.[49]

The principal source of the attack was jealousy over the female organization's greater success in fund-raising and membership; ZOA participation declined during the 1920s while the Hadassah roster grew to thirty-five thousand by 1930.[50] Above all, the ZOA felt threatened by the women's demand for equality and autonomy. Through the twenties this issue surfaced repeatedly as its leaders bucked the Zionist establishment at home and abroad to support Brandeis against Lipsky and Weizmann and even the Labor Zionist Pioneer Women in America.[51]

New Challenges

In internal deliberations Szold herself was a moderate, bent upon retaining Hadassah's partial autonomy but reluctant to create an irreparable split with the general Zionist movement. But she would brook no rival to Hadassah in America. The year 1921 was pivotal in the development of Jewish Palestine; it saw the first graduation from the Hadassah Training School for Nurses and the formation of the general fund known as *Keren Hayesod*. At that time Szold confronted two sisters, Eva Leon and Emma Gottheil. Gottheil was a Hadassah founder and Leon had secured funds to send Hadassah's first American nurses to Palestine. Nevertheless Szold had long been at loggerheads with the two women, probably because of their overheated patriotism during the recent war, when Emma's husband, Professor Richard Gottheil had attacked her friends Friedlaender and Seligsberg for disloyalty to the Allied cause.[52] When the sisters proposed a second American women's Zionist organization, the Women's *Keren Hayesod* Committee, Szold declared her opposition on two grounds. The first was disapproval of *Keren Hayesod*; despite her culturalist bent, she argued that a fund that intermixed donations and investments "seems to offer no guarantee of immediacy, or efficiency, or vigor."[53] Under that plan, all Hadassah contributions would go to the central Zionist office in London, which, even under current conditions, did not dedicate all of them to the projects for which they were collected. (To emphasize *Keren Hayesod's* inadequacy on another score, Szold noted Zionist leader Ussiskin's recommendation of an opthamologist on the basis of his prowess in Zionist speechmaking rather than his skill as a physician.[54]) Equally important was her determination that Hadassah remain the sole agency for Zionist work among American women. A second general Zionist women's organization, she insisted, would yield "two distinctive Palestinian purposes,—all [sic] failures!"[55]

When Szold left the Hadassah presidency in 1926, she encouraged her successor Irma Lindheim's political challenge to the ZOA;

this set the stage for Hadassah's near-total sovereignty, achieved some nine years later.[56]

Szold eschewed politics and always defined her own Zionism in spiritual terms, yet, after moving to Jerusalem in 1920, she flourished in the intensely political atmosphere of the *yishuv*. Under her leadership, Hadassah established the Hadassah Medical Organization, the Nurses Training School, *Tippat Halav* (milk stations for babies), and an internationally famed hospital. Ironically, it was largely because of her political neutrality that in 1927 she was chosen one of three members of the Palestine Executive Committee, the shadow government of the *yishuv*, in charge of health and education. By this time, she no longer controlled Hadassah in America, and indeed was happy to pass the torch to a new generation. But she was still expected to address annual conventions, either in person or by mail. Hadassah women venerated her even when they disregarded the content of her message. When, well into her seventies, she dedicated her remaining strength to Youth Aliyah, salvaging European youth from the Nazi fury, the entire Jewish world placed her on a pedestal. Though the iconic position was unwelcome, even embarrassing, there is no question that Szold achieved the self-sufficiency and recognition previously denied her.[57] In that sense, the life that she had "written" to Ginzberg had come to pass.

Modernizing the Synagogue

One issue discussed in the Ginzberg correspondence remains: the nexus between Jewish religious tradition and the role of women in the modern world. Letters to Ginzberg indicated the inappropriateness of certain traditional prayers for unmarried women. Sophie Szold's death in 1916 brought the issue of women's participation in synagogue life into sharper focus. At that point Henrietta's newfound independence found expression in an answer to Haym Peretz's offer to recite the kaddish, the synagogue prayer conventionally intoned by sons after their parents' death. In 1897, it will be recalled, Szold justified women's exemption from time-based religious obligations. Reforged in the Ginzberg crucible, Szold now maintained that Judaism no longer required women to submit to religious surrogacy:

> I cannot ask you to say Kaddish after my mother . . . I believe that the elimination of women from such duties was never intended by our law and custom—women were freed from

331

positive duties when they could not perform them, but not when they could. It was never intended that, if they could perform them, their performance of them should not be considered as valuable and valid as when one of the male sex performed them. And of the Kaddish I feel sure this is particularly true.[58]

Having established responsibility for her own religious life at a time of personal crisis, Szold tackled the broader issue of the place of women in the synagogue. By the time of her mother's death she had lost interest in the *Tehines*, in part because Schechter, her sponsor, had died and Ginzberg, source of the data, had been "dead" to her for eight years. Furthermore, her wholehearted dedication to organizational work left little time for serious scholarship. Still, even after she withdrew from the seminary circle, she remained an observant Jew. A 1907 letter to Ginzberg had scoffed at a prayerbook issued by the Reform movement for use in summer resorts, and while she lived in America she would not tamper with the basic liturgical structure. At the same time, unsightly and old-fashioned Orthodox services disturbed her; she found them "unlovely," "harrowing" to the nerves, and replete with "unaesthetic concomitants."[59]

Her disappointment in the synagogues of Jerusalem was even more poignant. Like Israel Friedlaender, she had hoped that Jewish resettlement of the land would bring about a religious renaissance. The very opposite was the case for a woman seeking spirituality in Jerusalem synagogues, which either ignored or demeaned her. In disgust, Szold reported to an American audience:

> *One Sabbath morning when I went to a Synagogue in Jerusalem, I caused a commotion. The Shamash was very much excited to see a woman at services, and directed me to the Woman's room, the furniture of which was a dusty little table. After some delay, he brought in a rickety old chair for me to sit on. The room was separated from the Congregation by a curtain hung over a narrow door. Fortunately for me, the curtain was about a foot from the floor, which enabled me to see the shuffling of the men's feet, the sign that they were reciting the "Borchu" and the "Amidah."*

Apparently this experience kept her away from synagogue until she underwent another ordeal at the *Yahrzeit* for one of her parents.

> *There was a narrow opening in the curtain of this window, which permitted a view of the Congregation, but there was so much noise*

*and we were so cut off from the men that I could not hear when
the Kaddish was recited.*[60]

Szold's reports of both incidents emphasized the wide gap separating the "Congregation" from women, regarded as outsiders and nuisances. Rebelling against Ginzberg's conservatism on ritual matters, Szold helped create religious services for like-minded Jews from western countries.

*We formed a Congregation, meeting in the home of one of the
group. Men, women, and children pray together and each person
takes part in the service, even in the reading of the law. The hope
is that gradually there may evolve from this and other similar
meeting-places the kind of service that will satisfy the needs of
those who long for a well-ordered public worship.*[61]

The congregation included American and British expatriots Jessie Sampter, Sophia Berger, Judah Magnes, Alexander Duskin, Norman Bentwich and two of his sisters. The prayerbook compiled by Szold and Berger featured nonliturgical readings in which women fully participated and men and women sang songs in unison. The liturgy was shortened and modified; in the tradition of the Szold-Jastrow prayerbook which Szold had helped revise in 1907, it eliminated hopes for the reestablishment of temple sacrifice and even for the restoration of Jewish national sovereignty. On some Sabbath mornings reading circles convened at Szold or Sampter's house; there were also Saturday afternoon discussions on Jewish issues, including, as Sampter put it, "women's questions in particular" with the wife of Sir Herbert Samuel, the British High Commissioner, who was a Jew.[62]

Swimming Against the Tide

Szold's push toward personal autonomy extended beyond synagogue rituals and women's concerns to a generalized spiritual, prophetic Zionism. On issues of war and peace and Arab-Jewish relations, she recurrently assumed the position of an independent intellectual swimming against the popular tide. During World War I, along with Alice Seligsberg and Jessie Sampter, she joined the People's Council of America for Peace and Democracy, Scott Nearing's pacifist organization. Only when respected Zionist colleagues Wise and Friedenwald, Mack and Brandeis convinced her that this affiliation harmed the cause did she reluctantly submit her resignation.

In Palestine her idealism was tempered with realism. Among Zionists, she was almost unique in her unhappiness with the British from the start, deploring the fact that they entered Palestine through military conquest and ruled with an imperialist fist. She extended a hand to urban Arabs; Hadassah Hospital and its auxiliary clinics catered to all Jerusalemites. When relations with Arabs worsened, she condemned all three parties, Jews as well as Arabs and the British administration. During the 1930s Szold considered herself in "platonic sympathy" with Brit Shalom (Covenant of Peace), led by Czech and German savants Hugo Bergman, Hans Kohn, Robert Weltsch, Gershom Scholem, and Ernst Simon. But she did not join the organization, which advocated an autonomous Palestine where Jews and Arabs would enjoy full equality. Upholding this position, she criticized the Peel Report of 1937 which recommended the partition of Palestine into Jewish and Arab sectors. Only in 1942, when the official Zionist movement, including Hadassah, openly promoted a Jewish state, did she act upon her convictions, largely out of fear of war with the Arabs. Encouraged by her old friend Judah Magnes, chancellor of the Hebrew University, she joined the committee which founded *Ihud* (Union), champion of Arab-Jewish rapprochement and a binational state in Palestine. Despite pleas from Hadassah leaders, Szold clung to her position, assuring critics that this was a matter of personal conviction rather than politics. So firm was her pacifism that she refused to sanction the enlistment of Youth Aliyah graduates into military service on the eve of World War II.[63]

A History-Making Life

On one score, then, Fineman was correct; the Ginzberg "trial" did produce a "transfiguration" but not the kind he intended. "Masculine" intellectualism did not give way to "feminine" pragmatism; instead, independent thought and action replaced compliance with authority. Summoning inner resources after the Ginzberg debacle, Szold learned to rely on her own instincts and live a life that reflected her own values: Zionist, cultural, practical, religious, and feminist. We have seen how this woman, in her fifties, sixties, and seventies, took on opponents of women's full participation in Zionism and religious ritual and stood her ground against those who did not share her vision of Jewish Palestine restored in peace and harmony. Bravely and not without pain, she challenged deeply cherished institutions and people whose convictions she shared: the traditional synagogue, the male-dominated Zionist organizations, other women Zionists, advocates of partition, even Hadassah itself.

In *Writing a Woman's Life* Carolyn Heilbrun quotes an evaluation of George Eliot that pertains in equal measure to Henrietta Szold. Like Eliot, the English novelist, Szold, the American Zionist, "whether deliberately, unconsciously, or accidentally . . . composed her own life so that its fitful, rudderless, and self-doubting first half was alchemized into gold in the second half."[64] After nearly four years of soul-searching, Henrietta Szold was ready to tackle issues introduced in the Ginzberg correspondence; decisions reached between 1912 and 1916 dictated subsequent ventures. Despite the painful cost to her physical and emotional well-being, the dialogue with Ginzberg had unconsciously formulated an agenda for three golden decades of a history-making life.

ABBREVIATIONS
GLOSSARY OF PROPER NAMES
ENDNOTES

Abbreviations

AH—*American Hebrew*
AI—*American Israelite*
AJHS—American Jewish Historical Society, Waltham, MA
BJC—(Baltimore) *Jewish Comment*
CAAC—Carmel Agranat Autograph Collection, private
   papers of Israel and Lilian Friedlaender, at the home
   of their daughter Carmel Agranat, Jerusalem, Israel.
CZA—Central Zionist Archives, Jerusalem, Israel
FAZ—Federation of American Zionists
HA—Henrietta Szold Papers, Hadassah Archives, New
   York City
HUC—Hebrew Union College
ITO—Jewish Territorial Organization
JC—*Jewish Chronicle* (London)
JHSM—Jewish Historical Society of Maryland (Henrietta
   Szold Papers), Baltimore, MD
JPS—Jewish Publication Society
JPSP—Jewish Publication Society Papers, Philadelphia
   Jewish Archives Center, The Balch Institute,
   Philadelphia, PA
JQR—*Jewish Quarterly Review*
JTS—Jewish Theological Seminary of America
JTSL—Jewish Theological Seminary Library
MWAC—Maxwell Whiteman Autograph Collection,
   Philadelphia, PA
NYT—*New York Times*
SL—Schlesinger Library (Henrietta Szold Papers),
   Radcliffe College, Cambridge, MA
ZOA—Zionist Organization of America

Glossary of Proper Names

Adler, Cyrus (1863–1940). Semitist and national communal leader, rooted in Philadelphia and its Jewish institutions (Maimonides College, JPS), first president of Dropsie College, 1906–1912, and Schechter's successor as president of the Jewish Theological Seminary, 1916–1940.

Benderly, Samson (1876–1944). Palestine-born Hebrew educator who abandoned medicine for Jewish education in Baltimore after completing a medical degree at Johns Hopkins University. In 1910 became head of the new Bureau of Jewish Education under sponsorship of the New York Kehillah.

Davidson, Israel (1870–1939). Lithuanian-born, American-educated scholar of medieval Hebrew literature, an expert in medieval liturgical poetry; a longtime acquaintance of Ginzberg when he assumed a teaching position at the Jewish Theological Seminary in 1905.

Friedenwald, Harry (1864–1950). Baltimore opthamologist and expert on Jews in medicine, lifelong friend of Henrietta Szold, supporter of the Jewish Theological Seminary. Between 1904 and 1908 he was president of the Federation of American Zionists.

Friedlaender, Israel (1876–1920). Polish-born, German-educated Semitist, professor of Bible at the Jewish Theological Seminary from 1903 until his tragic early death, colleague of Ginzberg, fellow Zionist worker and personal friend of Henrietta Szold.

Jastrow, Rachel Szold (1865–1926). The Szold sister closest to Henrietta in age, married to Joseph Jastrow, a pioneering psychologist who taught at the University of Wisconsin.

Kohler, Kaufmann (1843–1926). Theoretician and champion of "classical" Reform Judaism, author of the Pittsburgh Platform, 1885. As president of the Hebrew Union College between 1903 and 1921, he made anti-Zionism an important plank in the institution's platform.

Levin, Benjamin. The eldest child of Bertha and Louis H. Levin, Henrietta's much beloved nephew, born in 1902.

Levin, Bertha Szold (1873–1958). Henrietta's sister, born on her thirteenth birthday; mother of five children doted over by their childless aunt and widowed grandmother.

Levin, Louis H. (1866–1948). Merchant, lawyer, author, and editor of the *Jewish Comment* (Baltimore) who worked with Henrietta Szold even before his marriage to her sister Bertha in 1900.

Magnes, Judah L. (1877–1948). American-born graduate of the Hebrew Union College who served as assistant rabbi of Temple Emanu-el, between 1906 and 1910. In 1908 he formed the New York Kehillah and served at its head. Magnes and his family immigrated to Palestine in 1922 where he served as chancellor, then president of the Hebrew University in Jerusalem. He and Szold were lifelong close friends who shared common values of spiritual Zionism and pacifism.

Malter, Henry (1864–1925). Galician-born medievalist who taught at the Hebrew Union College from 1900 to 1907 when differences with Kaufmann Kohler caused his resignation. After Dropsie College opened in 1909, he assumed the chair of Talmudic literature, continuing there until his last days.

Margolis, Max (1866–1932). Biblicist and historian, editor-in-chief of the 1917 JPS Bible translation. Margolis was one of three professors at the Hebrew Union College who resigned in 1907 because of Zionist sympathies. He spent the rest of his teaching career at Dropsie College.

Marx, Alexander (1878–1953). Master of historical detail and Jewish manuscripts, professor of history and librarian of the Jewish Theological Seminary. Through fifty-year teaching careers at the seminary (1903–1953), Ginzberg and Marx remained close colleagues and friends. Marx and his wife Hannah Hoffman Marx were also good friends of Henrietta Szold.

Marshall, Louis (1856–1929). Prominent American-born lawyer, national Jewish communal leader, and supporter of the Jewish Theological Seminary; headed the American Jewish Committee between 1912 and his death.

Radin, Adolph Moses (1848–1909). Lithuanian-born rabbi and communal worker. Radin was rabbi of the People's Synagogue of the Educational Alliance and founder of the Russian American Hebrew Association. He was an active Zionist, a member of the Tannersville circle.

Rosenau, William (1865–1943). Baltimore rabbi and professor of postbiblical literature at Johns Hopkins University. An English-speaking rabbi, he replaced Henrietta's father, Rabbi Benjamin Szold, who was forced to retire in 1892.

Schechter, Solomon (1847–1915). Romanian-born scholar whose discovery of the Cairo Geniza, a treasurehouse of medieval manuscripts preserved in a medieval synagogue, brought him fame, not only at Cambridge University, where he was a reader in rabbinics, but worldwide. In 1902 he assumed the presidency of the Jewish Theological Seminary, a post he held until his death.

Seltzer, Adele Szold (1876–1940). Youngest sister of Henrietta who left the Szold home after her marriage in 1907. A socially aware woman and an intellectual, she worked with unfortunates on the Lower East Side, translated several books for the Jewish Publication Society, and delivered lectures on Jewish women.

Seltzer, Thomas (1875–1943). Publisher, journalist, translator, first editor of the *New Masses;* in the 1920s published books of D. H. Lawrence; husband of Adele Szold.

Schiff, Jacob H. (1847–1920). German-born, American multimillionaire financier who sustained every major Jewish institution and organization. With his support the Jewish Theological Seminary was reorganized and Ginzberg and other major faculty members given positions.

Schloessinger, Max (1877–1944). Semitist born in Heidelberg and educated in Berlin and Vienna. Between 1904 and 1907 he taught at the Hebrew Union College but resigned because of the administration's anti-Zionist stance. Returning to Europe, he established an import-export business, then moved to Palestine where he was active in the Hebrew University, sometimes serving as Judah Magnes's deputy.

Sulzberger, Mayer (1843–1923). Prominent Philadelphia judge, Hebraist, bibliophile and rare book collector, founder and supporter of many Jewish institutions in Philadelphia and New York, and president of the American Jewish Committee, 1906–1912. Chairman of the publication committee of the Jewish Publication Society from its formation until his death, and Henrietta Szold's immediate superior.

Szold, Sophie Schaar (1839–1916). Henrietta's mother, who moved to New York with her oldest daughters Henrietta and Adele in 1903. In 1909 she accompanied Henrietta to Palestine. The two women lived together until Sophie's death.

Notes

INTRODUCTION

1. Three biographers of Szold and Ginzberg have discussed the relationship. See Irvin Fineman, *Woman of Valor: The Life of Henrietta Szold, 1860–1945* (New York: Simon and Schuster, 1961): 117–202 and Joan Dash, *Summoned to Jerusalem: the Life of Henrietta Szold* (New York: Harper and Row, 1979): 47–78. A chapter in Eli Ginzberg's biography of his father, *Keeper of the Law* (Philadelphia: JPS, 1966): 105–29, is entitled "An Exceptional Friendship"; hence the title of this chapter. Equally noteworthy is the fact that their other biographers do not mention the friendship.
2. See Steven J. Zipperstein, *Elusive Prophet: Ahad Ha'am and the Origins of Zionism* (Berkeley and Los Angeles: University of California Press 1993): 201.
3. See Simon Kuznets, "Immigration of Russian Jews to the United States: Background and Structure," *Perspectives in American History* 9 (1975): 35–124; Gerald Sorin, A Time for Building; the Third Migration, 1880–1920 (Baltimore: the Johns Hopkins University Press, 1992): 58.
4. See this author's *Practical Dreamer: Israel Friedlaender and the Shaping of American Judaism* (New York: JTS, 1985): xxv–xxvi and Mel Scult's article "Schechter's Seminary," in *Tradition Renewed: A History of the Jewish Theological Seminary*, ed. Jack Wertheimer (JTS, 1997). Scult effectively demonstrates a lack of continuity between the "old" seminary under Sabato Morais and the "new" seminary, reorganized in 1901–1902.
5. For a discussion of Ginzberg's contribution to the *Jewish Encyclopedia*, see Shuly Rubin Schwartz, *The Emergence of Jewish Scholarship in America: The Publication of the Jewish Encyclopedia*

(Cincinnati: Hebrew Union College Press, 1991): especially chapers 3 and 4. For a general survey of his scholarship see David Druck, *Rabbi Levi Ginzberg* (Hebrew) (Jersey City, N.J., 1933): 73–105.

6. 11 May 1900; JPSP, Box 12, f7.
7. Rebekah Kohut, "Henrietta Szold," *Hadassah News Letter* xi: 3 (December, 1930): 11.
8. See her article "Early Zionist Days in Baltimore," *The Maccabean* 30 (1917): 265–66.
9. Louis Lipsky, "A Leader in Service," idem: 5.
10. Cyrus Adler was the coeditor of the 1904–1905 and the 1905–1906 volumes; Szold edited the 1906–1907 and 1907–1908 volumes alone.
11. *Abodath Israel, a Prayer Book for the Services of the Year at the Synagogue*, 1910. For full citation see p. 356, f27.
12. Even words of thanks were rare. Early in her tenure a letter from Szold to Sulzberger, dated 23 May 1895, indicated appreciation of the words of "a chief whose approval is not lightly given, whose approval is discrimination and whose approval I had no suspicion I was winning." JPSP, Box 12, f12.
13. See Jonathan Sarna, *JPS, The Americanization of Jewish Culture, 1888–1988* (Philadelphia: JPS, 1989): 48.
14. JPSP, Box 12, f7, passim.
15. See Szold's letters to Mayer Sulzberger, dated 19 July 1897, MWAC and the response of 20 July 1897, JPSP, Box 12, f7.
16. 25 December 1900, JHSM, Box 1, f14.
17. See Szold's letters to Sulzberger (14 February 1903) and Adler (18 February 1903) and Adler's response of 22 February 1903 in JPSP, Box 12, f12 and f24. The original request to Schechter, also dated 14 February, is in JHSM, Box 1. Adler's approval was narrowly based upon the right of "The President of the Faculty (i.e., Schechter) . . . in his discretion to admit to the classes in the Seminary special students not candidates for degrees who in his opinion are capable of profiting by the instruction given in the Seminary."
18. Herman H. Rubenovitz and Magnon L. Rubenovitz, *The Waking Heart* (Cambridge, Mass.: Nathaniel Dame & Co., 1967): 24.
19. The Schechter Report to the Board of the JTS (28 January 1906), Board Minutes, JTSL, characterized two of twenty-six junior students as "ladies." Myra Mildred Friedenrich was

twenty-three years old, with an M.A. from the University of California. But whereas Szold was absent only six times that year, less than many of the male students, Friedenrich's name is crossed out from "Dr. Joffe's Report," 1905–1906, JTSL General Files, Box 13. My thanks to Jerry Schwarzbard of the Seminary Library staff for locating these data.

20. *The Waking Heart*, 24.
21. See JTS Registers of 1903–1907, where Szold's name is listed. The register for 1906–1907 must have been printed before September 1906, when she decided to discontinue attendance.
22. Sarna, *JPS*, 36–37.
23. 25 October 1903, Henrietta Szold Papers, CZA/A125/308. Thanks to Mel Scult for directing my attention to this datum.
24. Szold to brother-in-law Louis H. Levin (13 January 1905), CZA/A125/254.
25. See Dash, *Summoned*, 17–18.
26. The letter is dated 21 August 1905; CAAC.
27. See below, Ginzberg to Szold (10 October 1904). This and all letters from Ginzberg to Szold are in CZA/A125/303.
28. Referred to in the "Meditation" and the letters as the "Introduction."
29. Szold to Ginzberg, July 1908. Louis Ginzberg Papers, JTSL, Box 12. Letters from Szold to Ginzberg cited in this volume are from this source, unless otherwise indicated.
30. Letter of 7 August 1908.
31. Letter of 11 September 1908.
32. See Eli Ginzberg, *Keeper of the Faith*, 107–11.
33. See Walter Lord, *The Good Years: from 1900 to the First World War* (New York: Harper and Brothers, 1960): 218, 220.
34. Szold to Ginzberg (16 August 1908).
35. Szold to Ginzberg (15 September 1908).
36. "The Dynamo and the Virgin" is a central chapter in *The Education of Henry Adams: A Biography* (Boston: Houghton Mifflin Co., 1946): 379–90.
37. Szold to Ginzberg (21 August 1907).
38. Szold to Ginzberg (14 August 1907).
39. He called them "primitive" religions. Ginzberg to Szold (4 September 1908), Henrietta Szold Papers, CZA/A125/303. Unless otherwise indicated, all letters from Ginzberg to Szold are from this source.

40. Mary S. Favret, *Romantic Correspondence: Women, Politics, and the Fiction of Letters* (New York: Cambridge University Press, 1993): 107.

41. Leonard Pearson, *The Use of Written Communication in Psychotherapy* (Springfield, Ill.: Charles C. Thomas, 1964): 16; Michael White and David Epson, *Narrative Means to Therapeutic Ends* (New York and London: W.W. Norton & Co., 1990): 6–17, 34–35.

42. Dorothy Tennov, *Love and Limerence: The Experience of Being in Love* (New York: Stein and Day, 1980). I've put together sentences from 23–24, 45–46.

43. The letter of 2 September 1906 indicates that she had not taken a vacation in eight years; CAAC.

44. She subscribed to *Die Welt, Revue des Etudes Juives,* and *The Nation.* Christological allusions were "a thorny crown of sorrows," "Work at his book was hourly crucifixious," and "bleeding from a thousand crucifixions."

45. Theodor Reik, *Of Love and Lust: On the Psychoanalysis of Romantic and Sexual Emotions* (New York: Farrar, Straus, and Cudahy, 1957): 148.

46. The Hertz correspondence is in Szold Papers, HA and CZA; Friedenwald correspondence in JPSP, Box 12 and CZA. Hertz was the seminary's first graduate. He continued to correspond with Szold after he left New York to serve a South African congregation. Friedenwald was a childhood friend four years her junior. They wrote to each other in the 1880s during his medical school days in Germany and continued to do so long after his return to Baltimore and his marriage, indeed for the remainder of their long lives. For the connection to Morris Jastrow see Fineman, *Woman of Valor,* 52–63.

47. For Aaronson, see Szold's journal of 1910, CZA/A125/989, (24 March 1910) (Szold Papers, SL also contain a copy). For Beyth see Dash, *Summoned to Jerusalem,* 251–285.

48. See Janet Malcolm, "A House of One's Own," *New Yorker* 71 (June 1995): 78.

49. Though the subject is covered in the "Meditation," the quotation is taken from her 1910 journal (10 April 1910): 142.

50. Her brother-in-law Louis H. Levin advised her to place her name on the volume "as a matter of truth and history," letter from Levin to Szold (24 March 1909), Szold Papers, JHSM, Box 1. Paul Radin is credited with translating the third volume but not

the fourth. Internal evidence reveals that Szold worked on materials included in both volumes. The title page of volume IV bears an enigmatic "translated from the German manuscript." It consists of translation and editorial work that Szold completed (with great pain) after 20 October 1908. The JPS published volume III in 1911 and volume IV in 1913. The notes, which Szold had happily envisioned as another joint effort between her and Ginzberg, appeared much later, in 1925 and 1928 (volumes V and VI). The opus was completed only in 1938, with an index (volume VII), by Boaz Cohen.

51. See Ira Progoff, *At a Journal Workshop: the Basic Text and Guide for Using the Intensive Journal* (New York: Dialogue House Library, 1975).

AWAKENING LOVE, 1903–1906

1. Pronouns in the masculine singular (he, him, his) that do not refer to a previously mentioned male denote Louis Ginzberg; Szold mentions his full name only once in the entire document, and that is not part of the narrative, but in a citation.

2. Clara de Hirsch Home for Working Girls, home for young female workers from poor families established by the German Jewish elite on the Lower East Side at the turn of the century.

3. Marcus Mordecai Jastrow (1829–1903), author of the well-known *Dictionary of the Targumim, the Talmud Babli and Yerushalmi, and the Midrashic Literature* (Philadelphia, 1903). In her years in Philadelphia, JPS Henrietta had boarded with the Jastrows who had ties of family and friendship with the Szold family. Jastrow and Benjamin Szold had written a prayer book together. See below, p. 356, f27.

4. Adele (1876–1940) was the youngest and spunkiest Szold sister. When the Szolds moved to New York in 1903, Adele was as yet unmarried.

5. Henrietta's sister Rachel (1866–1926) was married to Rabbi Morris Jastrow's younger son Joseph. The couple lived in Madison, Wisconsin, where Joseph was a pioneering professor of psychology at the University of Wisconsin (1888–1927).

6. This letter is found in JPSP, Box 12. It was published in Eli Ginzberg, *Keeper*, 73.

7. Solomon Schechter, born in Rumania in 1848, was president of the JTS from 1902 until his death in November, 1915.

8. Alexander Marx (1878–1953), librarian of the JTS and professor of history, Schechter's second major choice for the new seminary faculty, after Ginzberg.

9. Louis H. Levin (1866–1948), lawyer, author, and editor of the *Jewish Comment* (Baltimore), married to Henrietta's sister Bertha.

10. Probably Rabbi Charles Hoffman (1864–1945), a 1904 seminary graduate. Because of his age—forty at graduation—and experience —he was a founder of the Philadelphia Jewish Exponent—he was, in Mel Scult's words "as much a colleague of Schechter's [and hence of the entire faculty] as a student," in "Schechter's Seminary," forthcoming.

11. Israel Friedlaender (1876–1920), Sabato Morias Professor of Biblical Exegesis at the JTS and Zionist associate of Szold's.

12. The (Baltimore) *Jewish Comment*, hereafter BJC.

13. Nathans, prominent Jewish family of the old Sephardic aristocracy and longtime seminary supporters.

14. Elvira Solis, daughter of a venerable Philadelphia Sephardic family and a dear friend of Henrietta's.

15. Asher Ginzberg.

16. The *American Jewish Year Book,* coedited with Cyrus Adler in 1904 and 1905 and by Szold alone in 1906 and 1907.

17. Ignaz Goldziher (1850–1921), University of Budapest Semitist, a pioneer in Islamic studies and contributor to the study of Judaism in Islamic lands. Both Ginzberg and Friedlaender knew him from their student days in Germany.

18. *Kiddushin* focuses on marriage in all its aspects, including the sexual.

19. Rabbinic statement that a teacher learns more from his students than from his teachers. See Babylonian Talmud, Ta'anit 7a and Makkot 10a.

20. This is the only letter from Szold to Ginzberg in the Szold Papers (A125/303) at the CZA. All other letters deposited in that file are from Ginzberg to Szold or her mother.

21. Ginzberg's essay "The Talmud Student" was first delivered as a public lecture at the JTS, 23 February, 1905, and later reprinted under the title "The Disciple of the Wise," in *Students, Scholars, and Saints* (Philadelphia: JPS, 1928): 104–07.

22. Joseph Michael Asher (1872–1909), British-born professor of homiletics at the JTS, served as rabbi of the B'nai Jeshurum Synagogue, 1900–1906.

23. i.e., the *Jewish Quarterly Review* (JQR). See letter from Ginzberg at the end of this paragraph.
24. Ginzberg's "Geniza Studies" appeared first in the *JQR OS*, volumes 16 to 20 and later were reprinted in the second volume of his *Geonica*, published by JTS in 1909. The reference here is probably to volume 18, 102–03 on a twelfth-century responsum by Hai Gaon, partially destroyed by "water and dampness." Most sources from the Geniza were fragmentary, or as Ginzberg put it, "the remainder of a collection of Geniza Responsa" (19: 257); hence the quip about "remainders" and "remnants." What is called the "Old Series" of the JQR was published in England before 1908. Adler and Schechter resumed its publication in the United States in 1910 (JQR NS).
25. Max Schloessinger (1877–1944). Semitics scholar, who would resign from the faculty of the Hebrew Union College in 1907 and subsequently return to Europe. In 1909 he would marry Miriam Schaar, Szold's cousin.
26. i.e., lectures on Jewish law prepared for class. Szold translated them, had them typed, and then collected them. They have been preserved on microfilm in the JTS Library.
27. Simon Jacobson (1857–1921), cantor of the seminary synagogue. He held the title "Hazan and Instructor in Hazanuth at the Seminary. JTS." JTS Register, 1904–1905 (New York, 1904): 4.
28. There were no German letters addressed to Szold from Ginzberg in the CZA or any American archives available to me.
29. Mrs. Friedenwald, probably the wife of Harry Friedenwald (1864–1950), Baltimore friend of the Szold family, supporter of the Seminary, and president of the Federation of American Zionists, 1904–1908.
30. This letter was printed in Eli Ginzberg, *Keeper*, 113–14.
31. i.e., he is going around the issue rather than confronting head-on his hesitation about writing in English. Since Szold was his instructor in that language, he feels obliged to use it as the medium of their correspondence.
32. Hannah Marx (1880–1962) was the daughter of Bible scholar David Hoffmann, rector of the Rabbiner Seminary in Berlin.
33. Itzkowski was Ginzberg's European typesetter of Hebrew type. The letters contain many references to this man.
34. Moses Aaron Dropsie (1821–1905), Philadelphia attorney, businessman, and Jewish communal activist, willed his fortune to "The Dropsie College for Hebrew and Cognate Learning," a

postgraduate academic rather than a theological institution, with the stipulation that it be established in Philadelphia.

35. Joseph Krauskopf (1858–1923), Philadelphia Reform rabbi, a founder of the JPS, where he clashed often with Mayer Sulzberger and other more conservative Jews. See Jonathan Sarna, *JPS*, 17–23, 53–54.

36. i.e., to attend the Seventh Zionist Congress of 1905, as a delegate of the Federation of American Zionists.

37. When the Sixth Zionist Congress (1903) declined a possible British offer of an East African territory for Jewish settlement, the Anglo-Jewish writer Israel Zangwill (1864–1926) abandoned official Zionism. He then founded the Jewish Territorial Organization (ITO), which looked for sites in other countries as temporary Jewish "territories." Mainstream Zionists rejected his proposals out of hand.

38. *Ken Yovdu kol oyvekhah*: "So may all your enemies be destroyed." Judges 5:31, concluding words of the biblical Song of Deborah, expressing joy at the Israelite defeat of a Canaanite army.

39. A play the two had discussed, possibly written by Adele Szold.

40. Antonia Labriola (1843–1904), the first Italian Marxist philosopher, a strong influence upon Georges Sorel and Benedetto Croce. Sorel collected the essays mentioned in the letter and published them in Paris in 1897.

41. Karl Kautsky (1854–1939), after Marx and Engels, the leading Marxist theoretician of the pre-World War I period. Like Marx and Engels, he held that religion, philosophy, and ethics were reflections of economic conditions. Ginzberg was on stronger ground when he quoted Kautsky's opponent Eduard Bernstein in support of his own idealistic position.

42. Eduard Bernstein (1850–1932), leader of the revisionist group within German socialism that opposed Orthodox Marxist doctrines, arguing for social reform rather than the overthrow of capitalism. When this letter was written, Bernstein held a seat in the Reichstag.

43. Benjamin Hartogensis (1865–1939), the man with whom Szold had worked at the Russian Night School in Baltimore. In 1905 he was a widower and the purpose of his visit was probably a marriage proposal.

44. "The Rabbinical Student," public lecture delivered at JTS, 11 January 1906. Reprinted in *Students, Scholars, and Saints*, 59–87.

45. Judah Magnes (1877–1948), was rabbi of Temple Israel in Brooklyn, 1904–1906; then he accepted the position of associate rabbi at Temple Emanu-El in Manhattan. The Szold-Ginzberg correspondence of 1907 contained many references to his efforts to defend three Zionist professors dismissed from the HUC faculty. The identity of "the Magneses" mentioned here is unclear, as Judah did not marry Beatrice Lowenstein until 1908.

46. Jalkut, probably *Yalkut Shim'oni* [The Compilation of Simon (of Frankfort)], a medieval collection of interpretations of passages in the Hebrew Bible, arranged in sequence.

47. "Jewish Sympathy for Animals," *The Nation* 83:117, 9 August 1906. The article appeared the same day in the *New York Evening Post* and was reprinted a week later in *AH*, 17 August 1906: 270. See also my article, "Louis Ginzberg as Apologist," *American Jewish History* 79:2 (Winter 1989–90): 210–20.

48. See below, Ginzberg letter of 22 August 1906.

49. Israel Davidson (1870–1939) was the last major Schechter appointee to the seminary faculty. He became instructor in Talmud in 1905, registrar in 1915, and professor of medieval literature in 1917. A letter dated 2 September 1906 (CAAC) from Szold to Israel and Lillian Friedlaender indicates that the entire seminary circle returned to New York for his wedding. Carrie Dreyfus was the bride.

50. On a postal card, postmarked New York, 3 August 1906, spacing as it appears on the card. This was apparently a stab at the low level of American Jewish taste and the braggadoccio of men who called themselves Jewish scholars.

51. Samson Benderly (1876–1944), Palestinian-born physician who abandoned medicine for Jewish education after completing a medical degree at Columbia University. In 1907 he was a Baltimore educator, but would move to New York in 1910 to assume directorship of the new Bureau of Jewish Education under *Kehillah* sponsorship.

52. Henry Malter (1864–1925), Galician-born medievalist who taught at the Hebrew Union College from 1900 to 1907 when differences with Kaufmann Kohler over Zionism led to his resignation.

53. Ezekiel 37:4.

54. Anna was the live-in maid during the years that the Szolds lived on 123rd Street. She was a young Jewish woman from the Lower East Side.

55. The Radins were a scholarly family. Adolph Radin (1845–1909) served as rabbi of the People's Synagogue of the Educational Alliance. Max (1880–1950), his oldest son, was a jurist and law professor. Herman, the middle son became a physician. Paul (1883–1959), an anthropologist, translated volume III of the *Legends*.

56. Ahad Ha-am was the pseudonym name of Asher Ginzberg (1856–1927), preeminent Hebrew essayist and cultural Zionist of his day. See pp: 321–22.

57. Nahum Abramovich Pereferkovich (1871–1940), author of a critical translation of the Mishnah, the Talmud, and other rabbinic works into Russian.

58. See p. 352, f37. Both Szold and Ginzberg held the ITO in contempt.

CRITICAL YEARS, 1906–1908

1. Wife of Ginzberg's brother Abraham. Ginzberg lived with his brother's family until his marriage in 1909.

2. Here the Diary picks up from the previous entry.

3. On Mount Desert Island, where her sister Rachel rented a cottage.

4. There are no available personal letters from Szold to Ginzberg dated before 1907.

5. i.e., streetcar.

6. See "A Specimen of Jewish Learning at American Universities," *AH* 9 November 1906: i–v. The "specimen" was William Rosenau's *Jewish Biblical Commentators* (Baltimore, 1906). Ginzberg attacked Rosenau, Baltimore Reform rabbi and professor of Oriental languages at Johns Hopkins University, for his narrow focus. Rosenau, Ginzberg argued, ignored commentators "of an allegorical, philosophical and mystical character," as well as the foremost medieval commentators, and preferred second-rate German exegetes of the modern period to great men such as the Vilna Gaon, Eybeschutz, Landau, Luzatto, and the Malbin.

7. Benjamin Szold had been forced into retirement in September 1892, when his Baltimore congregation, Oheb Shalom Synagogue, opted for a more modern, English-speaking rabbi. Six months later William Rosenau replaced him. See Marcia L. Rozenblit, "Choosing a Synagogue: The Social Composition of

Two German Congregations in Nineteenth-Century Baltimore," in Jack Wertheimer, ed., *The American Synagogue Transformed* (New York: Cambridge University Press, 1987): 334.

8. "The Jewish Primary School," public lecture at the JTS, 31 January 1907, reprinted in *Students, Scholars, and Saints*, 1–34.

9. The full name of the volume was *Herev Nokemet Nekam Berit* [A Sword that Revenges the Quarrel of the Covenant].

10. Schechter reported on Ginzberg's leave of absence "from the first of May, owing to the sickness of his aged father, living in Amsterdam, who is in a very critical state." "Report of President Schechter to the Board of Directors Meeting of Sunday, May 26, 1907," General Files, JTSL.

11. Szold traveled to Philadelphia on a regular basis to attend meetings of the Publication Committee of the JPS.

12. Census Year Book, Szold prepared census figures for the American Jewish Year Book, working with statistics from the United States Census Bureau.

13. This is Szold's title, centered on the page.

14. "What Our Grandmothers Read," *The Hebrew Standard* (5 April 1907): 1–2, Szold's article on literature for women. After the Ginzberg debacle, Schechter encouraged her to compose a full study of this literature.

15. Helena Frank's translation of stories by Isaac Loeb Perez was published by JPS under the title *Stories and Pictures*.

16. Adele Szold married Thomas Seltzer in 1907.

17. The letter appears to be dated April 8, but since Ginzberg wrote of his imminent departure on April 23, it must have been written in May. Ginzberg's son, in *Keeper*, 116, dates it May 9; I prefer to keep the "8."

18. Sadie American (1862–1944), social worker and founder of the National Council of Jewish Women, an almost exact contemporary of Henrietta Szold.

19. Horace Hart, of the University Press in England, which printed the Geniza Studies. A discussion about publication follows.

20. Szold seems to be responding to a postcard as well as Ginzberg's letter of 8 May 1907.

21. Joseph Jacobs (1854–1916), Jewish historian and folklorist, Australian born, Cambridge educated, a disciple of Steinschneider. In America an editor of the *Jewish Encyclopedia*, later the *American Jewish Year Book* and the *American Hebrew*.

After the Ginzberg debacle he was Szold's first choice to take her place as translator and editor of the final unedited volume of the *Legends of the Jews*. (Letters from Szold to Jacobs and Israel Davidson, both dated 10 June 1910, JPSP Box 12, f3.) His refusal was probably due to his busy schedule—he also was registrar and professor of English at the Jewish Theological Seminary—but may have also reflected his disapproval of the title.

22. The wife of Professor Ginzberg's brother Abraham.

23. When three professors at the Hebrew Union College (Henry Malter, Max Margolis, and Max Schloessinger) were forced to resign from the faculty of the Hebrew Union College for pro-Zionist sentiments. The feud continued from the pulpit of Temple Emanu-el, the flagship congregation of Reform Judaism. See Szold letter of 20 May 1907.

24. *Tehines*, woman's prayer book, a subject which interested Szold at the time. See p. 355, f14.

25. Probably Szold-Seltzers.

26. See *AH* (24 May 1907): 55, 61–62. Adolph Kraus (1850–1938) was international president of IOBB (B'nai B'rith) from 1905 to 1925. Simon Wolf (1836–1923) headed the Committee on Civil and Religious Rights of the Union of American Hebrew Congregations. Both organizations were distressed at losing power to the new American Jewish Committee.

27. Prayer Book, a third edition of the Szold-Jastrow Prayerbook, *Avodath Yisroel: The Order of Prayer for the Israelitish Divine Service on Every Day of the Year*, 1865. The second edition was a joint effort: *Avodath Yisroel; Isrealitish Prayerbook for all the Public Services of the Year*, revised by Revs. Drs. M. Jastrow and H. Hochheimer, and translated by Marcus Jastrow, 1873. The third edition, *Abodath Israel, a Prayerbook for the Services of the Year at the Synagogue prepared by Benjamin Szold and Marcus Jastrow*, was published in 1910. A publisher's note explaining minor revisions is dated August 1907; these must have been the ones that Szold prepared during her "spare time."

28. "The Cincinnati imbroglio" refers to the three HUC professors pressured to resign by anti-Zionist President Kaufmann Kohler on account of their Zionist sympathies and activities. See p. 357, f30 and Naomi W. Cohen, "The Reaction of Reform Judaism in America to Political Zionism (1897–1922)," *PAJHS* 40 (June

1951): 372–82; Samuel E. Karff, ed. *Hebrew Union College—Jewish Institute of Religion at One Hundred Years* (Cincinnati, 1975): 62–67.

29. The letter argued for *Lehrfreiheit* [academic freedom] and asked the president to inquire into the attitude of the alumni. It was printed in *AI* (28 March 1907): 5.

30. "Dr. Kohler," Kaufmann Kohler (1843–1926) was president of the Hebrew Union College (1903–1921) and a strong opponent of Zionism. His series on Zionism appeared in the *Reform Advocate* in 1907. The article to which Szold is probably referring appeared in volume 33, 199–200 and was reprinted in *AH* (12 April 1907): 606.

31. In *AH* (17 May 1907): 39; *BJC* (7 May 1907): 88–89.

32. Maximillian Heller (1860–1929), prominent New Orleans Reform rabbi who would be elected president of the CCAR in 1909, despite his outspoken Zionism. His letter, "Freedom of Thought Should be Permitted at the H.U.C.," appeared in *AI* (16 May 1907): 5.

33. Leo Wise, (1849–1933) "Publisher and Proprietor" of *AI*, published in Cincinnati with a Reform perspective.

34. "The H.U.C.: Shall Control Pass out of the Hand of Its Friends?" *AI* (16 May 1907): 4. Emil G. Hirsh (1851–1923), radical Reform rabbi in Chicago, is scored because he "abolished the traditional Sabbath,"—he instituted a Sunday Sabbath service—and because he criticized I.M. Wise, the recently deceased paragon of Reform Judaism, for his moderate views.

35. Ibid. The claim is made that I.M. Wise refused to accept Ginzberg on the faculty of the HUC because the latter espoused biblical criticism.

36. Louis Marshall (1856–1929), New York corporation lawyer, important supporter of all Jewish communal endeavors and vocal promoter of the seminary.

37. In 1907 the Eighth Zionist Congress met in the Science and Art Institute of that city. They chose the Hague rather than Basle that year "to bring the matter of Zionism to the attention of the Hague Peace Conference and the Hague Tribunal," *AH* (10 May 1907): 33.

38. Alexander Marx.

39. Israel Friedlaender.

40. See p. 354, f6.

41. Mr. Dooley, the creation of the journalist Finley Peter Dunne. "Mr. Dooley" uttered "wise" sayings in a thick Irish brogue.
42. Sarah, third child of Bertha and Louis H. Levin.
43. In 1907 the scholarly Jewish world was titilated with the "discovery" of a medieval manuscript of *Kodashim*, one of the orders of the Jerusalem Talmud, previously unknown. For a while, Ginzberg was one of many taken in by this forgery and brought *Bekhorot*, one of two tractates published in 1907, to his father.
44. The *NYT* did not print anything about the Temple Emanu-el controversy of 1907. Ginzberg may have been referring to an article in the British or South African press paper excerpted by his South African brother.
45. The JPS published *Philo-Judaeus of Alexandria* in 1910. The author was Norman de Mattos Bentwich (1883–1971), scion of an English Zionist family and brother of Lilian Ruth Friedlaender. He would become attorney general of the Mandate government of Palestine during the 1920s, and in his later years, professor of international relations at the Hebrew University in Jerusalem.
46. Ecclesiastes 4:12.
47. Ruth Schechter was the daughter of Solomon Schechter and his wife Mathilde. Ruth married Morris Alexander, a lawyer living in Capetown, South Africa on 9 June 1907 at the seminary synagogue. In a letter to her family, dated 5 June 1907, Szold wrote: "Monday afternoon, I shopped for Ruth Schechter's present. I got an exquisite one, but of course I went beyond the limit set by us. It is an olive dish of cut glass set in a silver case, and the silver case is of beautiful design—the copy of an old French pattern. I spent some more money that afternoon for myself. I had to buy another hat to wear at the function," JPSP, Box 12, f17.
48. *Studies in Judaism, Second Series*, published by JPS in 1908.
49. Max Margolis (1866–1932) was general editor of the 1917 JPS Bible translation, completed in 1917. Reference here is to his translation of Micha, published in 1908.
50. Eliyahu Ze'ev Lewin-Epstein (1863–1932), Zionist pioneer born in Lithuania and lived in Palestine, but spent much of his time in the United States, marketing wine for the Carmel Society and promoting Zionism.
51. For the Zionist Congress.
52. Abraham Elijah Lubarsky (1856–1920), journalist and Hebraist, emigrated to the United States in 1903. In this country Lubarsky

founded the *Histadrut Ivrit* and edited its newspaper. In Eastern Europe he had been a close associate of Ahad Ha-am and was understandably distressed to learn of the violence perpetrated against his friend. See below, f57.

53. And therefore no longer needed to demonstrate progress in granting rights to the populations living in Russia.

54. Ginzberg, distraught over his father's illness, wrote the wrong date. Contextually, this letter responds to Szold's missives of May 20 and June 17.

55. J.P.C.—Publication Committee of the JPS.

56. At the same time that Ginzberg was working on the *Legends* and *Geonica*, he was also preparing another study, *Yerushalmi Fragments from the Geniza*. See p. 361, f73.

57. In May and June, 1907, rioting broke out in Odessa following the assassination of three police officials. Members of the fiercely nationalistic Black Hundreds ran wild, beating innocent civilians, especially targeting Jews. When Ahad Ha-am (Asher Ginzberg) stopped to see a gathering mob, a policeman rushed over to him and beat him about the head until he fell unconscious. Ginzberg was taken to the hospital, where he received numerous inquiries, including one from a St. Petersburg newspaper. He recovered completely. See *Igrot Ahad Ha-am* 4 (24 February 1910): 24; *AH* (24 May 1907): 59, and (14 June 1907): 149–150. Oddly, Steven J. Zipperstein, Ahad Ha-am's latest biographer, devotes only two half-sentences to what must have been a momentous experience in his subject's life: *Elusive Prophet*, 68, 226.

58. i.e., the four-letter biblical designation for the Lord.

59. The JPS did publish a collection of Ginzberg's essays, *Students, Scholars, and Saints*, but not until 1928.

60. *AH* (17 June 1907): 113–114. Cyrus Adler's speech, delivered at the 1907 commencement exercises of the Jewish Theological Seminary, argued for organizing all Jewish institutions in America into a Jewish University of America, with a single governing body.

61. Bertha Raynor Frank (1847–1913) was the daughter of a prominent Baltimore magnate, the disabled widow of a physician of that city, and the sister of a United States senator from Maryland. In May 1907, the management of an Atlantic City hotel informed her that her nieces would not be welcome there. The incident was reported widely in the Jewish press. See *BJC* (24 May 1907): 106, 114; *AH* (24 May 1907): 73; *AI* (23 May 1907): 7.

62. An apparent dig at Reform Jews whose rejection of distinguishing Jewish religious strictures do not gain them acceptance in gentile society.

63. Psalm 119:92.

64. Among the ritual objects used in the *Havdalah* service that ushers out the Sabbath is a small box containing spices (*besamim*). *Besamim* boxes were often worked out of fine metal or attractively decorated wood.

65. Central Conference of American Rabbis, organization of Reform rabbis in North America.

66. The reference was to a short notice published in *AH* (21 June 1907): 178. It read as follows: "The Central Conference of American Rabbis announces that a special edition of the Union Prayer Book has been prepared, suitable for Friday evening and Saturday morning services, to be held at the summer resorts. The book is neatly bound, the price being 25 cents, postpaid, and can be had in any quantity from the agents, the Bloch Publishing Co."

67. The section of Baltimore where Louis H. Levin, editor of the *Jewish Comment*, his wife Bertha, sister of Henrietta, and their family lived.

68. "Tendencies in a Seminary," *AI* (18 April 1907): 4. Max Heller, a Reform rabbi and a Zionist, writing in the aftermath of the Zionist professors' resignation, insisted that a liberal seminary be tolerant of all points of view.

69. Probably from "The Union and Zionism," an editorial in *AI* (23 May 1907): 5, dealing with the official pronouncement of the Union of American Hebrew Congregations, that the Jews are "not a nation but a religious community." This followed the unequivocal statement "America is our Zion . . . the home of religious liberty."

70. One of two secretaries who worked in the Szold house helping Henrietta Szold with her editorial responsibilities.

71. Moses Mielziner (1828–1903), a professor of Talmud at the Hebrew Union College, was the author of a popular *Introduction to the Talmud* (1894) and shorter studies on Jewish law. The reference here is to the latter.

72. Hermann Strack (1848–1922), a Protestant theologian and scholar at the University of Berlin. The reference is probably to his *Einleitung in den Talmud*, Munich, 1887.

73. The Geniza Studies consisted of three volumes. Drawing on Ginzberg's work with Geniza fragments, they were published under the rubric *Texts and Studies of the Jewish Theological Seminary of America*. Volumes I and II, entitled *Geonica*, were translated by Szold. Volume III, *Yerushalmi Fragments from the Genizah*, was less ambitious than this 1907 proposal. Throughout his life, Ginzberg would devote most of his efforts to the Jerusalem Talmud, culminating in his majestic *A Commentary on the Palestinian Talmud. A Study of the Development of the Halakah and Haggadah in Palestine and Babylon* (1941), volumes X–XII of the *Text and Studies* series. It contains an English language introduction, reprinted in 1941 as "The Palestinian Talmud."

74. i.e., a legal means of evading a rabbinic interdiction.

75. *AI* (16 May 1907): 4. Hirsch's statement was "At least the Theological Seminary is a graduate school and has shown its love for scientific teaching by calling Dr. Ginzburg (sic) whom Dr. Wise refused to call to the Hebrew Union College because of his disbelief in the authenticity of the Pentateuch." That issue contains no mention of Magnes' opinion of Ginzberg.

76. Samuel Schulman (1864–1955), a rabbi of Temple Beth El in New York, later of Temple Emanu-el, a classical Reformer and an anti-Zionist at the time, was born in eastern Europe, but brought to America in early childhood.

77. European rabbis of minor accomplishment and modest means provided for their families by accepting money for answers to questions of Jewish law. Ginzberg poses here, in jest, as that kind of rabbi rather than the scholar that he truly was. Thanks to Emanuel S. Goldsmith for this information.

78. Jacob Schiff (1847–1920), financeer, philanthropist, and pre-eminent leader of the Jewish community. His speech was reported in *AH* (21 June 1907): 117–78 and *AI* (27 June 1907): 4. Louis Marshall (1856–1929) was a prominent constitutional and corporate attorney and national Jewish leader.

79. i.e., before the mass migration of East Europeans to the American continent. "I found more warm-hearted Judaism forty years ago in this country," Schiff pronounced, to Szold's dismay, "than I find to-day when there are so many more orthodox Jews here. I see the sons and daughters of the orthodox Jews slip away from their religion and I am frank in saying that your yeshibas and your cheders will never maintain orthodox Judaism in the

United States. If you feel as warm-hearted down here as we do in the cause of Judaism, and I have no doubt that you do, you must support the Seminary."

80. i.e., Purim, which falls in late winter, when the scroll (*Megillah*) of Esther is read in the synagogue and not late summer, the time when the scroll of Lamentations (*Echah*) is read in synagogue in commemoration of the destruction of the temple on the fast day of Tish'a B'av. Esther is a much longer book than *Echah*.

81. Checking U.S. government statistics utilized for the Year Book.

82. Seven-day mourning period following the death of a close relative.

83. Isaiah 40:29. Isaiah chapter 40, which offers consolation to Israel after the destruction of the First Temple, is read on the first Sabbath after *Tish'a B'Av*.

84. In the letters of consolation, written over a period of six days (July 24–29) and apparently sent in two envelopes, the subscription "Sincerely yours" is omitted.

85. The 1907 Chautauqua Summer Assembly was held in Atlantic City, July 23–28 and reported verbatim in *AI* (1 August 1907): 7. What must have angered Szold and her fellow Zionists even more was Schiff's pronouncement that "the hope of the restoration of the Jewish nation in Palestine was not the guiding star of Israel's hope," was his insistence that the promised land was now America.

86. Rabbi Emil Ludwig Cohn (1881–1948), *Prediger* [official preacher and teacher] of the Berlin Jewish community, was suspended in 1907 because of his outspoken Zionism. He subsequently studied jurisprudence and wrote plays and essays on the problems of modern Judaism. It was not until 1926 that he would once again receive a call to a Berlin synagogue. For a contemporary report in the Anglo-Jewish press see "The Cohn Affair," *AH* (31 May 1907): 92.

87. Cranz (Kranz), a Baltic seaside resort, seventeen miles north of Königsberg.

88. Solomon Judah Friedlaender (Friedland), (c. 1860–c. 1912) was a literary charlatan who posed as a Sephardi Jew descended from the distinguished Algazi family. He forged several rabbinic and hasidic texts, the most notorious of which was his "discovery" of a medieval Spanish manuscript of the long-lost *Seder Kodashim* of the Jerusalem Talmud. In 1907 he published two tractates (followed by two more in 1909), along with his own commen-

tary, *Heshek Shelomo*. At the time many regarded it as a spectacular find. For Ginzberg's opinion on this matter see his last European letter to Szold, dated 24 September 1908.

89. Baer Abraham Ratner (1852–1916), author of a series of twelve books on the Talmud. *Varianten zum Jerusalemischen Talmud* (Vilna, 1901–1914). Ratner was one of the first to challenge the genuineness of the Friedland-Algazi manuscript. (He was later proven correct.)

90. On the death and rebirth of the JQR, see p. 351, f24.

91. Ethics of the Fathers, 2:6.

92. The reference is to recent graduates of the seminary's rabbinical department: Abraham M. Hershman, Abraham E. Dobrin, Nathan Blechman, and Nathan A. Lublin in 1906 and Jacob Kohn in 1907.

93. Two Raisin brothers were Reform rabbis. Jacob Zalman Raisin (1877–1946) was a Hebraist and author of *The Haskalah Movement in Russia* (JPS, 1913). Max Raisin (1881–1957), a HUC graduate, was also a prolific writer, in three languages. Unlike many of his peers, he was an ardent Zionist. Neither brother "crawled out of the rabbinate": Jacob served a Charleston, S.C., congregation from 1915 to 1944; Max remained in Paterson, N.J., for over thirty years (1921–1953).

94. Published in Schechter's *Studies in Judaism, Second Series* (Philadelphia, 1908): 202–85.

95. Israel Abraham, Schecter's English Jewish colleague.

96. David Philipson (1862–1949), *The Reform Movement in Judaism* (New York: Macmillan Co., 1907). Philipson was a leading Reform rabbi of his day, a founder of the Central Conference of Reform Rabbis, an editor of the JPS 1917 Bible translation, an instructor at the Hebrew Union College, and a major proponent of classical Reform Judaism. Schechter's review was never published, nor is it found in his papers in the JTS Library.

97. A review by Hebrew Union College Professor Gotthard Deutsch's (1859–1921) appeared in *AI* 53:51 (20 June 1907): 4–5. The "swipes" at Schechter were mostly recitals of misspellings and misquotations, intended to demonstrate Schechter's lack of sophistication, "to show that he never unlearned *cheder* habits." Deutsch was hardly more charitable to Philipson and equally pedantic, scoring the book for omissions and imbalance, as he put it "no proper assignments of space."

98. See letter of 17 July 1907. This is a rare instance of repetition of the same facts during the 1907 correspondence with Ginzberg.
99. "Rabbi Explains Attitude of Orthodox Union," *AH* (16 August 1907): 366. n.b. Earlier the director of an institution designated "Rabbinical School of the East Side" had responded to Schiff by insisting that the 300,000 recent immigrants to whom he alluded preferred rabbis "trained after the fashion of their fathers and grandfathers," *AI* (20 June 1907): 4.
100. Hershman was moving from Syracuse to Detroit, and Schechter would install him in his new rabbinical post. See Szold's letter of 18 August 1907, p. 119.
101. *Siyum* means completion in Hebrew. The term, generally applied to completing study of a Talmudic tractate, is used ironically here.
102. Confession of Sins, a litany of collective sins recited many times during Yom Kippur prayers.
103. Thirty-day period of mourning after the death of a loved one, less intensive than the seven days of *Shiv'a* that follow the interment.
104. Felix Perles (1874–1933), son of Joseph Perles, a nineteenth-century Aramaic and Hebrew philologist and lexicographer. The younger Rabbi Perles shared his father's scholarly interests and was, in addition, an active Zionist.
105. Wishes that she be inscribed and sealed (in the Book of Life for the coming Jewish calendar year).
106. Mrs. Jastrow, the widow of Marcus Jastrow, was Henrietta's sister Rachel's mother-in-law.
107. Five-year-old Benjamin Levin overturned a steam machine while in the Szold apartment and received a severe burn on his arm.
108. "Mr. Schiff Declares in Letter to Dr. Schechter That a True American Cannot Be a Good Zionist," *AH* (23 August 1907): 385.
109. *Die Welt* was the German-language organ of the Zionist movement. These issues of the journal discussed the Eighth Zionist Congress.
110. Herzl, eldest son of the Friedlaenders, was born in December 1906, and died in February 1995.
111. In *AH* (30 August 1907): 406.
112. i.e., Mayer Sulzberger.
113. Julian Mack, (1866–1943) respected Chicago jurist active in national Jewish affairs. In 1916 Judge Mack would create the fund that enabled Szold to resign from the JPS and continue her Zionist work on a full-time basis.

114. Marshall did reply; first in *AI*, reprinted under the title "The J.T.S. and Zionism," in *AH* (20 September 1907): 488.
115. Lamentations 1:18.
116. Address delivered at the Jewish Chautauqua Society, in which Schiff envisioned a future of "Jews in faith but at one in sentiment with their surroundings," and railed against Zionism. Ginzberg was responding to Szold's rendition of the speech, from which the words in the last sentence are taken.
117. Ginzberg feared that the absence from the Congress of two J.T.S. professors who were spending the summer in Europe might be misinterpreted to indicate the institution's agreement with Schiff's anti-Zionism.
118. That Ginzberg requested a $500 increase in salary soon after his return from Europe is indicated in the "Report of President Schechter to the Board of Directors," 20 October 1907, General Files, JTSL. Schechter recommended approval of the request, which would raise his salary to the level of the two married professors, Marx and Friedlaender.
119. Creole was the Szold family's elderly dog.
120. Alexander Cohen, slated for graduation from JTS that very month was "one of the most promising of our pupils . . . taken away by a sad and early death." Report of President Schechter to Board of Directors," 1 November 1908, General Files, JTSL. The report notes that Cohen's "colleagues" established a prize in his honor, probably the memorial fund mentioned here.
121. "Pother" means a choking cloud of smoke, similar to "bother."
122. Gal and Gak, Shat and Shash, Hag with and without a dot—diacritical points.
123. Albargeloni, Aaron of Lunel, Isaac, Rabbi Jehudai—important figures in Geonic literature.
124. Rabbi Sherira and his letters—Sherira ben Hanina Gaon—*Gaon* of Pumbedita, 986–1006, a prolific writer of Responsa.
125. Rabbi Hai and his garrulous Responsa—Sherira's son, generally considered the last of the *Geonim*.
126. Gischala, or Giscala, historic city in the Upper Galilee, a center of olive oil manufacture until the late Middle Ages. Rabbis who composed the Mishnah and the Palestinian Talmud lived there. Henrietta's playful remark refers to Giscala's Hebrew name *Gush Halav*, which means district rich in milk.

127. Scholars of Kairwan, or Kairouan, Tunisian city where Jewish life and learning flourished between the eighth and the tenth centuries. The academy of Kairouan was a famous center of Talmudic scholarship.

128. At the time Szold was translating Nahum Slouschz' study of Haskalah literature from the French. In 1909, the JPS published the book under the title *The Renascence of Hebrew Literature*.

129. *The Baltimore Jewish Comment*, edited for many years by Bertha Szold's husband, Louis H. Levin.

130. David Neumark (1866–1924), Galician-born, German-educated professor of philosophy at the Hebrew Union College, 1907–1924 and philosopher of Reform Judaism. The work referred to was Neumark's *Jehuda Halevi's Philosophy in its Principles*, first published in 1907 and reprinted in *Essays in Jewish Philosophy* (Cincinnati, 1929): 219–300.

131. The Twelfth Annual Summer Assembly of the Jewish Chautauqua Society took place between July 14 and July 20 in Buffalo, New York. See *AI* (9 July 1908): 6.

132. Christiansand (Kristiansand) is a city in southern Norway on the Skagerrak, a small inlet at the mouth of the Otra River, 150 miles southwest of Oslo (then called Christiania).

133. Maurice Bloomfield (1855–1928), professor of Sanskrit and comparative linguistics at Johns Hopkins University. In 1910–1911 he would serve as the president of the American Oriental Society.

134. The post cards were unavailable to me.

135. Ernst Bernhaim (1850–1942), *Einleitung in die Geschichtwissenschaft* [Introduction to Critical History] Berlin, 1905.

136. Solomon Zusha Prokesch received a Seminary DHL (Doctor of Hebrew Letters) in 1907; Elias Nathan Rabinowitz was ordained in 1908. They served as chaplains of the Hawthorne School for Delinquent Jewish Boys in Hawthorne, New York, then newly established under the auspices of the New York Jewish Protectory and Aid Society. See Baila R. Shargel and Harold L. Drimmer, *The Jews of Westchester, A Social History* (Fleischmanns, New York, 1994): 99 and Stanley Burnshaw, *The Epic of the Jews* (New York: Horizon Press, 1981), part III.

137. Butt of Lewis, a promotory at northern extremity of Lewis with Harris, the largest and most northerly island of the Outer Hebrides.

138. Haskalah, movement for Jewish enlightenment in nineteenth-century eastern Europe and subject of Slouschz' book.
139. Elvira Solis, see p. 350, f14. Apparently the two friends took the automotive spin through New Jersey with two older women, Sophie Szold and someone from the Solis family.
140. Seebad Heringsdorf, popular seaside and health resort village in Prussian Pomerania.
141. Conference of Semitists held in Copenhagen, August 1908. See *JC* (28 August 1908): 14–15.
142. Paul Haupt (1858–1926), German-born professor of Semitics at Johns Hopkins University, a non-Jew. A few days later Haupt delivered a paper entitled "The Ethnology of Galilee" or "Was Jesus a Jew by Race?" at the Oxford Congress of Religions. Haham Moses Gaster responded forcefully. See *JC* (25 September 1908): 30.
143. Abraham Shalom Yehuda (1877–1951), Arabist born in Palestine, lecturer at the *Hochschule fuer Wissenschaft des Judentums*, Berlin 1904–1914; later a professor at the University of Madrid (1914–1922).
144. Saul Chajes (1884–1935), East European bibliographer, author of *Ozar Beduyei ha-Shem*, a compilation of pseudonyms used in Hebrew literature.
145. i.e., wishes that the ocean liner *Minneapolis* would bring him back safely to America.
146. Philip Cowen (1853–1943), founder of the *American Hebrew* and its editor for twenty-seven years, also an immigration official at Ellis Island and gatherer of statistics and other facts about Jewish immigrants. Dubbing him "diacritical" must have been an inside joke about his personality. Ginzberg did not much like Cowen and refused several offers to write for his journal.
147. Paul Radin, Rabbi Adolph Radin's son, was a follower of the pioneering anthropologist Franz Boas. Radin was an anthropologist and a linguist who transcribed texts of Winnebago and other American Indian languages.
148. Presumably promoting territorialism, which Szold and Ginzberg spruned.
149. Isaac Leib Perez (1852–1915), Yiddish and Hebrew poet and author, some of whose stories Szold commissioned Helena Frank to translate. The JPS published *Stories and Pictures* in 1904 and *Yiddish Tales* in 1912.

150. "Foreign Criminals in New York," *North American Review* 188 (September, 1908): 383–94.

151. Leopold Zunz (1794–1886), an important founder of *Wissenschaft des Judentums*, "the Science of Judaism," i.e., the application of critical historical methods to the study of rabbinic literature.

152. In 1908 twenty-three charges were filed against District Attorney William Travers Jerome. Among other things, he was charged with having neglected to take action against people who took bribes in jury trials of the Metropolitan Railway Company and who stole the profits from sale of the company's bonds. Jerome was exonerated on all counts. See "Jerome Exonerated" in *NYT* (25 August 1908): 1–2.

153. *Nil admirari*, the attitude of being astonished at nothing.

154. 28 August 1908, 14–15.

155. See pp. 115–116, and f87 and 88 on p. 362.

156. A German printer of Jewish books.

157. Leopold Zunz (1794–1886), a founder of *Wissenschaft des Judentums*, the "Science of Judaism," pinned his hopes for Jewish renewal on Jewish scholarship.

158. *Lusitania*, the fastest ship afloat. In 1915 the sinking of this British vessel, with many American passengers on board, would help prepare the United States for a declaration of hostilities against Germany two years later.

159. Elul, the month before the Jewish New Year, is the traditional preparatory time for the High Holydays.

160. The servant Anna was vociferously angry at everyone who arrived late for dinner, with the exception of her favorite dinner guest, Professor Ginzberg.

161. Simon Jacobson (1857–1921) was cantor of the JTS synagogue.

162. Maimonides' *Yad ha-Hazakah* or *Mishnah Torah* is a code encompassing the entire Jewish legal system.

163. i.e., the U.S. Post Office.

164. Elkan Nathan Adler (1861–1946), English Jew, a lawyer by profession, a bibliophile and book collector who would donate his extensive and valuable Judaica library to the JTS. Ginzberg's attitude toward Adler indicates his contempt for the non-specialist.

165. The man under discussion was Christian David Ginsburg (1831–1914), an important scholar whose books, *The Massorah*,

Compiled from Manuscripts (1880) and *Introduction to the Massoretico-Critical Edition of the Hebrew Bible* (1894) were reissued in 1971 and 1966 respectively. Commenting on this encounter, Eli Ginzberg remembered: "My father often remarked that a gentleman does not change his name, his religion, or his bank," *Keeper*, 127.

166. Literally "holy names," obviously an ironic comment on recipients of British university degrees.
167. Even Ginzberg's qualified acceptance of Friedland's "discovery" proved wrong when the manuscript turned out to be a forgery. Ultimately Ratner was proved correct. Ginzberg was hardly alone in embracing the new discovery; Schechter also fell into the trap. This section's importance lies in Ginzberg's disdain for the London reporter, and, by extension, all non-experts who poked long noses into scholarly matters that they did not understand.
168. Solomon Schechter.
169. Joshua A. Joffe (1862–1935) was a Talmud instructor at JTS both before and after the reorganization of the seminary.
170. *Tageblatt*, Yiddish newspaper.
171. Nissim Behar (1848–1931), innovative Hebrew educator in Palestine who migrated to the United States in 1901 to represent the *Alliance Israelite Universelle*. American Jewish leaders objected to his fervent propaganda and loud public meetings.
172. I found it necessary to change the punctuation in this paragraph. It is uncharacteristically full of run-on sentences and changes in tense. Whether this reflects deep emotion about the subject or the lateness of the hour I leave to the reader to decide.
173. Protocol of the day demanded that a young suitor write to the father of his beloved rather than the woman herself.
174. Joseph Felsenstein (1835–1914), community leader in several Jewish communities; died in St. Joseph, Missouri.
175. The letter includes such revealing statements as the following: "You are the last person I need to tell what a fortunate woman you are to have won the love of such an extraordinary man. I have been in almost daily contact with him for five years and I know every fibre of his being for true and upright . . . For you, life at his side will be a sacred and beautiful feast." Eli Ginzberg published it as proof that his father's "hope and expectation that his engagement and marriage would not affect their friendship

would be fulfilled," *Keeper,* 128–29. Dash republished most of the letter as well, *Summoned to Jerusalem,* 73.

176. Miss Adams was one of the owners of the finishing school in Baltimore where the young Henrietta Szold taught.

177. Alice Seligsberg (1873–1940), American Jewish social worker. Under the influence of her dear friend Henrietta Szold, she would become active in Hadassah and administrator of the 1917 American Zionist Medical Unit in Palestine. Seligsberg was one of the few outside Henrietta's family and the seminary faculty to whom Szold unburdened herself after the Ginzberg rejection. See Seligsberg to Szold, 14 March 1909, CZA/A125/986.

178. Probably Arnold Ehrlich (1848–1919), Bible scholar, an expert in textual explication and reconstruction, radical for his day.

179. Schaetzilein, literally "little treasure." Throughout their long marriage, Adele Ginzberg called her husband "Schatzi" in public, to the entertainment of his students who looked upon the venerable professor with awe; from an interview with Arthur Hertzberg, July 1988.

180. Probably Arnold Ehrlich (1873–1940), lower critic of the Bible, an expert in textual explication and reconstruction, unusually radical for a Jewish scholar.

RECONSIDERATIONS: "DARK CHRONICLE OF A BROKEN HEART"

1. George Dobsevage, secretary of the JPS (as distinct from Henrietta Szold, who was secretary of the organization's publication committee).

2. Szold wrote "Dr. D" by mistake.

3. The Oheb Shalom Synagogue of Baltimore, which Benjamin Szold served for thirty-two years, forced him to retire in favor of a more Americanized rabbi and did little for his widow after his death.

4. "Mrs. Grundy," indicates social disapproval or narrow-mindedness. From a query often repeated in Tom Morton's 1798 play *Speed the Plough:* "What will Mrs. Grundy say?"

5. An early play by Henrik Ibsen (1858), its title is commonly translated as "The Vikings of Helgeland." See *The Oxford Ibsen,* volume II (London: Oxford University Press, 1962): 89.

6. An entire section of the *NYT* Sunday, 24 January 1909, Part 2, deals with the accident and the rescue. The headline reads "Liner Republic Rammed at Sea; Four Lives Lost." The White Star Line *Republic* sank, while the SS *Florida* of the Lloyd Italiano Line, with which it collided in fog twenty-six miles off Nantucket, thought badly damaged, did not. An editorial on page 4 credited the wireless for reporting the collision and making the rescue possible. On January 25 Gugliemo Marconi himself commented on the role of trans-Atlantic wireless signals in saving lives of the two ships' passengers and crews (*NYT*, 1).

7. From MWAC. This is the only letter published in this volume that is not verifiably authentic. The late Mr. Whiteman had in his possession only a typescript copy with no signature. In the printed edition of *The Legends* volumes 1 (1909) and 2 (1910) are marked "translated from the German Ms by Henrietta Szold." At end of the Preface to volume I, p. xv, Ginzberg writes that the first three volumes "are in the hands of the printer almost in their entirety." The date is 24 March 1909, two months after this putative letter. In volume 4 (1913), *Joshua to Esther*, no translator's name is given, because Szold refused to put her name on it, although the letters indicate that the translation was her work. Only volume 3 (1911) carries another translator's name, Paul Radin. I suspect that this is the material Szold wanted to have done by all those people who refused to do it: Jacobs, Davidson, etc. (See letters from Szold to Sulzberger, JPSP, Box 12.) If this letter is indeed the work of Professor Ginzberg, its brittle tone certainly indicates anger at the position in which Miss Szold's very public angst had placed him. The syntax also fits Szold's description.

8. Reading of *Shirat Ha-Yam*, song of rejoicing Exodus after the Israelites safely crossed the Red Sea.

9. "The Legends of the Church Fathers in the Apocryphal Literature," Berlin, 1900.

10. See *Seminary Addresses and Other Papers* (New York: Burning Book Press, 1959): 145–69.

11. Allusion to Psalm 126:5.

12. Small gifts usually of sweets and fruits exchanged between friends on Purim.

13. The one bears no resemblance to the other.

14. Szold was correct, to a point. For a long time, the subject was "taboo" in the Ginzberg household, *Keeper*, 128.

15. Mania Wilbushewitz Shochat (1880–1961), early collective farmer, central figure in the Ha-Shomer movement, pacifist. After Szold moved to Palestine in 1920, the two women became fast friends.
16. Henrietta's sister Bertha's husband Louis H. Levin and second child.
17. Israel Shochat, born in 1886, was a founder of the Haganah, a controversial figure in the labor movement of Palestine and a lawyer. He was known to be unfaithful to his wife Mania. They never divorced, however, and both of them survived until 1961.
18. Joseph Jacobs.
19. A way of life instead of death.
20. See p. 371, f7.
21. Ibid. This statement seems to verify the authenticity of Ginzberg's letter of 26 January 1909.
22. Morley Roberts, *David Bran* (Boston: L.C. Page & Co., 1908) was reviewed in *The Nation*, 18 March 1909: 281–82; William Dana Orcutt, *The Spell* (Harper & Bros., 1908) was reviewed in *The Nation*, 1 April 1909: 337. The hero of Roberts' novel is a fisherman who sets up a "Biblical" household with two women. Orcutt's hero is a scholar who loves his wife but maintains an intimate intellectual friendship with her best friend.
23. David Hoffmann, rector of the Rabbiner Seminary in Berlin.
24. Shabuot, Festival of Weeks, celebrating Israel's receiving the Torah at Mount Sinai.
25. A paraphrase of Szold's letter of 30 August 1907. There is no Hebrew greeting in this letter, but a translation of the traditional formula: "a good writing and sealing." The last thing on the page is actually a request of Ginzberg to mail enclosed New Year's greetings to the Marxes.
26. The original word, scratched out, was "retreat."
27. Richard Gottheil (1862–1936), professor of semitic languages at Columbia University and a prominent Zionist, as was his wife, Emma Leon Gottheil, one of the founders of Hadassah in 1912. Her later advocacy of a rival women's Zionist organization is discussed in the Epilogue.
28. Else Jerusalem, *Der heilege Skarabaens* Berlin: S. Fischer, 1909; Hermann Sudermann, *Das Hohe Lied* [Song of Songs] Berlin, 1908; Margarete Boehme, *Tagebuch einer Verlorenen von einer Toten*, Berlin: Karl Voegel, 1905.
29. Madison Cawein (1865–1914), was a popular poet of the day. "The Solitary" first appeared in *Harper's Monthly* 94 (April 1905):

718; since Szold recorded it with her "Renunciation" of that summer, one can assume that it was copied from the magazine.

30. The "Renunciation" and the Cawein poem, both handwritten in Szold's neat script, are located in CZA/A125/986.

EPILOGUE

1. Dash, *Summoned to Jerusalem*, 7; *The Jewish Encyclopedia* (New York: Funk and Wagnalls, 1910), volume VI; 336–367. For a more critical discussion of Henriette Herz, see Michael A. Meyer, *The Origins of the Modern Jew: Jewish Identity and European Culture in Germany, 1749–1824* (Detroit: Wayne State University Press, 1967): 101–08.

2. Carolyn G. Heilbrun, *Writing a Woman's Life* (New York: Ballantine Books, 1988): 12.

3. Szold to Felsenthal, 28 August 1905, Bernard Felsenthal Papers, AJHS.

4. The story is found in *The Pagan Rabbi and Other Stories* (New York: Alfred A. Knopf, 1969). Thanks to Deborah Dash Moore for the observation.

5. The essay was published in *Judaism at the World's Parliament of Religions* (Cincinnati: Union of Hebrew Congregations, 1894): 305–10. The same publication contained Szold's report on the work of the JPS. The only other author with more than one article in the volume was Issac M. Wise, leader of Reform Judaism.

6. Schechter's suggestion is recorded in a letter to Sulzberger, written on 8 March 1909 and published by Meyer Ben Horin: "Solomon Schechter to Judge Mayer Sulzberger," *Jewish Social Studies* 28:2 (1965): 95–96). Norman Bentwich cites part of the letter in his biography, *Solomon Schechter* (Philadelphia: JPS, 1948): 247.

7. Entry of 15 December 1908.

8. Fineman, *Woman of Valor*, 151; Ginzberg, *Keeper of the Law*, 128.

9. From author's interview in 1978 and often repeated to others. For Eli Ginzberg's reference to his father as the father of Hadassah, see *Keeper of the Law*, 128.

10. An essential ingredient of the Szold legend; see Lowenthal, *Henrietta Szold*, 68.

11. See Szold Papers, JHSM, Box 2.

12. Eric L. Goldstein, "The Practical as Spiritual, Henrietta Szold's American Zionist Ideology, 1878–1920," in Barry Kessler, ed., *Daughter of Zion: Henrietta Szold and American Jewish Womanhood*, 19–21; Szold's translation of Ahad Ha'am's "The Holy and the Secular" appeared in *Jewish Comment* 27 (May 1904): 4.
13. 26 March 1899, Steven Wise Papers, AJHS.
14. 2 September 1906, CAAC.
15. See Zipperstein, *Elusive Prophet*, 192.
16. See Szold's thank you note to Friedlaender, 5 December 1904, CAAC.
17. "The Practical Idealist," in *The Maccabean* 6 (4 August 1904): 94.
18. See Shargel, *Practical Dreamer*, 132–33.
19. Szold's journal of 1910, Monday, April 18, CZA/125/989. Just how busy they were is indicated by a letter from Szold to Friedlaender, 6 September 1910, suggesting that since a Kehillah meeting was scheduled for Monday afternoon, "therefore it would hardly be advisable to have an Administrative meeting (of the JPS Publication Committee) Monday night." Friedlaender Papers, JTSL, Box 2.
20. Szold to Schechter, 10 November 1910, quoted in Lowenthal, *Henrietta Szold: Life and Letters*, 74.
21. See Letterhead of the Agricultural Experimental Station at Athlit, *Encyclopedia Judaica*, Volume 2: 26. For evidence of Szold's personal attachment to Aaronsohn, see her 1910 journal, 121–37. For her regard for his scientific discoveries, see her lecture "The Discovery of Primitive Wheat," meeting of the Judeans, NYC (2 April 1914). MJHS, Box 2. After Aaronsohn's tragically early death in an airplane crash, Szold eulogized him. See "Aaron Aaronsohn," *Young Judean* 9 (June 1919): 294–99.
22. Song of Songs 1:6; 1910 journal, 10 May 1910.
23. The letter was written from Somesville, Mt. Desert, Maine (28 July 1911) CZA/A125/280.
24. Interview with Eli Ginzberg, 28 February 1996; 1910 journal.
25. The friendship began just after the Ginzberg rejection. A letter to Seligsberg, dated 1 January 1909, regrets the fact that the two were not well acquainted "before the shock came this fall," HA, Box 5, f45. Subsequent letters (idem) from Seligsberg offered advice and consolation. See also Joyce Antler, "Zion in Our Hearts, Henrietta Szold and the American Jewish Women's Movement," in *Daughters of Zion*, 44–48.

26. Jeremiah 8:22. See Shargel, *Practical Dreamer*, 7.
27. See Michael Berkowitz, *Zionist Culture and West European Jewry Before the First World War* (Cambridge University Press, 1993): 99, 105–08.
28. Hadassah's path from semiautonomy to submission to the ZOA to total independence is the subject of Donald H. Miller's Ph.D. dissertation. "A History of Hadassah 1912–1935" (New York University, 1968).
29. See *American Zionism from Herzl to the Holocaust* (Lincoln: University of Nebraska Press, 1995): 127–33.
30. Felix Danziger, "Die separatorische Tendenz der Hadassah," in *Judische Rundschau* (25 May 1927): 297–98.
31. Miller, *A History of Hadassah*, 51; radio address of 28 February 1937, CZA/A125/213 (also in SL, Box 1).
32. See Friedlaender's essay, "Palestine and the Diaspora," in *Past and Present* (Cincinnati: Ark Publishing Co., 1919): 470–72.
33. Carol Kutscher, *The Early Years of Hadassah, 1912–1921* (Brandeis University Ph.D. dissertation, 1976): 136.
34. See SL, Box 1.
35. Arthur A. Goren, "Spiritual Zionists and Jewish Sovereignty," in *The Americanization of the Jews*, eds. Robert M. Seltzer and Norman J. Cohen (New York: New York University Press, 1995): 169; Shargel, *Practical Dreamer*, 158–82.
36. Szold to Seligsberg, 13 October 1913, published in Lowenthal, *Henrietta Szold*, 82.
37. Ellen Umansky, "Jewish Women in the 20th-Century U.S." in *Jewish Women in Historical Perspective*. ed. Judith R. Baskin (Detroit: Wayne State University Press, 1991): 273. (Carrying her argument a step further, Umansky urged contemporary women to follow Szold's lead): Allon Gal, "Hadassah and the American Jewish Political Tradition," in Jeffrey S. Gurock and Marc Lee Raphael, eds., *An Inventory of Promises; Essays on American Jewish History in Honor of Moses Rischin* (Brooklyn: Carlson Publishing, Inc., 1995): 91.
38. Kutscher, *Early Years of Hadassah*, 156.
39. Ibid., 157; Shargel, *Practical Dreamer*, 160.
40. Ibid., 159 and Szold to Friedenwald, 13 February 1908, Szold Papers, JHSM, Box 8.
41. See Lowenthal, *Henrietta Szold*, 80–84; Kutscher, *Early Years of Hadassah*, 173–77; Bertha Badt-Strauss, *White Fire: The Life and*

Works of Jessie Sampter (New York: The Reconstructionist Press, 1956): 40–52.

42. Szold to Mrs. Brodie, 10 April 1913, JHSM, Box 1, f29.
43. See Irma Lindheim, *Parallel Quest, A Search of a Person and a People* (New York, Thomas Yoseloff, 1962): 218.
44. See letters exchanged between Szold and Seligsberg, 30 August 1915 and 8 September 1915, CZA/375/292.
45. See Rose Jacobs, "Beginning of Hadassah," in Isidore S. Meyer, ed., *Early History of Zionism in America* (New York, AJHS 1958): 239.
46. Szold to Seligsberg, 7 January 1920, CZA/A125/267, quoted in Miller, "History of Hadassah," 112.
47. Kutscher, *Early Years of Hadassah*, 208–22; Miller, *History of Hadassah*, 105–09; Yonathan Shapiro, *Leadership of the American Zionist Organization, 1897–1930* (Chicago: University of Illinois Press, 1971): 180.
48. See *Leadership*, passim. Shapiro read the ZOA's accusations uncritically and accepted its perspective, viz: "Hadassah, while affiliated with the Zionist Organization, was a Palestinian organization . . . the goals of the organization were restricted to the building of health services and welfare institutions in Palestine," 204.
49. Unveiled resentment of Hadassah was evident in many of Lipsky's pronouncements and in statements by Maurice Samuel, viz: "Women's Rights in Zionism, Equality and Special Privileges—But not Domination," *New Palestine* (15 June 1928): 627, 640. See Michael Berkowitz, "Cool Embrace: The Inter-Zionist Reception of Hadassah in Western Europe and the United States, 1914–1933," (paper delivered at the Gender and Judaism Conference, April 25–27, 1993): 11–12. For the term "Diaper Zionism," see Lindheim, *Parallel Quest*, 215.
50. Shapiro, *Leadership*, 204.
51. Berkowitz, "Cool Embrace," 9–11; Miller, *History of Hadassah*, 118–45; Kutscher, *Early Years*, 222–243.
52. Compelling Friedlaender to resign from a Red Cross mission to Palestine and causing the British to detain the American Zionist Medical Unit, headed by Seligsberg, for several months. See Shargel, *Practical Dreamer*, 23–31; Kutscher, *Early Years of Hadassah*, 165–167.

53. Letter to Seligsberg, 20 June 1921, JHSM, Box 1, f47. On American Zionists and *Keren Hayesod* see Urofsky, *American Zionism*, 283–98 and Shapiro, *Leadership*, 161–94.
54. Kutscher, *Early Years of Hadassah*, 229.
55. Szold to Emma Gottheil, 26 October 1922, SL Box 1, f9.
56. Lindheim, *Parallel Quest*, 211–12.
57. See Jenna Weissman Joselit, "The Canonization of Henrietta Szold," lecture delivered at a symposium on Szold entitled "A Deeper Look at the Daughter of Zion," at the JHSM, 17 September 1995.
58. Lowenthal, *Henrietta Szold*, 92–93.
59. Szold to Sampter, 8 March 1917 and 29 July 1922, quoted in Kutscher, *Early Years of Hadassah*, 75.
60. Both excerpts are from "Our Own Women," *United Synagogue Recorder* 3:3 (July 1923): 17.
61. Ibid.
62. Szold to Seligsberg (3 January 1921): 3, CZA/A125/283; Kutscher, *Early Years of Hadassah*, 75–77. (No copy of the prayer book was made available to Kutscher, who relayed its contents, or to me); Bertha Badt-Straus, *White Fire: the Life and Works of Jessie Sampter* (New York: The Reconstructionist Press, 1956): 78; Szold to Sampter (29 July 1922), HA, Box 5, f42.
63. See SL, Box 1, passim, and Susan Lee Hattis, *The Bi-National Idea in Palestine during Mandatory Times* (Tel Aviv: Ben Nun Press, 1970): 38–58, 171–72, 258–68.
64. *Writing a Woman's Life*, 48. The quotation is taken from Nina Auerbach, *Woman and the Demon* (Cambridge: Harvard University Press, 1982): 183.

Index of Personal Names